W9-CPD-167

Differentiating Instruction

Instruction for Learners Gaining Proficiency, English Language Learners, and Learners with Diverse Needs

Third Course

HOLT, RINEHART AND WINSTON

Reviewers for Grade 9 Differentiating Instruction

Melissa Bowell
Ft. Walton Beach High School
Ft. Walton Beach, Florida

M. Ann Capuzello
Bluffton High School
Bluffton, South Carolina

Yolanda Fernandez
Del Rio High School
Del Rio, Texas

Andrea Gallagher
Wando High School
Mt. Pleasant, South Carolina

Holly Hillgardner
South Bronx Prep
New York, New York

Dana Clark Howard
D.W. Daniel High School
Central, South Carolina

Barbara Kimbrough
Kane Area High School
Kane, Pennsylvania

Lynn Mason
Newark High School
Newark, Ohio

April Volponi
Francis Lewis High School
Fresh Meadows, New York

Susan Watson-Bell
Fort Dorchester High School
North Charleston, South Carolina

Karen Wukovitz
Bluffton High School
Bluffton, South Carolina

Copyright © by Holt, Rinehart and Winston

All rights reserved. No part of this publication may be reproduced or transmitted in any form or by any means, electronic or mechanical, including photocopy, recording, or any information storage and retrieval system, without permission in writing from the publisher.

Teachers using ELEMENTS OF LITERATURE may photocopy blackline masters in complete pages in sufficient quantities for classroom use only and not for resale.

ELEMENTS OF LITERATURE, HOLT, HRW, and the "Owl Design" are trademarks licensed to Holt, Rinehart and Winston, registered in the United States of America and/or other jurisdictions.

Printed in the United States of America

If you have received these materials as examination copies free of charge, Holt, Rinehart and Winston retains title to the materials and they may not be resold. Resale of examination copies is strictly prohibited.

Possession of this publication in print format does not entitle users to convert this publication, or any portion of it, into electronic format.

ISBN 978-0-55-400078-7
ISBN 0-55-400078-4

1 2 3 4 5 6 7 8 9 179 12 11 10 09 08

Contents

Unit 1: Short Stories

Collection 1: Plot and Setting

Original content Copyright © by Holt, Rinehart and Winston. Additions and changes to the original content are the responsibility of the instructor.

Collection 2: Character

Collection 3: Narrator and Voice

Original content Copyright © by Holt, Rinehart and Winston. Additions and changes to the original content are the responsibility of the instructor.

Collection 4: Symbolism and Irony

Original content Copyright © by Holt, Rinehart and Winston. Additions and changes to the original content are the responsibility of the instructor.

Unit 2: Nonfiction

Collection 5: Form and Style

Original content Copyright © by Holt, Rinehart and Winston. Additions and changes to the original content are the responsibility of the instructor.

Collection 6: Persuasion

Original content Copyright © by Holt, Rinehart and Winston. Additions and changes to the original content are the responsibility of the instructor.

Unit 3: Poetry

Collection 7: Poetry

Original content Copyright © by Holt, Rinehart and Winston. Additions and changes to the original content are the responsibility of the instructor.

Unit 4: Drama

Collection 8: Drama

Original content Copyright © by Holt, Rinehart and Winston. Additions and changes to the original content are the responsibility of the instructor.

Unit 5: Epic

Collection 9: Epic and Myth

Original content Copyright © by Holt, Rinehart and Winston. Additions and changes to the original content are the responsibility of the instructor.

Unit 6: Reading for Life

Collection 10: Reading for Life

Original content Copyright © by Holt, Rinehart and Winston. Additions and changes to the original content are the responsibility of the instructor.

Differentiating Instruction

To the Teacher

Throughout this guide you will find strategies and activities designed to help English-language learners and struggling students become active participants in classroom learning communities with their English-speaking peers. Based on current and proven practices for teaching content area subject matter to English-language learners, these strategies and activities reflect important ideas about the learner's role and about language and communication, which are at the heart of the program.

More specifically, the strategies in this guide address the needs of struggling students and English-language learners who are in the beginning through advanced stages of English language acquisition.

ABOUT *DIFFERENTIATING INSTRUCTION*

Differentiating Instruction is designed to provide differentiating instruction and to help teachers meet the needs of all struggling learners—those who need to gain proficiency in reading or writing, those for whom English is a second language, and those who have other learning needs that require special attention. This book contains the following types of teacher and student materials:

Teaching Support The front matter of this book contains materials on the following topics:

- essays by experts on teaching English-language learners, learners with diverse needs, and other struggling readers
- research articles summarizing research findings related to instruction for struggling students and English-language learners
- general strategies and routines to help meet the needs of struggling learners
- contrastive analysis chart of English sounds and those of other languages
- tools for improving fluency

LESSON PLANS

All lesson plans provide alternative activities for preteaching, reteaching, and scaffolding instruction. Activities that are especially useful for a specific group of struggling learners are called out in the minor column with the following acronyms: **RGP** for Readers Gaining Proficiency, **WGP** for Writers Gaining Proficiency, **ELL** for English-Language Learners, and **LDN** for Learners with Diverse Needs.

Reading, Literature, and Vocabulary A three-page lesson plan for all Minimum Course of Study selections in the Student Edition

Writing A two-page lesson plan for every Writing Workshop in the Student Edition that aligns with the writing process

Speaking and Listening A one-page lesson for every Speaking and Listening Workshop in the Student Edition, including alternative forms of presentation and assessment for students with disabilities

Targeted Strategies for Learners with Diverse Needs A one-page lesson plan for each collection in the Student Edition, providing additional/alternative practice

Original content Copyright © by Holt, Rinehart and Winston. Additions and changes to the original content are the responsibility of the instructor.

Differentiating Instruction

for the primary learning standards and skills covered in the Minimum Course of Study for the collection

SKILL BUILDERS AND GRAPHIC ORGANIZERS

Differentiating Instruction includes black line masters of the following types of practice pages:

Academic and Selection Vocabulary Skill Builder One page of vocabulary practice for the academic vocabulary in the collection and for the selection vocabulary associated with the Minimum Course of Study

Oral Language Skill Builder Two pages of oral language practice for each collection, often providing learners with opportunities for academic conversations about their reading and writing

English Language Skill Builder Two pages of English-language practice for each collection, usually focusing on elements of language that are especially challenging to English learners

Graphic Organizers To accompany all non-Minimum Course of Study selections, a one-page graphic organizer that helps students organize, interpret, and understand the selection as well as master learning standards and literary skills

Fluency On-level reading passages and below-level reading passages that can be given to students for fluency practice and informal assessment

ASSESSMENT

Differentiating Instruction includes two types of leveled assessment that are appropriate for struggling learners.

Selection Test A one-page assessment for every Minimum Course of Study selection, including objective items as well as one constructed-response item

Collection Summative Test A one-page assessment that covers the Minimum Course of Study for the collection—the MCOS literature and vocabulary; the academic vocabulary; and the reading, vocabulary, and literary standards and skills

Unit Test A two-page assessment that covers the Minimum Course of Study for the unit—the reading and literary standards and skills

PACING

Differentiating Instruction is designed to provide you with the information you need for pacing along with maximum flexibility. This program can be used in any of the following situations:

- A heterogeneous class
- A class for struggling learners of any or all types
- In 10- or 15-minute segments
- In regular class periods of any length

Original content Copyright © by Holt, Rinehart and Winston. Additions and changes to the original content are the responsibility of the instructor.

You will notice in the lesson plans in *Differentiating Instruction* that we have identified the estimated duration of each activity. As you plan your instruction with your learners and your class schedule in mind, you can choose as many or as few of the suggested activities as needed. In addition, with the cross-references provided to other materials that are appropriate for all types of struggling learners, you can expand instruction beyond what is provided in this book.

For example, look at the following excerpts from a lesson plan in *Differentiating Instruction, Third Course (Grade 9):*

LISTENING COMPREHENSION SKILLS *(10 minutes)*
Build Background/Set a Purpose Tell students that O. Henry is known for stories that have an unexpected twist at the end. Explain that . . .

LITERARY FOCUS *(20 minutes)*
Omniscient Point of View Explain that *omni-* means "all" and *-scien-* means "knowledge." So an omniscient narrator is "all-knowing. . . ."

READING/WRITING *(20 minutes)*
Especially for ELL
(15 minutes)
Have students practice sentence-combining. Model how to combine two sentences:
1. Justin was surprised that he was chosen to be on the...

RESOURCES
In *The Holt Reader:* "The Gift of the Magi" for students who need more scaffolding in a workbook format

In this book: Vocabulary Skill Builder, page 112; "The Gift of the Magi" Selection Test, page 117

Holt Audio Library, Disc Two, Track 19: a recording of the selection

These excerpts include examples of suggested activities and teaching strategies, and their suggested duration, as well as examples of references to other resources that can be used to differentiate instruction. As you preview lesson plans in this book, you can create plans for 5, 10, 15, or 20 minutes segments or for complete daily lesson plans.

Original content Copyright © by Holt, Rinehart and Winston. Additions and changes to the original content are the responsibility of the instructor.

Differentiating Instruction

Recognizing the Needs of English-Language Learners

Robin Scarcella, Ph.D.

BEGINNING LEARNERS

Beginning learners are just beginning to acquire English and have difficulty writing even the most basic sentences in English. They may not know how to write or may write with short sentences—sometimes just a word or two in length—, make many errors, and have very limited vocabulary. They have trouble understanding others without great effort. Their speech lacks fluency and often contains many pauses. Sometimes they are unable to read or they read very poorly. These learners should be receiving intensive English instruction. They lack the English proficiency required to attain the same high standards as all your other students, but can make significant gains once they begin to understand English.

INTERMEDIATE ENGLISH-LANGUAGE LEARNERS

Intermediate English-language learners constitute the largest group of students enrolled in middle school and high school. You can identify intermediate English language learners by their ability to communicate their ideas in everyday situations both in speech and in writing. Their writing contains simple sentences and even sentences with complex clauses. However, it is often riddled with errors. These students can use basic vocabulary words, but have difficulty using terms accurately.

Learners with an intermediate level of English proficiency are able to read basic, everyday materials, but find reading academic materials enormously challenging. They read them inaccurately, often glossing over difficult terms, misunderstanding sentence structures, and failing to notice logical connections between words. Without sufficient instruction, these learners often give up trying to access academic text. It is easy to overlook their reading problems, especially if they have developed strategies that enable them to look more proficient in English than they really are! They may rely on their teachers' explanations of readings, pre-reading activities, titles, headings and illustrations to guess the content of the readings.

You will find that intermediate learners often have little trouble communicating orally in informal situations, using an informal variety of English or a variety of language called learner language. They can say virtually anything they want in everyday situations, without putting out much effort. They often speak quickly and fluently with few hesitations. Their main language difficulties concern the ability to read and write and to communicate orally in academic situations. Unfortunately, they may reach an intermediate level of English proficiency and stay at that level. This happens when they hit a plateau in language development. When you talk to intermediate-level English language learners, it is easy to treat them as though they have mastered English, even when they have not.

Many native English speakers believe that it is rude to explain words to these learners or correct the learners' language. They unwittingly help the learners to maintain their intermediate level of English proficiency. Without instruction or

Original content Copyright © by Holt, Rinehart and Winston. Additions and changes to the original content are the responsibility of the instructor.

feedback, these learners never acquire enough English to graduate from high school or go on to college. This is particularly the case when learners live in areas where they are likely to interact with other learners who have not acquired English. In their communities and in their homes, they listen to English and they interact in English. But the variety of English that they use and to which they are exposed does not represent Standard English. It is a variety of Nonstandard English, immigrant English (sometimes called learner English or interlanguage). These students' knowledge of English does not develop through mere exposure to reading; they are especially in need of solid instruction.

ADVANCED LEARNERS

Advanced learners who have an advanced level of English are able to communicate accurately in both informal situations and academic ones. They often excel on standardized tests of content knowledge. When they speak and write, they continue to make some grammatical and vocabulary mistakes. Without instructional support, their grammar and vocabulary will not improve. Although they are able to read academic texts with some effort, they have difficulty accessing subtle meanings.

A Word of Caution Students' language proficiencies change as they live in the United States and receive instruction. It is important to remember that students are capable of making remarkable progress acquiring English. A student who enters your classroom at an intermediate level may even become advanced after a few months.

Also, it is important to remember that this book, *Differentiating Instruction,* is not designed for, or targeting, students at the beginning level, students who would benefit from participating in an ELD or ESL support program. Nevertheless, the materials provided in this book may also be beneficial to students at the beginning level and the Lesson Plans for Newcomers, on page 307, are especially designed for these students.

Original content Copyright © by Holt, Rinehart and Winston. Additions and changes to the original content are the responsibility of the instructor.

Differentiating Instruction

Literacy for All: Ten Guiding Principles

Patrick Schwarz, Ph.D.

All students can learn, and teachers must believe all students will learn. Having taught students with learning disabilities, ADHD, emotional/behavior support needs, autism/Asperger attributes, cognitive challenges and sensory support needs, I know that all will benefit from a literacy-rich environment guided by clear principles that provide a backbone for learning. Dignity and respect for all learner abilities are embedded in the following principles:

1. Student diversity strengthens a classroom and strengthens literacy due to educators trying out a greater array of varied teaching and learning approaches.
2. We should not make assumptions about the literacy of a learner: Everyday that I teach, a student surprises me with his or her ability, strengths, capacities, and gifts.
3. Focusing on a learner's abilities and possibilities rather than disabilities and deficits is an important concept in promoting literacy for all, since disability and deficit information do not help an educator teach.
4. Innovative diverse learning strategies such as universal design, differentiated instruction, cooperative learning, curricular adaptations, literature circles, educational technologies, cross-age peer tutoring and peer mediation will promote literacy for all. Once the door is opened, a wider learning spectrum is welcomed and greater learning success is achieved.
5. Using everything in education's bag of tricks will promote literacy for all.
6. All literacy approaches that help a learner gain skills are valuable.
7. Certain learners are more complex to assess and identify literacy support approaches for, but the effort is entirely worth it. It is critical to always believe in all learners and not to give up!
8. One educator should not shoulder all the responsibility for a student's literacy; rather, varied approaches and input must be a collaborative effort from a team, thereby gaining meaning and success.
9. Using a student's interests, fascinations, and passions in the curriculum will promote literacy.
10. Making education work for all is what good teaching and quality literacy are about.

Original content Copyright © by Holt, Rinehart and Winston. Additions and changes to the original content are the responsibility of the instructor.

What Research Tells Us About Effective Strategies for All Learners with Diverse Needs and English-Language Learners

. . . Those who suffer most from unsound teaching methods are the students most in need: learning disabled, impoverished, and nonnative speakers of English—the so-called at-risk students.

—Doug Carnine

TODAY'S CLASSROOM

Diversity defines today's classroom. Today's teacher in the mainstream classroom faces students with diverse needs. According to Swanson, "the number of children classified as having learning disabilities has increased substantially, from roughly three-quarters of a million in 1976 to more than 2.6 million in 1997." A decade later, the number had increased to 2.9 million. In their executive summary to the research, Gersten et al. point to the rise in English-language learners (ELLs). They say, "Projections indicate that one student in four will be Latino in 2020, compared to only one in ten in 1982." Which students are most at risk for reading failure? According to Lyon, they are "those who enter school with limited exposure to the English language."

Considering all the other demands on the classroom teacher's time and attention, meeting the needs of struggling students and ELLs may sound overwhelming. What can the classroom teacher with no special training in teaching these students do? What does the research tell us about creating more effective programs for these students? What special needs must be met?

WHAT THE RESEARCH SAYS

We know that reading instruction is affected positively when direct instruction is combined with strategy instruction. In their synthesis of the research, Collins et al. show how "contemporary reforms in reading curricula [. . .] emphasize integrating metacognition, motivation, and strategies."

Why are reading strategies so important? A key difference between strategic readers and struggling students is that strategic readers know how to choose strategies to apply to reading, while struggling students do not. These students need systematic and explicit instruction showing them how to choose strategies that fit their text, their purpose, and the occasion. Struggling students benefit from strategies that help them overcome problems in

- comprehending what they read
- recognizing text patterns
- distinguishing between relevant and irrelevant information
- recalling information

Original content Copyright © by Holt, Rinehart and Winston. Additions and changes to the original content are the responsibility of the instructor.

Differentiating Instruction

PRINCIPLES

Dickson, Carmine, and Kameenui's research for the National Center to Improve the Tools of Educators at the University of Oregon reveals six instructional principles for meeting the needs of struggling students. They are

- big ideas
- conspicuous strategies
- mediated scaffolding
- strategic integration
- primed background knowledge
- judicious review

BIG IDEAS

Big ideas are "concepts and principles that facilitate the most efficient and broadest acquisition of knowledge across a range of examples in a domain." In other words, some ideas are more important than others and serve as umbrellas under which other ideas fit. By concentrating on big ideas, struggling students will spend time mastering what is essential. This is particularly helpful since these students generally have more "catch-up" to do and face the "tyranny of time."

For struggling students a big idea for instruction concerns the importance of text structure. Good readers know how to use the structure of the text and its special features to make sense from that text. Students with learning difficulties do not. According to Seidenberg, struggling students benefit from instruction in how to do this.

CONSPICUOUS STRATEGIES

What is a strategy? Dickson et al. define a strategy as "an organized set of actions designed to accomplish a task." Conspicuous strategies are just that—conspicuous. In other words, they are made apparent to the student through identification and definition, modeling, guided practice, and appropriate feedback. To be effective, conspicuous strategies should be neither too narrow nor too broad and they should be generalizable. Conspicuous strategies are essential for struggling students, who need an array of strategies to enhance their understanding of the narrative and expository material they read."

MEDIATED SCAFFOLDING

Dickson et al. define mediated scaffolding as "the external support provided by teacher/peers, content, tasks, and materials during initial instruction." The first method of mediated scaffolding involves the way teachers interact with students and the way peers interact. It is called teacher-peer scaffolding. When the teacher models, he or she shows how to do something and then guides students' practice. In addition, the teacher may have students, or peers, tutor one another or share work with one another. Gersten et al. find the benefits of peer-assisted learning strategies promising.

Original content Copyright © by Holt, Rinehart and Winston. Additions and changes to the original content are the responsibility of the instructor.

Differentiating Instruction

The next three methods of mediated scaffolding concern content, tasks, and materials. In other words, how should teachers differentiate the content they present, the tasks they ask students to do, and the materials they give students to use in order to meet the needs of diverse students? *Content scaffolding* involves easier content before more difficult content. *Task control scaffolding* involves starting with easier tasks and building toward more difficult tasks. *Material scaffolding* involves providing materials—such as key words, think sheets, and interactive graphic organizers—to guide students' thinking.

STRATEGIC INTEGRATION

Diverse learners benefit from material that is strategically integrated, since they have difficulty making these connections on their own. In other words, they find it helpful when connections between materials are pointed out or made clear. Dickson et al. define strategic integration as "the integrating of content, skills, or concepts that (a) mutually support each other, (b) communicate generalizations, or (c) transfer to areas further and further removed from the original area of instruction." Strategic integration, then, is the "careful combination of new information with what the learner already knows to produce a more generalizable, higher order skill."

PRIMED BACKGROUND KNOWLEDGE

The research of Weaver and Kintsch has shown the importance of activating prior knowledge. Prior knowledge consists of not only background information about topics, themes, and concepts, but also knowledge about text structure, academic language, and the conventions of English. In citing the converging evidence, Lyon says, "Students who comprehend well are able to activate their relevant background knowledge when reading—they can relate what has been read to their own experiences and background." On the other hand, struggling students are not skilled at this. Effective instruction for these students includes ample time spent developing background knowledge, since that addresses the students' "memory and strategy deficits."

JUDICIOUS REVIEW

According to Dickson et al., judicious review refers to "the sequence and schedule of opportunities students receive to apply and develop facility with the conventions of well-presented text and the organizational patterns of text structures." To be effective, review should be sufficient, distributed over time, cumulative, and varied.

GOOD CLASSROOM PRACTICES

How do these principles translate into good classroom practices? Most likely, they describe things you and other good teachers you know have already been doing, including the following practices:

- spending more time on big ideas, or umbrella concepts

Original content Copyright © by Holt, Rinehart and Winston. Additions and changes to the original content are the responsibility of the instructor.

Differentiating Instruction

- identifying and modeling strategies to use, explaining them step-by-step in learner-friendly language, by teachers' talking aloud as they model them, purposefully partnering students to provide ample opportunities for students to practice using the strategies

- scaffolding instruction, moving from heavy support to lighter support or from easier concepts, tasks, and materials to more challenging concepts, tasks, and materials

- showing connections

- activating prior knowledge and building background

- reviewing often and regularly

BIBLIOGRAPHY

August, D. & Shanahan. T. (eds). (2006). *Developing literacy in second-language learners: Report of the National Literacy Panel on Language-Minority Children and Youth.* Mahwah, NJ: Lawrence Erlbaum Associations, Publishers. Executive summary retrieved November 5, 2007, from www.cal.org/projects/archive/nlpreports/Executive_Summary.pdf

Carnine, D. (1994). Introduction to the mini-series: Diverse learners and prevailing, emerging and research-based educational approaches and three tools. *School Psychology Review,* 23 (3), 341-350.

Collins, V.L., Dickson, S.V., Simmons, D.C., & Kameenui, E.J. (1996). Metacognition and its relation to reading comprehension: A synthesis of the research. Retrieved December 19, 2007, from http://idea.uoregon.edu/~ncite/documents/techrep/tech23.html

Dickson, S.V., Simmons, D.C., & Kameenui, E.J. (1995). Text organizational and its relation to reading comprehension: A synthesis of the research. Retrieved December 19, 2007, from http://idea.uoregon.edu/~ncite/documents/techrep/tech17.html

Francis, David F., et al. (2006). *Practical guidelines for the education of English language learners: Research-based recommendations for instruction and academic interventions.* Under cooperative agreement grant S283B050034 for U.S. Department of Education). Portsmouth, NH: RMC Research Corporation, Center on Instruction (COI), 2006. (Book 1 of 3) Retrieved November 6, 2007, from www.centeroninstruction.org/resources.cfm?category=ell&grade_start+grade_n=12&subcategory=research

Francis, David F., et al. (2006). *Practical guidelines for the education of English language learners: Research-based recommendations for serving adolescent newcomers.* Under cooperative agreement grant S283B050034 for U.S. Department of Education). Portsmouth, NH: RMC Research Corporation, Center on Instruction (COI), 2006. (Book 2 of 3)

Gersten, R. et al. (2007). *Effective literacy and English language instruction for English learners in the elementary grades: A practice guide.* (NCEE 2007-4011). Washington, DC: National Center for Education Evaluation and Regional Assistance, Institute of Education Sciences, U.S. Department of Education.

Original content Copyright © by Holt, Rinehart and Winston. Additions and changes to the original content are the responsibility of the instructor.

Differentiating Instruction

Gersten, R., Baker, S., Unok Marks, S., & Smith, S.B. (1999). *Effective instruction for learning disabled or at-risk English language learners: An integrative synthesis of the empirical and professional knowledge bases.* Retrieved December 19, 2007, from http://www.ncld.org/content/view/519

Lyon, G.R. (1999). *The NICHD research program in reading development, reading disorders, and reading instruction.* Retrieved December 19, 2007, from www.bartonreading.com/pages/keys99_nichd.cfm.html

National Center for Learning Disabilities. (1999-2007). Learning disabilities at a glance. Retrieved December 18, 2007, from http://www.ncld.org/content/view/447/391

Siedenberg, P.L. (1989). *Relating text-processing research to reading and writing instruction for learning disabled students.* Learning Disabilities Focus, 5 (1), 4-12.

Swanson, L.H. (1999). *Intervention research for adolescents with learning disabilities: A meta-analysis of outcomes related to high-order processing.* Retrieved December 19, 2007, from http://www.ncld.org/content/view/523

Swanson, L.H. (1999). *Intervention research for students with learning disabilities: A meta-analysis of outcomes.* Retrieved December 19, 2007, from http://www.ncld.org/content/view/517

Torgesen, J.K., Rashotte, C.A., Alexander, A., Alexander, J., & MacPhee, K. (2003). Progress towards understanding the instructional conditions necessary for remediating reading difficulties in older children. In B. Foorman (Ed.), *Preventing and remediating reading difficulties: Bringing science to scale.* (pp. 275-298). Parkton, MD: York Press.

Weaver III, C.A. & Kintsch, W. (1991). Expository text. In R. Barr, M.L. Kamil, P.B. Mosenthal, & P.D. Pearson (Eds.), *Handbook of Reading Research* (pp. 230-244). White Plains, NY: Longman.

Original content Copyright © by Holt, Rinehart and Winston. Additions and changes to the original content are the responsibility of the instructor.

Differentiating Instruction

What Research Tells Us About Learners with Diverse Needs

WHO IS THE LEARNER WITH DIVERSE NEEDS?

The profile of a student with diverse needs may include economic poverty, other sociological risk factors, neurological impairment, language delays, motivational factors, or simple lack of exposure to print and to educational aspirations in the home.

Learners with diverse needs may include:

- students with dyslexia or other reading disabilities
- low-achieving students
- students with learning disabilities
- students receiving services under Title I of Improving America's Schools

WHY IS READING IMPORTANT?

"[L]earning to read is the gateway to achieving future success." The California Special Education Reading Task Force states the issue in those stark terms. The medium in which the statement is made—a printed document—proves the point.

Despite the information revolution, there are no signs of the appearance of a postliterate society, in which oral or visual communication will dislodge written communication as the means through which the most important ideas are spread and the most important business is conducted. On the contrary, masses of working people who, a generation ago, might have been laboring on farms or on assembly lines now spend their working hours at computer screens. There, amid the bells and whistles of Web design, print still dominates the content.

The teen or preteen of today who lacks proficient reading skills is in all likelihood going to be deprived of the chance to take full advantage of the economic and social opportunities of coming decades. The youngster with poor reading skills will not acquire either the workplace competence or the paper credentials necessary to get good jobs—"good" in the sense of both earning power and personal satisfaction. Yet 30 to 40 percent of today's children have reading difficulties.

WHAT IS THE SOLUTION?

Difficulty with reading is a handicap not only for individuals but also for the entire society, which needs these people to keep itself functioning. Fortunately the solution is known. Reading difficulties can be overcome through an intensive emphasis on early intervention to prevent their development and on continuing instruction to remedy existing reading problems and keep secondary students in the "reading pool." Given such prevention and intervention, it has been estimated that some 85 to 90 percent of poor readers can be brought to average proficiency levels. The state of California is putting this solution into action.

WHAT IS A TEACHER TO DO?

The teacher who is not an expert in the problems of learners with diverse needs in a classroom of students with varying levels of reading ability need not feel overwhelmed. Increasingly, research shows that a fundamental-skills approach,

Original content Copyright © by Holt, Rinehart and Winston. Additions and changes to the original content are the responsibility of the instructor.

Differentiating Instruction

embedded in appropriate reading materials, can alleviate a wide range of reading problems regardless of their labels.

This view should come as a relief to the classroom teacher, whose attention can now be focused not so much on whether Jenny comes from a deprived background but on whether Jenny has trouble distinguishing between similarly spelled words or is able to extract a main idea from a paragraph. Research has shown that struggling readers benefit most from appropriate teaching practices—systematic and explicit instruction, frequent assessment linked to instruction, and curriculum modification.

WHAT DOES THE RESEARCH SAY?

For decades, struggling readers have been the subject of a tug of war between traditional and experimental philosophies in education. With the adoption of the California Reading Initiative, there is at last reason to believe that a broad consensus can be achieved among parents and educators across the spectrum. Certain approaches have been discarded as ineffective, specifically the modality-based approach, which posited that visual learners and auditory learners required essentially different instructional strategies. Modality-based instruction, which had arrived in the guise of the latest trend, is now known not to be effective.

Proponents of outmoded theories may protest that research can be found to support any given instructional style. Such research, though, varies widely in its reliability. Reliable research adheres to the methods of science—it uses controls; produces consistent, replicable results; and is objectively reviewed by the peers of the researchers. Given those guidelines, the wheat can be more easily separated from the chaff in the sometimes confusing field of educational research. Innovations in instruction that work can be extracted from the mass of innovations that do not work.

For this reason, there is cause to hope that the familiar pendulum movement in pedagogical trends can be interrupted.

Systematic and Explicit Instruction

Among the key beliefs that have been displaced by recent research in reading is that struggling readers require intrinsically different instruction practices than on-level learners do. In fact, the same tried-and-true methods that enable average readers to recognize letters, sounds, and words and to draw meaning from texts also enable struggling readers to do so. The difference is that for these students more instruction time is needed, teaching should be more precisely sequenced, and immediate, specific feedback is of paramount importance. The learner with diverse needs follows the same path toward reading proficiency as the on-level learner, except that the journey is more time-consuming, more systematically planned, and more reliant on explicit directions.

Curriculum Modification

It should be evident from this research that even within a mainstream classroom, the learner with diverse needs requires a specially tailored and scheduled curriculum. Too often struggling readers are expected to work with the same materials the rest of

Original content Copyright © by Holt, Rinehart and Winston. Additions and changes to the original content are the responsibility of the instructor.

Differentiating Instruction

the class is using, but to do so perhaps at a lower level of comprehension. Whether those materials are trade books, general textbooks, or commercially designed phonics programs, the mismatch between the text provided and the student's readiness for it causes the learner with diverse needs to work constantly at the frustration level (reading accuracy of 89 percent or less) rather than the instructional level (90 to 94 percent) or the independent level (95 percent or higher). To the learners' preexisting difficulties is added the extra difficulty of not being able to keep up with the assigned materials. From these circumstances, a loss of motivation and self-esteem can arise, contributing to a vicious cycle.

Frequent Assessment Tied to Instruction

To avoid the mismatch between student abilities and instructional materials, an individualized education program (IEP) should be developed for each student. Accurate assessment of each learner's reading skills is essential in order to establish goals and monitor progress. Standardized assessment can play a role here. More detailed diagnostic information is relatively easy to obtain by going over the assigned materials with the student. For example, fluency—defined as the number of words read correctly per minute—can be easily measured by timing the oral reading of a selected passage with the second hand of a watch and keeping a tally of errors.

Balanced Reading Instruction

Given the intensive extra attention devoted to basics for struggling readers, the concept of balanced reading instruction must be modified for them. Balance does not have to mean equal time for all subjects. Rather, it may include much more time devoted to decoding and fluency, depending on the students' needs.

This also does not mean that comprehension is given short shrift. Research indicates that comprehension and decoding are dependent on one another. For example, a reader can't comprehend words until he or she has recognized and decoded them. There is no need to worry that an emphasis on fundamental skills will deprive students of the joyful experience of reading a story.

Scaffolding

Where an advanced student might simply charge through a text and then become involved in postreading analysis, the struggling reader will require more extensive scaffolding at all points in the reading of a selection. That might include review of previously learned materials that have bearing on a new text. It might include extensive attention to text structures, such as the title, subheadings, and captions, during previewing. It might include explicit instruction in the organizational structure of the text, such as the basic story grammar of character-problem-resolution or problem-solution structure in nonfiction. Instruction in text organization—including physical presentation of the text and organization of the contents—can be a valuable way to prime the student's background knowledge. Understanding of textual clues can facilitate students' recall of main ideas and relationships among ideas.

Scaffolding for the struggling reader also includes extensive modeling, for both

Original content Copyright © by Holt, Rinehart and Winston. Additions and changes to the original content are the responsibility of the instructor.

content and decoding. The teacher might model any of the innumerable skills used and decisions made in the course of confronting a text, including but not limited to sounding out a word, guessing a word's or idiom's meaning through context clues, examining a physical structure of a text, self-questioning the meaning of an unclear passage, and deciding to use a certain reading strategy.

Modeling and Direct Instruction

Modeling and other forms of direct instruction can occur before or during the reading of a text. Frequent pauses for instruction are often called for, requiring extra time for the reading assignment. It is a misconception, though, to think that pausing within a story to examine vocabulary or use a reading strategy decreases students' enjoyment or appreciation of a story. Such instructive pauses are a part of interactive reading. Advanced readers break into their own reading flow continually to pursue questions and to self-monitor. Direct instruction creates the learning space in which the struggling reader can do the same.

Direct instruction should by no means be confused with mindless drill or rote learning or with lectures in which students are passive recipients of a teacher's pronouncements. That sort of caricatured direct instruction would doubtless be as ineffective as its critics maintain. The goal of effective direct instruction is, from the outset, to prepare students for independent understanding. The processes taught in direct instruction are, for the most part, reading and thinking strategies that will ultimately be used by the learner on his or her own. (Effective direct instruction may also include providing specific background information about a text.) In instruction of this type, modeling is followed up by a monitored and guided student practice, in which focused teacher-student interactions make immediately clear to the student which tasks have been performed correctly and which tasks, skills, or strategies need further review. Reteaching of weaker skills is incorporated as the next step.

The Role of Review

For learners with diverse needs, review should be ongoing. Review is not saved for the end of a collection or unit; it is pursued more frequently and for the most part in smaller batches distributed at regular, natural intervals throughout the learning process. Review methods can be flexible and creative, tailored to students' individual error patterns, and may rely on review of the same passages on multiple occasions. Review in many cases should be cumulative. Instructional items should not be deleted from the review process too early, for mastery requires frequent review after initial success.

Where Metacognition Fits In

As students progress in their mastery of particular skills, the balance can be shifted gradually from direct instruction to self-monitored learning. At what point can students be expected to begin integrating instruction into independent reading and activities? Students' metacognitive abilities come into play here. The student who thinks to ask, "Is this a good spot in which to use this strategy?" or "Should I go back and read that paragraph more slowly?" or "Am I clear about what this

Original content Copyright © by Holt, Rinehart and Winston. Additions and changes to the original content are the responsibility of the instructor.

question asks?" is well on the road to independent reading and response.

Metacognition, or thinking about thinking, is a broad term that includes students' knowledge and awareness of their own learning processes and may also involve students' motivation. Metacognition grows slowly over time, well into the teenage years. This makes it of particular interest for middle- and upper-grade teachers. Contrary to the idea that learners with diverse needs can't handle this level of cognitive sophistication, getting them, as they read, to think about and articulate what they are doing and why they are doing it can be a key to engaging them in reading. Metacognition turns the reading process into an intelligently directed pursuit rather than a frustrating game of blind man's bluff. This is an area of research where the findings converge rather clearly. As reviewed by Dickson et al., the research literature offers "evidence that metacognitive instruction enhances reading comprehension for [struggling readers]. . . . [They] may require instruction on 'more' rather than less metacognitive components than average achievers."

Metacognitive instruction has been found particularly beneficial for learners with diverse needs in determining how to decide on the use of a reading strategy, how to self-question and self-monitor, and how to assess one's readiness to meet the demands of a task.

MISCONCEPTIONS AND CORRECTIONS: AN OVERVIEW

The above is a brief overview of some of the major issues in the teaching of reading to learners with diverse needs and of some prominent misconceptions regarding those issues. Several of those ongoing misconceptions have resulted from a misunderstanding of what direct instruction involves. Some have resulted from misguided attempts to create a unique pedagogy for learners with diverse needs, while others, in contrast, have resulted from equally misguided attempts to have learners with diverse needs read exactly the same materials as their on-level classmates.

A more truly balanced approach is needed. Its underlying premise must be that learners with diverse needs can develop the mental habits of good readers but that a systematic, intense, direct, long-lasting effort is required to enable them to do so.

An educational world completely free of misconceptions on the part of students, parents, teachers, administrators, public officials, and researchers is no doubt an impossibility. In recent years it has become very possible, however, to close the gap between free-ranging misconception and reasonable understanding based on valid findings.

The following chart shows the current state of misconception and correction in reading instruction for learners with diverse needs and how the accurate conceptions can be transferred into the classroom.

Original content Copyright © by Holt, Rinehart and Winston. Additions and changes to the original content are the responsibility of the instructor.

Differentiating Instruction

COMMON MISCONCEPTIONS ABOUT INSTRUCTION FOR LEARNERS WITH DIVERSE NEEDS

Misconception	What Research Shows	Implications for Instruction
Most students with serious reading difficulties can never catch up.	The vast majority of students with serious reading difficulties can learn to read. Even the effects of neurological difficulties can be reduced.	Use intensive instruction and research-based practices to bridge the reading gap.
A student's socioeconomic level is an accurate measure of the student's potential as a reader.	Reading achievement depends on parental aspirations for the student, reading materials available in the home, attitudes toward education, and other aspects of family life rather than on socioeconomic status alone.	Avoid simple assumptions based on students' socioeconomic levels. Thorough awareness of social context is required.
In order to teach a learner with diverse needs to read, it is necessary to apply a specific diagnostic label to the student.	Reading success often depends more on the nature of the instruction than on the nature of the diagnosis. In fact, lack of effective instruction can lead to misdiagnosed problems.	Your goal is to diagnose and alleviate reading difficulties, not their underlying causes.
Learners with diverse needs require intrinsically different kinds of reading instruction than other learners require.	Learners with diverse needs learn best when instructed intensively in the same fundamental skills taught to average learners.	You can make the difference for learners with diverse needs in your regular classroom by giving them enough individual attention.
Intensive instructional time in reading is mainly an issue for the early grades.	Substantial reading progress may require three or more hours of daily instruction at all grade levels.	Give learners with diverse needs a large daily allotment of reading-instruction time, including immediate, precise, feedback.
Serious reading difficulties can be solved in the context of whole-group instruction using grade-level materials.	Reading remediation requires instruction in specific fundamental skills at the appropriate level of difficulty.	Assess students' individual skill deficiencies, and choose materials to focus on those.
Learners with diverse needs need to make due with the materials generally available.	A core reading curriculum at the appropriate difficulty level is crucial in teaching learners with diverse needs.	Districts must provide appropriate materials for teaching reading to learners with diverse needs. The individual teacher cannot be expected to provide adequate materials.

Original content Copyright © by Holt, Rinehart and Winston. Additions and changes to the original content are the responsibility of the instructor.

Differentiating Instruction

After the early grades, students have already acquired the fundamental reading skills.	After the early grades, instruction has tended to shift away from fundamental skills, with the result that students who did not acquire skills early may never acquire them.	Even in middle and higher grades, be prepared to spend lots of time on essential skills.
Balanced education means that each skill or standard receives equal emphasis for each student.	Each learner with diverse needs has individual needs that require individual assessment and balancing.	Determine the relative priority of a given skill or standard for a given student based on the student's language and literacy levels.
Direct instruction is another term for rote drill or lecturing.	Direct instruction aims to develop strategies for independent reading.	Make heavy use of direct instructional interactions, including modeling, guided practice, and feedback, to prepare students for independent reading.
Direct instruction may work for decoding but not for comprehension.	Direct instruction can provide the language skills, reading strategies, and knowledge (of content and genre) that are required for comprehension.	Cut through the underbrush that blocks the student's way to comprehension. Scaffold with intensive previewing, background information, and skill or strategy review.
Instruction focusing on the "basics," such as decoding, makes learning to read a decontextualized process, depriving students of meaningful encounters with stories and books.	Research shows that a blend of approaches combining reading for comprehension with decoding can be an effective strategy.	Integrate mini-lessons (for example, on vocabulary, decoding, or reading strategy) into reading for content and enjoyment.
Text presentation is a secondary issue in reading comprehension.	Student awareness of text structure and of the conventions of the physical presentation of the text is strongly related to comprehension.	Devote ample time to physical text clues and macro-level text organization (for example, story structure and problem-solution structure) when previewing a text.
Learners with diverse needs don't benefit from instruction in metacognition.	Research suggests that metacognitive instruction may benefit learners with diverse needs more than it does average students.	Explicitly teach learners with diverse needs metacognitive skills, such as self-monitoring, self-questioning, and strategy choice.

Original content Copyright © by Holt, Rinehart and Winston. Additions and changes to the original content are the responsibility of the instructor.

Differentiating Instruction

Modality-based instruction (for example, phonics for auditory learners, sight word for visual learners) is effective, scientific, and up-to-date.	As early as 1977, a body of research had shown that modality-based instruction is ineffective.	Discard modality-based instruction.
Research is ambiguous; it proves whatever the researcher wants to prove.	Research can provide clear results when it follows accepted rules of scientific inquiry.	Research can play a role in your decisions about classroom curriculum and practices.

BIBLIOGRAPHY

August, D. & Shanahan. T. (eds). (2006). *Developing literacy in second-language learners: Report of the National Literacy Panel on Language-Minority Children and Youth.* Mahwah, NJ: Lawrence Erlbaum Associations, Publishers. Executive summary retrieved November 5, 2007, from www.cal.org/projects/archive/nlpreports/Executive_Summary.pdf

California reading initiative and special education in California. (1999). Sacramento: California Special Education Reading Task Force, California Department of Education.

Carnine, D. W. (ed.) Torgesen, J.K., Rashotte, C.A., Alexander, A., Alexander, J., & MacPhee, K. (2003). Progress towards understanding the instructional conditions necessary for remediating reading difficulties in older children. In B. Foorman (Ed.). Preventing and Remediating Reading Difficulties: Bringing Science to Scale. (pp. 275-298). Parkton, MD: York Press.

Dickson, S.V., Collins, V.L., Simmons, D.C., & Kameenui, E.J. (1998). Metacognitive strategies: Research bases. In Simmons and Kameeenui (Eds.), What reading research tells us about children with diverse learning needs. (295-360). Mahway, NJ: Lawrence Erlbaum Associates.

Gersten, R. et al. (2007). *Effective literacy and English language instruction for English learners in the elementary grades: A practice guide.* (NCEE 2007-4011). Washington, DC: National Center for Education Evaluation and Regional Assistance, Institute of Education Sciences, U.S. Department of Education.

Francis, David F., et al. (2006). Practical guidelines for the education of English language learners: Research-based recommendations for instruction and academic interventions. Under cooperative agreement grant S283B050034 for U.S. Department of Education). Portsmouth, NH: RMC Research Corporation, Center on Instruction (COI), 2006. (Book 1 of 3) Retrieved November 6, 2007, from www.centeroninstruction.org/resources.cfm?category=ell&grade_start+grade_n=12&subcategory=research

Francis, David F., et al. (2006). Practical guidelines for the education of English language learners: Research-based recommendations for serving adolescent newcomers. Under cooperative agreement grant S283B050034 for U.S. Department of Education). Portsmouth, NH: RMC Research Corporation, Center on Instruction (COI), 2006. (Book 2 of 3)

Original content Copyright © by Holt, Rinehart and Winston. Additions and changes to the original content are the responsibility of the instructor.

Differentiating Instruction

Gersten, R. et al. (2007). Effective literacy and English language instruction for English learners in the elementary grades: A practice guide. (NCEE 2007-4011). Washington, DC: National Center for Education Evaluation and Regional Assistance, Institute of Education Sciences, U.S. Department of Education.

Kameenui, E.J., Carnine. D. W., Dixon, R., Simmons, D., & Coyne, M. (Eds.). (2001). Second edition. Effective teaching strategies that accommodate diverse learners. Upper Saddle River, New Jersey: Prentice-Hall.

Simmons, D.C, E.J.& Kameenui, E.J. (1998). Introduction. What reading research tells us about children with diverse learning needs. Mahway, NJ: Lawrence Erlbaum Associates.

Original content Copyright © by Holt, Rinehart and Winston. Additions and changes to the original content are the responsibility of the instructor.

Differentiating Instruction

What Research Tells Us About English-Language Learners

While other factors—such as motivation, persistence, and quantitative skills—play important roles in the learning process, it is not possible to overstate the role that language plays in determining students' success with academic content.

(Francis et al., 2006, Book 1, page 7)

WHAT REGULAR TEACHERS FACE: A PROFILE OF ENGLISH LEARNERS

The present wave of immigration has radically changed the nature of education in middle schools and high schools throughout the United States. Nearly all teachers at the secondary level will at some point teach English learners. The term "English-language learners" is shorthand for many types of students, regardless of their educational needs or backgrounds. The term refers to students of different levels of English proficiency, schooling, socioeconomic status, linguistic and cultural backgrounds, and immigration histories. These learners come from language backgrounds other than English, and their English proficiency is not yet developed to the point in which they can fully profit from English-only instruction without assistance (August & Hakuta, 1997).

THE NEEDS OF ENGLISH-LANGUAGE LEARNERS

Teaching English Language Arts to English-language learners is both a challenge and an opportunity, especially at the middle school and high school levels. It is a challenge because students face a demanding curriculum and require advanced academic literacy. It is an opportunity because English Language Arts offers English learners ways to think, listen, speak, read, and write critically, which enables them to learn about the world and develop advanced skills in English.

To instruct English-language learners effectively, teachers must recognize their instructional needs—needs often based on student preparation, proficiency in English, and length of residence in the United States. Many groups of English-language learners are highly prepared for instruction. Those who have been schooled in their home countries enter schools in the United States with strong academic preparation and excellent literacy skills in their first language. Some are even better prepared than their native-English-speaking peers. It is relatively easy for these students to learn English, since they are simply learning the language for concepts that they already know. Also, because they can read and write well in their first languages, they quickly learn to read and write in English. Many literacy skills transfer from one language to another (Gersten et. al., 2007; August & Shanahan, 2006). Peregroy and Boyle (2001) explain transfer this way:

> … [reading] is essentially the same [process] whether reading English as a first or a second language. In other words, both first and second language readers look at the page and the print and use their knowledge of sound/symbol relationships, word order, grammar, and knowledge about the text's topic and structure along with their linguistic knowledge and reading strategies to arrive at an interpretation and to achieve their purpose for reading. (p. 259)

Original content Copyright © by Holt, Rinehart and Winston. Additions and changes to the original content are the responsibility of the instructor.

Differentiating Instruction

- **English Learners with Disrupted Schooling** These students may not have received a solid education in their home countries. They may have moved frequently from one school to the next or made frequent trips between their home country and the United States. They may never have learned to read or write well in their first languages. Through no fault of their own, they often fail to attain success in our schools are at risk of dropping out. Students who are under-schooled need intensive, comprehensive and thorough content-area instruction.

- **"Newcomers"** English-language learners can also be classified in terms of the amount of time they have spent in the United States. Recent arrivals to the United States, or "newcomers," are just beginning to learn English and have difficulty conveying even their most basic needs in English. This group requires survival English instruction, including the instruction of school "navigational language," such as "Raise your hands if you have a question" and "Time's up!" and emergency language, such as "Help!" "Fire!" and "Call the police!" In addition, recent arrivals require a basic introduction to the traditions and norms of the United States, information about school culture, and instruction in the fundamentals of the English language. They can best receive this type of intensive instruction and an introduction to the United States in ESL or ELD classrooms, programs, and services designed for newcomers. See *Holt English Language Development* for a guide to teaching English to newcomers.

- **Residents or Second-Generation Learners** The largest group of English-language learners consists of long-term residents and second-generation immigrant students whose parents were born in the United States. These students may consider themselves bilingual, but they may be losing their first language; or English may be the only language that they know. They have received most, if not all, of their education in schools in the United States, but they may still have a relatively low or intermediate level of English language proficiency. Although they can communicate in conversational English, instruction in academic English is essential for these students; and additional instructional time may be required for them to learn it. Without this instruction, these learners may fail to attain the advanced proficiency in English required to reach content standards, pass large-scale statewide assessments, complete course requirements, and satisfy college admission requirements.

ACADEMIC ENGLISH

Academic English is the formal language used in classrooms; it is the language of school-based learning and extended, reasoned discourse. It entails knowledge of the structure of the language and the precise way in which words and phrases are used. To illustrate the difference between academic English and informal English, consider the ways the two varieties of English are used by middle school students. For instance, the following would typify informal use of English: *Gimme it [pointing to a cell phone]. I gotta go. My mom say I gotta get home.* The student only needs to point to the cell phone to convey her meaning to her friend. In contrast, students who have learned the more sophisticated features of academic English might tell an adult, *Could you please give me the cell phone because I*

Original content Copyright © by Holt, Rinehart and Winston. Additions and changes to the original content are the responsibility of the instructor.

have to leave? My mother says I am needed at home. Notice that informal expressions such as *gimme* and *gotta* are absent in academic English. Also, academic English is grammatically correct and characterized by subordination (*because I have to leave*), rather than short, simple sentences. The academic English version is more abstract, complex, and grammatically accurate. It does not depend on context to convey meaning.

TIME TO GAIN FLUENCY

The length of time it takes to learn academic English is related to the amount of instruction students receive. Students who never receive instruction in it will probably never acquire it. The strong consensus of expert opinion is that English learners require considerable explicit, systematic, and deliberate instruction to learn the features of the type of formal English used in the schools and used in academic discourse. Teachers can maximize students' success by carefully monitoring their students' use and development of academic English. They can use the instructional tools and resources that are designed to teach English-language learners academic English.

WRITTEN WORK

When it comes to evaluating the academic writing of students with strong literacy skills in their first language, teachers have to be attuned to the ways students may have been trained to write in their home countries. Andrea Lunsford of Stanford University explains that teachers' expectations are often not clear to someone new to schooling in the United States. She points out that instructors expect students to present a highly explicit progression of ideas in a piece of writing—an introduction with a thesis, background on the topic, an overview of what will follow, generalizations and specifics logically laid out, a consideration of counterarguments, and a conclusion. According to Lunsford, a student from Chile would consider that progression childish, having been taught to be digressive. Likewise, a Korean student would have been taught to be indirect, presenting an introduction, the topic, a tangential topic, and only in the conclusion the thesis of the piece.

Teachers in the United States mostly expect factual evidence. Teachers and students in other parts of the world—for example, in China—place more trust in everyday wisdom, in what they consider authoritative philosophical or religious texts, and in people they judge authoritative. Lunsford's other observation about authority is that teachers in the United States expect students to become authorities on a topic, but other cultures, such as Japanese, Indonesian, and Navajo, "position student writers as novices whose job is to reflect what they learn from their teachers," not to present their own perspectives.

GENERAL ADVICE FOR TEACHING ENGLISH-LANGUAGE LEARNERS

Given the student profile and predilections discussed above, what can regular English teachers do to integrate English-language learners into their classes successfully? Clearly, both the instruction and the assignments need to be matched

Original content Copyright © by Holt, Rinehart and Winston. Additions and changes to the original content are the responsibility of the instructor.

to the instructional needs of students. To accomplish this objective, teachers will want to consider a series of language issues.

Language Issues

- *Comprehension Difficulties.* Many English learners have difficulty understanding their instructor and classmates. They might not understand the teachers' directions, hear or understand certain sounds, understand common idioms such as "make up your mind" and "let's hit the books" or the language used in explanations, definitions, and classroom discussions. English learners also have difficulty making sense of the vocabulary, grammar, and discourse patterns of their reading. They may face reading obstacles due to limitations in their background knowledge or lack of familiarity with English text structures.

- *Production Difficulties.* English learners often face language-production problems. In speech, they might not pronounce words correctly, or they might not know the vocabulary to respond to their teachers' questions. They may know a single definition of a word but not know the word's literal meaning or connotations. They may not know the other words that commonly precede and follow it. For example, English learners often have difficulty learning collocations—word groups such as "peanut butter and jelly" or "comment on" and words with multiple meanings—such as "table" and "fault" (August et al., 2005).

SUPPORTIVE, HIGH-QUALITY INSTRUCTION WITH HIGH EXPECTATIONS

A goal for a regular English teacher is to create a classroom atmosphere that is supportive of English-language learners and that accelerates their acquisition not only of conversational skills but also academic language. It involves providing high-quality instruction that is explicit and carefully designed, implemented, and monitored. It also involves having high expectations of English learners and providing all students with challenging and engaging learning experiences.

When teachers cushion learners, they prevent learners from addressing and improving these weaknesses. Teachers who tend to treat all English-language learners as though they have just arrived in the United States and are only just beginning to acquire English may provide their students with excessive encouragement and little accurate feedback. They may give English learners simplified tasks or set low expectations. As a result, they avoid giving the students advice that would improve their knowledge of English. Instead, teachers should make sure that English learners participate in supplemental and intervention programs (August & Hakuta, 1997).

ERROR CORRECTION

Teachers should correct students appropriately and avoid embarrassing them or giving confusing feedback. To support oral fluency activities, teachers can learn about students' native languages and be aware of student differences in pronunciation. They can understand that English learners may apply knowledge of their home languages when producing English sounds, words, grammar and discourse. If students read aloud, teachers can make notes on mispronunciations

Original content Copyright © by Holt, Rinehart and Winston. Additions and changes to the original content are the responsibility of the instructor.

and use these notes later when helping students in small groups or one-on-one conferences. To support writing activities, teachers can provide learners with effective feedback on their written assignments.

TEACHING LITERATURE AND OTHER READING

A review of the research on teaching literature and nonfiction to English-language learners integrated into regular English classes yields a variety of pointers. Some researchers recommend tried-and-true strategies that work with all students, not just English learners, but some also offer specific research-based guidance for teaching English learners specifically. Recent research has revealed evidence-based practices and instructional approaches that are theoretically sound for application to English learners. In 2006, a group of researchers analyzed the existing scientific research on second language learning and instruction. August and Shanahan, as well as Gersten and others, summarized this research in a series of reports. These reports discuss current and proven practices for teaching English learners. Francis et al. make the following recommendations:

1. **Increase opportunities for English learners to develop sophisticated vocabulary knowledge related to their classroom reading.** Include deliberate, systematic and explicit vocabulary instruction into daily lessons. Francis et al. even suggest that English learners and their classmates need about 12-14 exposures to a word and its meanings across many different contexts if they are to gain deep understanding of vocabulary. All researchers agree that you should teach useful, high frequency function words such as *nevertheless* and *although* as well as high utility academic words such as *examine* and *sequential*. Researchers concur that you should teach the ways words relate to one another (word families) and can be changed into different words by adding different word parts (roots, suffixes, and prefixes), levels of word knowledge, and word learning strategies (such as using word parts and the dictionary to unlock word meanings). This type of instruction helps English-language learners to become independent word learners.

2. **During reading instruction, equip English learners with strategies and knowledge to comprehend and analyze narrative and expository texts.** Provide effective comprehension instruction for English learners that is explicit and that actively engages the students in thinking about their own use of strategies. Francis et al. explain that it is important to help learners adjust the reading comprehension process to the type of text (e.g., expository or narrative), the purposes for the reading (e.g., to learn about a concept or to entertain), and the format of the content (e.g., the format of instructions, an argumentative essay, or a narrative). They emphasize the importance of promoting meta-cognition—"the students' ability to reflect on, monitor, and control their own thinking processes." Students who already use these strategies for reading in their native language may need reminders to use them in English as well.

Francis et al. explain how these research-based techniques can be used to foster the development of comprehension strategies:

- *Before Reading:* Ask students to make predictions about what the text involves before reading. Scaffold discussions about texts to help students understand purpose of their reading. Remind students of the knowledge they already have about the reading.

Original content Copyright © by Holt, Rinehart and Winston. Additions and changes to the original content are the responsibility of the instructor.

Differentiating Instruction

- *During Reading:* Teach students to monitor their understanding of the text, to ask questions during reading, to recognize when their reading comprehension falls apart, and to figure out what information they need to understand the text.

- *After Reading:* Help students summarize text after they read. Summarizing requires students to synthesize what they have read, to be aware of the difference between important and less important information, and to appropriate some of the authors' words and sentence structures into their speech or writing.

Two goals of these techniques are to get students to apply strategies effectively across texts and to use the strategies independently. In using the techniques, teachers need to make sure that students participate in structured conversations about the text. In these conversations, students can discuss their interpretations, comprehension strategies, purposes for reading, genre, and the ways genres affect the strategies they use.

3. **When developing English learners' reading fluency, focus on vocabulary and increased exposure to print.** Considerable research now indicates that English-language learners need to develop the ability to read literature and other texts with fluency in specific ways—with appropriate phrasing (pausing appropriately), appropriate prosody (with the correct rhythm, including stress and intonation), and good inflection (appropriately changing tone or pitch). To improve students' oral reading fluency, Francis et al. recommend that teachers help students develop "automaticity" in word-recognition skills and word meanings, so that the students can hold information in working memory while constructing and extracting meaning from text.

To help students develop fluency, teachers should also provide students with ample practice reading text that is at the students' instructional level (reading with 90% accuracy). Use repeated reading. In this activity, students read to the teacher or other students whose fluency skills are better than their own. Their teacher or partners provide them with useful corrective feedback. They read the passage repeatedly until they can read it with few errors with acceptable phrasing and expression. Vocabulary is pre-taught, and the teacher makes sure students understand the reading by drawing students into discussions about passage content beforehand.

4. **Give English learners significant opportunities to engage in structured academic talk about literature and other readings.** A significant factor in developing advanced language skills is the use of academic words and structures and feedback. Practice is optimized when connected to reading and writing activities focused on the literature and other class readings. Reading aloud and shared readings that are accompanied by structured discussion are excellent ways to promote language development and reading comprehension.

5. **Encourage students to engage in independent reading.** Francis et al. explain that the following conditions should be met: 1) there should be a careful match between the reader's ability and the characteristics of the text, and 2) explicit goals should be set for the independent reading activity. Independent reading can be connected to the writing activities—a written reflection or a structured discussion with peers. Follow-up activities promote increased student engagement with reading.

Original content Copyright © by Holt, Rinehart and Winston. Additions and changes to the original content are the responsibility of the instructor.

Differentiating Instruction

TEACHING VOCABULARY

Vocabulary development has long been considered important for reading comprehension. The National Reading Panel concluded that vocabulary should be taught both directly and indirectly. Learning in rich contexts, incidental learning, and the use of computer technology all help adolescents develop larger vocabularies. A combination of methods, rather than a single teaching method, leads to the best learning.

- **Use context-rich activities.** Demonstrate the use of new vocabulary in situations related to English learners' experiences. Where appropriate, use the context provided by concepts or literature the students have already learned.

- **Control the content.** When teaching new vocabulary, present words and phrases embedded in sentences or text well known to English learners. Each sentence or portion of text should focus on only one new word or phrase.

- **Control the vocabulary.** When introducing and developing new concepts, control the complexity of the language. Learning new concepts and new vocabulary at the same time is loaded with many unknowns, which tend to impede the acquisition of new material.

TEACHING SPEAKING AND LISTENING

English learners should be encouraged to practice their linguistic skills in oral situations. Oral activities in which English learners are prompted to voice their opinions or share personal experiences help them build confidence in their speaking abilities. These activities develop English learners' speaking skills.

- **Summarization and/or Paraphrasing.** Ask students to summarize and/or paraphrase parts of a text to a partner.

- **Think/Pair/Share.** Call on students to read a text and reflect on it. Tell them to think about a question or issue related to this text and share their thoughts with a partner for two to three minutes. Next, randomly select pairs of students to summarize their answers. When possible, structure these activities so that less proficient learners are partnered with more proficient ones.

- **Instructional Conversations.** Encourage students to talk to one another in ways that specifically improve their oral language development. Require students to respond orally to a specific text (e.g., explain it, defend ideas in it, or describe an aspect or feature of it). Tell students how to participate in conversations (e.g., explicitly teaching them ways to introduce new topics, keep conversations going, ask questions, and clarify). For instance, teach students to say *I'd like to hear Ramon's opinion. Who has a different idea? I have not heard Ana's ideas.*

PRONUNCIATION

Once English learners get used to the stress and intonation patterns of English, they will sound altogether more fluent. There are several activities teachers can use to help students internalize the intonation, rhythm, and stress patterns of English:

- **Gesturing intonation.** To teach in intonation and rhythm, you can make gestures in the air so that students can see intonation of a sentence.

Original content Copyright © by Holt, Rinehart and Winston. Additions and changes to the original content are the responsibility of the instructor.

Differentiating Instruction

- **Clapping rhythm.** You can clap so that the students hear the number of beats (syllables) in a word or sentence. The claps can be louder or quieter so that the students hear the different stress patterns. Ask the students to clap themselves. Practicing will make students sensitive to the different rhythms of English.

- **Humming.** You can also hum a sentence that the students have been working on and then direct students to say what sentence you have hummed.

- **Pointing to Fingers.** You can hold up a hand in front of the class. You can indicate by pointing to each finger that each finger represents a word of a sentence. By pointing to spaces between fingers, joining fingers, and separating fingers, you can indicate missing words, liaisons, phrases, and pauses. Using fingers in this way helps make the pronunciation of a sentence visible.

- **Thumbs Up.** To teach students where to place stress on multi-syllabic words, repeat words orally and ask the students to put their thumbs up when they hear the stress.

- **Songs, Chants, Poems and Tongue Twisters.** Use songs, chants, poems and tongue twisters to teach intonation, rhythm and stress. Students recite them aloud chorally after their teacher, practice them, and memorize them.

LISTENING DEVELOPMENT

Often teachers forget the importance of helping students improve their listening skills. Yet there are many useful activities that do just this.

- **Read Alouds.** By reading aloud to students on a regular basis and asking students to listen purposefully, you engage students' interest and build their listening skills. Students may summarize the passage, retell the important parts of the text, complete true/false exercises based on the passage, or answer a series of comprehension questions (both literal and inferential) based on the passage.

- **Guided Listening - Mini-Lecture Activity.** Give students brief oral mini-lectures on key subjects related to the lesson. As you lecture, ask students to use graphic organizers and/or another system of taking notes. Follow up by asking students questions. You can also ask students to summarize or critique the mini-lectures. This activity can be scaffolded for English learners.

- **Oral Cloze Activity.** Ask students to complete a cloze activity. Give students a short reading with missing words. As you read the text aloud to students, have them fill in the missing words. Or write five sentences on the board and erase four or five targeted words. Read the sentences aloud and invite students to say or write the missing words.

- **Direct Instruction, Modeling, and Practice.** In these activities, teachers explain specific listening skills, model these skills, and provide students with opportunities for them to practice using these skills in partners and groups. Gibbon suggests that teachers teach English learners how to ask for clarification when they do not understand what they have heard. Specifically, teachers demonstrate the use of the following locutions:

Original content Copyright © by Holt, Rinehart and Winston. Additions and changes to the original content are the responsibility of the instructor.

Differentiating Instruction

"When you said . . . did you mean . . . ?"

"Excuse me, what do you mean by . . . ?"

"Could you tell me again . . .?"

TEACHING WRITING

All students, especially English-language learners, benefit when teachers are explicit about the writing they want their students to produce. Teachers can teach students what constitutes cohesion, a logical progression of ideas, a thesis, background on a topic, generalizations, specifics, evidence, authority, counterarguments, and a conclusion. They can provide ample models to illustrate these terms, clear definitions of these terms, and sufficient scaffolded practice.

- **Guide the writing.** With English learners, brainstorm vocabulary related to a topic. Write the words and phrases on the board. Have students review the list and encourage them to use the vocabulary orally to discuss the target topic. Then, have each student write on the board a sentence that relates to the topic. With the group, organize the sentences into paragraphs. Correct the grammatical errors and explain them to students. Finally, have the students read the final product.

- **Modify writing assignments.** To help English-language learners with limited English proficiency, try shortening the assignment. For instance, an English learner writing a persuasive piece could state his or her opinion, fully elaborate on one reason, and provide a call to action in one paragraph.

- **Assign numerous short writing assignments.** When students have numerous opportunities to write on the same topic or text with teacher instruction and supportive feedback, they gain the writing proficiency to write longer texts.

- **Provide effective instructional feedback.** Try to provide feedback systematically, using student-friendly explanations and corrective feedback symbols, as appropriate. Don't forget to ask students to use your feedback to improve their writing.

- **Give multiple-draft essay assignments.** All students, and especially English learners benefit from the opportunity to draft, write, revise, and edit their work. You can give students time in class to write, revise, and edit their essays, so that they get into the habit of revising and editing and become good self-editors.

- **Hold teacher-student conferences.** Provide one-on-one conferences that focus on the students' strengths and weaknesses in writing.

- **Teach editing skills.** Teachers frequently provide students with short instruction on error correction and provide time in class for students to review their teachers' feedback on their writing and rewrite or edit their writing based on this feedback.

Original content Copyright © by Holt, Rinehart and Winston. Additions and changes to the original content are the responsibility of the instructor.

Differentiating Instruction

TEACHING ENGLISH-LANGUAGE LEARNERS

Misconception	Expert Opinion	Implications for Instruction
Teachers should always use the simplest English possible for English-language learners.	Learners need to hear examples of English that may be beyond what they can produce themselves but that can be understood from context.	Teach academic vocabulary. Consider using student-friendly definitions and diagrams as well as other visual aids to help English learners deal with more advanced vocabulary.
English-language learners should demonstrate mastery of one skill before going on to practice another skill.	Learning is gradual and recursive rather than strictly progressive.	Expose students to a wide variety of skills without waiting for total mastery of any one skill.
Errors should always be called to the attention of English-language learners.	Errors can provide valuable information concerning student learning.	Provide sensible error correction when necessary in order to facilitate language development.
Ability to converse fluently in informal, conversational English means learners should perform well in school.	Control of informal, conversational English does not correlate with literacy skills.	Remember that students who have mastered the ability to converse in informal situations still require intensive reading and writing instruction.
English-language learners eventually acquire academic English on their own, mainly through independent, pleasure reading.	Students learn academic English through direct instruction tied to reading and writing. Even with effective instruction, it may take students many years to learn academic English.	Teach academic English every day and encourage students to learn it and use it in their speech and writing.
Repetitive grammar and vocabulary drills are the best tools for expanding English learners' progress.	Extensive, scaffolded journal writing in lieu of drills is an effective tool for helping students gain proficiency in English.	Incorporate grammar and vocabulary drills, but do not limit students to the use of these tools alone.
English-language learners should be discouraged from using their first language in classrooms.	English learners perform better when allowed to use their first language to help them understand lessons and produce English.	Encourage English-speaking students to accept the need for English learners to express themselves in their first language for instructional reasons and emergency situations.

Original content Copyright © by Holt, Rinehart and Winston. Additions and changes to the original content are the responsibility of the instructor.

Differentiating Instruction

BIBLIOGRAPHY

August, D., Carlo, M., Dressler, C., & Snow, C. (2005). The critical role of vocabulary development for English language learners. *Learning Disabilities Research and Practice,* 20, 50-57.

August, D. & Hakuta, K. (1997). *Improving schooling for language-minority children.* Washington, D.C.: National Academy Press.

August, D. & Shanahan. T. (Eds), (2006). *Developing literacy in second-language learners: Report of the National Literacy Panel on Language-Minority Children and Youth.* Mahwah, NJ: Lawrence Erlbaum Associations, Publishers.

Carlo, M.S., August, D., McLaughlin, B., Snow, C.E., Dressler, C., Lippman, D., et al. (2004). Closing the gap: Addressing the vocabulary needs for English language learners in bilingual and mainstream classrooms. *Reading Research Quarterly,* 39, 188-215.

Davidson, J. & Koppenaver, D. (1993). *Adolescent literacy: What works and why* (2nd ed.). New York: Garland.

Echevarria, J., Vogt, M. & Short, D. (2003). Making content comprehensible for English learners: *The SIOP Model.* 2nd Edition. Boston, MA: Pearson/Allyn & Bacon, 2003.

Francis, David F., et al. (2006). *Practical Guidelines for the Education of English Language Learners: Research-Based Recommendations for Instruction and Academic Interventions.* Under cooperative agreement grant S283B050034 for U.S. Department of Education). Portsmouth, NH: RMC Research Corporation, Center on Instruction (COI), 2006. (Book 1 of 3)

Francis, David F., et al. (2006). *Practical Guidelines for the Education of English Language Learners: Research-Based Recommendations for Serving Adolescent Newcomers.* Under cooperative agreement grant S283B050034 for U.S. Department of Education). Portsmouth, NH: RMC Research Corporation, Center on Instruction (COI), 2006. (Book 2 of 3)

Gersten, R. et al. (2007). *Effective literacy and English language instruction for English learners in the elementary grades: A practice guide* (NCEE 2007-4011). Washington, DC: National Center for Education Evaluation and Regional Assistance, Institute of Education Sciences, U.S. Department of Education. Retrieved November 27, 2007, from http://ies.ed.gov/ncee/

Gibbons, P. (1993). *Learning to learn in a second language.* Portsmouth, NH: Heinemann.

Lunsford, A. A. (2004). *The everyday writer* (3rd ed.). New York: Bedford/St. Martin's.

Peregroy, S. F., & Boyle, O. F. (2001). *Reading, writing, and learning in ESL.* New York: Longman.

Roit, M. L. (2006). Essential comprehension strategies for English learners. In T.A. Young & N. L. Hadaway (Eds.), *Supporting the literacy development of English learners: Increasing success in all classrooms* (pp. 80-95). Newark, DE: International Reading Association.

Scarcella, R. (2003). *Accelerating academic English: A focus on the English learner.* Oakland, California: Regents of the University of California.

Van Gelderen, Amos, et al. (2007). Development of adolescent reading comprehension in language 1 and language 2: A longitudinal analysis of constituent components. *Journal of Educational Psychology,* 99, 3, 477-491.

Original content Copyright © by Holt, Rinehart and Winston. Additions and changes to the original content are the responsibility of the instructor.

Phonological Features

The Linguistic Contrastive Analysis chart identifies English sounds that will or will not pose difficulty for primary speakers of languages other than English. Examples of how the sounds transfer from English to students' primary languages are included.

English	Spanish	Vietnamese	Cantonese or Mandarin	Pilipino or Tagalog	Hmong	Korean
Initial Consonants						
/f/ fan	Little difficulty	/b/ ban	Little difficulty	/p/ pan	/p/ pan	/p/ pan
/v/ van	/b/, /f/ ban, fan (Note: Spanish has only one sound for /b/ and /v/.)	Little difficulty	/w/ wan	Little difficulty	Little difficulty	/w/, /b/ wan, ban
/th/ though	Little difficulty	/d/ doe	/d/ doe (Note: /th/ and /th/ do not exist.)	/b/, /f/ bow, foe	/d/ doe	(Note: /th/ and /th/ do not exist.)
/th/ think	/d/ dink	/d/, /z/ dink, zink	/d/ dink	/d/ dink	/d/ dink	/s/ sink
/sh/ sheet	/ch/ cheat (Note: /sh/ does not exist.)	/s/,/ch/ seat, cheat	/s/ seat	Little difficulty	Little difficulty	Little difficulty
/j/ jar	/h/,/y/ har, yar	/z/ zar	Little difficulty	/y/ yar	Little difficulty	/zh/ as in rouge
/y/ yes	/j/ jes	Little difficulty	Little difficulty	Little difficulty	Little difficulty	Little difficulty
/h/ house	The nearest sound to /h/ in Spanish sounds like the *ch* in *Bach*.	Little difficulty	The nearest sound to /h/ sounds like the *ch* in *Bach*.	Little difficulty	Little difficulty	Little difficulty
/n/ need	Little difficulty	Little difficulty	/l/ lead	Little difficulty	Little difficulty	Little difficulty
/r/ rock	rolled or trilled Rock	Little difficulty	/l/ lock (Note: Many speakers find /l/ and /r/ difficult to distinguish	Little difficulty	Little difficulty	/l/ lock (Note: /r/ does not exist.)
/s/ student	add /e/ before /s/ estudent	Little difficulty	Little difficulty	Little difficulty	Little difficulty	/sh/ shtudent

Original content Copyright © by Holt, Rinehart and Winston. Additions and changes to the original content are the responsibility of the instructor.

Differentiating Instruction

English	Spanish	Vietnamese	Cantonese or Mandarin	Pilipino or Tagalog	Hmong	Korean
Initial Consonants *(continued)*						
/z/ zoo	/s/ sue (Note: Initial /z/ does not exist.)	Little difficulty	/s/ sue (Note: /z/ does not exist.)	/s/ sue	/s/ sue	/j/,/ch/ choo
/p/,/t/,/k/ pot, tot, cot	/b/,/d/,/g/ bot, dot, got	Initial /t/ in Vietnamese sounds like /d/: dot	Little difficulty	/b/,/d/,/g/ bot, dot, got	Little difficulty	/p/ may be replaced by /f/: fought
/b/,/d/,/g/ bet, debt, get	Initial /b/ is sometimes replaced with /v/: vet	Little difficulty	/p/,/t/,/k/ pet, tet, ket	Little difficulty	Little difficulty	/b/ may be replaced by /v/: vet
Medial Consonants						
/zh/ measure	/z/ mezure	Little difficulty	/z/,/sh/ mezure, meashure	/z/ mezure	Little difficulty	/z/,/sh/ mezure, meashure
/r/ horrible	rolled or trilled hoRrible	Little difficulty	/l/ holible	Little difficulty	Little difficulty	/l/ holible
Final Consonants						
/p/,/k/,/t/ tip, sick, sit	Little difficulty	Little difficulty	Often dropped or replaced with a *schwa* sound. (Note: there are few final consonants.)	Little difficulty	/b/,/d/,/g/ tib, sid, sig	Often dropped or replaced with a *schwa* sound. (Note: there are few final consonants.)
/s/ after consonant cats, hats	Little difficulty	Not used in Vietnamese.	Little difficulty	Little difficulty	Little difficulty	Little difficulty
/v/ love	Usually no difficulty, but may be replaced with /b/ : lub	/b/, /p/ lub, lup	Often deleted.	Little difficulty	Often deleted.	Little difficulty, but may be replaced by /b/: lub
/j/ edge	/ch/ etch	Often deleted.	Little difficulty	/ə/ added at end edgeh	Little difficulty	/ə/ added at end edgeh
/m/ dream	/n/,/ng/ drean, dreang	Little difficulty	Little difficulty	Little difficulty	Little difficulty	Little difficulty
/ng/ thing	/n/ thin	Little difficulty	/n/ thin	/n/ thin	/n/ thin	/n/ thin
Vowels						
/ē/ sheep	Little difficulty	Little difficulty	Little difficulty	Little difficulty	Little difficulty	Little difficulty
/i/ lip	/ē/ leap	/ē/ leap	Little difficulty	/ē/ leap	Little difficulty	/ē/ leap

Original content Copyright © by Holt, Rinehart and Winston. Additions and changes to the original content are the responsibility of the instructor.

Differentiating Instruction

English	Spanish	Vietnamese	Cantonese or Mandarin	Pilipino or Tagalog	Hmong	Korean
Vowels *(continued)*						
/ā/ raid	Often substitute /e/: red	Little difficulty	Little difficulty	Little difficulty	Little difficulty	/e/ red
/e/ bet	/ā/ bait	/a/ bat	Vowel sounds might vary as a function of the surrounding consonant sounds	/ā/ bait	Little difficulty	/ē/ beat
/a/ cat	/o/ cot	/o/ cot	/a/ does not exist; cot, Kate, ket, cut. Learners might nasalize or replace with /o/: cot, /e/:bet, or /u/ : cup. Most frequently substitute /a/ with /e/.	/o/ cot	/o/ cot	Little difficulty
/o/ clock	/ō/ cloak	Little difficulty	Little difficulty	/ō/ cloak	Little difficulty	/ō/ cloak (There are no long-short vowel distinctions in Korean.)
/ə/ above	Does not exist. Often replaced by another vowel.	Little difficulty	Does not exist. Often replaced by another vowel.	Does not exist. Often replaced by another vowel.	Does not exist. Often replaced by another vowel.	Does not exist. Often replaced by another vowel.
/u/ cup	/o/, / ōō / cop, coop	Little difficulty	/o/ cop	/o/ cop	Little difficulty	/o/ cop
/ō/ boat	Little difficulty	Little difficulty	Little difficulty	Little difficulty	/ô/ bought	Little difficulty
/oo/ pull	/ ōō / pool	/ ōō / pool	/ ōō / pool	/ ōō / pool	Little difficulty	Little difficulty
/ ōō / pool	Little difficulty	Little difficulty	Little difficulty	Little difficulty	Little difficulty	Little difficulty

Original content Copyright © by Holt, Rinehart and Winston. Additions and changes to the original content are the responsibility of the instructor.

Differentiating Instruction

Grammatical Features

Grammar Point	Spanish	Vietnamese	Cantonese or Mandarin	Pilipino or Tagalog	Hmong	Korean
Nouns						
PLURAL FORMS Nouns do not change form to show the plural in the primary language or plurals are not used in the same way.		•	•		•	•
POSSESSIVE FORMS Prepositions are either inferred or are not formed in the same way.	•	•	•	•	•	•
The word order in the primary language is different.	•	•	•	•	•	•
COUNT VS. NONCOUNT Nouns that are count and noncount differ between English and primary language.	•	•	•	•	•	•
Articles						
Articles are either lacking or the distinction between *a* and *the* is not paralleled in the primary language.		•	•	•	•	•
Learners sometimes confuse the articles *a/an* with *one* since articles either do not exist in the primary language or serve a different function.		•			•	
Pronouns						
PERSONAL PRONOUNS, GENDER The third person pronoun in the primary language is gender-free. The same pronoun is used where English uses masculine, feminine, and neuter pronouns, resulting in confusion of pronoun forms in English.			•	•	•	
PERSONAL PRONOUN FORMS The same pronoun form is used for he/him, she/her, and in some primary languages for I/me and we/us.			•		•	
There is no number agreement in the primary language. In Vietnamese, plurality is never expressed.		•	•			

Original content Copyright © by Holt, Rinehart and Winston. Additions and changes to the original content are the responsibility of the instructor.

Differentiating Instruction

Grammar Point	Spanish	Vietnamese	Cantonese or Mandarin	Pilipino or Tagalog	Hmong	Korean
Pronouns continued						
Subject pronouns may be dropped in the primary language and the verb ending supplies information on number and/or gender.	•					
Direct objects are frequently dropped in the primary language.		•				
A subordinate clause at the beginning of a sentence does not require a subject in the primary language.		•	•			•
(Use of pronouns with subject nouns) This type of redundant structure reflects "topic-comment" approach used in the primary language: The speaker mentions a topic and then makes a comment on it.	•	•	•		•	•
It is common in the primary language to repeat nouns rather than to use pronouns.		•	•			•
POSSESSIVE FORMS Speakers tend to omit final *n*, creating confusion between *my* and *mine*.		•	•		•	•
Verbs						
SUBJECT–VERB AGREEMENT There is no subject-verb agreement in the primary language.		•	•	•	•	•
TENSE Verb forms do not change to indicate tense, or time is understood from context.		•	•	•	•	•
PAST TENSE Speakers of the primary language have difficulty recognizing that merely a vowel shift in the middle of the verb, rather than a change in the ending of the verb, is sufficient to produce a change of tense in irregular verbs.	•	•	•		•	•
IN NEGATIVE STATEMENTS Helping verbs are not used in negative statements in the primary language.	•		•	•		• (There are no helping verbs in Korean.)

Original content Copyright © by Holt, Rinehart and Winston. Additions and changes to the original content are the responsibility of the instructor.

Differentiating Instruction

Grammar Point	Spanish	Vietnamese	Cantonese or Mandarin	Pilipino or Tagalog	Hmong	Korean
Verbs (continued)						
VERB TENSE The verb form either doesn't exist in the primary language or has a different function. Vietnamese, Hmong, Cantonese, and Mandarin do not use verbs to express time.		•	•	•	•	•
PAST CONTINUOUS In the primary language, the past continuous form can be used in contexts in which English uses the expression *used to* or the simple past.	•			•		
VERB AS A NOUN Unlike English, Cantonese does not require an infinitive marker when using a verb as a noun.			•			
In Hmong verbs can be connected without *and* or any other conjunction (serial verbs).					•	
LINKING VERBS The verb *be* is not required in all sentences. In some primary languages, it is implied in the adjective form. In others the concept is expressed as a verb.		•	•		•	•
PASSIVE VOICE Passive voice in the primary language does not require a helping verb.		•	•			•
TRANSITIVE VERBS VERSUS INTRASITIVE VERBS Verbs that do and do not take a direct object differ between English and primary language.	•		•	•		
PHRASAL VERBS Phrasal verbs do not exist in the primary language. There is often confusion over their meaning in English.	•					
HAVE VERSUS *BE* Some Spanish constructions use *have* where English uses *be*.	•					

Original content Copyright © by Holt, Rinehart and Winston. Additions and changes to the original content are the responsibility of the instructor.

Differentiating Instruction

Grammar Point	Spanish	Vietnamese	Cantonese or Mandarin	Pilipino or Tagalog	Hmong	Korean
Adjectives						
WORD ORDER Adjectives commonly come after nouns in the primary language.	•	•			•	
Adjectives always come before words they modify in the primary language.			•			
COMPARISON Comparative and superlative are usually formed with separate words in the primary language, the equivalent of *more* and *most* in English.	•				•	•
CONFUSION OF –*ING* AND –*ED* FORMS The speakers of the primary language sometimes confuse these adjective forms, not distinguishing between *an interesting movie* and *an interested viewer*, for example.	•	•	•	•	•	•
Adverbs						
Adverbs usually come before verbs in the primary language, and this tendency is carried over into English.			•			
Prepositions						
English prepositions do not match the prepositions of the primary language precisely.			•			
Complex Sentences						
The primary language lacks tense markers so that matching the tenses of two verbs in one sentence correctly can be difficult. Learners may also try to analyze the tense needed in English according to meaning, which in some cases can result in the use of an incorrect tense.		•	•	•	•	•
IF VERSUS WHEN The primary language has one expression that covers the use of English if and when for the future.				•		

Original content Copyright © by Holt, Rinehart and Winston. Additions and changes to the original content are the responsibility of the instructor.

Differentiating Instruction

Grammar Point	Spanish	Vietnamese	Cantonese or Mandarin	Pilipino or Tagalog	Hmong	Korean
Sentence Structure						
The pattern in the primary language is to describe what happens first while later occurrences follow. This is not an error in English, but it leads to a lack of sentence variety.			•			
The phrase with the indirect object can come before the direct object in Spanish.	•					
Spanish requires double negatives in many sentence structures.	•					
Questions						
The Primary language doesn't use subject-verb inversion in questions.		•	•	•		•
In the primary language, word order is the same in some questions and statements, depending on the context.			•	•	•	•
In the primary language, there is no exact counterpart to the *do/did* verb in questions.	•			•	•	•
YES/NO QUESTIONS In the primary language, learners tend to answer yes by repeating the verb in question. They tend to say no by using *not* and repeating the verb.			•		•	
TAG QUESTIONS The primary language has no exact counterpart to a tag question, forms them differently, or does not add *do/did* to questions.		•	•			•

Original content Copyright © by Holt, Rinehart and Winston. Additions and changes to the original content are the responsibility of the instructor.

Fluency and *Differentiating Instruction*

ABOUT THE FLUENCY PASSAGES IN *DIFFERENTIATING INSTRUCTION*

Fluency refers to a reader's ability to read aloud a text quickly and accurately while rendering the words in an expressive way. A fluent reader renders a text in a way that both the reader and other listeners can comprehend. A fluent reader also has a good sense of pace, phrasing, expression, and vocal inflection. He or she uses cues in the text, such as punctuation and typesetting, to guide his or reading and "chunks" text into phrases rather than reading one word at a time.

Differentiating Instruction provides at- and below-level fluency reading passages at each grade level. The at-level passages are excerpted from the minimum course of study selections that appear in *Elements of Literature*. The below-level passages in grades 7-12 are excerpted from the minimum course of study selections that appear in the previous grade level of *Elements of Literature*. The below-level passages that appear in grade 6 were created specifically for that grade.

You can use these passages as informal diagnostic tools to gather information about your students' fluency. With the information gained through this diagnosis, you can address the individual needs of your students and improve student achievement in reading. As explained below, you can also use these passages as instructional tools to improve students' fluency.

IMPLEMENTING THE FLUENCY PASSAGES IN *DIFFERENTIATING INSTRUCTION*

You may implement the oral fluency passages in *Differentiating Instruction* in the following ways:

- **Modeling**—You or a proficient reader reads aloud a fluency passage in a meaningful and expressive way while students follow along silently. Then, as a class, you discuss how the reader sounded while reading the passage.

- **Echo reading**—You or a proficient student reads a passage aloud phrase-by-phrase or sentence-by-sentence. The rest of the class repeats each phrase or sentence, pronouncing the words in the same way as the reader.

- **Choral reading**—You and the class read a passage as one voice. While reading, students pay attention to the pace at which they read as a group.

- **Independent reading**—An individual student reads aloud by himself or herself. Or a student reads aloud to the class or to the teacher. The student focuses on pronouncing the words correctly and making the passage sound natural and engaging.

EVALUATING YOUR STUDENTS' ORAL FLUENCY

The fluency passages in this book may also be used to evaluate your students' oral fluency. Evaluation should involve only you and the student in a quiet environment. Before asking students to read a passage aloud, review the following steps:

- As a student reads, you may pronounce any proper nouns or specialized or foreign terms that the student may not know or recognize in print.

- If the student self-corrects, do not count an error.

Original content Copyright © by Holt, Rinehart and Winston. Additions and changes to the original content are the responsibility of the instructor.

- If a student makes the same mistake more than once, count only one error.
- If the student hesitates for more than five seconds, pronounce the word and count an error.
- If the student misreads or omits a word, draw a line through it and count one error.
- Draw an arrow to indicate that words were reversed and count one error.
- If a student repeats a word, do not count an error.

CALCULATING ORAL FLUENCY

To calculate a student's fluency (words correct per minute, or wcpm), follow these steps:

- Count the total number of words the student reads in one minute, using the numbers that appear in the fluency passage as a guide.
- Subtract the number of errors from the total number of words read. This number is the words correct per minute.

PRACTICE, PRACTICE, PRACTICE

Remind students that fluency is a skill that can only improve by engaging in lots of practice. Encourage students to read aloud at every opportunity—to partners or small groups in class, to family members at home, or into tape recorders when they are alone. Provide them with the following checklist to help them monitor their fluency—and its improvement—on their own.

FLUENCY SELF-EVALUATION

After reading aloud, work alone or with your teacher or a partner to give yourself a score for each item on the checklist below. Give a score of 1 to 4, 4 being the best.

____ I chunked words into phrases instead of reading word-by-word.

____ I read the passage at a steady pace (not too fast or too slow).

____ I read the passage smoothly without stopping or stumbling.

____ I used my voice to convey emotions and make meaning.

____ I read dialogue with an expressive voice that reflected the characters' feelings.

____ I used punctuation marks (commas, periods, question marks) to help me chunk words in groups.

____ I used punctuation marks (commas, periods, question marks) to help me read with expression.

____ I stressed certain words or phrases in order to emphasize their importance.

____ I repeated words or phrases that seemed important in order to understand them better.

Original content Copyright © by Holt, Rinehart and Winston. Additions and changes to the original content are the responsibility of the instructor.

Differentiating Instruction

Teaching Strategies That Work

STRATEGIES FOR TEACHING LEARNERS GAINING PROFICIENCY AND ENGLISH-LANGUAGE LEARNERS

As a teacher, by providing learners gaining proficiency and English-language learners with activities and strategies, you can help them achieve the goals of developing academic language, acquiring vocabulary to learn new concepts, and producing oral and written language. The following strategies help you to identify the signs of a student who is struggling with English or with comprehension. They also suggest ways to help learners gain proficiency as readers, writers, and speakers.

DETECTING ENGLISH-LANGUAGE LEARNERS' DIFFICULTIES

Since concept acquisition and development are intricately related to language ability, difficulties related to language acquisition may prevent students from developing new concepts fully. It is important to recognize when English-language learners experience such difficulties so that you can help them by reteaching a lesson, reinforcing a learning activity, or clarifying an idea previously presented. Below are some of the classroom behaviors that may be indicative of the difficulties related to the development of academic language.

BEHAVIORS THAT INDICATE PROBLEMS

Behavior	Example
Lack of participation	The student may put his or her head down or refuse to answer a question.
Incorrect responses	The student continually gives incorrect responses even when questions have been simplified or additional prompts have been provided.
Mixing native language and English	The student speaks or writes in both English and his or her native language because he or she does not completely understand a concept.
Over- or under-extension of concepts	The student fails to recognize examples of a concept (under-extension) or includes examples that are not part of the concept (over-extension).
Misunderstanding	The student may not be able to answer questions or follow directions because he or she does not understand what is being asked.
Difficulty in literal or inferential reading comprehension	The student may not be familiar with the words in the text or the ideas that the words represent. The student may not have prior knowledge of a concept.
Native language interference	The student may inappropriately generalize native language elements into English. For example, Spanish-speaking students may omit the verbs *do, does*, and *did* in interrogative phrases or sentences because in Spanish they are not used.
Cultural miscues	The student may not have prior knowledge or personal experiences from which to draw a correct response.
Inappropriate rhythm	The student may not be familiar with the words or punctuation within a text.
Uneasiness in using idioms and expressions	The student may translate an idiom word-for-word; therefore, the student may become confused.

Original content Copyright © by Holt, Rinehart and Winston. Additions and changes to the original content are the responsibility of the instructor.

Differentiating Instruction

GENERAL STRATEGIES FOR INSTRUCTING ENGLISH-LANGUAGE LEARNERS

By identifying English-language learners' difficulties, you can address their learning needs better. Following are general strategies you can use to motivate learners and support their learning.

- Note that English-language learners may show more ability to express themselves in a social situation than in an academic situation. Social and academic English vary considerably, so classroom practices should take this into account. Teachers can help their students express themselves in academic English, by showing them ways to replace colloquial expressions with academic ones and ways to replace simple sentences with complex ones.

- Recognize that English-language learners' prior knowledge bases may reflect disrupted schooling and/or be associated with different cultural experiences. Students will need help in developing strategies to build their own prior knowledge, which is important to constructing meaning.

- Draw analogies to past experiences and provide opportunities for students to share their own experiences. These analogies will help English-language learners to relate their reading and instruction to their prior knowledge.

- Help English-language learners deal with culturally unfamiliar topics by doing what you do when you introduce a new topic to the entire class—place it in a familiar context. Bring the topic to life and encourage students to draw upon their personal experiences and knowledge.

- For beginning English-language learners, use role-playing, objects, pictures, and graphic organizers to create associations and support meaning. Use gestures and facial expressions to cue feelings and moods.

- Paraphrase questions. By restating questions, you can English-language learners' existing knowledge and encourage the acquisition of new language.

- Ask questions and encourage English-language learners to offer explanations and summaries. These practices allow you to determine if students understand new material.

- For beginning English-language learners, try replacing lengthy or complex sentences with shorter, declarative phrases or sentences.

- When possible, pair English-language learners with more proficient English learners. Heterogeneous grouping allows the modeling of English to occur in a natural context. Well-structured cooperative-learning situations focused on the text help all students learn from text and gain academic literacy.

GENERAL STRATEGIES FOR INSTRUCTING ALL LEARNERS GAINING PROFICENCY

The following are strategies and activities that can be used for all struggling learners or for those students who require additional support in vocabulary and concept development, reading, writing, and understanding and producing oral language. When using any of these strategies, explain and model the strategies to students so that they can integrate these as part of their own learning strategies. The activities can be adapted to any unit or topic.

Original content Copyright © by Holt, Rinehart and Winston. Additions and changes to the original content are the responsibility of the instructor.

Differentiating Instruction

VOCABULARY DEVELOPMENT/ CONCEPT DEVELOPMENT

You can facilitate the acquisition of new vocabulary and new concepts by using activities or materials that provide a context familiar to the students.

- **Use context-rich activities.** Demonstrate the use of new vocabulary in situations related to students' experiences. Where appropriate, use the context provided by concepts or literature the students have already learned. The use of the classroom, the school, and the students' environment to build, develop, and exemplify new vocabulary and concepts provides the context in the present, which makes the activity more concrete to the student.

- **Control the content.** When teaching new vocabulary, present words and phrases embedded in sentences or text well known to students. Each sentence or portion of text should focus on only one new word or phrase. This allows the students to concentrate on the acquisition of the target language without having to be concerned with new vocabulary and new concepts at the same time.

- **Control the vocabulary.** When introducing and developing new concepts, control the complexity of the language. Learning new concepts and new vocabulary at the same time is loaded with many unknowns, which tend to impede the acquisition of new material. Therefore, use language that does not present difficulties so that the focus is on the new concept.

READING COMPREHENSION

The greatest challenge in the acquisition of new academic language and new concepts is to make text comprehensible to students so that concept development can proceed logically.

- **Group text in small units.** Break long text into smaller units such as paragraphs. Well-constructed paragraphs usually have one main idea with supporting details, so they can stand alone without losing meaning. Use the units to identify the students' difficulties and teach to those areas. After working with the target paragraphs, reconstruct the whole text and restate the active-reading questions or the goal of the reading.

- **Identify main ideas.** Identify the main idea in the text as well as the supporting details. Explain to students how the details support the main idea.

- **Paraphrase and rephrase text.** Simplify text by paraphrasing and rephrasing sections of text, such as sentences or short paragraphs, using language familiar to students. Break down complex sentences into simple sentences. Help clarify the intention and meaning of each sentence, and reconstruct the original sentence afterward.

WRITING

You can help students become more proficient with writing by teaching them the language they need to know in order to write and by using activities that simplify the writing process.

Original content Copyright © by Holt, Rinehart and Winston. Additions and changes to the original content are the responsibility of the instructor.

- **Guide the writing.** With all learners gaining proficiency, brainstorm vocabulary related to a topic. As students brainstorm, you or a scribe can write the words and phrases on the board. Have students review the list of words and phrases, and encourage them to use the vocabulary orally to describe, explain, or illustrate the target topic. Then, have each student write on the board a sentence that relates to the topic. With the group, organize the sentences into one or two paragraphs. Correct the grammatical errors and explain them to students. Finally, have the students read the final product. You can also help struggling students improve their writing by suggesting alternative language, more supporting details, or additional facts.

- **Modify writing assignments.** To help struggling students, use the Writing Workshop lesson plans to lead students through a shorter lesson. Consider also shortening the assignment. For instance, a writer gaining proficiency who must write a persuasive piece could state his or her opinion, fully elaborate on one reason, and provide a call to action in one paragraph. Also, English-language learners may benefit from developing shorter writing products so that they can concentrate on word choice, grammar, and punctuation.

- **Provide effective instructional feedback.** Struggling students benefit from the instructional feedback their teachers provide them on their writing. Try to provide this feedback systematically, using student-friendly explanations and corrective feedback symbols, as appropriate. Don't forget to ask students to use your feedback to improve their writing. The best feedback is often given during very short one-on-one teacher-student conferences.

LISTENING

Multiple opportunities for listening, with different goals, enhance the development of language comprehension.

- **Promote active, focused listening.** Provide different goals for listening. For example, ask English-language learners to listen for specific vocabulary related to a concept during an oral discussion. Then, have students write on a piece of paper the target words and the phrases or sentences in which the target words are embedded. Students can add to this list as you continue the discussion.

- **Use checklists.** Have students listen for vocabulary words that appear in the Word Banks or in the Language Coach activities that accompany each reading selection during a discussion or an oral reading activity. This strategy will reinforce the words that are necessary to understanding a concept.

- **Use text and cloze activities.** Provide struggling students with hard copy of the text with words blanked out. Have them fill in the words as you or a proficient speaker reads aloud. Have English-language learners focus on different elements of diction, such as emphasis, rhythm, and accentuation. For example, students can highlight words that they notice are emphasized during an oral reading.

Original content Copyright © by Holt, Rinehart and Winston. Additions and changes to the original content are the responsibility of the instructor.

Differentiating Instruction

- **Ask questions.** Provide questions to students that will need to be answered after listening to a discussion, an oral reading activity, or an audiotape. These activities allow you to check their understanding of what they have heard.

SPEAKING

Learners gaining proficiency should be encouraged to practice their linguistic skills in academic arenas. Oral activities in which English-language learners are prompted to voice their opinions or share personal experiences help them build confidence in their speaking abilities.

- **Model and tape the presentation.** Provide learners gaining proficiency and English learners with a taped model presentation of their material. (You or a proficient English-speaking student can record it.) Help students analyze the language in the presentation, and encourage several listening sessions. Have students practice their oral presentations with a group of peers. If they need help, provide them with lists of expressions and sentence stems they can use.

STUDENT SELF-MONITORING

By monitoring their own learning, learners gaining proficiency are able to recognize the strategies that work best for them when they encounter difficulties. Consider the following activities to help students monitor their learning:

- Encourage students to check their comprehension when reading or listening. To do this, they can summarize information or answer questions.

- Ask students to identify the difficulties they encounter when learning new lessons and the strategies that work for them. Then, assist students in developing a plan that includes specific strategies, which will help them achieve learning. Finally, have students evaluate their plans by discussing how their plans worked and what changes they may need to make in the future.

By using these strategies, you can help your students achieve their academic goals and become more proficient readers, writers, and speakers. More importantly, though, you provide students with a supportive environment in which they become more self-confident and capable of many levels of communication.

Original content Copyright © by Holt, Rinehart and Winston. Additions and changes to the original content are the responsibility of the instructor.

Differentiating Instruction

Collection 1
Graphic Organizer

The Sniper Liam O'Flaherty

Identify Type of Conflict Chart In the story "The Sniper," the main character faces different **conflicts**. Some conflicts are internal, which are within the character. Some conflicts are external, which come from outside the character.

Identify the kind of conflict the character faces in the following scenes by writing *internal* **or** *external* **in the second column. If the conflict is external, identify the source of the conflict. The first one is done for you.**

Scene	Type of Conflict	Source of external conflict
A bullet almost hits him while he is smoking.	External	The enemy sniper
He wants to smoke a cigarette, but he know it is risky.		
A woman points out his location to the armored car driver.		
He is shot in the arm.		
He must overcome the pain to plan his escape from the roof.		
His enemy on the opposite roof will shoot him if he tries to escape.		
He feels sick after he shoots his enemy dead.		

Original content Copyright © by Holt, Rinehart and Winston. Additions and changes to the original content are the responsibility of the instructor.

Differentiating Instruction

The Most Dangerous Game Richard Connell

Preteach

LISTENING COMPREHENSION SKILLS *(15 minutes)*

Build Background/Set a Purpose Discuss Build Background on p. 18. Make sure students understand what is meant by "big-game hunting." Explain that it refers to hunting large wild animals. A common big-game animal in the U.S. today is deer. Tell students that this story was written in the 1920s. Then use a world map to point out areas of sub-Sahara Africa, Southeast Asia, and around the Amazon River in South America as examples of the "foreign locales" that people traveled to for big-game hunting. Discuss types of animals in those regions that people might hunt, such as lions and tigers. Point out that most of those animals are now protected and the kind of big-game hunting described in the story is rare today.

Discuss the Preview the Selection feature on p. 18. Use the world map to help students place the setting of the story. Point out New York, where Rainsford lives. Highlight the Caribbean, where Rainsford and Whitney are sailing. Locate Rio de Janeiro, Brazil, and the Amazon River, where they are going to hunt. Preview these details of the plot:

- Rainsford is famous for his skills as a big-game hunter. He has hunted animals all over the world.

- Rainsford experiences something unexpected on a place called Ship-Trap Island. Have students use the art on p. 21 for ideas about the island and what it is like.

Discuss the title of the selection. Explain that "game" has two possible meanings. Have a volunteer explain the most common meaning of the word *game*, e.g. something you play for fun. Point out a different meaning of *game*, e.g. wild animals that are hunted. Ask students to share their ideas of what "the most dangerous game" might be. Have them compare their ideas to what they learn as they read.

VOCABULARY SKILLS *(10 minutes)*

Preteach Vocabulary Words Review the meanings of the vocabulary in the Word Bank. Then give students these sentences to complete.

1. The players were [invariably] disappointed any time it lost a game.

2. Although the dog looked fierce, it had a [disarming] wag to its tail.

3. I saw the lights of the train [receding] and knew I had missed it.

4. The patient [surmounted] all of her health problems and got well.

5. It would be [imprudent] for a large family to buy a small car.

Remind students to watch for these words as they read the story.

RESOURCES

In *The Holt Reader:* "The Most Dangerous Game" for students who need more scaffolding in a workbook format

In this book: *Vocabulary Skill Builder,* p. 16; "The Most Dangerous Game" Selection Test, p. 17

Consult *Holt Audio Library,* for recordings of most selections

WORD BANK
receding
disarming
imprudent
surmounted
invariably

VOCABULARY SKILL
Especially for ELL
(5 minutes or less)
Because the vocabulary in this story is so rich, English-language learners may benefit from practice with the additional words below. Pair English-language learners with more proficient partners who can read the words and definitions aloud. Ask those partners to employ facial expressions or mime to reinforce the meaning of each word:
palpable (p. 19) able to be felt by touching
tangible (p. 20) capable of being touched or felt
anguish (p. 21) very great pain or distress
discerned (p. 23) detected or recognized; made out
quizzically (p. 27) in a questioning way

Original content Copyright © by Holt, Rinehart and Winston. Additions and changes to the original content are the responsibility of the instructor.

Differentiating Instruction

LANGUAGE COACH SKILL *(10 minutes)*

Prefixes Tell students that a prefix is a word part added to the beginning of a base word, or root, to create a new word with a different meaning. Write the prefix *un-* on the board. Explain that it means "not." Give students these sentences from the story containing words with *un-*. Discuss how *un-* added to each root word creates the opposite meaning.

- "An *unbroken* front of snarled and ragged jungle fringed the shore." (p. 22).

- "The stone steps were real enough,…yet about it all hung an air of *unreality*." (p. 22)

- "But there was one small trait of the general's that made Rainsford *uncomfortable*." (p. 24)

Write these sentences on the board. Have students complete each one by adding a word from the box.

unbroken	uncomfortable	unreality

1. The heavy fog created a blurry, silent world of [unreality] outside.

2. When you get above the trees, you will have an [unbroken] view.

3. He is shy and [uncomfortable] around people he doesn't know.

LITERARY FOCUS *(45 minutes)*

Suspense and Foreshadowing Ask students to pay attention to how they feel as you read aloud the following example:

> Imagine I told you that we were going to have a special guest in class today. Some of you will be very happy about this guest. But some of you will think this guest is your worst nightmare. By the end of the day, you'll know which you are.

Discuss students' reactions. Point out that no one knows whether they will be very happy or very unhappy. The feeling of uncertainty is called *suspense.* Ask students to identify *clues,* or hints, you gave about what will happen (e.g. some students will be happy, some unhappy, they will know at the day's end). Identify those clues as examples of *foreshadowing.* Explain that writers plant clues in a story about what may happen. They use foreshadowing and suspense to make readers curious and to make them want to keep reading.

Help students use academic vocabulary and concepts. Show students the illustration on p. 31. Have students work with a partner to discuss the painting. Ask each pair to decide how they think the painting creates a feeling of suspense (e.g. cannot see the person's face; cannot tell if the person is running away or running after something). Have each pair also describe an event in the story that the painting may foreshadow. Bring all student pairs together to share their ideas with the class.

"The Most Dangerous Game" by Richard Connell. Copyright © 1924 by Richard Connell; copyright renewed © 1952 by Louise Fox Connell. Reproduced by permission of **Brandt & Hochman Literary Agents, Inc**. Any electronic copying or distribution of this text is strictly forbidden.

ACADEMIC VOCABULARY
Preteaching Academic Vocabulary
(5 minutes)
Write these terms and their meanings on a chalkboard or transparency. Review them with the students before previewing the selection.

Suspense: A feeling you get of being worried or anxious from not knowing what will happen next in a story.
Foreshadowing: Clues in a story that hint at what may happen
Outcome: Result; ending
Prediction: A guess that is based on what you learn or know from your own life

LANGUAGE SKILL
Especially for LDN
(5 minutes or less)
For students who benefit from visual representations of concepts, explain the term *foreshadowing* by shining a light on an object to create a shadow. Point out that the shadow gives you an idea of what the object is. Then explain the parts of the word *foreshadow:* the prefix *fore-*, which means "before," and *shadow.* Help students put the meanings of these word parts together to conclude that *foreshadowing* is getting an idea of something before it happens.

Original content Copyright © by Holt, Rinehart and Winston. Additions and changes to the original content are the responsibility of the instructor.

Differentiating Instruction

READING FOCUS *(20 minutes)*

Making Predictions Talk about a "wild guess" as a guess that is made without any information to back it up. Explain that a *prediction* is the opposite of a wild guess. A prediction is a guess based on information you learn or your own experiences. Have students respond to each question with a prediction, and explain what they base it on.

- What time will you eat lunch tomorrow?
- What will you do next summer?

Have students work in pairs to fill out a chart like the one at the right. As they read the story, prompt them to use clues to make predictions.

READING FOCUS
Predictions Chart

Page #	Clues	My Predic-tions

Direct Teach

(60 minutes)

Chunk the Text Help students pace their reading by dividing the selection into "chunks" or parts. After students read each part, stop to help them identify clues that foreshadow events and make predictions.

Part 1: ends p. 22, col.1: "…sleep of his life."
Part 2: ends p. 25, col 1 "I live for danger, Mr. Rainsford."
Part 3: ends p. 27, col 1: "…what you speak of is murder."
Part 4: ends p. 29, col 2: "I hope you have a good night's rest."
Part 5: ends p. 32, col 1 "…in the crimson sash about his waist."
Part 6: ends p. 33, col 2: "I will not lose my nerve. I will not."
Part 7: ends p. 35, col 1: "Thank you for a most amusing evening."
Part 8: ends p. 36, col 2: "…slept in a better bed, Rainsford decided."

Check for Understanding

WRITING FOCUS *(15 minutes)*

Descriptive Words Explain that the author uses words to describe the setting that create a feeling of danger. Discuss this example:

"The cry was pinched off short as the *blood-warm* waters of the Caribbean Sea closed over his head." (p. 20)

Read aloud the sentences below. Then have students write original sentences using the descriptive words *jagged* and *savagely*.

1. "Jagged crags appeared to jut into the opaqueness." (p. 21)
2. "…insects bit him savagely." (p. 34)

Think As A Reader/Writer Ask: *What places can be dangerous?* Have students brainstorm ideas, and then choose one place to write about. Have them write a few sentences about the place using words that describe why it is dangerous.

READING/WRITING
Especially for WGP
(5 minutes)
Writers gaining proficiency are likely to benefit from a word bank of descriptive words. Encourage these students to scan the selection for sensory words and details that create a feeling of danger. Have them list the words in five separate lists, one for each sense. Then ask them to add more words to the lists—words that evoke the danger of the place they will describe.

"The Most Dangerous Game" by Richard Connell. Copyright © 1924 by Richard Connell; copyright renewed © 1952 by Louise Fox Connell. Reproduced by permission of **Brandt & Hochman Literary Agents, Inc**. Any electronic copying or distribution of this text is strictly forbidden.

Original content Copyright © by Holt, Rinehart and Winston. Additions and changes to the original content are the responsibility of the instructor.

Collection 1
Graphic Organizer

Disguises Jean Fong Kwok

Time Line Most stories describe a **sequence of events** in chronological order. Sometimes a writer will interrupt a story with a **flashback** to a different time. Understanding the main sequence of events will help you grasp the story's plot.

"Disguises" tells of events that take place in two time periods. Clarify the sequence of events by filling in the time line below. Place the events in chronological order in which they actually happened. The first one is done for you.

Events
• She gives a homeless man a quarter • Mrs. Chen leaves the factory to go home • She dreams about her supervisor • She calls home from the pay phone • She gets off on the wrong stop • She tells her husband and son about the kind stranger	• She tries to ask the subway clerk for directions • She dreams about her childhood • Someone tries to steal her necklace • A Chinese student helps her get home • She gets on the subway and falls asleep • She dreams about being in a carriage

1. Mrs. Chen leaves the factory to go home	2	3	4
5	6	7	8
9	10	11	12

Original content Copyright © by Holt, Rinehart and Winston. Additions and changes to the original content are the responsibility of the instructor.

Lesson Plan and Teaching Strategies

Liberty Julia Alvarez

Preteach

LISTENING COMPREHENSION SKILLS *(15 minutes)*

Build Background/Set a Purpose Discuss the Build Background on p. 56. Have a volunteer find the Dominican Republic on a map of North America, using the small map for guidance, and the U.S. to show its location nearby. Provide this additional information to aid students' understanding. Explain that General Trujillo seized power in 1930 and had total control over the people for 31 years. He used "secret police," or police that spy on ordinary people inside a country, to find out who was against him. Many people were sent to prison or murdered. Discuss how those conditions would make people feel (e.g. fearful, anxious, suspicious of others) and why some people would take risks to obtain freedom. Explain that Trujillo was killed by military leaders in 1961, after the author's family had already escaped to America.

Discuss the Preview the Selection feature on p. 56. Use the small map to remind students where the story takes place. Explain that "political upheaval" often means efforts to change a country's leader by force and is dangerous for people involved. Preview these details of the plot:

- The story is told by a young girl, who is probably meant to be the author at the age when her family left the Dominican Republic. Have students use the photo on page 62 to help imagine this young girl.

- The family is given a puppy that the father names Liberty. Have students use the photo on page 61 to visualize the dog.

Discuss the title of the selection. Based on what they know, ask students to make predictions about why the story is called "Liberty." Have students state their ideas and explain their reasoning. For example, do they think the story is mainly about the dog or about achieving liberty? As students read, have them check their predictions for accuracy.

VOCABULARY SKILLS *(10 minutes)*

Preteach Vocabulary Words Review the meanings of the vocabulary in the Word Bank. Then give students these sentences to complete.

1. The batter was [distracted] by the noisy crowd and missed the ball.

2. Those kids look confused and give the [impression] they are lost.

3. If the car does not start, we will have to [resort] to walking.

4. The family was [inconsolable] after their house burned down.

5. The coach gave the team many [admonitions] to work harder.

6. The principal may [elect] to close school if the weather gets worse.

Remind students to watch for these words as they read the story.

RESOURCES

In *The Holt Reader:* "Liberty," for students who need more scaffolding in a workbook format

In this book: *Vocabulary Skill Builder,* p. 16; "Liberty," Selection Test, p. 18

Consult *Holt Audio Library* for recordings of most selections

WORD BANK

elect
distracted
admonitions
impression
inconsolable
resort

ACADEMIC VOCABULARY

Preteaching Academic Vocabulary

(5 minutes)
Write these terms and their meanings on a chalkboard or transparency. Review them with the students before previewing the selection.

Setting: The place and time of a story
Conflict: A problem that causes a clash between characters or between a character and a place
Convey: Suggest; communicate
Effect: Result

Original content Copyright © by Holt, Rinehart and Winston. Additions and changes to the original content are the responsibility of the instructor.

LANGUAGE COACH SKILL *(15 minutes)*

Multiple Meanings Explain that some words have more than one meaning. Hold up an ink pen, and write *pen* on the board. Have students give the meaning of "pen" (e.g. writing tool). Then read this sentence:

- " 'I'll take Liberty back to his *pen*,' I offered." (p. 58)

Ask a volunteer to draw a simple picture on the board of a pen used to hold a pet. Discuss the two meanings of pen and clues in the sentence that help students decide the correct meaning (e.g. an animal would not have a writing pen).

Write the words *spot*, *poor*, and *funny* on the board. Ask volunteers to explain two meanings of each word (e.g. *spot:* a place and a drip that makes a stain; *poor:* having little money and sad or unfortunate; *funny:* humorous and strange or odd). Discuss this sentence from the story. Have students use context clues to decide the meaning of the word:

- "Sure enough, as soon as he saw where we were headed . . .then swerved to the front yard to our favorite *spot*." (p. 58)

Have students write an original sentence for each word (*pen, spot, poor, funny*) and include context clues to show which meaning they use.

LITERARY FOCUS *(45 minutes)*

Setting and Conflict Ask a volunteer to explain what to look for to identify the *setting* of a story (e.g., where and when it takes places). Point out that details about the setting give clues to types of *conflict,* or problems, in a story. Have students think about this example.

> You go to an island on vacation. You expect days of fun on a sunny beach. But a day after you arrive, a ferocious storm such as a hurricane hits the island. When the storm passes, the island is like a different place. There is damage everywhere and it feels dangerous. Suddenly, you are struggling to stay safe and find a way to get out.

Discuss students' responses. Have them explain how the storm creates a different situation on the island (e.g., it's no longer about a fun vacation but about survival). Point out that when writers choose a setting, they think about more than just the place. They think about conditions in that setting that create conflicts for characters.

Help students use academic vocabulary and concepts. Show students the photo on p. 54. Point out that it's hard to tell when this photo was taken. Have students work with a partner. Ask each pair to imagine two different stories around this setting. One is about a family coming to New York in the early 2000s. The other story is about a family coming to New York in the early 1900s. Have students think about how the time period makes a difference in each story, and identify a realistic

"Liberty" by Julia Alvarez. Copyright © 1996 by Julia Alvarez. First published in *Writer's Harvest 2*, edited by Ethan Canin, published by Harcourt Brace and Company, 1996. All rights reserved. Reproduced by permission of **Susan Bergholz Literary Services, New York**.

LANGUAGE SKILL
Especially for WGP
(10 minutes)
Students who are writers gaining proficiency may benefit by working with a partner to write original sentences containing the multiple-meaning words *pen, spot, poor,* and *funny*. Ask each pair to write two sentences for each word, using a different meaning in each sentence.

LANGUAGE SKILL
Especially for ELL
(20 minutes)
Some English-language learners may be unfamiliar with some idioms in the story. Before they read, preview the following idioms. Read each one aloud and ask students what they think its literal meaning is. (It may help some students to draw a picture of the literal meaning.) Then explain the idiomatic meaning and ask students to use each idiom in a sentence.

light into (p. 58): attack verbally
changed her tune (p. 58): altered her thinking or attitude
live wire (p. 58): an energetic person
keep an eye on things (p. 60): observe closely
flunk out (p. 60): fail in schoolwork
break my heart (p. 61): make me extremely sad

Original content Copyright © by Holt, Rinehart and Winston. Additions and changes to the original content are the responsibility of the instructor.

Differentiating Instruction

conflict for today (e.g., making friends at school) and long ago (e.g., getting to go to school). Bring all groups together to compare story ideas and generalize on ways the setting influences conflicts in a story.

READING FOCUS *(20 minutes)*
Analyzing Details Explain that *details* are pieces of information about a person or a place, such as the color of a person's hair or the buildings in a city. Looking for details helps you know a person or a place better. Have students work with the same or a different partner from the previous activity. Ask students to record three positive *details* about their partner, using words or drawings. Discuss students' examples and how details help distinguish one person from another.

Point out that writers include many details to help a reader picture a setting or a character's appearance and actions. *Analyzing,* or thinking about, the details can help students understand the story better. Have students work in pairs to fill out a chart like the one at the right. As they record a detail, prompt them to *analyze* what it means.

Direct Teach

(30 minutes)
Chunk the Text Help students pace their reading by dividing the selection into "chunks" or parts. After students read each part, have them stop to identify and analyze details to understand the conflict.
Part 1: ends p. 59, col.2,: "…and tell them what I had seen."
Part 2: ends p. 61, col. 2,: "…book I got you on the Arabian nights."
Part 3: ends p. 62, col. 2,: "…my Liberty will be waiting for me here."

Check for Understanding

WRITING FOCUS *(20 minutes)*
Descriptive Details Discuss these examples of how the author uses details about the dog, Liberty, to bring him to life:

"A black-and-white-speckled electric current of energy." (p. 57)

"…that little hyperactive baton of a tail knocked things off the low coffee table…" (p. 58)

Have students use their own descriptive words to finish these sentences:

1. Liberty could be trouble because….

2. The girl loves Liberty because….

Think As A Reader/Writer Point out that "freedom" is another word for liberty. Ask: *How does it feel when you are free to do anything you want?* Guide students to connect the author's description of Liberty's energy with the excitement and sense of possibilities that freedom and liberty represent. Have them write a few sentences that compare the dog's behavior with the idea of what liberty means.

READING FOCUS
Details Chart

Detail	What It Tells Me

READING/WRITING
Especially for RGP
(5 minutes or less)
Some readers gaining proficiency may have difficulties understanding the subtleties of this story. Discuss the photo on p. 59, which shows the shadow of a man. Point out that the two men the narrator meets are like the man in this photo. They are watching and listening to what goes on in the house without revealing who they are. Remind students of the Build Background information on "secret police" and explain that the two men are most likely members of the secret police spying on the narrator's father.

As they continue to read, have students write down more details that explain why the father, and the whole family, might be in danger.

"Liberty" by Julia Alvarez. Copyright © 1996 by Julia Alvarez. First published in *Writer's Harvest 2,* edited by Ethan Canin, published by Harcourt Brace and Company, 1996. All rights reserved. Reproduced by permission of **Susan Bergholz Literary Services, New York.**

Original content Copyright © by Holt, Rinehart and Winston. Additions and changes to the original content are the responsibility of the instructor.

Differentiating Instruction

Collection 1
Graphic Organizer

Harrison Bergeron Kurt Vonnegut

Visualizing Chart As you read, sensory details can help you **visualize** the characters, setting, and events in a story.

Look at the passages from the story in the picture column. Complete the second column by writing the vivid words and phrases that help you create a mental picture. Most of these words will appeal to the sense of sight, but some of them might also appeal to another sense, such as hearing or touch.

Passage	Vivid Words and Phrases
"And to offset his good looks, the H-G men required that he wear at all times a red rubber ball for a nose, keep his eyebrows shaved off, and cover his even white teeth with black caps at snaggletooth random."	
"Harrison thrust his thumbs under the bar of the padlock that secured hid head harness. The bar snapped like celery. Harrison smashed his headphones and spectacles against the wall."	
"They leaped like deer on the moon. The studio ceiling was thirty feet high, but each leap brought the dancers nearer to it."	

From "Harrison Bergeron" from *Welcome to the Monkey House* by Kurt Vonnegut, Jr. Copyright © 1961 by Kurt Vonnegut, Jr. Reproduced by permission of **Dell Publishing, a division of Random House, Inc., www.randomhouse.com** and CD-ROM format by permission of **Donald C. Farber, Attorney for Kurt Vonnegut, Jr.**

Original content Copyright © by Holt, Rinehart and Winston. Additions and changes to the original content are the responsibility of the instructor.

Collection 1
Graphic Organizer

A Sound of Thunder/ Being Prey

Setting Comparison Chart The **setting** refers to the time, place, and social and historical conditions of a story or article. Writers use specific details to describe the setting.

Use this chart to compare the settings of the two selections. Find specific details that describe the times, places, and conditions of the different settings used by each author.

	Time	Place	Conditions
A Sound of Thunder			
Being Prey			

Original content Copyright © by Holt, Rinehart and Winston. Additions and changes to the original content are the responsibility of the instructor.

Differentiating Instruction

Lesson Plan and Teaching Strategies

The Great Escape   Thomas Fleming *from* Boys' Life

Preteach

LISTENING COMPREHENSION SKILLS *(15 minutes)*

Build Background/Set a Purpose Discuss the Build Background on p. 100. To help students place "The Great Escape" in history, review some basic facts about World War II. Use a world map to locate key countries in the war, including Germany and its chief enemies, England, Russia, and the U.S., known as the Allies. Also locate Australia, Canada, Czechoslovakia, the Netherlands, Norway, Poland, and South Africa as examples of countries where the prisoners involved in the escape were from. Explain that World War II began on September 1, 1939, when the Germans attacked Poland. Adolf Hitler was the leader of the Nazi party in Germany and a brutal dictator. Some students may be aware of Hilter's concentration camps where Jews and others were killed. Point out that the prisoners in this article were in a military camp called a *stalag*. They were fliers who were captured after their planes were shot down during bombing raids over Europe. Check for any questions about World War II before you proceed.

Preview these details to help students set a purpose for reading:

- The article describes a famous escape by 76 men from a prison camp called Stalag Luft III. Have students use the map to locate the camp in Sagan. Explain that this area of eastern Germany became part of Poland after the war ended.

- When prisoners escaped, they tried to reach neutral countries that were not in the war, such as Sweden, Switzerland, and Spain. Use a map to find each country and note its distance from western Poland.

- The escape took place on March 24, 1944, more than five years after the war began. Point out that the Germans controlled all of the territory through which the prisoners had to travel to reach safety.

- The men escaped by digging tunnels. Have students preview the images to help them visualize this challenge.

Discuss the title of the article. Based on what they know, what seems "great," or amazing, about this escape? Have students state their ideas and explain their reasoning. Have students read to confirm their ideas.

VOCABULARY SKILLS *(5-10 minutes)*

Preteach Vocabulary Words Review the meanings of the vocabulary in the Word Bank. Then give students these sentences to complete.

1. Thieves [prowled] around the neighborhood, planning a robbery.

2. The thieves robbed a house, and then were [pursued] by the police.

Remind students to watch for these words as they read the story.

RESOURCES

In *The Holt Reader:* "The Great Escape," for students who need more scaffolding in a workbook format

In this book: *Vocabulary Skill Builder,* p. 16; "The Great Escape," Selection Test, p. 19

Consult *Holt Audio Library* for recordings of most selections

WORD BANK
prowled
pursued

READING/WRITING
Especially for LDN
(20 minutes)
Learners with diverse needs may require more historical background on World War II in Europe to understand the significance of the Great Escape. Work with students to create a basic time line of the war in Europe. Guide students to use resources that summarize the war, such as American History textbooks and pictorial histories from the school library, to identify key events from September 1939 to May 1945, including the Great Escape. Have all LDN students contribute to one master time line.

Original content Copyright © by Holt, Rinehart and Winston. Additions and changes to the original content are the responsibility of the instructor.

Differentiating Instruction

LANGUAGE COACH SKILL *(20 minutes)*

Word Forms Explain that both vocabulary words are verbs that also have noun forms:

- *prowl* and *prowler* are both noun forms of *prowled*
- *pursuit* is the noun form of *pursued*

Point out that many words have different forms with related meanings. Read and discuss the following examples from the article:

- "The X Organization spotted weaklings among the ferrets and <u>bribed</u> them with chocolate from their Red Cross aid packages." (p. 102). Confirm that a *bribe* is the noun form of *bribed*.

- "All around the camp were dozens of 'stooges' who <u>signaled </u>when a ferret approached." (p. 102) Confirm that a *signal* is the noun form of *signaled*.

- "This was an outrageous <u>violation</u> of the rules of war." (p. 103) Confirm that to *violate* is the verb form of *violation*.

Review with students how to use context clues to understand the meaning of a word, including its form. Then have students work with a partner to write original sentences using each of these words: *bribe* (noun), *signal* (noun), *violate* (verb), and *investigate* (verb). As needed, have pairs check the word meanings in a dictionary before they write.

INFORMATIONAL TEXT FOCUS *(45 minutes)*

Main Idea Discuss the purpose of reading an article that provides information like "The Great Escape." Confirm that students will learn interesting details. However, their main purpose is to find the main idea. Explain that *main idea* is the most important idea the author wants to *convey* about a subject. Assure students that authors will *support* them in finding the main idea. Sometimes authors include a sentence that states the main idea. Writers always include clues to the main idea. Have students listen to this example for clues to the main idea:

> Let's say you are reading an article about soccer. The title is "Soccer: The New Number One High School Sport." In the article, the writer reports on the popularity of soccer. The writer includes statistics, or numbers, to show that more high school students are playing soccer and more high schools have soccer teams. The author includes facts about soccer, such as how it is played and why it is generally a safer sport for students to play than football. The author includes quotes from coaches and students around the U.S. talking about why soccer is a great game for both boys and girls to play.

From "The Great Escape" by Thomas Fleming from Boys' Life, March 1997. Copyright © 1997. Copyright © 1997 by **Thomas Fleming**. Reproduced by permission of the author.

Original content Copyright © by Holt, Rinehart and Winston. Additions and changes to the original content are the responsibility of the instructor.

LANGUAGE SKILL
Especially for ELL
(20 minutes)
English-language learners will benefit from models for how to pronounce difficult or unfamiliar words. Have students read several paragraphs from the article with you or with a fluent reader in the class. Stop after each paragraph to review the meaning and pronunciation of challenging words. Point out words that have related meanings when presented in different forms (see examples at the left).

ACADEMIC VOCABULARY
Preteaching Academic Vocabulary
(5 minutes)
Write these terms and their meanings on a chalkboard or transparency. Review them with the students before previewing the selection.

Main Idea: The most important or central message in a nonfiction text
Convey: Suggest; communicate
Support: Back up; strengthen by giving evidence

Differentiating Instruction

Ask: *What is this author's purpose in writing? What is the main message, or main idea, the author wants you to get from this article?* Guide students to identify clues to help find the main idea, such as the article title; statistics and facts that show more high school students are playing soccer and that it is a safer sport to play; and the quotations from people that give positive views of soccer. Help students conclude that the main idea is that soccer is the new top sport in high school.

Have students work with a partner to preview the "The Great Escape" for clues to the main idea. Explain that one tip for finding the main idea is to read the introduction. Have the student pairs read the first part, up to "The Escape Genius," and then use a chart like the one at right to take notes on what they read. For now, have them fill in the title and list key words and phrases in the "Repetition of Ideas" column that might explain why this was a "great escape." Then have students work in pairs to continue filling out the chart as they read the complete article.

Direct Teach

(30 minutes)

Chunk the Text Help students pace their reading by dividing the selection into "chunks" or parts. After students read each part, have them stop to fill in information in the chart.
Part 1: ends p. 102: "…the tunnel rats kept digging."
Part 2: ends p. 104: "…a goal once they agree to what that goal is.'"

Check for Understanding

WRITING FOCUS *(30 minutes)*
Including the Main Idea in a Summary To help students find the main idea of "The Great Escape," discuss important information they learned from the article. Prompt students with these points:

Digging the tunnels was difficult and dangerous work. The prisoners had to find a clever way to get rid of the tunnel dirt.

The prisoners were in constant danger of having the German guards discover the tunnels – and the Germans did find "Tom."

The prisoners had to make clothing for disguises and create phony documents to prepare for the escape.

The prisoners knew that if they escaped, they would be in great danger of being captured before they could reach safety. Only three of the 76 prisoners made it to freedom, and 50 were killed by the Gestapo.

Have students think about these and other details from the article. Then have them write a sentence explaining the main idea – the writer's most important point – about the Great Escape.
Constructed Response Explain that students are to write a summary of the article that includes a statement of the main idea. Remind students that a summary provides only the most important information, such as key people and events. Suggest that students begin the summary with their sentence explaining the main idea of the article.

Original content Copyright © by Holt, Rinehart and Winston. Additions and changes to the original content are the responsibility of the instructor.

Differentiating Instruction

READING FOCUS
Finding the Main Idea Chart

Text Feature	My Comments
Title of Article	
Headings	
Repetition of Ideas	
Conclusion	

READING/WRITING
Especially for WGP
(10 minutes)
Writers gaining proficiency will benefit from help in writing a summary. Have students list people and events from the article, and then choose only the most important to include. As students write, have them follow this outline for summarizing the article:
* What was the Great Escape?
* When did it take place?
* Who was involved?
* Why is it important?

Collection 1
Graphic Organizer

Did Animals Sense Tsunami Was Coming? *from* National

Geographic News

Main Idea and Supporting Details Diagram A **main idea** is the writer's most important message. Details that support a writer's main idea include facts, statistics, quotations, and examples.

Each diagram below lists a main idea from the selection. In the smaller ovals, list at least three details the writer uses to support the main idea.

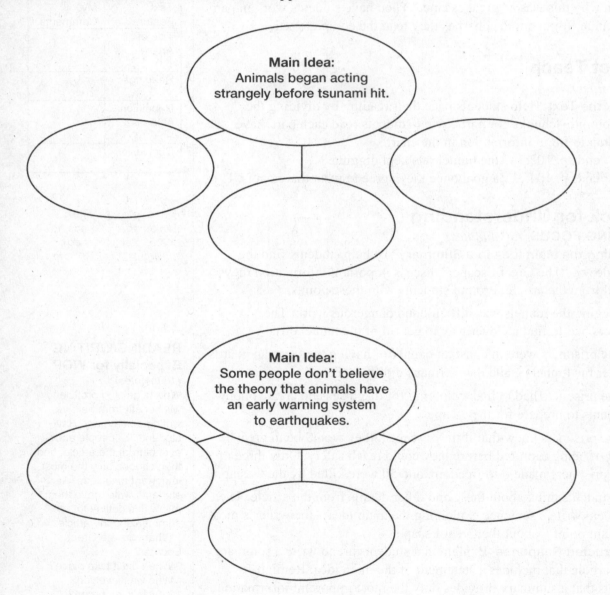

Main Idea:
Animals began acting
strangely before tsunami hit.

Main Idea:
Some people don't believe
the theory that animals have
an early warning system
to earthquakes.

Original content Copyright © by Holt, Rinehart and Winston. Additions and changes to the original content are the responsibility of the instructor.

Differentiating Instruction

Collection 1
Targeted Strategies for Learners with Diverse Needs

READING SKILLS

Main Ideas/Supporting Details *(15 minutes)* Explain to students that the main idea of a selection states what the selection is about. Help students understand that a sentence or title may state the main idea, but not always. To figure out what the main idea is, whether it's stated or unstated, good readers think about what the details have in common.

Detail 1	Detail 2	Detail 3
What do they have in common?		
Main Idea:		

Work together as a class to choose three details from "The Great Escape." Then find the topic they have in common. What is the most important thing that the author has to say? That's the main idea.

LITERARY SKILLS

Suspense and Foreshadowing *(15 minutes)* Explain that many authors use foreshadowing to create a feeling of suspense and excitement in their work. Foreshadowing offers the careful reader hints or clues about what is going to happen later. Good readers often use foreshadowing to make predictions. These clues might be:

- in dialogue: does a character make a prediction about the future, or make a statement that's either pessimistic or overly optimistic?

- in an action: does a character act nervous or tempt fate by doing something that is likely to bring about a negative outcome?

Have partners work together to list examples of foreshadowing on the first page of *The Most Dangerous Game*.

Setting and Conflict *(15 minutes)* Help students understand that setting is another way in which the author communicates the story. Help students connect the details given about the setting to the action, for example, ask: *What do these details tell you about the conflict in the* Liberty?

- dug up flower bulbs

- chain link fence and putrid green doghouse

- hedge where one can hide from punishment

- wires in the study

Have student pairs discuss the feeling each detail evokes. Then have them talk about each detail's connection to the plot.

Readings in Collection 1 Minimum Course of Study

- *The Most Dangerous Game,* p. 16
- *Liberty,* p. 54
- The Great Escape, p. 98

RESOURCES

In *The Holt Reader,* all three selections help students who need more scaffolding in a workbook format.

Consult *Holt Audio Library* for recordings of most selections.

TEACHING TIP

Help English-language learners recognize and use idioms. Point out the expression "to have in common" for example. Explain that it means "to share." Ask: *What do basketball, football, and soccer have in common?* Point the expression "to tempt fate" Explain that it means to behave in a risky way (which might include violating a superstition)...

ALTERNATIVE ASSESSMENT *(5 minutes)*

Discuss the following items with learners with diverse needs.

The most important point can be found in the [main idea/details].

You can use [foreshadowing] to guess what will happen next in a story.

The setting [might/might not] give you information about the conflict in the story.

Original content Copyright © by Holt, Rinehart and Winston. Additions and changes to the original content are the responsibility of the instructor.

Differentiating Instruction

Collection 1
Student Edition pages 16–111
Academic and Selection Vocabulary

The Most Dangerous Game   Liberty
The Great Escape

A. Circle the word that doesn't belong in each series.

1. imprudent, careful, thoughtless, unwise

2. distracted, attentive, unfocused, daydreaming

3. inconsolable, upset, delighted, brokenhearted

4. admonitions, scolding, warning, commendations

5. receding, withdrawing, advancing, retreating

6. disarming, annoying, charming, enchanting

B. Write a "T" for true or "F" for false next to each sentence below.

_____ 1. If you resort to something, you take it on vacation with you.

_____ 2. If you elect to see a movie with friends, then you make a choice to go.

_____ 3. A plan that is pursued is put into action.

_____ 4. A problem that is surmounted cannot be solved.

_____ 5. A surprise announcement is something that invariably arrives.

_____ 6. A cat that prowled around a backyard would probably be looking for a meal.

C. Use the academic vocabulary words to complete the following paragraph about "The Most Dangerous Game," by Richard Connell.

support   outcome   effect   excerpt   convey

The short story "The Most Dangerous Game" tries to (1) _____ how it

feels to be hunted. The (2) _____, or part, of the story that takes place in

the woods is especially intense. In the story, the author shows that General Zaroff lives like a

gentleman. The details that (3) _____ this include descriptions of his fine

house and custom clothes. The (4) _____ is chilling because the

General's hobby is so savage. Fortunately, in the final (5) _____ the

General is beaten at his own game.

Original content Copyright © by Holt, Rinehart and Winston. Additions and changes to the original content are the responsibility of the instructor.

Collection 1

Selection Test

The Most Dangerous Game   Richard Connell

COMPREHENSION, SKILLS, AND VOCABULARY Circle the letter of the best answer to each of the following items.

1. Why does General Zaroff hunt people instead of animals?

   A) He likes animals better than people.

   B) He felt bad about hunting animals.

   C) He wants the challenge of hunting something that can reason.

   D) He hopes to end the problem of sailors coming to his island home.

2. Rainsford provides the general with his greatest challenge because Rainsford—

   A) will also hunt anything

   B) makes friends with Ivan

   C) is also an expert with a gun

   D) is smart, cunning, and persistent

3. Which is an example of foreshadowing in the story?

   A) Rainsford falls into "blood-warm waters."

   B) Whitney and Rainsford are headed for the Amazon River.

   C) General Zaroff has read about Rainsford in books on hunting.

   D) General Zaroff knows Rainsford is hiding in a tree but doesn't shoot him.

4. Based on details about Rainsford, most readers might predict that—

   A) he would lose the game

   B) he would beat General Zaroff

   C) he would tame the general's hounds

   D) he would become a good friend of the general

5. Which of the following is the best example of a person who is **imprudent**?

   A) He never spends money.

   B) He saves part of his summer earnings for a car.

   C) He spends his allowance as soon as he gets it.

   D) He builds a great CD collection by buying one CD each month.

6. How do you think the experience of being hunted changed Rainsford? Did he become kinder or crueler? Think about clues in the story. Use the organizer below to collect your ideas. Then write a short paragraph.

Introductory statement: I think Rainsford became kinder/crueler...
Two or three supporting sentences: First...He also...For those reasons...
Concluding statement: As a result, Rainsford...

Original content Copyright © by Holt, Rinehart and Winston. Additions and changes to the original content are the responsibility of the instructor.

| Collection 1 **Selection Test** | *Student Edition pages 54–65* |

Liberty Julia Alvarez

COMPREHENSION, SKILLS, AND VOCABULARY Circle the letter of the best answer to each of the following items.

1. Which are details that explain the setting of the story?
   A) The mother does not like dogs.
   B) The family lives in a Spanish-speaking country.
   C) The narrator often gets in trouble with her mother.
   D) The father wants to go to a university in the United States.

2. Who is Mister Victor?
   A) an American official
   B) an uncle in the family
   C) one of the men who spies on the family
   D) a man who will deliver guns for hunting

3. What is the main conflict in this story?
   A) The girl does not want to give up the dog.
   B) The girl is so attached to the dog, she has no other friends.
   C) The parents cannot agree on whether they should go to America.
   D) The family is in danger of getting in trouble before they can get to America.

4. The father names the puppy Liberty. What does this tell you about him?
   A) that he wants the dog to be free
   B) that he likes unusual names for dogs
   C) that freedom for his family is the main thing on his mind
   D) that he thinks Liberty is what families in the U.S. name their dogs

5. Someone who is **inconsolable**—
   A) cannot be fooled
   B) cannot be understood
   C) cannot be cured of a sickness
   D) cannot be helped to overcome a sadness

6. The father says that "all liberty involves sacrifice." What do you think he means? What does the girl sacrifice for liberty? Do you agree or disagree with the father's statement? Think about clues in the story. Use the organizer below to collect your ideas. Then write a short paragraph.

| Introductory statement: I think the father means that… |
| Two supporting sentences: For example, the girl sacrifices…She also… |
| Concluding statements: For those reasons, I agree/disagree with the father… |

Original content Copyright © by Holt, Rinehart and Winston. Additions and changes to the original content are the responsibility of the instructor.

Differentiating Instruction

Name _____ Class _____ Date_____

Collection 1

Selection Test

Student Edition pages 98–105

The Great Escape Thomas Fleming *from* Boys' Life

COMPREHENSION, SKILLS, AND VOCABULARY Circle the letter of the best answer to each of the following items.

1. When did the Great Escape take place?

   A) during World War I

   B) during World War II

   C) in modern-day Poland

   D) in modern-day Germany

2. Which statement accurately describes the Great Escape?

   A) A few prisoners of war tried to escape.

   B) About 50 men were caught trying to escape.

   C) The men escaped by pretending to be guards and sneaking out.

   D) Only 3 of 76 prisoners who escaped were not recaptured or killed.

3. What was one of the biggest problems the prisoners had?

   A) learning to speak German

   B) building a factory in the prison camp

   C) getting rid of the sand from the tunnels they dug

   D) stealing the clothing they needed for their disguises

4. What is the main idea of the article "The Great Escape"?

   A) It is not that hard to escape from a prison camp.

   B) Few people who try to escape from a prison camp are successful.

   C) The prisoners' determination and their bravery made them heroic.

   D) This escape failed because it was poorly planned from the beginning.

5. Which describes what a person being **pursued** would most likely do?

   A) talk loudly

   B) walk slowly

   C) stop for a picnic

   D) look for a place to hide

6. The article describes Roger Bushell, who was called Big X, as an "escape genius." Based on what you learned about him, do you agree or disagree? Use the organizer to collect your ideas and details from the article to support your point of view. Then write a short paragraph.

| Introductory statement: I do/do not think Roger Bushell was an escape genius. |
| Two supporting sentences: To start with, … Also, …. In addition,… |
| Concluding statement: In conclusion, I believe … |

Original content Copyright © by Holt, Rinehart and Winston. Additions and changes to the original content are the responsibility of the instructor.

Differentiating Instruction

Collection 1
Collection Summative Test

VOCABULARY SKILLS Complete the sentences below by using the collection vocabulary words from the list below.

imprudent   receding   impression   resort
prowled   distracted   disarming

1. I got the _____from his voice that he was glad to talk to me.

2. We were too _____ by the beautiful sunset to notice that our boat was

   drifting away from shore.

3. The hungry teens _____ through the kitchen cupboard, looking for snacks.

4. We may _____ to writing a song if we can't find one we like.

5. It is _____ to leave without a coat when it's cold outside.

LITERARY AND READING SKILLS Circle the letter of the best answer.

6. Which statement best describes a story with **suspense**?

   A) You know how it is going to end.

   B) It has many humorous characters.

   C) You have the feeling that something bad may happen.

   D) There is a good character you like and a bad character you don't like.

7. To find the **main idea** of a nonfiction article,

   A) look for the most interesting details

   B) read the title, which always gives the main idea

   C) read for the sentence the writer always includes that states the main idea

   D) look for clues to the main message the writer communicates on the topic

8. When you **make a prediction,** you

   A) take a wild guess about what may happen

   B) take a guess about what may happen based on evidence

   C) decide what a story means based on the events that have occurred

   D) read between the lines to find the big idea about life the author wants to share

LANGUAGE AND WRITING SKILLS Choose the correct answer in each answer pair.

9. A word with multiple meanings has more than one _____ [definition/spelling]

10. A word with a prefix meaning "not" is _____ [under/unusual]

Original content Copyright © by Holt, Rinehart and Winston. Additions and changes to the original content are the responsibility of the instructor.

Old Man at the Bridge Ernest Hemingway

"Inferring Character Traits" Chart An **inference** is an educated guess based on clues. To make inferences about characters, look for their traits. Clues to their traits appear in their thoughts, actions, and words.

Read the box of character traits below. Which traits apply to the old man in the story? Which apply to the soldier? Some traits may apply to both characters. List the traits in the correct columns in the chart below, and find details in the story to support your answers.

Character Traits				
kind-hearted	watchful	confused	worried	responsible

The Old Man		The Soldier	
Character Trait	Story Details	Character Trait	Story Details

Original content Copyright © by Holt, Rinehart and Winston. Additions and changes to the original content are the responsibility of the instructor.

Lesson Plan and Teaching Strategies

Thank You, M'am Langston Hughes

Preteach

LISTENING COMPREHENSION SKILLS *(10 minutes)*
Build Background/Set a Purpose Talk about Build Background on
p. 136, simplifying words like *residents* (people who live there).
Explain that Langston Hughes lived in Harlem during the 1920s, and
point out that section of New York City on an available map. Share that
Hughes lived there at a time when it was crowded with newcomers
from the South and when it was also famous for its music and writing.
Discuss the Preview the Selection feature on p. 136. Have students look
at the photographs of Harlem on page 136 and on page 139. Preview
these details of the plot:

- A teenage boy named Roger tries to steal a purse from a woman who
  is walking home alone at night.

- The woman kicks him, holds him, and insists that he come home
  with her, where she can wash his face.

- The woman feeds Roger and gives him money. She tells him not to
  steal anything again. He leaves, without being able to thank her.

Point out that people can often act in unexpected ways. Ask: *Did you
ever get unexpected help from someone? What happened?*

VOCABULARY SKILLS *(10 minutes)*
Preteach Vocabulary Words Review the meanings of the vocabulary
in the Word Bank. Then give students these sentences to complete.

1. After everyone left the street festival, the street seemed [barren].

2. The teacher will not [permit] students to eat in her classroom.

3. The elderly man looked [frail] but was actually strong and healthy.

Remind students to watch for these words as they read the story.

LANGUAGE COACH SKILL *(10 minutes)*
Multiple-Meaning Words Explain that some words have more than
one meaning. Discuss the following words from the story—

- In Hughes's work, the word *blast* means "at full speed." (p. 137) The
  word can also mean "an explosion."

- The word *square* means "in the middle of" (p. 137). It can also mean
  "a shape with four equal lines and four right angles."

- *Stoop* means to crouch down (p. 138). It can also mean "the front
  steps of an apartment building."

Write these sentences on the board. Have students complete each one
by adding a word from the box.

RESOURCES
In *The Holt Reader:* "Thank
You, M'am" for students who
need more scaffolding in a
workbook format

In this book: *Vocabulary Skill
Builder*, p. 36; "Thank You,
M'am" Selection Test, p. 37.

Consult *Holt Audio Library*
for recordings of most
selections.

WORD BANK
permit
frail
barren

LANGUAGE SKILL
Especially for ELL
(5 minutes or less)
Explain that some of these
words from the story are
informal expressions, or
slang. Pronounce words with
students, discuss definitions,
and ask volunteers to use
words in sentences.
M'am (p. 137): contraction
for *Madam*, usually spelled
Ma'am.
sitter (p. 137): part of your
body used for sitting
roomers (p. 138): people
who rent rooms in a house
ain't: (138) nonstandard
contraction for *am not* or
has not
icebox (p. 140) refrigerator

Original content Copyright © by Holt, Rinehart and Winston. Additions and changes to the original content are the responsibility of the instructor.

Differentiating Instruction

blast	square	stoop

1. We sat on the [stoop], chatting with our neighbors.
2. The child drew a [square] house with a triangle for a roof.
3. The [blast] of the explosion could be felt for miles.

LITERARY FOCUS *(20 minutes)*

Character and Dialogue Explain: *Writers let us learn about their characters (the people in their stories, poems or plays) by showing us what they do and by describing what they look like. Good writers sometimes let us learn from what the characters say—that is, their dialogue.* Ask students how to identify dialogue in a story. *(Quotation marks usually set off characters' words.)* Review the following lines of dialogue from the story.

> "If I turn you loose, will you run?" asked the woman.
> "Yes'm," said the boy.
> "Then I won't turn you loose," said the woman. (page 138)

Discuss with students what they can tell about the woman from this piece of dialogue. *(She is firm and practical.)* Discuss what they can learn about the boy from his short answer to the woman. *(He is honest and respectful toward the woman.)*

Help students use academic vocabulary and concepts. Divide them into groups of three. Tell students to experiment with diction as they write their own description of a character from the story. Write the following lines of dialogue on the board.

"Maybe you ain't been to your supper either, late as it be. Have you?"

"There's nobody home at my house." (page 139)

Have students identify which character said each line. Then have them note what the dialogue reveals about the characters.

READING FOCUS *(45 minutes)*

Make Inferences Explain that when you *make inferences,* you use clues from the story in combination with your own experience to make a guess about something in the story. Now read the following passages: …*"You ought to be my son. I would teach you right from wrong. Least I can do right now is to wash your face. Are you hungry?" (page 138)* Ask students what clues they can find in the text about Mrs. Luella Bates Washington Jones. *(She takes charge, and she wants Roger to be clean and fed.)* Based on their own experience with adults like Mrs. Luella Bates Washington Jones, what more can they infer about her? *(She is concerned about Roger, in spite of his bad behavior.)* What can they infer about how Roger is feeling? *(He is scared but impressed.)*

"Thank You, Ma'm" from *Short Stories* by Langston Hughes. Copyright © 1996 by Ramona Bass and Arnold Rampersad. All rights reserved. Reproduced by permission of **Hill and Wang, a division of Farrar, Straus, and Giroux, LLC.**

ACADEMIC VOCABULARY
Preteaching Academic Vocabulary
(5 minutes)
Write these terms and their meanings on a chalkboard or transparency. Review them with the students before previewing the selection.

Character: The people you find in a story, poem, or a play.
Dialogue: The conversation that takes place between people in a story or play.
Incident: Something that took place; event.
Inferences: Using clues from the text along with what you already know to make a guess about something in a story, poem, or play.

READING FOCUS
Make Inferences

Original content Copyright © by Holt, Rinehart and Winston. Additions and changes to the original content are the responsibility of the instructor.

Have students work in pairs to fill out graphic organizers like the one on the preceding page. First, ask students to choose different moments from the story, and have them note clues about the characters from the text. Next have them note what they already know about that kind of situation. Finally, have them write down their inferences. Encourage them to share their answers with the class.

Direct Teach

(45 minutes)

Think – Pair – Share English-language learners may benefit from completing a main event chart as they read. Write the words WHO, WHAT, WHEN, WHERE, and WHY in a list on the board or on an overhead projector. After reading the first paragraph of the story, ask, *What happened?* Add the appropriate answer to the right of the word WHAT. (A boy tried to steal a woman's purse, but he fell and she kicked him and shook him.) Continue with the following questions: *To whom did it happen?* (a boy and a large woman) *When did it happen?* (11:00 at night) *Where did it happen?* (on the sidewalk) *Why did it happen?* (The boy wanted to run away with the woman's purse.) Encourage students to continue using the chart as they read the story.

Check for Understanding

WRITING FOCUS *(15 minutes)*

Dialogue and Dialect Point out that every area in the United States has a different dialect; that is, people who live in different places have their own special way of speaking English. Explain that few people speak formal English all the time, and when writers create dialogue they often use dialect of the region where the characters live. This helps to make the characters sound real. Write these sentences on the board:

"Ain't you got nobody home to tell you to wash your face?" (p. 140)

"Don't you have anyone at home to tell you to wash your face?"

Have a volunteer read both sentences. Ask students to point out differences between the dialect and formal English.

Read aloud each sentence below. Have students write their own versions, either in formal English or in a regional dialect.

1. *"Now ain't you ashamed of yourself?"* (p. 138) *(Aren't you ashamed of yourself?)*

2. *"You a lie!"* (p. 138) *(You are a liar!)*

Think As A Reader/Writer Ask: *If Roger saw Mrs. Jones on the street the next day, what might he say?* Ask students to think about what they know of his character and then write two or three sentences of the dialogue he might have with Mrs. Jones.

"Thank You, Ma'm" from *Short Stories* by Langston Hughes. Copyright © 1996 by Ramona Bass and Arnold Rampersad. All rights reserved. Reproduced by permission of **Hill and Wang, a division of Farrar, Straus, and Giroux, LLC.**

VOCABULARY SKILL
Especially for ELL

Students may be unfamiliar with the term half nelson (page 138). Explain that this is a wrestling hold that involves passing one arm under the opponent's arm from behind, and placing the hand on the back of the opponent's neck, in order to prevent the opponent from moving.

READING/WRITING
Especially for ELL
(5 minutes)

Explain that all languages have dialects, or variations that show up in different regions. Ask English-language learners to suggest examples from their first language or native country. Have them explain how the dialect differs from the formal language.

Original content Copyright © by Holt, Rinehart and Winston. Additions and changes to the original content are the responsibility of the instructor.

Differentiating Instruction

To Da-duh, in Memoriam Paule Marshall

Character Interactions Chart The relationships that characters have with each other are often revealed in their **interactions** with each other. These interactions can also give the reader clues to a character's personality or motivation.

Use this chart to describe what the following interactions reveal about the characters and their motivations.

Interaction	Why the Character Takes the Action (Motivation)
The narrator's mother grabs her hand as Da-duh approaches.	
Da-duh gives the narrator's mother only a quick hug when greeting her at the airport.	
Da-duh hushes the family for making such a fuss over the family's arrival.	
Da-duh takes the narrator to see the canes.	
The narrator tells Da-duh about the snow in New York City.	

Original content Copyright © by Holt, Rinehart and Winston. Additions and changes to the original content are the responsibility of the instructor.

American History   Judith Ortiz Cofer

Preteach

LISTENING COMPREHENSION SKILLS *(10 minutes)*
Build Background/Set a Purpose   Discuss Build Background on p. 162. Make sure students understand that President Kennedy was killed. Explain that the selection is about a girl and a boy who were in high school the day this happened. Explain that the assassination is an event in American history. Point out the title of the selection.

Discuss Preview the Selection on p. 162. Have students look ahead at the photographs. Preview these details of the plot:

- Elena's family is from Puerto Rico. They live in a large apartment building like those shown on pages 164 and 167.

- Elena likes Eugene.

- Eugene's family is white. His family lives in a house near Elena's apartment building.

Explain that a historical event affects people in different ways, especially if they are not directly influenced by it. Ask volunteers to talk about where they were and what they felt immediately after an important historical event or crisis, such as 9/11 or Hurricane Katrina. As students read, ask them to compare their reactions to Elena's feelings after President Kennedy dies.

VOCABULARY SKILLS *(10 minutes)*
Preteach Vocabulary Words   Review the meanings of the vocabulary in the Word Bank. Then give students these sentences to complete.

1. Winning the game filled the team with [elation].

2. [Infatuated] with his new girlfriend, Martin kept saying her name.

3. My friend was too [discreet] to shout in the restaurant.

4. It was a tiny cut, but the boy needed [solace] from his mother.

5. If teachers are [vigilant], they catch the students who cheat.

Remind students to watch for these words as they read the story.

LANGUAGE COACH SKILL *(10 minutes)*
Word Origins   Explain that understanding the origins of words can help students learn new words. Discuss these words from the story.

- The Latin word *profundus* means "deep" or "limitless." In English, a *profound* silence is a deep silence (p. 163).

- The Latin word *emergere* means "to rise out of the water." The word *emerge* is often used to describe how a person comes out from somewhere and into view (p. 165).

RESOURCES

In *The Holt Reader:*
"American History" for students who need more scaffolding in a workbook format

In this book: *Vocabulary Skill Builder,* p. 36; "American History" Selection Test, p. 38

Consult *Holt Audio Library* for recordings of most selections.

WORD BANK

discreet
infatuated
vigilant
elation
solace

ACADEMIC VOCABULARY
Preteaching Academic Vocabulary *(5 minutes)*
Write these terms and their meanings on a chalkboard or transparency. Review them with the students before previewing the selection.

Major Character: A character whom the story is mostly about
Minor Character: A character who is part of the story but not someone the story is mostly about
Traits: Details about someone; particularly details about how they talk or act
Personality: Who someone is; the whole way a person talks and acts
Complex: Having more than one part or aspect; complicated

Original content Copyright © by Holt, Rinehart and Winston. Additions and changes to the original content are the responsibility of the instructor.

Differentiating Instruction

- The Greek word *topos* means "a place" or "a subject." The word *topic* in English means a subject (p. 166).

The Middle English word *thrall* means "to make a slave." Today, the word *enthralled* implies that someone feels captured by a feeling or an activity (p. 166).

Write these sentences on the board. Have students complete each one by adding a word from the box.

profound	emerged	enthralled	topic

1. We started studying a new [topic] in our history class.
2. She was [enthralled] by movies and saw a new one every weekend.
3. The puppy [emerged] soaking wet from the stream.
4. When I turned off my flashlight, the darkness was [profound].

LITERARY FOCUS *(20 minutes)*

Round and Flat Characters Explain: *A character is a person in a story. Flat characters are people readers don't learn a lot about. They are usually minor characters. Round characters are people readers do learn a lot about. They are usually major characters.* As an example, read aloud a description of two characters:

> Angela talked softly and worked quietly at her desk. Frank talked too loudly, but he was so funny he could make you spill your drink at lunch. Whenever he walked past a mirror he always checked his hair, and whenever the teacher asked a question in class—whatever she asked about—he answered by talking about baseball.

Explain that Angela is a flat character, and Frank is a round character. Readers can picture Frank clearly because they learn a lot of traits, or details, about his personality. Tell students that in "American History" Elena is an example of a round character.

Help students use academic vocabulary and concepts. Divide them into groups of three. Have them create a two-column chart with the headings *Round* and *Flat*. Tell students to spend five minutes talking about favorite characters from books, movies, television, or comics. Students should identify the characters as flat or round and give reasons for their choices. Expect students to use academic vocabulary, and prompt them if they do not. Ask volunteers for examples from their charts.

READING FOCUS *(45 minutes)*

Make Inferences About Characters Explain that an inference is when students use clues to figure out information someone did not actually say. Offer this example: *I was hungry when I got home, but I was full an hour later.* Ask: *What happened?* (You ate a snack.) Explain that students used clues and drew on their own experiences to infer what you did not actually say. The clues were that you were hungry but that

LANGUAGE SKILL
Especially for ELL
(5 minutes or less)
Some English Learners may have difficulty with the technical terms round characters and flat characters. Display a ball or a marble and a piece of paper. Point out that the round ball or marble is more interesting to look at it than the flat paper. Explain that a round character is more interesting to read about than a flat one.

READING FOCUS
Inferences Chart

Page #	Words, Thoughts, Actions	My Infer-ences

Original content Copyright © by Holt, Rinehart and Winston. Additions and changes to the original content are the responsibility of the instructor.

Differentiating Instruction

you did something to change how you felt. Their experience should tell them that a hungry person eats and then feels full. Tell students that they can also make inferences about characters based on their words, thoughts, and actions.

Have students work in pairs to fill out a chart like the one at the right. As they read the selection, prompt them to use clues and draw on their own experiences to make inferences about the characters of Elena, Eugene, their mothers, and Mr. DePalma.

Direct Teach
(60 minutes)

Chunk the Text Help students pace their reading by dividing the selection into "chunks" or parts. After the students have read each part, stop to help them make inferences about characters.

Part 1: ends p. 164, col. 2: "while I froze."
Part 2: ends p. 165, col 2: "…my stomach was doing somersaults."
Part 3: ends p. 167, col 2: "…at school when we were seen together."
Part 4: ends p. 169, col 2: "…a white handkerchief to her face."
Part 5: ends p. 170, col 2: "…gray as it touched the ground below."

Check for Comprehension
WRITING FOCUS *(15 minutes)*

Dialogue and Narrative Explain that an author can use dialogue to quote a character's exact words. An author can also use narrative to describe what a person said. In "American History," Judith Ortiz Cofer uses both dialogue and narrative. Use dialogue from the story to model the difference between dialogue and narrative.

> **Dialogue** "I have a test to study for, Mama." (p. 169)
> **Rewritten as Narrative** I told my mother I had a test to study for.

Read aloud each sentence below. If it is dialogue, have students rewrite it as narrative. If it is narrative, have students rewrite it as a dialogue.

1. I hated the city, especially in the winter. (p. 164)
2. "You are heading for humiliation and pain." (p. 169)
3. His mother was very unhappy, Eugene said. (p. 167)
4. "I don't know how you people do it." (p. 170)

Think As A Reader/Writer Ask: *What might Elena say to Eugene when she sees him at school the next day?* Ask students to think about her personality and character traits and then write two or three sentences of the dialogue she might have with Eugene.

VOCABULARY SKILL
Especially for ELL
(15 minutes)

Students learn new words more easily if the words are presented in meaningful categories. Define these words from the selection. Explain that these words all can be used to describe characters' actions or attitudes.

snobbery (p. 165): acting like you're better than someone else
nag (p. 166): to remind someone again and again of what they should do
titters (p. 167): nervous laughter
distraught (p. 168): completely overcome with sadness
trance (p. 170): staring without moving or seeming to see anything

Organize students in groups of four or five to think of examples for each of these words from their own experience. Provide corrective feedback.

READING/WRITING
Especially for WPG
(15 minutes)

Work with writers gaining proficiency before they begin to write to brainstorm a list of Elena's personality and character traits. Encourage student pairs to then act out a scene between Elena and Eugene. Critique the scene to be sure students stay "in character." Then have students write or transcribe the scene they just enacted. Check to be sure they use correct punctuation when transcribing spoken language to print.

Slight adaptation of "American History" from *The Latin Deli: Prose and Poetry* by Judith Ortiz Cofer. Copyright © 1993 by Judith Ortiz Cofer. Reproduced by permission of **The University of Georgia Press**.

Original content Copyright © by Holt, Rinehart and Winston. Additions and changes to the original content are the responsibility of the instructor.

Differentiating Instruction

Lesson Plan and Teaching Strategies

An Interview with Dave Eggers

Preteach

LISTENING COMPREHENSION SKILLS *(10 minutes)*

Build Background/Set a Purpose Discuss Build Background on p. 200. Explain that Dave Eggers became famous when he was a young man in his twenties, and that he has shown an interest in helping children and young people ever since. Note that in the interview, Eggers gives advice to readers about reading and writing.

. Preview these details of the selection:

- A journalist from a magazine called *Writing* asks Dave Eggers questions. They talk about how often Eggers writes.

- Eggers explains that he thinks fame is useful in that someone famous can have more influence to do good.

- Eggers advises students to read a lot, and, along with their schoolwork, to read books that they enjoy.

Have students look ahead at the photographs. Explain that 826 Valencia is Eggers's tutoring program in San Francisco. Discuss with students whether 826 Valencia looks like a place they would like to go.

VOCABULARY SKILLS *(10 minutes)*

Preteach Vocabulary Words Review the meanings of the vocabulary in the Word Bank. Then give students these sentences to complete.

1. The band's music was surprising and [unconventional].

2. Earning money at a summer job [enabled] Ciara to buy an MP3 player.

Remind students to watch for these words as they read the story.

LANGUAGE COACH SKILL *(10 minutes)*

Word Origins Explain that many words have long histories, and that knowing where a word comes from can help you to understand it more fully.

- The Latin word *memoria* means "mindful, remembering." In English, the word *memoir* means a person's written account of his life. *p. 200*

- The Latin word *literarius* means "belonging to letters or learning." In English, a literary work is a worthwhile work of fiction or nonfiction. *p.200*

- In Latin, the word *illustrationen* means a *vivid representation*. In English the word *illustrate* means to draw pictures for a book, greeting card, magazine or advertisement. *p.201*

RESOURCES
In *The Holt Reader:* "An interview with Dave Eggers" for students who need more scaffolding in a workbook format

In this book: *Vocabulary Skill Builder,* p. 36; "An Interview with Dave Eggers" Selection Test, p. 39

Consult *Holt Audio Library* for recordings of most selections.

WORD BANK
unconventional
enabled

ACADEMIC VOCABULARY
Preteaching Academic Vocabulary
(5 minutes)
Write these terms and their meanings on a chalkboard or transparency. Review them with the students before previewing the selection.
Synthesize: To pull together many pieces of evidence to gain a more complete understanding
Audience: The people who will read the writer's work.
Purpose: The writer's reason for writing the work.
Main Idea: The main point of a piece of writing.
Observation: Statement about what one sees.
Significant: Important.

Original content Copyright © by Holt, Rinehart and Winston. Additions and changes to the original content are the responsibility of the instructor.

Differentiating Instruction

Write these sentences on the board. Have students complete each one by adding a word from the box.

memoir	literary	illustrate

1. David tried to [illustrate] his report with funny pictures.
2. My favorite [literary] work is *Pride and Prejudice* by Jane Austen.
3. The author's [memoir] covered his childhood in Philadelphia.

INFORMATIONAL TEXT FOCUS *(20 minutes)*

Audience and Purpose Explain: *Writers keep in mind the people who will read their work. These people are known as the audience. A writer might think about who his or her audience is likely to be, when thinking about the purpose, or main reason, for a piece of writing. Look at the following questions from the selection.*

> "When and why did you starting writing?" (page 201)
> "How do you write?" (page 201)
> "Why did you want to help young people learn to write?" (page 202)

Explain that these questions indicate that the journalist is interested in Eggers as a writer—both in his life as a writer and in his help toward other writers. You can infer that the purpose of the piece is to communicate Dave Eggers's ideas about writing.

Draw student's attention to the boxed text on page 204. Ask: *What audience did Dave Eggers have in mind when he wrote this text? (young writers). Do you think Eggers would have different advice for more experienced adult writers? (Students will probably say yes—for example, he might not talk about zombies.)*

Help students use academic vocabulary and concepts. Divide them into groups of three. Tell students to work together to make notes in graphic organizers like the ones on the right. Have them jot down their ideas about the audience and purpose of the main selection and the boxed text. Then have them share their ideas with the class.

Direct Teach

(45 minutes)

Build Fluency Read parts of the interview aloud to students, stopping frequently to restate and summarize the information. Then invite pairs of volunteers to read aloud, with one student reading the questions and the other reading the answers.

LANGUAGE SKILL
Especially for ELL
(5 minutes or less)
Some English-language learners may have difficulty with the technical term *purpose*. Remind students that *purpose* involves the author's reasons for writing the piece. Connect the idea of the selection's purpose to student's reasons for doing things in their everyday life. For example, you might ask questions like the following:

"What was your purpose in coming to school today?"

"What is the purpose of eating lunch?"

"What is the purpose of exercise?"

INFORMATIONAL TEXT FOCUS
Audience and Purpose

Interview with Dave Eggers	
Audience	Purpose

Dave's Advice for Young Writers	
Audience	Purpose

From "A Staggering Genius Talks About Writing, Fame, and . . . Trout An Interview with Dave Eggers" from *Writing Magazine*, vol. 27, no 4, January 2005. Copyright © 2005 by Weekly Reader Corporation. All rights reserved. Reproduced by permission of **Weekly Reader Corporation**.

Original content Copyright © by Holt, Rinehart and Winston. Additions and changes to the original content are the responsibility of the instructor.

Differentiating Instruction

Check for Understanding

WRITING FOCUS *(15 minutes)*

Purpose and Audience Explain that in an article that has the purpose of sharing information about writing, the content might change depending on whom the writer believes the audience for the piece is. For example, look at the following lines from "An Interview with Dave Eggers."

> The point is to begin to love books. I guarantee there are at least 100 books out there for everyone—100 books that will knock you over and change your life—so get started looking for those. (That doesn't mean you shouldn't finish the books you're reading in class. Your teachers know why they're asking you to read a certain book. You have to trust them.) (page 204)

What It Tells About Purpose and Audience Based on the fact that Eggers mentions reading books for class, we can infer that the writer expected the audience for this piece to be students. Have students state or write similar advice, but this time to "would-be" writers who are the age of their parents or grandparents. [*Students may write that adults should use their own experiences in their writing, and what they have learned about life. They may also encourage adults to read widely.*]

Think As A Reader/Writer Have students work in pairs. Ask: *What do you like to do? How could you get other people excited about what you like to do?* Then have students interview each other about their interests. Have them imagine that other students their age will be reading the interview, and have them write the interview with that in mind. Make sure that students understand that the purpose of their writing is to share information and advice about their field of interest.

READING/WRITING
Especially for ELL
(15 minutes)

Comprehending an interview may be difficult for students just learning English. Encourage English-language learners to review the passages with you or a teaching assistant, taking note of any words or phrases that are unfamiliar to them. Then have students use a dictionary to look up the words, and encourage them to ask questions about phrases that are still unclear.

READING/WRITING
Especially for WGP
(5 minutes)

Point out that when people conduct interviews, they usually have a list of questions to ask the person they are interviewing, and that they take careful notes of the answers. Note that when writing the interview, the writer can choose what to include in order to make the interview interesting and appropriate for the audience. Work with students to help them edit their list of questions. Then have them work in pairs to select the most appropriate information to include in the final draft of their interviews.

From "A Staggering Genius Talks About Writing, Fame, and . . . Trout An Interview with Dave Eggers" from *Writing Magazine*, vol. 27, no 4, January 2005. Copyright © 2005 by Weekly Reader Corporation. All rights reserved. Reproduced by permission of **Weekly Reader Corporation**.

Original content Copyright © by Holt, Rinehart and Winston. Additions and changes to the original content are the responsibility of the instructor.

Collection 2
Graphic Organizer

An Interview with Dave Eggers/Teaching Chess, and Life

"Synthesize Main Ideas" Chart To **synthesize** ideas from more than one source, you consider how the sources fit together. Then you develop an idea or a conclusion drawn from considering all the sources.

The chart below contains passages from the two selections. Read the two passages and consider the main idea in each. Then synthesize the main ideas into one statement. One box is completed for you.

Selection	Passage	Main Idea	Synthesizing Idea
"An Interview with Dave Eggers"	"I had a string of great teachers and enjoyed my time there. English and art were my favorite subjects, and I would take after-school art classes to learn more."		
"Teaching Chess, and Life"	"As an eighth-grader at a gang-infested junior high school, I joined the chess team as a way to stay out of trouble. I already knew the coach, Mr. Chiappetta, because he was my social studies teacher."	The author is influenced to participate in after-school activities.	
"An Interview with Dave Eggers"	"I learned a lot of what I know about writing and design while I was in high school, so I think if we at 826 Valencia can help aspiring writers when they're very young and if we can introduce them to actual writers who have been successful, then those students can get a clear idea of a writer's life."		
"Teaching Chess, and Life"	"With Chia's mentorship, I learned from my mistake. As a coach at I.S. 90, I've had to teach the same lesson to others. It makes me feel good about myself because I like helping younger kids learn the game Chia taught me to love."		

From "A 'Staggering Genius' Talks About Writing, Fame, and ...Trout. An Interview With Dave Eggers" from *Writing Magazine,* vol. 27, no. 4, January 2005. Copyright © 2005 by Weekly Reader Corporation. All rights reserved. Reproduced by permission of **Weekly Reader Corporation.**

Original content Copyright © by Holt, Rinehart and Winston. Additions and changes to the original content are the responsibility of the instructor.

Targeted Strategies for Learners with Diverse Needs

READING SKILLS

Audience and Purpose *(15 minutes)* Explain that writers have three main purposes for writing: to inform, to persuade, and to entertain. Usually one purpose is highlighted. However, it's possible to balance all three. For example, have students think of an ad that is funny, gives information about a product and tries to convince people to buy that product. Share chart below with students:

Purpose: to inform	Purpose: to persuade	Purpose: to entertain
wants to give you information	wants you to believe or do something	wants to create feelings in you
Audience: anyone, experts, beginners, fans, customers, coworkers, children, teens, adults, geographic groups, cultural groups, etc.		

Have students work in small groups using articles and ads in a newspaper to practice identifying audience and purpose.

LITERARY SKILLS

Character and Dialogue *(15 minutes)* Help students connect their "people skills" to their developing reading skills. Find a piece of dialogue from a story you have read together as a class and guide students as they attempt to answer these questions.

- What information do the characters give about themselves?
- What can you tell about them from their style of speaking?
- What can you tell about them from what they chose not to say?

Then have partners work together on a different piece of dialogue, each analyzing one of the characters engaged.

Round and Flat Characters *(15 minutes)* Explain to students that the more information they have about characters, the more they seem like people in real life. Round characters seem like they could step off the page. Flat ones are more like sketches. Review the list of characters in *American History*. Then brainstorm what you know about each from the story.

- The narrator
- Eugene
- The narrator's mother
- Mr. DePalma

Have students work in small groups to put the characters in order from roundest to flattest. Ask students to give evidence for their ranking.

Readings in Collection 2 Minimum Course of Study

- "Thank You, M'am", p. 134
- "American History", p. 160
- "An Interview with Dave Eggers", p. 198

RESOURCES

In *The Holt Reader,* all three selections help students who need more scaffolding in a workbook format.

Consult *Holt Audio Library* for recordings of most selections.

TEACHING TIP

English-language learners may have trouble with the vernacular speech in "Thank You, M'am". Explain that in order to make the dialogue sound realistic the author used slang, contractions, and other colloquial expressions. Help students with any language they find difficult.

ALTERNATIVE ASSESSMENT *(5 minutes)*
Have students provide answers for these items.

He doesn't know how to talk to girls is an example of [direct/indirect] characterization.

The most interesting character will be a [round/flat] character.

The main purpose of a short story is [to entertain].

Original content Copyright © by Holt, Rinehart and Winston. Additions and changes to the original content are the responsibility of the instructor.

Differentiating Instruction

Thank You, M'am   American History
Interview with Dave Eggers

A. Match words and definitions. Write the letter of the correct definition next to each word.

_____ 1. enabled

_____ 2. unconventional

_____ 3. barren

_____ 4. permit

_____ 5. frail

a. allow

b. thin and weak

c. empty and deserted

d. not what people usually do

e. gave the power to do something

f. developed more fully

g. advice from a wise teacher

B. Complete each sentence with one of the vocabulary words below.

discreet   solace   vigilant   infatuated   elation

1. We experienced a feeling of _____ when our team won game.

2. After I lost my pet, my one _____ was walking my neighbor's dog.

3. Jenna was always _____ about the secrets that Sam shared with her.

4. The adoring fans were _____ with the handsome movie star.

5. We were _____ about picking up our trash while we camped.

C. Use the academic vocabulary words to complete the following paragraph about "American History" by Judith Ortiz Cofer.

observation   incident   complex   significant

The main character in "American History" has (1) _____ feelings about

her family. Elena is proud of her Puerto Rican heritage but feels caught between two cultures.

From her window, she often watches her neighbors. They are unaware of her constant

(2) _____. The story ends with an upsetting (3) _____

that happens on the day that President Kennedy was killed. Elena goes to study with her

neighbor Eugene, and his mother will not allow her into the house. This

(4) _____ event introduces her to some difficult truths about prejudice.

Original content Copyright © by Holt, Rinehart and Winston. Additions and changes to the original content are the responsibility of the instructor.

Differentiating Instruction

Thank You, M'am Langston Hughes

COMPREHENSION, SKILLS, AND VOCABULARY Circle the letter of the best
answer to each of the following items.

1. How does Roger meet Mrs. Jones?

    A) He tries to help her across the street.

    B) He asks her for money.

    C) He tries to steal her purse.

    D) He goes to the beauty shop where she works.

2. Mrs. Jones brings Roger back to her home because—

    A) she wants to call the police

    B) she wants to feed him

    C) she wants him to move in with her

    D) she wants him to do chores for her

3. By the end of the story, you can infer that Roger feels the following toward Mrs. Jones—

    A) gratitude

    B) anger

    C) pity

    D) jealousy

4. Which sentence uses correct standard English and means the same as the sentence below?

    "…You gonna take me to jail?"

    A) You going to took me to jail?

    B) Are you going to take me to jail?

    C) Do you wanna take me to jail?

    D) Are you going to jail?

5. Which of the following is the best example of someone who is **frail**?

    A) After working out for months, Miguel felt very strong.

    B) After his long illness, Miguel still did not feel strong.

    C) After practicing every day, Miguel could run very fast.

    D) After practicing every day, Miguel could run very far.

6. Write a character sketch of Roger. Use the organizer below to note your ideas.
   Then write your answer in a paragraph.

Introductory statement: Based on his actions, Roger seems to be ….
Supporting sentences: From what he tells Mrs. Jones, his home life seems…
Concluding statement: All in all, Roger seems to be….

Original content Copyright © by Holt, Rinehart and Winston. Additions and changes to the original content are the responsibility of the instructor.

American History Judith Ortiz Cofer

COMPREHENSION, SKILLS, AND VOCABULARY Circle the letter of the best answer to each of the following items.

1. In the selection, what is one emotion that every adult seems to share?

   A) grief over the President's death

   B) hatred of the bone-chilling cold weather

   C) suspicion about the families in the El Building

   D) dislike for anyone who moved to Paterson from somewhere else

2. Elena first decides that she likes Eugene when she notices that he—

   A) spends a lot of time reading

   B) speaks with an interesting accent

   C) lives in a two-story house with backyard

   D) is popular with the girls who jump rope

3. Why does Elena's mother warn her daughter that she is "heading for humiliation and pain"?

   A) Elena is too young to drive.

   B) Elena spends too much time reading.

   C) Elena likes a boy who is different from her.

   D) Elena wants to go to college and become a teacher.

4. What is the lesson Elena learns when Eugene's mother sends her away?

   A) Eugene was only pretending to like her.

   B) The President's death has made people react strangely.

   C) Eugene's family will be moving back to Georgia.

   D) Prejudice is ugly and hurtful.

5. Which of the following is the best example of someone who is **infatuated**?

   A) She watched for him to do something wrong.

   B) She felt her heart beat faster every time he came near her.

   C) She did her homework and never talked back to her teachers.

   D) She patted him on the back and told him he would feel better.

6. Think about people today. Would it be a problem for a girl from one ethnic group to fall in love with a boy from another group? Use the organizer below to collect your ideas. Then write a short paragraph.

| Introductory statement: Today, it would/would not be a problem… |
| Two or three supporting sentences: First….In addition…For that reason… |
| Concluding statement: Thus I believe that a girl from one ethnic group… |

Original content Copyright © by Holt, Rinehart and Winston. Additions and changes to the original content are the responsibility of the instructor.

Differentiating Instruction

Selection Test

An Interview with Dave Eggers

COMPREHENSION, SKILLS, AND VOCABULARY Circle the letter of the best answer to each of the following items.

1. How does Dave Eggers become famous?
   A) He writes a bestselling book of cartoons.
   B) He writes a bestselling book about his own life.
   C) He writes a bestselling children's book.
   D) He writes a bestselling online how-to book.

2. How does Dave Eggers try to help others?
   A) He draws cartoons about current events.
   B) He teaches mathematics at a local high school.
   C) He has a tutoring center to help young writers.
   D) He gives all of his money to the poor.

3. What is the purpose of this interview?
   A) to share Eggers' ideas about writing
   B) to share Eggers' ideas about drawing
   C) to share Eggers' ideas about the Internet
   D) to share Eggers' ideas about math

4. Who is the audience for the interview?
   A) children ages 5-10
   B) older adults ready to change careers
   C) creative writing teachers
   D) teenagers and young adults

5. What is the best example of someone who is **unconventional**?
   A) a musician who plays like everyone else
   B) a musician who plays like nobody else
   C) a musician who takes lessons every week
   D) a musician who teaches others

6. Write a paragraph about the best piece of advice Dave Eggers shares about writing. Use the graphic organizer below to collect your ideas.

Introductory statement: I think that the best piece of advice that Dave Eggers shares is ….
Two or three supporting sentences: From my own experience, I know that… Also, it makes sense that…
Concluding statement: All in all, Eggers' advice seems important because….

Original content Copyright © by Holt, Rinehart and Winston. Additions and changes to the original content are the responsibility of the instructor.

Differentiating Instruction

Collection 2
Collection Summative Test

VOCABULARY SKILLS Complete the sentences below by using the collection
vocabulary words from the list below.

permit   discreet   enabled   solace

vigilant   frail   barren

1. The farmers could not grow crops on the _____ land.

2. If she were _____, how could she lift a hundred pound weight?

3. The guards would not _____ anyone to enter the building.

4. My friends were all quiet, calm, and _____ at the museum.

5. The Secret Service is _____ about protecting our President at all times.

LITERARY AND READING SKILLS Circle the letter of the best answer.

6. Which statement is the best description of a **round character**?

   A) He never changed. He played a lot of sports and had many friends.

   B) She studied all day. She read all her books for school. Then she read more books.

   C) She talked in a high, little-girl voice. She was the best hardball pitcher in town.

   D) He was very quiet in class. He never talked to anyone.

7. The **protagonist** of a story is the character

   A) who keeps other characters from getting what they want

   B) who hardly changes during the story

   C) who interests readers the most

   D) who always tells the story

8. When you **synthesize** sources, you

   A) persuade an audience to think a certain way

   B) draw information together from different texts

   C) give a firsthand account of your experiences

   D) tell a story about something that happened to you

LANGUAGE AND WRITING SKILLS Choose the correct answer in each
answer pair.

9. The adults were upset, _____ [and/but] the children were still happy.

10. I forgot my homework, _____ [so/or] I returned home to get it.

Original content Copyright © by Holt, Rinehart and Winston. Additions and changes to the original content are the responsibility of the instructor.

Differentiating Instruction

Collection 3
Graphic Organizer

In the Family María Elena Llano

Narrator Profile Chart A **first-person narrator** is a character in the story who tells the story from his or her view, using the pronouns *I, we, my, us,* etc. As the narrator tells the story, you can ask questions to help you understand the narrator's perspective.

Use this chart to answer questions about the story's narrator.

How old is the narrator?	
What is the narrator's attitude about seeing dead family members in the mirror?	
How does the narrator feel about Clara?	
How does the narrator feel about Clara's death?	
What is the narrator most worried about?	

Original content Copyright © by Holt, Rinehart and Winston. Additions and changes to the original content are the responsibility of the instructor.

Differentiating Instruction

Lesson Plan and Teaching Strategies

The Interlopers Saki

Preteach

PREREADING SKILLS *(10 minutes)*
Build Background/Set a Purpose Explain that the setting, or where and when the story takes place, plays an important part in this particular story. To help prepare students for the setting of the story, draw a map on the board that shows two areas of adjoining land. Mark the map with symbols of trees to show forests. Where the two areas come together, use cross-hatching to show the disputed strip of land. Label one area "Ulrich Von Gradwitz" and the other section "Geor Znaeym," Pronounce the names and explain that these are the two characters in the story.

Tell students that the two characters have been fighting over the narrow strip of forestland indicated by the cross-hatch. It belongs to Ulrich, but Georg believes that it rightfully belongs to him. Therefore, Georg hunts on the land, killing animals that belong to Ulrich.

VOCABULARY SKILLS *(10 minutes)*
Preteach Vocabulary Words Review the meanings of the vocabulary in the Word Bank. Then give students these sentences to complete.

1. We expressed our [condolences] to the dead man's family.
2. [Marauders] broke into the house and stole everything of value.
3. Not being able to solve the puzzle caused her great [exasperation].
4. The causes of the accident were [disputed] in court.
5. The enemies forgave each other and reached a [reconciliation].

Remind students to watch for these words as they read the story.

LANGUAGE COACH SKILL *(10 minutes)*
Oral Fluency Display the Vocabulary Words. Read each word aloud and have students repeat the word after you. Say each word slowly and have students count the number of syllables they heard. Then say the word normally and have students indicate, by using an ordinal number, which syllable is stressed. Have students decide which words on the list:

- have three syllables (disputed; marauders)
- have more than four syllables (exasperation; reconciliation)
- are said with the greatest stress on the second syllable (disputed; marauders; condolences)
- are said with the greatest stress on the next to last syllable (marauders; disputed; reconciliation)

Have students work together to explore other similarities in the pronunciation of the Vocabulary Words.

RESOURCES
In *The Holt Reader:* "The Interlopers" for students who need more scaffolding in a workbook format

In this book: *Vocabulary Skill Builder,* p. 56; "The Interlopers" Selection Test, p. 57

Consult *Holt Audio Library* for recordings of most selections

TEACHER TIP
Point out to students that the title of the story gives readers a clue about the ending. Ask students to look up *interloper* (someone who interferes in other people's lives) in a dictionary and to keep the meaning in mind as they read.

WORD BANK
disputed
marauders
exasperation
condolences
reconciliation

ACADEMIC VOCABULARY
Preteaching Academic Vocabulary
(5 minutes)
Write these terms and their meanings on a chalkboard or transparency. Review them with the students before previewing the selection.

First-person narrator. A character in the story who talks to us, using the pronoun I

Original content Copyright © by Holt, Rinehart and Winston. Additions and changes to the original content are the responsibility of the instructor.

Differentiating Instruction

LITERARY FOCUS *(20 minutes)*

Omniscient Narrator Explain that an omniscient narrator knows everything about the characters and their problems. This all-knowing narrator can tell about the characters' past, present, and future. This kind of narrator can even tell what the characters are thinking or what is happening in other places. This narrator is not a character in the story. Instead, he or she stands above the action, like a god.

Point out that the omniscient narrator is very familiar to all of us. We have heard this narrator, telling us fairy tales since we were very young. Begin to tell the story of "Cinderella," or another universal tale. Ask students for a show of hands to determine how many have heard this story or a variation of it from their native culture. Then ask how the story would be different if Cinderella was the narrator; if one of the stepsisters was the narrator; if the Prince was the narrator. Guide students to understand that any one of these characters would be more limited in their knowledge than an omniscient narrator, and would only know what was going on from his or her point of view. That character would only know about his or her own thoughts and feelings.

Remind students that, because an omniscient narrator knows what is in the characters' future, he or she is usually one step ahead of the reader. Sometimes, an omniscient narrator will save a key piece of information until the very end of the story. Ask students to think about whether or not Saki gives readers a surprise ending in "The Interlopers."

Help students use academic vocabulary and concepts. As a follow up to the preceding discussion of Cinderella stories, have a volunteer retell a Cinderella story from his or her culture from the omniscient point of view. Have another volunteer choose one character from the story and retell it from his or her point of view. Guide students to see how different points of view create differences in how the story unfolds.

READING FOCUS *(30 minutes)*

Drawing Conclusions Explain that when you draw conclusions, you use information that is presented to you together with your own knowledge to figure something out. Provide this example by saying: *Imagine that there is snow covering the ground. You see one set of footprints leading up to a house and two sets of footprints going away from the house.* Ask: *What do the footprints tell you?* (Someone came to call for a person in the house, and they both left the house together.) Encourage students to talk about how they used the footprints to figure this out. Ask: *What other information did you use?*

Have students work in pairs to complete a chart like the one at the right. After reading each chunk of the selection, have the partners discuss what conclusions they were able to draw as they read. Have them write their conclusions on the right, and the evidence from the text that allowed them to draw that conclusion on the left.

Third-person-limited narrator: He or she plays no part in the story but just tells it, focusing on just one character.

READING SKILL
Especially for RGP
(5 minutes or less)
To help readers gain proficiency in evaluating a surprise ending, ask: *Why is the last word in the story such a shock—especially after the conversation that took place between the two men?* Have students report on how they imagined the story would end. Then ask: *What do you think will happen next to the two men?*

LANGUAGE SKILL
Especially for LDN
(5 minutes or less)
For students who learn by listening, read aloud excerpts from selections in the Student Edition. Have students listen carefully to determine if the story is being told by a first-person narrator, e.g. "Teaching Chess, and Life;" a third-person limited narrator e.g. "The Most Dangerous Game;" or an omniscient narrator, e.g. "The Interlopers."

READING FOCUS
Conclusions Chart

Conclusion	Evidence

Original content Copyright © by Holt, Rinehart and Winston. Additions and changes to the original content are the responsibility of the instructor.

Differentiating Instruction

Direct Teach

(60 minutes)

Chunk the Text Help students pace their reading by dividing the selection into "chunks" or parts. After the students have read each part, stop to help them draw conclusions based on the evidence presented.

Part 1: ends p. 235, col. 2: "...the quarter from whence it came."

Part 2: ends p. 236, col 2: "...splintered branches and broken twigs."

Part 3: ends p. 238, col 1: "...first on the scene."

Part 4: ends p. 239, col 2: "...for an answering halloo."

Part 5: ends p. 240, col 2: "'*Wolves.*'"

Oral Fluency Because the descriptive portions of "The Interlopers" contains some long and challenging sentences, help students "chunk" the sentences, too. By reading in meaningful phrases (rather than word by word) students will gain understanding and catch many more of the subtleties of the text. Model reading in meaningful phrases or chunks, for example:

In a forest of mixed growth / somewhere on the eastern spurs of the Carpathians, / a man stood one winter night/ watching and listening, / as though he waited for some beast of the woods / to come within the range of his vision / and, / later, / of his rifle.(p. 234)

Check for Understanding

WRITING FOCUS *(15 minutes)*

Omniscient Narrator Remind students that an **omniscient narrator** knows the thoughts and innermost feelings of every character in the story. Use an excerpt from the story to explore the kinds of information that can only be revealed by an omniscient narrator. Read this paragraph from the story aloud. Then have students identify the information that a narrator who was only an observer could not know.

Relief at being alive and exasperation at his captive plight brought a strange medley of pious thank offerings and sharp curses to Ulrich's lips. Georg, who was nearly blinded with the blood which trickled across his eyes, stopped his struggling for a moment to listen, and then gave a short, snarling laugh.(p. 236)

Help students recognize that a narrator who was only an observer could not know the mix of emotions that caused Ulrich to say the things he did.

Think As A Reader/Writer Ask: *What would the story be like if it were told from the point of view of one of the characters?* Explore with students how that change in narrator would affect the surprise ending. Then ask students to rewrite the paragraph quoted above as though Ulrich himself were telling the story.

LANGUAGE SKILL
Especially for ELL
(15 minutes)
Hearing the story read aloud will help students who are having difficulty with the language. As you read aloud each chunk of the story, help English-language learners to summarize each part. Encourage the students to note how the emotions of the two main characters change during the course of the story and how the author builds suspense at the climax.

READING/WRITING
Especially for WGP
(5 minutes)
Remind writers who are gaining proficiency that, if the story is now to be told by a first-person narrator that the personal pronoun "I" will be used to tell the story. Work with these student writers to help them distinguish Ulrich from Georg by making a T-chart like the one below and recording the thoughts, feelings, and actions of the character in each column.

Ulrich	Georg

Especially for RGP
(5 minutes or less)
Have students return to the story to find other places where the omniscient narrator tells the reader what Ulrich and Georg are thinking. Ask: *How would the story be different if you did not know these details?*

Original content Copyright © by Holt, Rinehart and Winston. Additions and changes to the original content are the responsibility of the instructor.

Differentiating Instruction

Collection 3
Graphic Organizer

Initiation Sylvia Plath

"Identifying Types of Characterization Techniques" Chart Authors use both **direct characterization** and **indirect characterization** to create their characters. In direct characterization, the writer tells us directly what the character is like. In indirect characterization, you watch what the character says or does to form an opinion about the character.

Read the passages below and then identify the type of characterization the author is using by writing *direct* or *indirect* in the second column.

Character	Passage	Type of Characterization
Louise Fullerton	"It was Louise Fullerton behind her, Louise who had always before been very nice, very polite, friendlier than the rest, even long ago, before the invitation had come."	
Louise Fullerton	"I know it doesn't sound like much, but well, it's things like that which set someone apart. I mean, you know that no girl at Lansing would be seen dead wearing knee socks, no matter how cold it gets, and it's kiddish and kind of green to carry a bookbag," said Louise.	
Bev	"Bev was suddenly there in the doorway. 'Wipe that smile off your face,' she commanded."	
Tracy	"Generally, the girls who were outsiders now, as Millicent had been, scoffed at the initiation antics as childish and absurd to hide their secret envy. But Tracy was understanding, as ever."	
Tracy	"'I know, but even so,' Tracy had said quietly, 'you'll change, whether you think you will or not. Nothing ever stays the same.'"	

From "Initiation" from *Johnny Panic and the Bible of Dreams* by Sylvia Plath. Copyright © 1952, 1953, 1954, 1955, 1956, 1957, 1960, 1961, 1962, 1963 by Sylvia Plath. Copyright © 1977, 1979 by Ted Hughes. Reproduced by permission of **HarperCollins Publishers, Inc.**

Collection 3
Graphic Organizer

Marigolds Eugenia W. Collier

Analyzing Perspectives Chart When characters have different ideas about a topic, person, or event, they are displaying different viewpoints or **perspectives.** Sometimes one character can show different perspectives on the same topic, especially if they are looking at it from different times in their lives.

The narrator in the story shows different perspectives about events and people. Sometimes she writes from the perspective of a teenager. Sometimes her perspective is that of an adult, seeing the same event through the maturity of an adult. For each passage below, indicate which perspective the narrator is using – by writing teenager or adult in the second column.

Passage	Perspective
"'Tell you what,' said Joey finally, his eyes sparkling. 'Let's us go over to Miss Lottie's.' The idea caught on at once, for annoying Miss Lottie was always fun."	
"I cursed and spat on the ground – my favorite gesture of phony bravado. 'Ya'll children get the stones, I'll show you how to use 'em.'"	
"I said before that we children were not consciously aware of how thick were the bars of our cage. I wonder now, though, whether we were not more aware of it than I thought. Perhaps we had some dim notion of what we were, and how little chance we had of being anything else."	
"The witch was no longer a witch but only a broken old woman who had dared to create beauty in the midst of ugliness and sterility. She had been born in squalor and lived in it all her life."	

Slightly adapted from "Marigolds" by Eugenia W. Collier from *Negro Digest,* November 1969.
Copyright © 1969 by **Eugenia W. Collier.** Reproduced by permission of the author.

Original content Copyright © by Holt, Rinehart and Winston. Additions and changes to the original content are the responsibility of the instructor.

Differentiating Instruction

Collection 3
Graphic Organizer

The Wife's Story Ursula K. LeGuin

Elements of Voice Chart A narrator's **voice** is defined by his or her speaking style, word choice, and **tone**, or attitude. Writers use voice to reveal a narrator's personality.

Read the following passage from the story. Then using the words listed, describe the elements of the narrator's voice. Then write one sentence that describes the narrator's personality.

Simple	Informal	Short	Surprised	Sad	Honest	Repetitive
He was a good husband, a good father. I don't understand it. I don't believe in it. I don't believe that I happened. I saw it happen but it isn't true. It can't be. He was always gentle. If you'd seen him playing with the children, anybody who saw him with the children would have known that there wasn't any bad in him, not one mean bone.							

Word Choice	Sentence Structure	Tone	Style

Narrator's Personality:

From "The Wife's Story" from *The Compass Rose: Short Stories* by Ursula K. LeGuin. Copyright © 1982 by Ursula K. LeGuin. Reproduced by permission of **Virginia Kidd Literary Agency.**

Original content Copyright © by Holt, Rinehart and Winston. Additions and changes to the original content are the responsibility of the instructor.

Collection 3
Graphic Organizer

Letter to John Allan / Alone Edgar Allan Poe

Biographical Analysis Chart Writers are shaped by the events of their lives. When you make connections between an author's life and works, you are looking at literature from a **biographical approach.**

Complete this chart to increase your understanding and appreciation of "Letter to John Allan" and "Alone."

When and where is Poe's letter written? **When and where is his poem written?**
What background from Poe's life help you understand the letter better?
What details in "Alone" reflect Poe's background?
What similar attitudes are expressed in both the letter and the poem?

Original content Copyright © by Holt, Rinehart and Winston. Additions and changes to the original content are the responsibility of the instructor.

Differentiating Instruction

The Cask of Amontillado Edgar Allan Poe

Preteach

PREREADING SKILLS *(10 minutes)*
Build Background/Set a Purpose Discuss Build Background on page 286 with students, and invite them to preview the selection by examining the illustration of Carnival in Venice on page 287, and the photo of the Christian catacombs on page 291. Encourage students to describe the feeling that the painting evokes about carnival season, as well as their ideas about the dual purpose of the catacombs—as a place to bury the dead and a place to store fine wine. Ask: *How might these two purposes overlap in Poe's story—given that the story is set during a season of wild celebration?*

Point out to students that the author of the story, Edgar Allan Poe, was a major American writer during the 1800s. Review the timeline of his life on pages 278 and 279 with students, embellishing each event with details from Meet the Writer (e.g. Poe was always in debt, drank heavily, suffered many personal disappointments, and became both famous and infamous for his tales of horror). Ask students to keep this in mind as they read "The Cask of Amontillado."

VOCABULARY SKILLS *(10 minutes)*
Preteach Vocabulary Words Review the meanings of the vocabulary in the Word Bank. Then give students these sentences to complete.

1. We [implore] you not to do anything you will regret.
2. She didn't want to [impose] upon him by asking him to do a favor.
3. It isn't fair when people who do bad things do so with [impunity].
4. The man was [obstinate] and refused to listen to reason.
5. The injured parties sought [retribution] for the harm done to them.

Remind students to watch for these words as they read the story.

LANGUAGE COACH SKILL *(10 minutes)*
Denotations/Connotations Explain that a word's **denotation** is the definition given for it in a dictionary and a word's **connotations** are the feelings associated with the word. Point out that authors often think about the connotations of the words they use to make a more precise picture in the reader's mind. Ask students to think of the words *sheepishly* and *shyly*. Ask: Which one creates a clearer image in your mind?

Display these pairs of words and read them aloud. Explain that the words in each pair have similar meanings. Ask which one creates a clearer image in the listener's mind.

RESOURCES
In *The Holt Reader:* "The Cask of Amontillado" for students who need more scaffolding in a workbook format

In this book: *Vocabulary Skill Builder,* p. 56; "The Cask of Amontillado" Selection Test, p. 58

Consult Holt *Audio Library* for recordings of most selections

TEACHER TIP
Show additional pictures of ancient catacombs from a resource book in your school library. Ask students to describe how they would feel in such a place.

WORD BANK
impunity
retribution
impose
implore
obstinate

ACADEMIC VOCABULARY
Preteaching Academic Vocabulary
(5 minutes)
Write these terms and their meanings on a chalkboard or transparency. Review them with the students before previewing the selection.

Distinct: Unique; obviously different.
Impression: Overall effect.

Original content Copyright © by Holt, Rinehart and Winston. Additions and changes to the original content are the responsibility of the instructor.

Differentiating Instruction

- *lingered   stayed*
- *belief   conviction*
- *scrawny   thin*

Read aloud the word pairs again. This time ask students to label each word in the pair as having a positive, negative, or neutral connotation.

LITERARY FOCUS *(20 minutes)*

Unreliable Narrator Explain that the narrator is the reader's only source of information about characters and events in a story. Readers usually assume that what the narrator tells them is true, but this is not always the case. Sometimes, the narrator does not know the whole truth. Some- times, the narrator deliberately tries to fool or trick the reader. When this happens, we have an **unreliable narrator**. Ask: *What are some reasons a narrator might have for not being truthful in telling a story?*

Explain that there are ways that a reader can decide if the narrator is trustworthy. Tell students that the narrator's words and actions can help the reader judge his or her reliability. Point out that when the narrator's words and actions seem phony, or unreasonable, or just plain crazy, readers can conclude that the narrator is unreliable.

Help students use academic vocabulary and concepts in the context of this story. For example, have students pause at the end of each chunk of text to record their *impressions* of the narrator. At the end of the story, brainstorm elements of the story that make it distinct from other stories the students have read. Use the words *impression* and *distinct* to talk about the story, its narrator, and its author. Poll students to determine how many would like to read more by Edgar Allan Poe. Conclude from the survey if Poe has left a positive or negative *impression* on the class.

READING FOCUS *(30 minutes)*

Drawing Conclusions Explain that when you read, you need to act like a detective. You need to look for clues and gather evidence in order to make judgments or **draw conclusions** about the story.

Tell students that they will need to conclude whether or not the narrator in this story is reliable. Remind them that what the narrator says and does can be clues to help them determine his reliability. Ask students to think about the following: *Does the narrator's way of speaking, his choice of words, and his attitude seem sincere?*

Explain that one good way to determine this is to compare the narrator to another character in the story. Have students work in pairs to complete a Venn diagram like the one on the right. Ask them to compare and contrast the words and actions of the narrator to those of his enemy, Fortunato. Encourage students to use the similarities and differences to help them determine the reliability of the narrator. Finally, divide the class into two teams to debate whether this narrator can be trusted or not.

Ask students to use their Venn diagrams as the springboard for debate.

LANGUAGE SKILL
Especially for ELL
(5 minutes or less)
Explain that the spelling pattern *vowel-consonant-e* is usually the signal that the vowel preceding the consonant has a long sound. The Vocabulary Word *impose* is an example. The *o* in *impose* has the long sound. The word *obstinate* is an exception. The final syllable, although spelled *vowel-consonant-e*, is an unaccented syllable, so the vowel sound is /uh/ not /oh/.

READING SKILL
Especially for RGP
(5 minutes or less)
Remind students that in a first-person narrative, a character in the story is telling the story. When the pronoun *I* appears in the narration, it refers to the narrator, Montresor. Within the first-person narration, there is also dialogue, the words that the two characters say to each other. Dialogue is set within quotation marks. In dialogue, the pronoun *I* refers to the character who is speaking— the narrator or Fortuato.

READING FOCUS
Venn Diagram

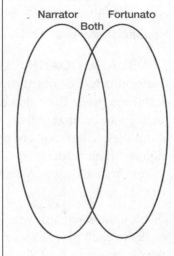

Narrator   Fortunato
Both

Original content Copyright © by Holt, Rinehart and Winston. Additions and changes to the original content are the responsibility of the instructor.

Differentiating Instruction

Direct Teach

(60 minutes)

Chunk the Text Help students pace their reading by dividing the selection into "chunks" or parts. After the students have read each part, stop to help them draw conclusions based on the evidence presented.

Part 1: ends p. 286, col. 1: "…the thought of his immolation."

Part 2: ends p. 288, col 2: "…to hurry me to my *palazzo*."

Part 3: ends p. 289, col 2: "'Good!' he said."

Part 4: ends p. 291, col 1: "…I stepped back from the recess."

Part 5: ends p. 292, col 2: "*In pace requiescat.*"

Check for Understanding

WRITING FOCUS *(15 minutes)*

Powerful Words and Images To give students further practice in analyzing the narrator of the story, read aloud these examples of Poe's use of words and images to reveal the personality of his narrator. After reading each one, ask: *What does this reveal about the narrator?*

- "I must not only punish, but punish with impunity. A wrong is unredressed when retribution overtakes its redresser." *(p. 286, col. 1: These statements reveal how calculating the narrator is. He wants to punish Fortunato for the wrongs he had done to him, but he wants to do so without being caught and punished himself.)*

- "Once more let me *implore* you to return. No? Then I must positively leave you. But I must first render you all the little attentions in my power." *(p. 291, col. 1: At this point, the narrator has already chained Fortunato to the wall, so the idea of his returning is completely absurd. As the reader is soon to learn, "all the little attentions in my power" include walling him up.)*

- "The noise lasted for several minutes, during which, that I might hearken to it with more satisfaction, I ceased my labors and sat down upon the bones." *(p, 292, col. 1: The idea that the narrator enjoys listening to his victim struggling and sits down among the bones of his ancestors to enjoy it better makes readers question his sanity.)*

- "There came forth in return only a jingling of the bells. My heart grew sick—on account of the dampness of the catacombs." *(p. 292, col. 2: This statement reveals the monstrous nature of the narrator. He has just sealed a human being into a living tomb, and he complains that the dampness of the place makes him sick at heart.)*

Think as a Reader/Writer Ask: Given what you know about Montresor, how do you think he will behave the first time someone mentions to him that Fortunato has mysteriously disappeared? Discuss Montresor's likely reaction. Then have students write a brief dialogue between Montresor and the person who tells him about Fortunato's disappearance.

READING SKILL

Especially for LDN

Because the story language is especially difficult, students might benefit from following along in their books as they listen to an audio recording. Pause after each chunk and help students summarize what happened in that part of the story.

ORAL LANGUAGE SKILLS

Especially for RGP

Invite students to express their opinions about the narrator and his actions. Ask: *Is he insane, or is he a cold-blooded murderer consumed by revenge?* Remind students to give details from the story to support their opinions.

READING/WRITING

Especially for WGP

(5 minutes or less)

Remind students that there are two ways to write dialogue:

- A direct quotation gives a speaker's exact words and must be placed within quotation marks: "I am beside myself with grief that the respected and admired Fortunato is missing?" said Montresor.
- An indirect quotation is not the exact words of a speaker and is not placed within quotation marks. It is often introduced by the word *that*: Montresor said **that** he was beside himself with grief . . .

Original content Copyright © by Holt, Rinehart and Winston. Additions and changes to the original content are the responsibility of the instructor.

Differentiating Instruction

Lesson Plan and Teaching Strategies

Four Readings About Poe's Death

Preteach

PREREADING SKILLS *(10 minutes)*

Build Background/Set a Purpose Remind students that *informational sources* are nonfiction materials which, instead of telling a story that someone invented, explain or give information about something that really existed or happened. Explain that all informational materials are either **primary sources** or **secondary sources**. To make the distinction, point out the Mississippi River on a classroom map. Point to the source of the river, Lake Itasca in northwest Minnesota. Explain that this is where the river begins. Like the source of a river, a *primary* source is where the information begins. It is a firsthand account of events. As you follow the flow of the Mississippi, point out its tributaries (the Ohio, Missouri, Arkansas, and Tennessee Rivers). Explain that, like a tributary, a *secondary* source is an extension of the primary source. It provides an explanation, an analysis, or a restatement of the primary source.

Tell students that they will be reading varying accounts of the death of Edgar Allan Poe. Explain that each account is a secondary source that interprets information found in the only primary source that exists about the death of Poe: the account of the doctor who attended him in his final days. This account is referred to in "Poe's Final Days," an excerpt from a biography of Edgar Allan Poe.

VOCABULARY SKILLS *(10 minutes)*

Preteach Vocabulary Words Review the meanings of the vocabulary in the Word Bank. Then give students these sentences to complete.

1. A [chronic] cough can be a symptom of a serious problem.

2. Wearing bright red would make you [conspicuous] at a funeral.

3. Banks are located in large [imposing] buildings to inspire trust.

4. Flu sufferers often remain asleep and [insensible] for hours.

5. The flu virus is easily [transmitted] from one person to another.

Remind students to watch for these words as they read the story.

LANGUAGE COACH SKILL *(10 minutes)*

Antonyms Remind students that **antonyms** are words that have the opposite meanings. *Light* and *dark* are antonyms. So are *ill* and *healthy*. Display the Vocabulary Words and read each word aloud. Then one at a time, say the following words and explain their meanings. Have students decide which Vocabulary Word is an antonym for each one:

- *alert*: watchful, prepared, ready to act (antonym: *insensible*)

- *humble*: modest or lowly (antonym: *imposing*)

RESOURCES

In *The Holt Reader:* Four Readings About Poe's Death for students who need more scaffolding in a workbook format

In this book: *Vocabulary Skill Builder,* p. 56; Four Readings About Poe's Death Selection Test, p. 59

Consult *Holt Audio Library* for recordings of most selections

TEACHER TIP

Before students read the four theories about Poe's death, review the biographical material on pages 278-279 in the Student Edition.

WORD BANK

insensible
imposing
conspicuous
chronic
transmitted

ACADEMIC VOCABULARY

Preteaching Academic Vocabulary

(5 minutes)

Write these terms and their meanings on a chalkboard or transparency. Review them with the students before previewing the selection.

Portray: Describe with words or other means; show

Insight: Clear understanding

Original content Copyright © by Holt, Rinehart and Winston. Additions and changes to the original content are the responsibility of the instructor.

Differentiating Instruction

- *occasional*: occurring from time to time   (antonym: *chronic*)
- *isolated*: kept out of contact   (antonym: *transmitted*)
- *ordinary*: not likely to attract attention   (antonym: *conspicuous*)

Have students work together to think of other antonym pairs.

INFORMATIONAL TEXT FOCUS *(30 minutes)*

Synthesizing Sources Help students understand what it means to synthesize sources by modeling with this Think Aloud: *You want to understand what the Vietnam Memorial in Washington, D.C. means to people, so you ask a lot of people what their reaction is to it. You ask visitors, Vietnam veterans, and the artist who created it. Then you take all the responses into consideration—**synthesize** them—and give an overall impression, or big picture, of what the memorial means.*

Explain to students that they will be synthesizing information when they read four different texts on the same topic: the death of Edgar Allan Poe. Review with students these guidelines, which they should follow as they read each text and prepare to synthesize the information.

1. **Find the main idea.** Ask yourself: *What does this writer think was the cause of Poe's death?* Be able to state what the author thinks in your own words.

2. **Look for supporting evidence.** Ask yourself: *Why does this writer think this was the cause of Poe's death? What supports this opinion?* Consider whether or not the evidence is convincing.

3. **Compare and contrast.** Make connections among the four texts you will be reading. Ask yourself: *In what ways are all four sources in agreement? In what ways to they differ?*

4. **Synthesize.** Pull everything you read together to give an overall impression of the mystery and disagreement about the cause of Poe's death.

Have students work in pairs to complete a chart like the one at the right. After reading each selection, have partners discuss the main idea of the selection and the evidence the writer uses to support the idea. Have them write the main idea of each selection in the left column and the evidence offered in support of the idea in the right column.

When students have completed their reading, have them scan the four reading selections again to ensure that they have captured all the supporting evidence for each main idea. Have students take turns summarizing each article with his or her partner, and try to synthesize the information from all four sources.

Finally, lead a class discussion of which sources seem most credible and why. Encourage students to use the academic vocabulary and concepts in the whole class discussion. Have volunteers articulate their overall impressions of circumstances surrounding Poe's death.

READING SKILL
Especially for RGP
(5 minutes or less)
Point out the different types of informational materials represented by these readings. The first is an excerpt from a biography. Explain what a biography is and point out that the excerpt is just a few pages from a whole book about the life of Poe. Make sure that students understand what a "Letter to the Editor" is and why people write them. Point out that the first letter (p. 304) is in response to the newspaper article (pp. 302-303), and the second letter (p. 305) is in response to the first letter.

READING FOCUS
Main Idea Chart

Main Idea	Supporting Evidence

Original content Copyright © by Holt, Rinehart and Winston. Additions and changes to the original content are the responsibility of the instructor.

Direct Teach

(60 minutes)

Chunk the Text Help students pace their reading by dividing the two longer selections into "chunks" or parts. The newspaper article and the two letters to the editor can each be read as a chunk. After the students have read each part, stop to help them summarize the text and consider how it contributes to the main idea of the piece.

"Poe's Final Days"

Part 1: ends p. 299, col. 2: "'an object of unusual regard.'"

Part 2: ends p. 301, col 1: "'…and expired!'"

Part 3: ends p. 301, col 2: "…against the wind and rain."

Part 4: "Poe's Death Rewritten as Case of Rabies …"

Part 5: "If Only Poe Had Succeeded When He Said Nevermore to Drink"

Part 6: "Rabies Death Theory"

Check for Understanding

WRITING FOCUS *(20 minutes)*

Synthesize Sources To assist students with the task of synthesizing information and writing their own statement about which account of Poe's death they find most convincing, organize students into groups of three. Have each group member choose a different explanation of how Poe died: alcoholism, encephalitis, or rabies. Have them find evidence to support their position in the four readings. Point out that the evidence may appear in more than one of the selections. Encourage students to use their main idea/supporting evidence chart to help them organize their evidence and their case for how Poe died.

After students have gathered their evidence, have the groups debate their positions and try to reach consensus about Poe's death.

Think As A Reader/Writer Ask: *Which explanation of Poe's death do you think is right?* Explore with students the three possible causes that have been offered up in the four readings. Review the evidence in support of each. Then have students write a brief paragraph stating their opinion and supporting it with evidence from one or more of the selections.

LANGUAGE SKILL
Especially for ELL

(15 minutes)

Graphic organizers are a great way to summarize information for English language learners. Create a timeline of Poe's Final Days in order to capture the details between September 27th and October 7th. Have students work in blue pen and allow enough space so that students can annotate the timeline with notes from the other articles in different color ink: black, green, red. Students can then compare and contrast information in all four selections in order to synthesize and draw conclusions about how they think Poe really died.

READING/WRITING SKILL
Especially for WGP

To help students get started, provide a thesis statement, such as: *Having read several accounts of the death of Edgar Allan Poe, I have come to the conclusion that Poe's death was caused by* . . . Review the point-by-point method of comparing and contrasting information from more than one source, and work with students to use this method to build a solid argument for their position on the cause of Poe's death.

Original content Copyright © by Holt, Rinehart and Winston. Additions and changes to the original content are the responsibility of the instructor.

Differentiating Instruction

Targeted Strategies for Learners with Diverse Needs

READING SKILLS

Synthesizing Sources *(15 minutes)* Explain that students synthesize when they put together several different pieces of information. The point of synthesizing information is to get a better understanding of a subject. Demonstrate the process of synthesis by asking three volunteers to stand up in front of the class and briefly tell what they learned from the articles about Poe. Students who are listening should fill in an organizer like the one below:

Student 1's remarks	Student 2's remarks:	Student 3's remarks:
Synthesis:		

Work together as a class to write one or two sentences that synthesize all three students' remarks. Write the sentences on the board. Challenge students to identify the source of the information in the sentences.

LITERARY SKILLS

Omniscient Narrator *(15 minutes)* Help students understand the concept of a narrator that stands outside the action. Explain that this kind of narrator is like a sportscaster announcing a game. However, an omniscient narrator would be able to do things a real-life sportscaster couldn't do. For example:

- read the minds of all the players
- know everything about their past
- know everything about their future

Have students work in groups to create a short skit showing what it might be like if an omniscient sportscaster were announcing a game.

Unreliable Narrator *(15 minutes)* Have students recall how they analyzed characters by looking at dialogue. Explain to students that they can analyze a narrator, just like any other character in a story. Have them use these questions to help them test the narrator's reliability.

- Is the narrator part of the action? If so, how might the narrator be biased against other characters?
- Does the narrator seem to be truthful and have good judgment? If not, why?

Have students work with a partner to answer these questions about the narrator of "The Cask of Amontillado", citing specific examples from the story.

Readings in Collection 3 Minimum Course of Study

- "The Interlopers", p. 232
- "The Cask of Amontillado", p. 285
- "Four Readings About Poe's Death", p. 297

RESOURCES

In *The Holt Reader,* all three selections help students who need more scaffolding in a workbook format.
Consult *Holt Audio Library* for recordings of most selections.

TEACHING TIP

Students with diverse needs may have difficulty separating the information the narrator offers from the quality of the narration. Work with students one-on-one to show them what they can believe and what they can question about the narrator in "The Cask of Amontillado".

ALTERNATIVE ASSESSMENT *(5 minutes)*
Have students provide answers for these items.

You may not want to trust an [omniscient/unreliable] narrator.

Taking information from more than one place and putting it together is an example of [synthesis].

Original content Copyright © by Holt, Rinehart and Winston. Additions and changes to the original content are the responsibility of the instructor.

Differentiating Instruction

Chapter 3
Academic and Selection Vocabulary

The Interlopers   The Cask of Amontillado
Four Readings About Poe's Death

A. Choose the word that best fits into each category.

exasperation	reconciliation	retribution	obstinate	conspicuous

1. Bold appearance: striking, obvious, noticeable, _____

2. Ending arguments: compromise, settle, resolution, _____

3. Feeling impatient: frustration, annoyance, anger, _____

4. Seeking punishment for a wrong: justice, revenge, payback, _____

5. Being stubborn: determined, unmoved, inflexible, _____

B. Read the phrase beside each vocabulary word. Write E for example or N for non-example.

_____ 1, Chronic: a permanent condition, like asthma

_____ 2. Imposing: a small stuffed animal

_____ 3. Transmitted: a message that never arrives

_____ 4. Condolences: flowers sent to a funeral

_____ 5. Disputed: a case being argued in court

C. Use the academic vocabulary words to complete the following paragraph about "The Cask of Amontillado," by Edgar Allan Poe.

portrays   impression   insight   distinct

The two main characters in "The Cask of Amontillado" are very (1) _____

from one another. Fortunato is in a costume and celebrating while the narrator is secretly

plotting revenge. Poe (2) _____ Fortunato as a proud man. The narrator

tries to give the (3) _____ that he cares about Fortunato. But the narrator

uses Fortunato's pride to lead him into a trap. Poe give some hints about what's going happen,

but the reader only gets (4) _____ into the plan when the narrator begins

to build the wall.

Original content Copyright © by Holt, Rinehart and Winston. Additions and changes to the original content are the responsibility of the instructor.

Differentiating Instruction

Collection 3
Selection Test

The Interlopers Saki

COMPREHENSION, SKILLS, AND VOCABULARY Circle the letter of the best answer to each of the following items.

1. Why are the two characters in the story sworn enemies?

   A) They used to fight as boys.

   B) Their grandfathers had fought in opposing armies.

   C) They each believe they are the rightful owners of the same forest land.

   D) Georg's family has cut trees for generations on Ulrich's family's land.

2. Who are the interlopers in the story?

   A) the wolves

   B) Ulrich's men

   C) Georg's ancestors

   D) Ulrich von Gradwitz and Georg Znaeyn

3. Which sentence from the story tells something that only an omniscient narrator could reveal?

   A) The two raised their voices in a prolonged hunting call.

   B) The two enemies stood glaring at one another for a long silent moment.

   C) And each prayed a private prayer that his men would be the first to arrive.

   D) All around them lay a thick strewn wreckage of splintered branched and broken twigs.

4. What makes the surprise ending so effective?

   A) Wolves are an endangered species.

   B) The story had led the reader to hope for a happy ending.

   C) The reader has no idea what will happen to Ulrich and Georg.

   D) A forest setting is not a place where you would expect to encounter wolves.

5. Which is the first hint that Ulrich and Georg might reach some kind of **reconciliation**?

   A) Ulrich offers Georg some wine.

   B) Ulrich addresses Georg as "Forest thief."

   C) Ulrich suggests that they try shouting for help together.

   D) Georg says he will send condolences to Ulrich's family when he is found dead.

6. In the story, two men are in conflict with each other and with nature. Think of a modern situation in which a conflict with nature might bring people who are strangers—or even enemies—together. Use the graphic organizer below to collect your ideas. Then write a short paragraph.

Introductory statement: Today, weather and natural disasters bring people together.
Two or three supporting sentences: For example….Also…In addition…
Concluding statement: As I have shown…

Original content Copyright © by Holt, Rinehart and Winston. Additions and changes to the original content are the responsibility of the instructor.

Differentiating Instruction

Collection 3
Student Edition pages 285–295
Selection Test

The Cask of Amontillado Edgar Allan Poe

**COMPREHENSION, SKILLS, AND VOCABULARY Circle the letter of the best
answer to each of the following items.**

1. The narrator promises revenge against Fortunato because—

   A) Fortunato insulted him

   B) Fortunato had finer *palazzo* and a happier life

   C) Fortunato knew more about old wines

   D) Fortunato doubted his claim to be one of the Masons

2. What weak point does the narrator use to get Fortunato down into the catacombs?

   A) Fortunato's tendency to drink too much

   B) Fortunato's pride in his knowledge of old wines

   C) Fortunato's jealousy of their friend Luchesi

   D) Fortunato's poor health and dislike of damp places

3. Who is narrator in this story?

   A) Luchesi

   B) Fortunato

   C) Montresor

   D) Edgar Allan Poe

4. Which sentence from the story raises the most doubt about the narrator's **reliability**?

   A) He accosted me with excessive warmth, for he had been drinking too much.

   B) "You are rich, respected, admitted, beloved; you are happy, as I once was."

   C) Throwing the links about his waist, it was but the work of a few seconds to secure it.

   D) The noise lasted for several minutes, during which, that I might hearken to it with more
   satisfaction, I ceased my labors and sat down among the bones.

5. What detail tells readers that the narrator punished his enemy with **impunity**?

   A) All the servants were out when the narrator arrived with Fortunato.

   B) The narrator wore a mask when he hurried to his *palazzo* with Fortunato.

   C) The bones he piled against the wall he built remained undisturbed for fifty years.

   D) The narrator was satisfied that the solid walls of the catacombs would muffle all sound.

6. How would you persuade Montresor that his revenge on Fortunato was extreme and wrong?
   Use the organizer below to collect your ideas. Then write a short paragraph.

Introductory statement: What you did was …
Two or three supporting sentences: First…In addition…Besides…
Concluding statement: For these reasons, I believe that you…

Original content Copyright © by Holt, Rinehart and Winston. Additions and changes to the original content are the responsibility of the instructor.

Collection 3
Selection Test

Four Readings About Poe's Death

COMPREHENSION, SKILLS, AND VOCABULARY Circle the letter of the best answer to each of the following items.

1. In what city did Edgar Allan Poe die?

    A) Boston

    B) Baltimore

    C) Richmond

    D) Philadelphia

2. Which three things are suggested as causes of death in these four selections?

    A) heart disease, rabies, alcoholism

    B) brain congestion, alcoholism, rabies

    C) alcoholism, brain congestion, suicide

    D) tuberculosis, alcoholism, brain congestion

3. Elmira Shelton recalled that Poe had a fever when he left Richmond. Which theory does this support?

    A) Poe died as a result of rabies.

    B) Poe died from delirium tremens.

    C) Poe died from drinking too much alcohol.

    D) Poe died from an inflammation of the brain.

4. Why does Dr. R. Michael Benitez believe that Poe died from rabies?

    A) Poe was never known to drink alcohol in any form.

    B) His cat Caterina had died of rabies three months earlier.

    C) At the time of Poe's death, doctors did not know how rabies was transmitted.

    D) According to eyewitnesses, Poe had all the symptoms of a classic case of rabies.

5. "There was a <u>conspicuous</u> lack in this report of things like CT scans." **Conspicuous** means

    A) sensible

    B) noticeable

    C) criminal

    D) unprofessional

6. Do you think we will ever know for sure the cause of Poe's death? Use the graphic organizer to collect your ideas. Then write a paragraph to answer the question.

Introductory statement: We will eventually/will never know for sure how Poe died, because…
Two or three reasons: At that time, doctors…while doctors…Also, the evidence…
Concluding statement: For these reasons, I believe that…

Original content Copyright © by Holt, Rinehart and Winston. Additions and changes to the original content are the responsibility of the instructor.

Differentiating Instruction

Collection 3
Collection Summative Test

VOCABULARY SKILLS **Complete the sentences below by using the collection vocabulary words from the list below.**

disputed	exasperation	reconciliation	imposing
obstinate	implore	conspicuous	chronic

1. No one _____ the fact that Andre was brilliant.

2. What made everyone crazy was how stubborn and _____ he could be.

3. His refusal to consider another opinion filled everyone with _____.

4. His _____ rudeness was also cause for outrage.

5. At 7 feet 6 inches tall the player presented an _____ figure on the court.

LITERARY AND READING SKILLS **Circle the letter of the best answer.**

6. Which sentence is a clue that the story is being told by a **first-person narrator**?

    A) The sun came up slowly, poking fingers of light through the leaves of the trees.

    B) Before the week was over, it was clear to everyone that things were going terribly wrong.

    C) I can still remember how it felt to be the only kid to miss the signal to stop singing.

    D) On the way home, Nancy told everyone what had happened in the principal's office.

7. Which sentence is a clue that the story is being told by an **omniscient narrator**?

    A) I think I knew all along that I didn't have a chance at winning.

    B) Morris stared at him with hatred in his eye, but Benjy didn't back down.

    C) They sat side by side, in uneasy silence, each wishing desperately to be someplace else.

    D) The corners of her mouth betrayed her amusement as she tried to speak sternly.

8. Which sentence is a clue that the story is being told by an **unreliable narrator**?

    A) "It must be understood that neither by word not deed had I given Fortunato cause to doubt my goodwill."

    B) "He prided himself on his connoisseurship in wine."

    C) "In this respect I did not differ from him materially."

    D) "It was about dusk one evening, during the supreme madness of carnival season, that I encountered my friend."

LANGUAGE AND WRITING SKILLS **Choose the word in each pair that completes the sentence and has a more positive connotation.**

9. The bank was located in an _____ [imposing/impressive] granite building.

10. The man's red hair was his most _____ [conspicuous/striking] feature.

Original content Copyright © by Holt, Rinehart and Winston. Additions and changes to the original content are the responsibility of the instructor.

Peter and Rosa Isak Dinesen

Ambiguity Chart Ambiguity is an element of uncertainty in a text, in which something can be interpreted in a number of ways. It adds a layer of complexity to a story because it presents readers with a variety of possible interpretations.

The chart below contains story details that are ambiguous. Next to each detail from the story, provide a reasonable interpretation that conflicts with the one already filled in.

Story Details	Interpretation 1	Interpretation 2
The skipper's wife is jealous of the figurehead.		The wife resents the time her husband spends on the ship.
The wife wants the blue stones to wear as earrings.	The wife thinks the stones would look prettier as earrings.	
The wife begins to lose her eyesight after removing the stones from the figurehead.	She has a rare disease that is causing her to go blind, which has nothing to do with the blue stones.	
The husband's ship runs into a tall rock and sinks.		The husband wasn't paying enough attention in sailing the ship and it crashed accidentally.

Original content Copyright © by Holt, Rinehart and Winston. Additions and changes to the original content are the responsibility of the instructor.

Lesson Plan and Teaching Strategies

The Scarlet Ibis James Hurst

Preteach

LISTENING COMPREHENSION SKILLS *(20 minutes)*

Build Background/Set a Purpose Discuss Build Background on
p. 332. Have students use a U.S. map to locate states in the Southeast.
Point out that the author does not specify where the story takes place,
but clues such as the family growing cotton and the trees and flowers
the narrator describes set the story in the South. Check for students'
knowledge of World War I (1914–1918). Use a map of Europe to locate
France, where the battles mentioned in the story were fought. Identify
the main countries in the war: France, England, and Russia against
Germany. Explain that the U.S. under President Woodrow Wilson (who
is mentioned in the story) entered the war in 1917, fighting against
Germany. Point out that World War I was a very bloody war, with
millions of soldiers and civilians killed and wounded.

Discuss the Preview the Selection feature on p. 332. Preview these
details about the story:

- Doodle is the younger brother of the narrator.

- Doodle had a problem when he was born that makes him different.

- The narrator wants to change Doodle to be more like other kids.

- A scarlet ibis, a kind of tropical bird, makes a surprise appearance.
  Refer students to the picture on p. 332 for an image of the bird.

Read aloud the Meet the Writer information on p. 332, especially the
"Brothers at War" paragraph. Ask students to give ideas about what one
brother might try to change about another (e.g., the way the person acts
or thinks) and what might happen as a result (e.g., the brothers might
fight or one brother might be helped by the other). Have students read
to find out what the narrator wants to change about Doodle, what the
outcome is, and what the scarlet ibis has to do with the story.

VOCABULARY SKILLS *(15 minutes)*

Preteach Vocabulary Words Review the meanings of the vocabulary
in the Word Bank. Then give students these sentences to complete.

1. The oil in the puddles was easy to see because it was [iridescent].

2. Don't hit the table with that stick because you will [mar] the wood.

3. The darkening sky suggested that a storm was [imminent].

4. We never question his [infallibility] because he is always right.

5. She [reiterated] the plan, although we understood it the first time.

Remind students to watch for these words as they read the story.

RESOURCES

In *The Holt Reader:* "The
Scarlet Ibis," for students
who need more scaffolding
in a workbook format

In this book: *Vocabulary Skill
Builder,* p. 75; "The Scarlet
Ibis," Selection Test, p. 76

Consult *Holt Audio Library*
for recordings of most
selections

WORD BANK
imminent
iridescent
infallibility
reiterated
mar

VOCABULARY SKILLS
Especially for ELL
(10 minutes)
English-language learners
will benefit from previewing
figures of speech used in the
story. After students learn
each expression, have them
use it in an original sentence.
all there (p. 334): mentally
normal and capable
for heaven's sake (p. 335):
an expression of annoyance
or impatience
paint a picture (p. 337):
describe by creating visual
images
*cross their hearts and hope
to die* (p. 337): an expression
of willingness, honesty, good
intentions, or seriousness
had left no crumbs behind (p.
340): had not left a trail to
follow back to where they
started; a reference to the
story of Hansel and Gretel

Original content Copyright © by Holt, Rinehart and Winston. Additions and changes to the original content are the responsibility of the instructor.

Differentiating Instruction

LANGUAGE COACH SKILL *(30 minutes)*

Oral Fluency Point out to students that one way to be comfortable with new words is to use them in everyday conversations about their own activities. As an example, read this sentence from the story:

- "With success so *imminent,* we decided not to tell anyone until he could actually walk." (p. 337)

Review the meaning of *imminent.* Give an example of a holiday or school event that is imminent. Confirm the word meaning by giving the date of the event to show its nearness in time. Ask volunteers to share events that are imminent in their lives (e.g. trips; sports competitions).

Then have students work with a partner to use each vocabulary word in a short conversation. Write the following sentences on the board as discussion prompts. Have students repeat each sentence, then complete it to reflect their own ideas and activities:

- Something that could *mar* my plans for the weekend is … because …
- I should have *reiterated* … because …
- I do/do not believe that anyone can show *infallibility* because …
- Something that is *imminent* for me is …
- When I think of something *iridescent,* I think of …

Encourage students to continue using these words in conversation.

LITERARY FOCUS *(30 minutes)*

Symbols and Theme Explain that a **symbol** is something that is used to stand for something else. Identify the classroom clock as an object associated with time and, therefore, a symbol of the concept of time. Point out that a person can be a symbol. For example, the principal is the main person in charge and a symbol of authority at school. Have students give examples of other symbols (e.g. a flag for patriotism).

Explain that writers include symbols in a story to communicate important ideas. The central, or most important, idea in a story is called the **theme.** It is a lesson about life that the writer wants to share. As an example, discuss the theme of the story "Liberty" from Collection 1. (e.g., Achieving something important can require making sacrifices.) Point out that writers usually don't state the theme in a story. They *imply* it from story events and clues, such as symbols, they include. Explain that figuring out the theme can be very personal. Each reader may state the theme differently from others, and that's okay.

Have students work with a partner to discuss what the scarlet ibis might symbolize in this story. Have students study the images on pp. 330, 332, and 341. Remind students that in the story setting, it is unusual to see a scarlet ibis. Ask students to think about what a bird might symbolize (e.g., freedom, escape, fragility) and what this bird's color might mean (e.g., danger, blood). Have each pair record ideas to check as they read.

ACADEMIC VOCABULARY
Preteaching Academic Vocabulary
(5 minutes)
Write these terms and their meanings on a chalkboard or transparency. Review them with the students before introducing the literary and reading focus skills.
Symbol: An object, person, animal, or event that stands for something else, such as a concept or an emotion
Theme: The central idea of a work of literature
Imply: Suggest; hint at
Literal: Based on the ordinary meaning of the actual words

READING/WRITING
Especially for ELL
(5 minutes in class; 15 minutes or more for individual students)
Invite English-language learners to explain examples of symbols from their own cultures, such as objects and people that stand for a place or important ideas. To help ELL students connect to the symbolism of the scarlet ibis, have students use art and writing to identify an animal that is an important symbol in their native culture.

Original content Copyright © by Holt, Rinehart and Winston. Additions and changes to the original content are the responsibility of the instructor.

Differentiating Instruction

READING FOCUS *(15 minutes)*

Analyzing Details Discuss the painting on p. 339. Confirm that the *literal* scene is of two children, and the title is *The Carefree Days of Childhood*. Explain that details in the painting can have a larger, or more important, meaning. For example, the children running might represent the idea that the carefree days of childhood go by quickly.

Remind students to look for details a writer includes that show what a person, place, or an event is like. Explain that students need to think about why the writer is including those details and analyze what larger meaning they may have for understanding the story. Have students prepare a T-chart like the one at right to fill in as they read.

Direct Teach

(45 minutes)

Chunk the Text Help students pace their reading by dividing the selection into "chunks" or parts. After students read each part, have them work with a partner to fill in the Story Details Chart.
Part 1: ends p. 335, col. 1: "…from someone called Doodle."
Part 2: ends p. 336, col. 2: "…Don't leave me.'"
Part 3: ends p. 337, col. 2: "…having a crippled brother."
Part 4: ends p. 340, col. 1: "…and I helped him up."
Part 5: ends p. 342, col. 2: " 'Specially *red* dead birds.' "
Part 6: ends p. 344, col. 2: "…from the heresy of rain."

Check for Understanding

WRITING FOCUS *(30 minutes)*
Dialogue Explain that **dialogue** is conversation between characters. Authors quote characters' exact words to reveal their thoughts and personalities. Discuss with students what this dialogue reveals:

" 'Don't hurt me, Brother,' he warned.

'Shut up. I'm not going to hurt you. I'm going to teach you to walk.' I heaved him up again, and again he collapsed. (p. 336)

Model rewriting a narrative sentence as dialogue by changing the last sentence to: " 'Here, I'll pick you up again.'" But again he collapsed.

Have students practice by rewriting this sentence as dialogue:

"If I so much as picked up my cap, he'd start crying to go with me…" (p. 335)

Think as a Reader/Writer Tell students that they will rewrite a small part of the story to include more dialogue. Use the first paragraph on p. 336 as an example. Discuss how students could rewrite this scene as a conversation between the narrator and Doodle. Then have students find another passage to rewrite as dialogue, offering guidance as needed.

READING FOCUS
Story Details Chart

Story Details	Larger Meanings

READING/WRITING
Especially for RGP
(15 minutes or more)
For readers who are gaining proficiency, check comprehension and guide their understanding of the story using these questions: *What details about Doodle and the ibis show that they are alike?* (e. g. Doodle is weak and survives only a short time; the ibis dies soon after it arrives. The ibis dies trying to fly; Doodle dies trying to run home. The red ibis dies under the bleeding tree; Doodle dies, bleeding, beneath a red bush.) *On p. 337, the narrator says, "Pride is a wonderful, terrible thing, a seed that bears two vines, life and death." What wonderful thing does pride drive the narrator to do?* (He refuses to accept Doodle's limitations and teaches him to walk.) *What terrible thing does pride do?* (It drives the narrator to push Doodle beyond his limits, leading to Doodle's death)

"The Scarlet Ibis" by James R. Hurst from *The Atlantic Monthly*, July 1960. Copyright © 1960 by **James R. Hurst**. Reproduced by permission of the author.

Original content Copyright © by Holt, Rinehart and Winston. Additions and changes to the original content are the responsibility of the instructor.

Differentiating Instruction

Collection 4
Graphic Organizer

Student Edition pages 348–359
IDENTIFYING SYMBOLS

The Necklace Guy de Maupassant

Symbol Chart A **symbol** is an object, event, person, or animal that stands both for itself and also for something else.

Fill out the chart below to analyze symbols from "The Necklace." In the first column are passages from the story. Locate a symbol from each passage, and write it in the second column. Then, write the meaning of the symbol in the third column.

Story Passage	Symbol	Meaning
"All at once she found, in a black satin box, a superb diamond necklace; and her pulse beat faster with longing. Her hands trembled as she took it up. Clasping it around her throat, outside her high-necked dress, she stood in ecstasy looking at her reflection."		
"He threw over her shoulders the wraps he had brought for going home, modest garments of everyday life whose shabbiness clashed with the stylishness of her evening clothes. She felt this and longed to escape unseen by the other women, who were draped in expensive furs."		
"They walked toward the Seine, disconsolate and shivering. Finally, on the docks, they found one of those carriages that one sees in Paris only after nightfall, as if they were ashamed to show their drabness during the daylight hours."		

Original content Copyright © by Holt, Rinehart and Winston. Additions and changes to the original content are the responsibility of the instructor.

Differentiating Instruction

Lesson Plan and Teaching Strategies

The Gift of the Magi O. Henry

Preteach

LISTENING COMPREHENSION SKILLS *(10 minutes)*
Build Background/Set a Purpose Discuss Build Background on p. 362. Explain to students that the Magi were a class of priests from an ancient kingdom in what is now northern Iran. (Find Iran on a world map to confirm its location.) Both frankincense and myrrh are resins, or sticky matter, from trees found in that area. They were burned for the fragrant odor they gave off, just as incense is burned today. Both frankincense and myrrh were considered very precious gifts, along with gold, to give the baby Jesus. Be sure students understand that the Magi are not characters in this story. Explain that appreciating the importance of the Magi's gifts, however, will help them understand the story.

Discuss the Preview the Selection feature on p. 362. Use the Meet the Writer information on page 362 to explain that this story is one of the many tales that O. Henry set in New York City. Find New York on a U.S. map. Discuss the image of New York on the page to help students imagine the city as it looked in the early 1900s, when this story takes place. Preview these story details with students:

- Della and Jim are a young couple living in New York. Della has long hair that falls below her knees. Jim has a prized pocket watch.

- Della and Jim are very much in love. They would do anything for each other.

- The story takes place on Christmas Eve Day. Della and Jim have little money to buy Christmas presents for each other.

Ask students to predict what the Magi and their gifts have to do with Della and Jim. Have students state their ideas and explain their reasoning. Remind them to check their ideas for accuracy as they read.

VOCABULARY SKILLS *(10 minutes)*
Preteach Vocabulary Words Review the meanings of the vocabulary in the Word Bank. Then give students these sentences to complete.

1. You need to be [agile] to do back flips and cartwheels.

2. The front-row seats at the concert are [coveted] because they're the best.

3. The students used [prudence] in setting goals they could achieve.

4. Almost everyone at school is an [ardent] supporter of at least one sports team.

5. You should give an old car careful [scrutiny] before you buy it.

Remind students to watch for these words as they read the story.

RESOURCES
In *The Holt Reader:* "The Gift of the Magi," for students who need more scaffolding in a workbook format

In this book: *Vocabulary Skill Builder,* p. 75; "The Gift of the Magi," Selection Test, p. 77

Consult *Holt Audio Library* for recordings of most selections

WORD BANK
agile
prudence
scrutiny
coveted
ardent

VOCABULARY AND LANGUAGE SKILLS
Especially for ELL
(10 minutes)
Extend vocabulary and oral-language development for English-language learners. Have ELL students work with a partner to review what they have learned about the story from the preview discussion, using the words *coveted* and *ardent* to describe the characters, and other vocabulary words as they can, in their conversation.

Original content Copyright © by Holt, Rinehart and Winston. Additions and changes to the original content are the responsibility of the instructor.

Differentiating Instruction

LANGUAGE COACH SKILL *(20 minutes)*

Word Derivations Write these sentences from the story on the board:

- "He looked thin and *serious*." (p. 366)

- ". . . the letters of 'Dillingham' looked blurred, as though they were thinking *seriously* of contracting to . . . *D*." (p. 364)

Explain that adding the suffix *–ly* to a word changes its form. *Serious* is an adjective that describes a man, the character Jim. Ask a volunteer to explain what *seriously* describes in the second sentence. Confirm that it's the verb *thinking*. Adding *–ly* changes the adjective *serious* to the adverb *seriously*. Point out that the word meaning does not change. A *serious* person and thinking *seriously* both mean thoughtful and grave.

Now write *chill* and *chilly* on the board. Read this partial sentence:

- "Madame, large, too white, *chilly* . . ." (p. 366)

Explain that adding *–y* to a word also changes the form. A *chill* is a noun that means a feeling of coldness. Adding *–y* creates the adjective *chilly* that describes Madame, who acts in a cold way toward others.

Write these sentences on the board. Point out that each word in the box appears in the story. Have students complete each sentence by adding an adjective or adverb from the box.

nervously	worthy	gradually	carefully

1. It took some time, but his scores [gradually] improved.
2. The painting is beautiful and [worthy] of praise.
3. There is ice on the sidewalk, so walk [carefully].
4. The children waited [nervously] to find out if their dog was okay.

LITERARY FOCUS *(20 minutes)*

Situational Irony Explain that when we expect one thing to happen, but something entirely different happens instead, that is called *situational irony*. As an example of irony, discuss the information in the first paragraph of Meet the Writer on p. 362. Point out that when O. Henry ran away, it made him look guilty. However, if he had stayed in Austin, he might not have gone to jail because the bank was careless with money. The bank's carelessness is the twist that might have given O. Henry's personal story a surprising ending. Instead, he became a writer whom readers *associate* with the literary technique of *situational irony*. Many of his stories have plots with unexpected outcomes.

Have students check their understanding of situational irony with this activity. Have students work with a partner to think of a movie or a book they know in which the story has an unexpected outcome. Have each pair describe the plot, what is expected to happen, and the surprise "ironic" ending. Bring all pairs together to share their examples.

ACADEMIC VOCABULARY
Preteaching Academic Vocabulary
(5 minutes)
Write these terms and their meanings on a chalkboard or transparency. Review them with the students before introducing the literary and reading focus skills.
Situational Irony: A literary technique that uses an unexpected outcome to surprise the reader
Associate: Mentally make a link
Ambiguous: Not clearly defined; capable of having two outcomes

READING/WRITING
Especially for RGP
(15 minutes)
After students read the story, re-read key passages to help them develop an appreciation for the way in which O. Henry sets up a situation and then surprises readers with an ironic ending. On p. 366, re-read the section in which Della purchases the watch chain with excitement and joy. Re-read the passage on p. 367 and p. 368 in which "The Combs" are described. Then work with students to complete a chart like the one below to identify the situational irony in the story.

Back-ground	Della's hair and Jim's watch: their most prized possessions
Situation	They have no money to buy gifts
Solution	Della sells her hair and Jim sells his watch to get money
Irony	They cannot use the gifts they receive

Original content Copyright © by Holt, Rinehart and Winston. Additions and changes to the original content are the responsibility of the instructor.

Differentiating Instruction

READING FOCUS *(20 minutes)*

Analyzing Details Discuss the painting on p. 365. Have students identify details in the scene (e.g. the woman has very long hair; she is fixing her hair; the window is open). Then talk about the significance of the details and the information they give about the scene. For example, the open window shows it is probably warm out. The woman's face and figure suggest that she is fairly young. Point out that the way she is holding her hair is *ambiguous*. She could be braiding her hair or removing the braid. Clearly, she takes pride in her beautiful hair.

Explain that when students read a story, they need to look for details a writer includes that show what a person, place, or an event is like. Then students need to think about why the writer is including those details and analyze why they may be important for understanding the story. Have students work in pairs to fill out a chart like the one at right. As they record a detail, prompt them to analyze its significance.

Direct Teach

(20 minutes)

Chunk the Text Help students pace their reading by dividing the selection into "chunks" or parts. After students read each part, have them stop to add story details to the chart and explain their significance.
Part 1: ends p. 364, col. 2: "…and collected herself, panting."
Part 2: ends p. 367, col. 2: "and threw it upon the table."
Part 3: ends p. 368, col. 2: "They are the Magi."

Check for Understanding

WRITING FOCUS *(30 minutes)*
Narrator's Voice Read this passage as an example of how O. Henry uses the narrator to speak directly to the reader:

> "While the mistress of the house . . . take a look at the home. A furnished flat at $8 per week. It did not . . . the squad." (p. 363)

Discuss the effect of the narrator's voice and how it helps to draw the reader into the story. Point out, though, that this third-person narrator comments but is not experiencing the situation directly. Discuss how the story would be different if told by Della, for example. Have students write a description of the apartment, using Della as the narrator.

Think as a Reader/Writer Explain that students are to write a paragraph from the point of view of Jim as the narrator. Have students review the story for details about what Jim is like (e.g. serious, loving). Have them re-read p. 367 and p. 368 and pay attention to how Jim speaks and reacts. Then have students choose a scene to rewrite with Jim as the narrator, such as his reaction to Della's hair or receiving the chain knowing he has sold the watch. Remind students to use the first-person *I* to represent Jim speaking and to aim to capture his feelings and personality in what he says.

READING FOCUS
Story Details Chart

Story Details	Significance

READING/WRITING
Especially for LDN
(15 minutes or more)
Learners with diverse needs may benefit from role-playing to experience being a narrator. Have two or three students act out a scenario, such as two people trying to keep a secret from a third person. Have another student take the role of the narrator and comment on what the others are doing for the audience, the rest of the group. Ask several teams of students to try a role-play. In keeping with the writing activity, have at least one role-play in which the narrator is a character involved in the action. Discuss how the narrator helps explain and highlight different aspects of what is happening in each scenario.

The Golden Kite, the Silver Wind Ray Bradbury

Cause and Effects Chains A **cause** explains why something happens, and an **effect** is the result of something that happens. Often in stories, events have both a cause and then an effect that leads to another event.

In "The Golden Kite, the Silver Wind," the events have a cause that lead to another event. In the chains below, look at the event in the middle circle. Then write in the cause for that event in the first circle. In the third circle, write the effect of that event.

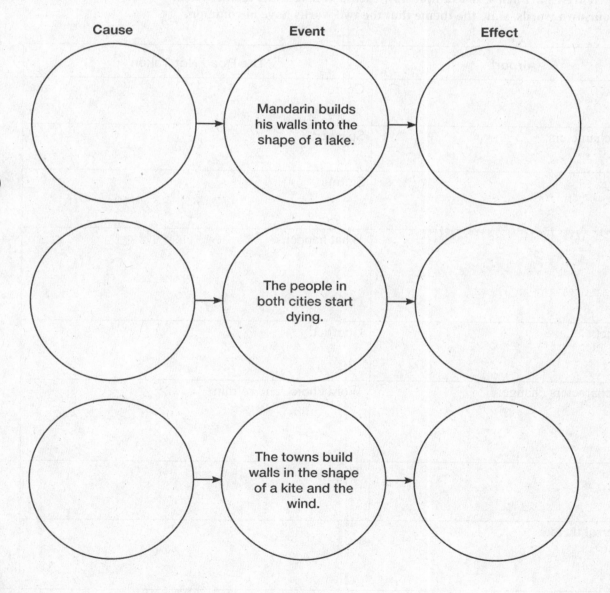

Cause   Event   Effect

Mandarin builds his walls into the shape of a lake.

The people in both cities start dying.

The towns build walls in the shape of a kite and the wind.

Original content Copyright © by Holt, Rinehart and Winston. Additions and changes to the original content are the responsibility of the instructor.

Collection 4
Graphic Organizer

Airport Pauline Kaldas

The Road Not Taken Robert Frost

Genre Chart The **theme** is what a story or poem reveals about life or human nature. Although different **genres** use different elements to reveal theme, they often share a common theme.

Both "Airport" and "The Road Not Taken" reveal something about life choices. Use the Genre Chart below to examine how each text reveals its theme. Then, using your own words, state the theme that the two works have in common.

Airport	The Road Not Taken
Genre:	Genre:
Main characters:	Speaker:
Setting:	Setting:
Plot:	What happens?
Conflict:	Conflict:
How characters change:	Word choice and refrain
Theme:	Theme:
Universal theme:	

Original content Copyright © by Holt, Rinehart and Winston. Additions and changes to the original content are the responsibility of the instructor.

Differentiating Instruction

Lesson Plan and Teaching Strategies

Synthesizing Works by One Author Albert Einstein

Preteach

LISTENING COMPREHENSION SKILLS *(15 minutes)*

Build Background/Set a Purpose Discuss Build Background on p. 398. Refer students to the photo of Einstein on p. 396 to help them picture him, and then check for what they know about Einstein (e.g., his famous formula: $E = mc^2$). Fill in details, as needed, about Nazi Germany's policies against Jews to explain why Einstein was forced to leave Germany and settle in the U.S. Point out that the first piece by Einstein is from 1931, two years before the Nazis came to power in 1933. In that work, the "World War" he refers to is World War I. His letter to President Roosevelt was written a month before World War II began in September 1939, when Germany attacked Poland. Review the Build Background on p. 399. Use the photo to identify Franklin Roosevelt (and confirm that Einstein is not in the picture). Explain that the third article was written in 1952, seven years after atomic bombs were dropped on two Japanese cities, ending World War II. Invite students to share knowledge they have about how atomic bombs were developed or used in World War II. Check for questions students have about Einstein, World War II, or nuclear weapons before you proceed.

Preview these details to help students set a purpose for reading:

- Even before World War II began, Einstein was a pacifist – someone who does not believe in war and will not fight in a war.

- Einstein was in favor of the U.S. developing nuclear weapons because he believed Nazi Germany was trying to do the same.

- Atomic bombs created destruction on a greater scale than ever before. Have students preview the images on p. 401 to imagine Einstein's views of this terrible weapon.

Discuss the titles of the first article on p. 398 and the third article on p. 401. (Be sure students know that abolition means elimination or ending.) Based on these two titles, do students think Einstein's views about war changed? If so, how? Have students state their ideas and explain their reasoning. Have students read to check their ideas.

VOCABULARY SKILLS *(10 minutes or less)*

Preteach Vocabulary Words Review the meanings of the vocabulary in the Word Bank. Then give students these sentences to complete.

1. They look like a better team, so it's [conceivable] that they'll win.

2. We must get rid of this garbage to [eradicate] the terrible odor.

3. Flying from cold and snow to a sunny beach is a [radical] change.

Remind students to watch for these words as they read the articles.

RESOURCES

In *The Holt Reader:* "Synthesizing Works by One Author," for students who need more scaffolding in a workbook format

In this book: *Vocabulary Skill Builder,* p. 75; "Synthesizing Works by One Author," Selection Test, p. 78

Consult *Holt Audio Library* for recordings of most selections

WORD BANK
eradicate
conceivable
radical

VOCABULARY SKILLS
Especially for ELL
(10 minutes or less)
English-language learners will benefit from reviewing the following additional words from the selections. Read each word and definition with students, and have them use the word in an original sentence.
suffice (p. 398): be enough; be sufficient
ungrudgingly (p. 398): willingly; heartily
detestable (p. 402): deserving to be hated

Original content Copyright © by Holt, Rinehart and Winston. Additions and changes to the original content are the responsibility of the instructor.

LANGUAGE COACH SKILL *(30 minutes)*

Word Origins Explain that understanding the origins of words can help students learn new words. Discuss these words from the selections:

- *Instinct* is from the Latin *instinctus* and *instinguere,* meaning to "impel, instigate." When you impel, you push or force something to happen. When you instigate, you start or set off something. In English, an instinct is something natural from within that makes one act in a certain way ("combative instinct," p. 398).

- *Moderate* is from the Latin *moderare,* "to keep within bounds, restrain." In English, moderate means not too much; average ("moderate quantities," p. 400).

- *Abolish* is from the Latin *abolescere,* "to decay little by little," and *abolere,* "to retard, destroy." In English, abolish means to put an end to ("abolish war," p. 402).

- *Universal* is from the Latin *universus,* which means "all together." In English, something that is universal happens everywhere or affects everyone ("universal destruction," p. 402).

Write these sentences on the board. Have students complete each one by adding a word from the box.

abolish	universal	moderate	instinct

1. We need a [moderate] leader who does not have extreme ideas.
2. Food, clothing, and shelter are [universal] needs of all people.
3. A cat's [instinct] is to hunt mice, birds, and other small animals.
4. To [abolish] a rule, everyone must agree that it's no longer needed.

INFORMATIONAL TEXT FOCUS *(45 minutes)*

Synthesizing Sources: Works by One Author Explain that reading nonfiction text sometimes requires taking information from different articles and putting it together to understand a topic. It can also mean reading articles on the same topic by the same author, to understand the person's point of view. Give students this example to discuss:

> Your favorite musical group is playing two concerts on different nights. You have tickets for the second night. You want to know what to expect. So you read a newspaper article about the first concert. Then you go online to read some blogs from kids who were at the concert. You take the information from the article and the information in the blogs and you *synthesize* it – you put it together in your mind – to get a picture of what the concert will be like.

Talk about the value of reading more than one source on a topic (e.g. you get different points of view and learn more information). Take students through the skills they can use to synthesize information. They **paraphrase**, or put someone's ideas in their own words to be sure they

---

ACADEMIC VOCABULARY
Preteaching Academic Vocabulary
(5 minutes)
Write these terms and their meanings on a chalkboard or transparency. Review them with the students before presenting the informational text focus skills.

Paraphrase: To restate an idea in your own words
Compare and Contrast: To look for similarities (compare) and differences (contrast)
Synthesize: To put together information from different articles or sources

READING/WRITING
Especially for RGP
(10 minutes or less)
Readers who are gaining proficiency will benefit from a brief discussion to clarify the genre of each article by Einstein, for help in understanding the probable purpose and audience:
* Einstein's purpose in the interview is to express his ideas; the audience is listeners or readers;
* The purpose of the letter is to express his views to President Roosevelt;
* The purpose of the magazine article is to state his opinions to readers.

Original content Copyright © by Holt, Rinehart and Winston. Additions and changes to the original content are the responsibility of the instructor.

Differentiating Instruction

understand. They *compare* to find similarities and *contrast* to find differences in views. They connect ideas to what they know – in this case, about the musical group. Then they **synthesize** – put all the sources together – to decide what they can tell about the concert. Explain that with the articles by Einstein, they are reading three works by one author on a similar topic – weapons in war. Students will use these same skills to understand Einstein's ideas. Read the explanations for how to use each skill to synthesize works by one author on p. 397.

Have students work with a partner to practice paraphrasing sentences from the first two paragraphs of "Weapons of the Spirit," p. 398. Have them read a sentence then restate the idea in their own words. Circulate to guide and assist students. Have the student partners each create a chart like the one at right. Have the pairs fill in a problem and solution Einstein identified in the first two paragraphs, using their own words.

Direct Teach

(60 minutes—or one class period for each selection)

Think-Pair-Share As students read each selection by Einstein, have them consider the problem he poses in each one, as well as the solution he suggests. Ask students to make notes in a Problem-Solution Chart like the one on the right. After reading each selection, have students partner with another student to discuss and formulate a shared response. Have volunteers share their responses with the entire class.

Check for Understanding

WRITING FOCUS *(40 minutes)*

Writing from Historical Perspective Review with students the date of each piece and the chief view Einstein expresses in it. For example:

The interview is from 1931. He states that war is a waste of energy and that people should fight with weapons of the spirit, not real ones.

The letter is from August 1939. He urges the president to support the development of nuclear arms because the Germans may be doing so.

The article is from 1952. He calls for an end to all war.

Re-read and discuss the first two paragraphs of Einstein's article on p. 402. Point out that he is looking back at the letter he wrote in 1939. Confirm as a group that Einstein still believed in 1952 that he had no choice about encouraging the production of atomic weapons. Have each student write a sentence that paraphrases Einstein's view.

Constructed Response Ask: *If you could go back to July 1939, before Einstein wrote his letter to President Roosevelt, what would you advise Einstein to do?* Have students use their historical knowledge and what they have learned about Einstein's views on war to write a paragraph explaining what they would tell Einstein. For the second part of the question, have them explain if they think Einstein would have acted differently, such as asking Roosevelt to stop all experimentation with nuclear weapons, using Einstein's views to support their ideas.

Original content Copyright © by Holt, Rinehart and Winston. Additions and changes to the original content are the responsibility of the instructor.

READING FOCUS
Problem-Solution Chart

What is the problem?	What are some solutions?

READING/WRITING
Especially for LDN
(10 minutes)
Learners with diverse needs may require help with historical background to develop their Constructed Response. Check for what students know about the outcome of World War II and the nuclear age that followed the war. Have them take notes as you discuss these key points:
* Nazi Germany never produced an atomic weapon.
* America was the first nation to produce atomic bombs.
* Today, many nations have nuclear weapons, creating much concern in the world.
*To date, the U.S. is the only country to have dropped atomic bombs on an enemy in war.

Differentiating Instruction

Collection 4
Targeted Strategies for Learners with Diverse Needs

READING SKILLS

Synthesizing Sources: Works by One Author *(15 minutes)* Explain that writers often have a message or theme that reappears in their different works. Discuss with students that Einstein had a role in the creation of the atomic bomb, but he considered himself a man of peace. Point out that in the four selections by Einstein, he addressed his ideas about peace, war, and weapons. After students have read these selections work with them to fill in an organizer like the one below:

Peace	War	Weapons
Synthesis:		

Ask: *Reading across the four selections, what did Einstein say about these ideas?* Challenge students to identify the source of the information in the sentences.

LITERARY SKILLS

Symbols and Theme *(15 minutes)* Fables can be used to help students understand the concepts of **symbol** and **theme**. Retell the fable of the tortoise and the hare. Explain that the theme of the fable is stated in the moral of the story: *Slow and steady wins the race*. Be sure students understand that in other genres the theme is often not stated. Explain that this fable also includes symbols. The rabbit represents speed and the tortoise represents slowness. Ask: *What else do these two creatures represent? (laziness, overconfidence; perseverance, humility)* Ask:

- *Which other animals might also serve as symbols of speed and slowness? (jaguar/snail, gazelle/three-toed sloth)*

- *How would the message change if the rabbit had won the race instead? (Accept all reasonable answers.)*

Once students understand the concepts, have them work with partners to say what the ibis represents in "The Scarlet Ibis". Have them state the message of that story. Ask volunteers to share their ideas with the class.

Situational Irony *(15 minutes)* Help students understand that irony is when the opposite of what was expected happens. What is expected from the following situation?

- Someone scores the game-winning goal

After students respond, have them give the same situation an ironic twist. Have them think about how that goal might have been scored (by accident) or who might have scored it (the most underrated player).

- **Readings in Collection 4 Minimum Course of Study**
- "The Scarlet Ibis", p. 330
- "The Gift of the Magi", p. 360
- Synthesizing Works by One Author, p. 396

RESOURCES

In *The Holt Reader,* all three selections help students who need more scaffolding in a workbook format.

Consult *Holt Audio Library* for recordings of most selections.

TEACHING TIP

Some students with diverse needs may have trouble with the concept of irony. Help them make the connection between irony and sarcasm. Show how words have the opposite meaning if they are said in a sarcastic tone of voice: *great, no problem,* and *thanks a lot.* Also explain that irony leads people to think while typically sarcasm is used to hurt or insult.

ALTERNATIVE ASSESSMENT *(5 minutes)*
Ask students to answer these questions.

- Preserving peace is a [theme/symbol] in Einstein's writing.

- A team mascot is a type of [symbol/theme].

- You drop your books and find a dollar bill on the ground when you bend down to pick them up. That's an example of [situational irony].

Original content Copyright © by Holt, Rinehart and Winston. Additions and changes to the original content are the responsibility of the instructor.

Differentiating Instruction

Collection 4
Academic and Selection Vocabulary

The Scarlet Ibis The Gift of the Magi
Weapons of the Spirit/Letter to President Roosevelt.
Albert Einstein/On the Abolition of the Threat of War...

A. Write a "U" for unrelated, an "S" for synonym or an "A" for antonym next to each pair of words.

_____ 1. reiterated, repeated

_____ 2. agile, clumsy

_____ 3. radical, drastic

_____ 4. eradicate, remove

____ 5. infallibility, perfection

____ 6. conceivable, impossible

____ 7. mar, damage

____ 8. ardent, devoted

B. Choose the best answer to each question.

1. How would someone feel about receiving a coveted gift?

   A. happy   B. unhappy

2. If the end of an exciting game is imminent what should you do?

   A. get a snack   B. stay in your seat

3. Which situation requires more prudence?

   A. riding a bike   B. watching TV

4. Which object is more likely to come under scrutiny?

   A. a bug under a microscope   B. a pillow on a chair

C. Use the academic vocabulary words to complete the following paragraph about "The Scarlet Ibis," by James Hurst.

ambiguous   associated   literal   imply

The narrator names his brother "Doodle" because he (1) _____ the way his

brother crawls with a certain kind of bug. The narrator wanted Doodle to be normal and was

worried that Doodle's health problems would (2) _____ that there was

something wrong with his family. In the story, the ending is (3) _____ .

The author doesn't tell us if Doodle recovers or not. I believe the bird was symbolic of Doodle,

however. Thus, the bird's death was not only (4) _____ but also symbolic of

Doodle's death.

Original content Copyright © by Holt, Rinehart and Winston. Additions and changes to the original content are the responsibility of the instructor.

Differentiating Instruction

Collection 4
Selection Test

The Scarlet Ibis James Hurst

COMPREHENSION, SKILLS, AND VOCABULARY **Circle the letter of the best answer to each of the following items.**

1. The narrator teaches his brother Doodle to

    A) walk

    B) crawl

    C) drive a go-cart

    D) tell outrageous lies

2. What first motivates the narrator to try to change Doodle?

    A) his deep love for Doodle

    B) a doctor's orders to make Doodle try harder

    C) his embarrassment at what Doodle cannot do

    D) his parents' request to make Doodle like other kids

3. Which is a symbol of death and loss in the story?

    A) the scarlet ibis

    B) Doodle's go-cart

    C) Old Woman Swamp

    D Doodle's casket in the barn

4. Which is the best statement of the theme of this story?

    A) Death is a natural part of life.

    B) Change is a natural part of life.

    C) Being different causes many conflicts.

    D) Trying to change others leads to conflict and sorrow.

5. Which best describes someone who shows **infallibility**?

    A) The person is never right.

    B) The person is never wrong.

    C) The person is never organized.

    D) The person can never be trusted.

6. People believe that James Hurst wrote this story to comment on the bloodshed between nations in World War I. Do you agree with that point of view? Why or why not? Think of details in the story to support your opinion. Use the organizer to collect your ideas. Then write a short paragraph.

Introductory statement: I do/do not agree that James Hurst wrote …
Two or three supporting sentences: For one thing, … Also, … In addition, …
Concluding statement: So, in conclusion, I think the author…

Original content Copyright © by Holt, Rinehart and Winston. Additions and changes to the original content are the responsibility of the instructor.

Collection 4
Selection Test

The Gift of the Magi O. Henry

COMPREHENSION, SKILLS, AND VOCABULARY Circle the letter of the best answer to each of the following items.

1. What is the setting of the story?
   A) New York City today
   B) New York City long ago
   C) long ago in a far-away country
   D) a time when all woman had long hair

2. What is the main problem in the story?
   A) Della and Jim live in a shabby apartment.
   B) Della is tired of her long hair but Jim loves it.
   C) Jim does not try hard enough to get a good job.
   D) Della has only saved $1.87 to buy Jim a Christmas gift.

3. Which detail from the story is the most significant?
   A) The apartment costs $8 a week.
   B) Jim's middle name is Dillingham.
   C) Jim's most prized possession is a pocket watch.
   D) Della's hat is not nearly as beautiful as her hair.

4. Which detail is part of the situational irony in the story?
   A) Jim liked Della with short hair.
   B) Jim liked the leather watch strap he was using.
   C) Jim never wanted to exchange Christmas gifts.
   D) Jim knew that Della wanted a beautiful set of combs.

5. Which word best describes something that is **coveted?**
   A) wanted
   B) avoided
   C) forgotten
   D) ridiculous

6. At the end of the story, O. Henry implies that the greatest gift Della and Jim give each other is their love. Do you think that statement is correct? What events in the story support your point of view? Use the organizer to collect your ideas. Then write a short paragraph.

| Introductory statement: I do/do not think the greatest gift in the story is love. |
| Two or three supporting sentences: For example, Della…Jim also…They… |
| Concluding statement: So, in conclusion, I think the story shows… |

Original content Copyright © by Holt, Rinehart and Winston. Additions and changes to the original content are the responsibility of the instructor.

Differentiating Instruction

Selection Test

Synthesizing Works by One Author Albert Einstein

COMPREHENSION, SKILLS, AND VOCABULARY Circle the letter of the best answer to each of the following items.

1. How does Albert Einstein feel about war?

    A) He thinks it is the same as murder.

    B) He thinks the weapons cost too much money.

    C) He thinks it is a way for people to show patriotism.

    D) He thinks people should fight in wars for what they believe.

2. Einstein wants people to make heroic sacrifices—

    A) for science

    B) for President Roosevelt

    C) to defeat Nazi Germany

    D) to achieve peace in the world

3. Which would you do to paraphrase Einstein's ideas?

    A) copy his exact words

    B) memorize his exact words

    C) explain his ideas using your own words

    D) disagree with his ideas and explain why

4. Which statement is true about Einstein's views in these three works?

    A) He has the same views against all weapons in each one.

    B) He thinks that beyond abolishing weapons we must abolish the threat of war.

    C) He starts out believing nuclear weapons are necessary, and then is against war.

    D) He makes arguments for why countries must continue going to war in all three.

5. Which statement best explains what happens when you **eradicate** something?

    A) You cause it to spread.

    B) You make it smaller in size.

    C) You get rid of it completely.

    D) You increase the amount you have.

6. Synthesize what you've learned about Albert Einstein. What is your opinion of him from his works and the views he expresses in them? Use the graphicorganizer to collect your ideas. Then write a paragraph.

Introductory statement: I think Albert Einstein was…
Two supporting sentences: I feel this way because… I agree/disagree…
Concluding statement. In conclusion, my respect for him increased/decreased

Original content Copyright © by Holt, Rinehart and Winston. Additions and changes to the original content are the responsibility of the instructor.

Collection 4
Collection Summative Test

VOCABULARY SKILLS Complete the sentences below by using the collection vocabulary words from the list below.

mar   prudence   reiterated   imminent

ardent   scrutiny   conceivable

1. The coach _____.that the team must practice again today.

2. We need to give that idea more _____ to see if it can work.

3. He is a(n) _____ believer in loyalty and stands up for friends.

4. We'll show _____.by being careful where we walk at night.

5. It is _____ that our missing dog has been found and possible that we'll get him back today.

LITERARY AND READING SKILLS Circle the letter of the best answer.

6. Which statement best describes a story with **situational irony**?

   A) It has a happy ending.

   B) You can guess the ending.

   C) The characters are in a difficult situation.

   D) The ending is not what you expect it will be.

7. An author uses **symbols** in a story to—

   A) represent ideas or feelings

   B) take the place of important characters

   C) hint to the reader that someone will die

   D) set the story in a certain time and place

8. When you **synthesize** nonfiction sources, you—

   A) write a nonfiction article on a topic

   B) find the best source to read on a topic

   C) put ideas together from several sources to understand a topic

   D) double-check a source to see if it has accurate information on a topic

LANGUAGE AND WRITING SKILLS Choose the correct answer in each answer pair.

9. Knowing an English word comes from Greek or Latin tells you its _____

   [pronunciation/origin].

10. When you write dialogue, you put each character's words in _____ [narrative/quotations].

Original content Copyright © by Holt, Rinehart and Winston. Additions and changes to the original content are the responsibility of the instructor.

Differentiating Instruction

Lesson Plan and Teaching Strategies

Writing Workshop: Autobiographical Narrative

PREWRITING

Evaluate Your Memories *(15 minutes)*

Review the definition of an autobiographical narrative: *An autobiographical narrative tells about a personal experience that had some special meaning for you.* Once students think of a personal story that they remember well and would be willing to share, have them work with a partner to define the moment in time.

Have students discuss their experiences with a partner, using these questions.

1. What is the main thing that happens?

2. What other events make up this experience?

3. What do you need to tell your audience at the beginning? (If they don't know you well—what would they need to know?)

4. How does this experience end?

Then have students use this information to make a simple flowchart of their experience.

Gather Sensory Details/Thoughts and Feelings *(15 minutes)*

Explain that adding details makes a story more exciting for an audience. Have students add details by illustrating their flowchart with drawings that relate to what they could see, hear, touch, taste, and smell.

Then have students share their flowchart with a partner and interview each other, using these questions.

1. What thoughts and feelings did you have at that time?

2. What did you say? What did someone say to you?

3. How did this experience change you? What did you learn?

Have students use the answers to these questions to create speech and thought bubbles, and add them to their flowcharts.

DRAFTING

Organize and Draft Your Narrative *(10 minutes)*

Make sure students use their illustrated flowcharts to draft their essays. Review the autobiographical narrative structure on page 419 of the Student Edition. Remind students that their first paragraph should start the narrative in an interesting way. Students can go back and look at the beginnings of other selections in the unit for inspiration. The second paragraph should tell about the main part of the experience. The third paragraph should explain why this story is important. Have students then begin to draft their narrative.

TEACHING TIP

Before beginning this lesson, spend some extra time working with students on the writing model on page 416. Read it aloud to students and help them with difficult vocabulary, such as *enticed, idyll, backwaters,* and *glutted.* Help students number the events that take place in the story. Point out where action is inferred (for example the author left out a lot of details between one day and the next).

ESPECIALLY FOR ELL
(10 minutes)

After English-language learners illustrate the details of their stories, have them partner with proficient English speakers. Have proficient speakers help English-language learners label their illustrations to generate additional vocabulary. Give English-language learners time to look up the definitions of new words, as needed.

ESPECIALLY FOR WGP

Writers who are gaining proficiency may need extra help deciding how much information to include. If possible, spend a few minutes alone with students after each partner-discussion. Help students summarize the events that make up their experience, particularly beginning and end points. Help them to decide what kind of information their audience will need.

Original content Copyright © by Holt, Rinehart and Winston. Additions and changes to the original content are the responsibility of the instructor.

EVALUATING AND REVISING

Review Content and Organization *(20 minutes)*

Give students time to focus on the following points in Evaluation Questions 1, 2, 3, 4 and 6. Help them understand how they can use these points to make their stories better.

1. Have students turn to the first paragraph of the student draft on page 421 for an example of a strong beginning. What kind of information does the author include? Is it enough?

2. Remind students that they can use their imaginations to add more details. However, the details should be realistic. Ask students to supply examples of realistic details.

3. Point out the edits to the last paragraph of the draft on page 421. The author added her inner thoughts to the conclusion. How do the changes help the audience know what the experience meant to the author?

4. Have students compare the order of events they've numbered to the flowcharts they used in prewriting. Are the events in the right order? Have they left out anything important?

6. Have students read the final paragraph of the student draft before and after the revision on page 422. Ask them to think about which ending gave them a stronger feeling about the author's experience.

Pair students with a partner. Have each student discuss how they can use these guidelines to improve each other's drafts.

Grammar Link: Using Active Voice and Proofread *(15 Minutes)*

Students may have trouble knowing when to use the passive voice and when to use the active voice. Explain that the active voice is generally better and more exciting to read, and it gives more information. It's best to avoid the passive voice, if possible. Discuss the following scenarios and examples of how to improve sentences by using the active voice:

Passive	Active
The vase was broken.	*The excited dog broke the vase.*
Waiting for Thanksgiving is hard.	*I can't wait for Thanksgiving.*
The table was covered with a delicious feast.	*My grandmother covered the table with a delicious feast.*

Then ask students to reread their essays to find and fix sentences in the passive voice.

TEACHING TIP
Allow students to write their first draft before teaching the Grammar Link on page 419. This will avoid an overload of instructions. Instead, use both Grammar Links in the proofreading section, along with a review for any other errors.

ESPECIALLY FOR ELL
(10 minutes)

During the lesson on introductory adverb clauses (page 419), be sure that English language learners understand the time and causal relationships communicated by the subordinating conjunctions: *after, before, because, when, while, as, if although, since, while,* and *until.* Draw clocks, arrows, question marks and ordinal numbers (1st, 2nd), to communicate these relationships symbolically or have students look up words in their native language.

ESPECIALLY FOR LDN
When applying the lesson on introductory adverb clauses to their own writing, some students may begin to list events exhaustively or link events out of chronological order. Spend some time with these students individually to be sure they are using transitions logically and appropriately.

Original content Copyright © by Holt, Rinehart and Winston. Additions and changes to the original content are the responsibility of the instructor.

Differentiating Instruction

Listening and Speaking Workshop: Presenting an Oral Narrative

ADAPT YOUR NARRATIVE *(20 minutes)*

Explain that students will now take the autobiographical narrative they have written and prepare it for an oral presentation. Have them follow these steps:

1. Ask your partner to read your oral narrative to you. Listen for anything you'd like to change.

2. Your partner can stop and ask you questions about anything that is unclear. Work together to make corrections.

3. Number the events in your narrative and see if you have a transition between each one. Be sure the listener can tell when you change time or place.

4. Read your conclusion to your partner. Can your partner restate your thoughts and feelings in his or her own words? If not, your conclusion might be unclear.

Deliver Your Narrative

USE VERBAL AND NONVERBAL TECHNIQUES *(20 minutes)*

Explain how to use these techniques.

Use Your Voice Expressive reading will make the story more exciting. Remind students to use their voice to bring the story to life. Have them try speaking softly and making wide eyes to show suspense. Have them smile and take a short pause after something funny so the audience has time to think about it. Have them imitate characters.

Use Your Eyes Eye contact will help students make an emotional connection to their audience. Have students rehearse repeatedly in front of a mirror. Advise them to memorize as much as they can. Have them use the flowcharts they made in prewriting to create cue cards. Explain that it's easier to use cards than to find your spot in a script.

Have students practice their delivery with a partner. Have the partner fill out a checklist like the one below as feedback.

Non-verbal Techniques	Regularly	Sometimes	Never
Clear Meaning			
Verbal Techniques			
Nonverbal Techniques			
Smooth Use of Note Cards			

Teaching Tip

You may want to practice using the feedback chart (at the bottom of this page) with students by reading something to them. Model how to discuss the feedback in a positive manner, offering examples and suggestions.

ESPECIALLY FOR ELL

The pronunciation goal for English-language learners is intelligibility. Students do not need to strive for accent-free speech.

ESPECIALLY FOR LDN

Some learners with diverse needs have trouble making eye contact. Give them tips about where they can focus their eyes, such as the back wall of the classroom, so they don't read down into the page.

EVALUATION CRITERIA

Use these criteria to evaluate students' presentations:

- Gave their presentations smoothly with little hesitation
- Pronounced most words intelligibly
- Varied tone, volume, and rate of expression
- Focused on a single episode and was able to communicate its meaning
- Offered sensory details, thoughts, and feelings
- Demonstrated a command of non-verbal techniques

Original content Copyright © by Holt, Rinehart and Winston. Additions and changes to the original content are the responsibility of the instructor.

Differentiating Instruction

Unit 1, Skill Builder 1
Oral Language Skill Builder

Summarize

UNDERSTAND THE SKILL You can summarize the plot of a story to help you understand and remember events. Look for the problems that the main character has and his attempts to solve them.

Work with a partner to complete the chart. Then answer the discussion questions below. Afterwards, discuss your answers with other classmates.

Summarizing the Plot of "The Most Dangerous Game"	
What is the first problem?	The action begins when _____.
How does Rainsford solve this problem?	He decides to _____. So he _____.
What is the next problem?	Even though _____, his problems aren't over yet because_____.
How does he try to solve it?	_____ decides to _____. But that doesn't work so he tries_____ and _____.
What is the climax?	The situation is at its most exciting when _____ because_____.
What is the turning point?	Things began to change when _____ because_____.
What is the conclusion?	Finally the problem is solved when _____ _____. So _____.

Extend Discussion What other ways might the story have ended? Discuss these two different "what if" situations with a partner.

- Suppose the other man had been the better hunter. How would that change the ending of the story?

- Suppose both men had enjoyed the game. What other ending would be possible then?

Original content Copyright © by Holt, Rinehart and Winston. Additions and changes to the original content are the responsibility of the instructor.

Differentiating Instruction

Unit 1, Skill Builder 2
Oral Language Skill Builder

Comparisons

UNDERSTAND THE SKILL You can make comparisons between characters to understand them better. You reread what the author says directly about how the characters are similar and different. You also make inferences about what the author doesn't say directly.

Work with a partner to complete the chart. Then answer the discussion question below. When you are finished, explain your answers to different partners.

Comparing Mrs. Jones and Roger in "Thank You M'am"	
Who is stronger?	In comparison to Roger, Mrs. Jones is _____. We think this because she _____.
Who needs more help?	Compared to Mrs. Jones, Roger _____. We think this because he _____.
Who gives more help?	Even though Roger _____, Mrs. Jones _____.
Who is more trusting?	_____ is the character who is the more trusting. The part of the story that shows us this is _____.
Who needs to be trusted?	_____ is the character who needs to be trusted. The part of the story that shows us this is when _____.
Who learns more?	In our opinion, _____ is the character who learns more. One reason we think this is _____. Another reason we think this is _____.

Extend Discussion What if Mrs. Jones meets Roger again in three months? Discuss these two different "what if" situations with a partner.

- Suppose Roger is doing well in school. How will she feel? What will she say to him?
- Suppose Roger is trying to steal another purse. How will she feel? What will she say?

Original content Copyright © by Holt, Rinehart and Winston. Additions and changes to the original content are the responsibility of the instructor.

Unit 1, Skill Builder 3
English Language Skill Builder

Shades of Meaning

UNDERSTAND THE SKILL There are many words in English for the places where people live. There are also many words that describe how rich or poor people are. Although each group of words tells about the same kind of thing, the words themselves can actually have very different meanings.

Discuss each set of words with a partner. If you don't know a word, look it up in a dictionary. Then think carefully about the labels at the end of each line. Plot the words where you think they belong. Discuss your work with different partners.

Places People Live

hut	mansion	house	condominium
shack	apartment	rooming-house	tenement

more expensive ←————————————|————————————→ **less expensive**

richer ←————————————|————————————→ **poorer**

How Much Money People Have

affluent	comfortable	destitute	well-off
prosperous	wealthy	impoverished	middle class

EXTEND DISCUSSION Use these words to discuss the selections you have read. Support each answer with details from the selection.

1. Which of these words best describes where Mrs. Jones lives in "Thank You, M'am"?

   _____ Which word describes how rich or poor Roger is? _____

2. Which word describes where Elena lives in "American History"? _____ Which word describes where Eugene lives? _____

3. Which word best describes how rich or poor Elena's family is in "American History"?

   _____ Would you use a different word for Eugene's family?

   If so, what word? _____

4. What word best describes where Dave Eggers might live? _____ What word best describes how rich or poor he might be? _____

Original content Copyright © by Holt, Rinehart and Winston. Additions and changes to the original content are the responsibility of the instructor.

Unit 1, Skill Builder 4
English Language Skill Builder

Phonemic Awareness

UNDERSTAND THE SKILL The English language includes some sounds that other languages don't have. Hearing and pronouncing these sounds takes practice. The best way to learn these sounds is by paying attention to the difference between words that are very close in sound.

Practice saying the word pairs until you can hear and say the difference between them.

Contrasting Sounds

taught, thought   breathe, breeze   price, prize   seem, theme

sigh, shy   search, surge   harsh, hearth   face, faith

1. Which pairs have contrasting sounds at the beginning of the words?

   _____   _____   _____

2. Which pairs have contrasting sounds at the end of the words?

   _____   _____   _____

   _____   _____

EXTEND DISCUSSION Take turns reading the paragraph below with a partner. As you read, pronounce each pair of words carefully. Fill in each blank with the correct word choice. Then reread the paragraph aloud.

   You may have (1) _____ (taught/thought) that giving up a dog was a

high (2) _____ (price/prize) to pay for freedom. But some governments can be

(3) _____ (harsh/hearth). When families have lived through

(4) _____ (searches/surges) of their homes, they are often afraid to

(5) _____ (breathe/breeze) let alone (6) _____ (sigh/shy).

   In those moments, (7) _____ (face/faith) in liberty might

(8) _____ (seem/theme) like your only hope!

Unit 1
Summative Test

LITERARY AND READING SKILLS

A. Circle the letter of the best answer. *(25 points; 5 points each)*

1. Which statement is the best example of an **internal conflict**?

   A) Two men decide to end their feud, but they find themselves hunted by hungry wolves.

   B) Rainsford believes that he has caught General Zaroff in a trap, but the General is still alive and ready to chase.

   C) The young man in "Thank You, M'am" thinks about running away from the woman, but he decides to stay and eat dinner.

   D) The narrator of "The Cask of Amontillado" pretends to be concerned about Fortunato's health, but he is planning to murder the man.

2. Which question helps you determine a character's **motivation**?

   A) What is going to happen next to the character?

   B) Which character is telling the story?

   C) Where does the character live?

   D) What does the character want?

3. Which clue lets you know that a narrator is a **first-person narrator**?

   A) The narrator refers to himself or herself directly as "I."

   B) The narrator knows everything about all the characters.

   C) The narrator tells lies or half-truths about events.

   D) The narrator talks about one character as he or she.

4. Which of the following is an object, event, person, or animal that stands both for itself and also for something else?

   A) allegory

   B) inference

   C) narrator

   D) symbol

5. If a story or poem is **ambiguous**, then it

   A) has a narrator who speaks from his or her own experiences

   B) turns out differently than the way the reader expected

   C) contains an object or person that stands for itself and something else

   D) includes details with uncertain meaning or unclear events

Original content Copyright © by Holt, Rinehart and Winston. Additions and changes to the original content are the responsibility of the instructor.

Differentiating Instruction

Unit 1 Summative Test *continued*

B. Complete each sentence with one of the literary or reading skills shown below. *(25 points; 5 points each)*

visualizing	antagonist	flashback	mood	inference

6. A story's _____ is a character that creates conflict and keeps the hero from reaching his or her goal.

7. When you make a(n) _____ about characters, you make an educated guess about them based on details in the story.

8. Through the use of _____ storytellers fill in details about a character's past.

9. An important reading skill is _____ because it allows you to create a picture in your mind and helps you remember the details.

10. The _____ of a story can affect the way we feel as we read.

Read the question below. Then write a short response on the lines. *(50 points)*

Making Predictions

11. What do you predict will happen to Jim and Della, the main characters in O. Henry's story "The Gift of the Magi"? On what details do you base your predictions?

_____

_____

_____

_____

_____

_____

_____

_____

_____

Original content Copyright © by Holt, Rinehart and Winston. Additions and changes to the original content are the responsibility of the instructor.

Differentiating Instruction

Collection 5
Graphic Organizer

How to Eat a Guava Esmeralda Santiago

Imagery Diagram Imagery is language that appeals to the sense of sight, hearing, smell, taste, or touch.

Read the passage from the selection. Then fill out the diagram below with words and phrases that appeal to each sense. Not all senses may be used.

> A green guava is sour and hard. You bite into it at its widest point, because it's easier to grasp with your teeth. You hear the skin, meat and seeds crunching inside your head, while the inside of your mouth explodes in little spurts of sour.

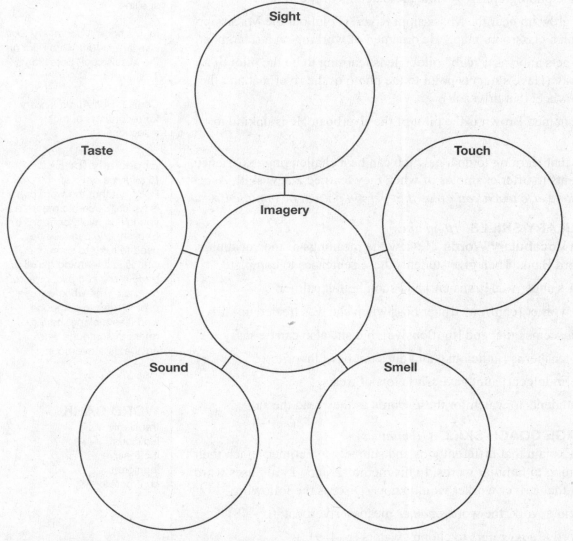

"Prologue: How to Eat a Guava" from *When I Was Puerto Rican* by Esmeralda Santiago. Copyright © 1993 by Esmeralda Santiago. Reproduced by permission of **Da Capo Press, a member of Perseus Books, L.L.C.**

Original content Copyright © by Holt, Rinehart and Winston. Additions and changes to the original content are the responsibility of the instructor.

Lesson Plan and Teaching Strategies

Cub Pilot on the Mississippi Mark Twain

Preteach

LISTENING COMPREHENSION SKILLS *(10 minutes)*
Build Background/Set a Purpose Discuss Build Background on
p. 446, simplifying words like *obstacles* (hurdles); *shallow* (mime
"low"), and *commercial* (for trade). Explain that Mark Twain lived in
the 1800s, and that he was famous for his humorous stories and novels.
Note that the selection is about Mark Twain's experiences as a young
man learning to become a riverboat pilot. Point out the selection title.

Discuss the Preview the Selection feature on p. 446. Have students look
ahead at the photographs. Preview these details of the plot:

- Twain grew up near the Mississippi River. (Point out the Mississippi
  River on a classroom map.) He dreamed of working on a steamboat.

- Twain gets a job as a "cub" pilot. He is learning to be the pilot of a
  riverboat. (Have students point to the photo of the riverboat and the
  paddle wheel that drives it.)

- A man named Brown is the pilot of the riverboat. He is unkind to
  Twain.

Point out that learning to do a new job can be a challenging experience.
Ask students to offer examples of when they learned a new skill. Ask:
Did someone else teach you? Was that person patient or impatient?

VOCABULARY SKILLS *(10 minutes)*
Preteach Vocabulary Words Review the meanings of the vocabulary
in the Word Bank. Then give students these sentences to complete.

1. Juan's anger was [transient] and soon he felt calmer.

2. The worker [confronted] her boss when she was treated unfairly.

3. Gina seems quiet and [inoffensive], but she also can be sassy.

4. Our teacher is [judicious], and does not have favorites.

5. Her [indulgent] aunt gave Carla lots of treats.

Remind students to watch for these words as they read the story.

LANGUAGE COACH SKILL *(10 minutes)*
Jargon Explain that different jobs and subjects sometimes attach their
own meaning to familiar words. In his memoir, Mark Twain uses word
meanings that a river worker would know. Discuss the following—

- In Twain's work, the word *steamer* means a riverboat. (p. 448)

- The word *breaks* refers to choppy waters (p. 449).

- *Leads* are weights that test how deep the river is (p. 450).

RESOURCES

In *The Holt Reader:* "Cub
Pilot on the Mississippi" for
students who need more
scaffolding in a workbook
format

In *Holt Pronunciation
Resources* video support of
phoneme sounds and
spelling

In this book: *Vocabulary Skill
Builder,* p. 104; "Cub Pilot on
the Mississippi" Selection
Test, p. 105.

Consult *Holt Audio Library*
for recordings of most
selections.

Especially for ELL
(5 minutes or less)
Point out that the word *cub*
is typically used to mean "a
young lion, wolf, or bear." In
English, *cub* can also be
used to refer to someone
who is just learning a skill or
trade like a *cub pilot* or a *cub
reporter.* And while we use
pilot to refer to someone
who flies a plane, here it
refers to someone who
navigates a riverboat.

WORD BANK
transient
judicious
inoffensive
indulgent
confronted

Original content Copyright © by Holt, Rinehart and Winston. Additions and changes to the original content are the responsibility of the instructor.

Differentiating Instruction

Even the pen name that Samuel Clemens chose for himself, "Mark Twain," is riverboat jargon. It means that the water is twelve feet deep, and should be safe for riverboat travel.

Write these sentences on the board. Have students complete each one by adding a word from the box.

leads	breaks	Mark Twain	steamer

1. The [steamer]is a wonderful boat.
2. The captain yelled, "[Mark twain,]" so that we knew the water was deep enough for the riverboat.
3. The pilot dropped the [leads] to see how deep the water was.
4. The boat began to shake when we hit the [breaks].

LITERARY FOCUS *(20 minutes)*
Style and Tone Explain: *The way in which a writer uses language is his or her style. Style is created mainly through diction, or word choice. We also look at the way the writer puts together sentences. Are they long and complicated? Are they short and simple? Listen to the following and think about the writer's style:*

> "He was a middle-aged, long, slim, bony, smooth-shaven, horse-faced, ignorant, stingy, malicious, snarling, fault hunting, mote-magnifying tyrant." (page 448)

Explain that this very long sentence becomes more and more humorous because readers can sense the writer's building anger toward the man he is describing. Words like "long" and "smooth-shaven" simply give a description of the man. But as the sentence continues, the words the writer chooses get more and more insulting. "Horse-faced," "ignorant," and "tyrant" are not words that anyone would use to describe a friend. Discuss with students what tone of voice they would expect the writer to have if he was telling the story to an audience.

Explain: *Another important part of a writer's style is the tone of the story. When we talk about tone, we look at how the writer feels toward the people and events in the story. The tone is the writer's attitude.*

Help students use academic vocabulary and concepts. Divide them into groups of three. Tell students to experiment with diction as they write their own description of a character from the story. Have students think about how long complicated sentences would compare to short direct sentences. Ask volunteers to read their descriptions. Then have them discuss the tone of their descriptions. Focus on how they established a particular attitude toward the character in their descriptions.

READING FOCUS *(45 minutes)*
Read Aloud and Paraphrase Explain that when you *paraphrase*, you put something in your own words. Offer a sentence from the selection: *By means of a dozen or so of pretty direct questions, he pumped my*

ACADEMIC VOCABULARY
Preteaching Academic Vocabulary
(5 minutes)
Write these terms and their meanings on a chalkboard or transparency. Review them with the students before previewing the selection.

Attitude: Way of thinking, acting, or feeling; outlook.
Diction: The words that a writer chooses to use.
Establish: Set up; create.

LANGUAGE SKILL
Especially for ELL
(5 minutes or less)
Some English-language learners may have difficulty with the technical term *tone*. Remind students that *tone* involves the writer's feelings about what he or she is telling the reader. Connect the idea of the story's tone to a speaker's tone of voice. For example, say the following sentence with the tone of voice indicated:

"Nice to see you." (enthusiastic and kind)

"Nice to see you. "(sarcastic)

"Nice to see you."(automatic, as if speaker is not really thinking about what he or she is saying.)

READING FOCUS
Read Aloud and Paraphrase

Passage	Paraphrase

family history out of me. (p. 450) Now read a paraphrase of the sentence: *He asked me a lot of questions about my family, and I told him what he wanted to know.* Ask students to volunteer their own paraphrase of the sentence. Discuss how the paraphrases are different from the original sentence. Ask: *Do they reveal the same attitude toward the pilot and his relationship to the narrator?*

Have students work in pairs to fill out a chart like the one at the bottom of page 91. First, ask students to take turns reading passages from the selection out loud. Then have them work together to paraphrase what they have read. Encourage them to read their paraphrases aloud, too. Then compare and contrast the paraphrased passage to the original.

Direct Teach

(45 minutes)

Think – Pair – Share For struggling readers, diction in "Cub Pilot on the Mississippi" may impede understanding. Help foster understanding through the use of a Story Map like the one on the right. Review academic terms like "conflict" (the main problem in the story) and "resolution" (the way the problem is solved and the story ends). Have students work on the Story Maps individually. Then have them discuss their responses in pairs. Have partners work toward agreement on their answers to the Story Map and then share their responses with the class.

Check for Understanding

WRITING FOCUS *(15 minutes)*

Dialogue Explain that when an author uses a character's exact words, he or she is using *dialogue*. Point out that you can learn a lot about characters based on their dialogue. Use the following example in which Twain uses dialogue to show readers what the pilot is like:

Dialogue "Dern sight better staid there!" (p. 449)
What It Tells About the Character Based on Brown's remark, we can tell that he uses slang instead of using standard English. We can also tell that he is angry and expresses this in a straightforward manner.

Read aloud each sentence below. Have students state or write what each piece of dialogue tells about the character.

1. "Dod dern my skin, I'll learn you to swell yourself up and blow around here about your dodderned ORDERS!" (Brown) (p. 450) [Brown is angry and resentful of the narrator.]

2. "You lie, yourself. He did tell you." (narrator) (p. 452) [The narrator is brave in confronting Brown, and uses simple language.]

3. "I'm deuced glad of it!" (captain) (p. 454) [The captain is on the narrator's side, and expresses it openly.]

Think As A Reader/Writer Ask: *How might a man like Brown speak to the narrator today?* Then ask students to rewrite an example of Brown's dialogue so that it sounds like it could be spoken today, by a man with similar traits.

Original content Copyright © by Holt, Rinehart and Winston. Additions and changes to the original content are the responsibility of the instructor.

Differentiating Instruction

VOCABULARY SKILL
Especially for ELL
(15 minutes)
Paraphrasing passages may be difficult for students who have trouble understanding Twain's language. Encourage English-language learners to review the passages with you or a teaching assistant, taking note of any words or phrases that are unfamiliar to them. Then have students use a dictionary to look up the words, and encourage them to ask questions about phrases that are still unclear.

WRITING FOCUS
Story Map

Title	
Characters	
Setting	
Conflict	
Main Events	
Resolution	

READING/WRITING
Especially for WGP
(5 minutes)
Point out that although using correct grammar is very important in formal writing, a character's words should reflect his or her background
Informal English: "I'll learn you to swell yourself up. "
Standard English: "I'll teach you to act so superior . . ."

Point out that the story surrounding the dialogue should be written as clearly as possible.

Collection 5
Graphic Organizer

Student Edition pages 458–465
FIGURATIVE LANGUAGE

The Secret Latina Veronica Chambers

Figurative Language Chart When writers use words in an unusual way, they are often using **figurative language.** Three common types of figurative language are the **simile, metaphor,** and **personification.**

Read each passage in the left column. Underline the figurative language. Then decide which of the three figures of speech the passage contains. Place an X in the appropriate column.

Passage	Simile	Metaphor	Personification
"A Panamanian was a sort of fish with feathers. . . "			
"...She was homesick for Panama and for those names that sang like timbales on carnival day."			
"Panama, in Central America, is a narrow sliver of a county."			
"When she spoke Spanish, her words were a fast current, a stream of language that was colorful, passionate, fiery."			

Slightly adapted from "The Secret Latina" by Veronica Chambers from *Becoming American: Persona/Essays by First Generation Immigrant Women.* Copyright ©2000 By Veronica Chambers. Reproduced by permission of the author.

Original content Copyright © by Holt, Rinehart and Winston. Additions and changes to the original content are the responsibility of the instructor.

Differentiating Instruction

Lesson Plan and Teaching Strategies

The Grandfather Gary Soto

Preteach

LISTENING COMPREHENSION SKILLS *(10 minutes)*

Build Background/Set a Purpose Discuss Build Background on p. 468. Make sure that students understand that Gary Soto's grandfather is from Mexico, and that he has settled in Fresno, California. Point out that Soto's grandfather spent many years working in a factory where raisins were packed.

Discuss the Preview the Selection feature on p. 468. Have students look at the photograph on page 469. Preview these details of the selection:

- Soto's grandfather believes that growing fruit trees will save him money. As an immigrant to the country, he worries about money.

- Soto's grandfather has a favorite tree—an avocado tree. He loves it even when it does not bear avocados.

- Over the years, as Soto's grandfather watches the tree grow, his family grows and makes roots (becomes established) in the U. S.

Explain that Soto's grandfather loves the avocado tree and cares for it even though it does not grow fruit for a long time. Tell students that, like Soto's grandfather, avocado trees originally came from Mexico. Eventually, people in California started to grow the trees; now they are a favorite California fruit. Ask: *Have you ever had to move from one place to another? Was it helpful to bring something as a reminder of your former home?*

VOCABULARY SKILLS *(10 minutes)*

Preteach Vocabulary Words Review the meanings of the vocabulary in the Word Bank. Then give students these sentences to complete.

1. We were disappointed that we only made a [meager] amount of money from our garage sale.

2. The nervous child [hovered] close to his mother at the party.

3. The small girl [sulked] when she did not win an award.

4. We heard the stream [gurgle] close by our campsite.

Remind students to watch for these words as they read the story.

LANGUAGE COACH SKILL *(10 minutes)*

Onomatopoeia Explain that if a word sounds like what it means (for example, *boom* or *tinkle*), it is an example of onomatopoeia. Note that the vocabulary word *gurgle* is an example of onomatopoeia.

Write this sentence from the story on the board. Have students identify the word that is an onomatopoeia.

RESOURCES

In *The Holt Reader:* "The Grandfather" for students who need more scaffolding in a workbook format

In this book: *Vocabulary Skill Builder,* p. 104; "The Grandfather" Selection Test, p. 106

Consult *Holt Audio Library* for recordings of most selections

WORD BANK

gurgle
hovered
sulked
meager

ACADEMIC VOCABULARY

Preteaching Academic Vocabulary
(5 minutes)
Write these terms and their meanings on a chalkboard or transparency. Review them with the students before previewing the selection.

Personal Essay: A short, informal piece of nonfiction that tells about events in a writer's life, as well as his or her thoughts and feelings.
Appeal: Attract; interest
Enhance: Make greater; improve
Imagery: Words and phrases that help readers to see, hear, feel, smell, or taste something.

Original content Copyright © by Holt, Rinehart and Winston. Additions and changes to the original content are the responsibility of the instructor.

Differentiating Instruction

- "And wind reached all the way from the sea, which was blue and clean, unlike the oily water sloshing against a San Francisco pier." (p. 469) [sloshing].

Write these sentences on the board. Have students complete each one by adding an example of onomatopoeia from the box.

popped	slammed	hiss	stomp

1. We started to [stomp] our feet against the theater floor when the film stopped.
2. The kernels [popped] for several minutes in the microwave.
3. The audience started to [hiss] at the bad guy.
4. The angry girl [slammed] the door on her way out.

LITERARY FOCUS *(20 minutes)*

Style and Imagery Explain *"The Grandfather" is Gary Soto's personal essay. You can tell that it is a personal essay because Soto writes in the first person—that is, he tells his own story using words like* I, my, *or* me. *In essays like this, writers tell about a specific event or part of their life, and their feelings about it.*

Remind students that when we talk about a writer's style, we are talking about how he or she uses language. Explain: *Writers create their style by the words they choose and by the way they put sentences together.*

Another piece of the writers' style is how they use imagery. Explain: *Imagery is the words or phrases in a story that help us to see, hear, feel, smell, or taste something. Listen to the following from the selection.*

> The chile plants, which also saved him from giving up his hot, sweaty quarters, were propped up with sticks to support an abundance of red fruit.

Explain that this sentence appeals to two different senses: touch (*hot, sweaty quarters*) and sight (*an abundance of red fruit*). Ask students to find other examples of imagery in the story.

READING FOCUS *(45 minutes)*

Make Generalizations Explain that when you make a generalization, you are using specific details in a story to make a larger point. Offer this example: *From the story, we know that Grandfather likes fruit trees that can save him money and that he was an immigrant from Mexico.* Ask students to make generalizations about Grandfather from those details. (Grandfather worries about money.) Explain that students used these details to make a larger point about what Grandfather was like. Point out that students can also look at specific examples of Soto's writing style by looking at individual sentences. They can use these to make a generalization about Soto's style.

"The Grandfather" from A Summer Life by Gary Soto (Dell, 1991) Copyright © 1990 **University Press of New England** and electronic format by permission of **Gary Soto**.

Original content Copyright © by Holt, Rinehart and Winston. Additions and changes to the original content are the responsibility of the instructor.

Differentiating Instruction

LANGUAGE SKILL
Especially for ELL
(5 minutes or less)
Some English learners may have difficulty with the technical term *imagery*. Review the word *image* with students, and note that we often talk about images we see in photographs or paintings. Note that imagery can be thought of as a snapshot of what the writer senses. Have volunteers look for examples in the selection.

READING FOCUS
Generalization Chart

Details/ Evidence About Grandfather	General- ization

Have students work in pairs to fill out charts like those on the right. As they read the selection, prompt them to write down details from the story about Grandfather and to make notes about Soto's writing style. Then encourage them to make generalizations based on those details.

Details/ Evidence About Soto's style	Generaliz ation

Direct Teach

(60 minutes)

Chunk the Text Help students pace their reading by dividing the selection into "chunks" or parts. After the students have read each part, stop to help them make generalizations about what they have read.

Part 1: ends p. 469, col. 2: "...against a San Francisco pier."
Part 2: ends p. 470, col 1: "...dig themselves back into fresh air."
Part 3: ends p. 470, col 1: "...welcome ungry sparrows."
Part 4: ends p. 470, col 2: "...an ice cold watermelon."
Part 5: ends p. 470, col 2: "...hugged the ground."

Check for Understanding

WRITING FOCUS *(15 minutes)*

Personal Essay Explain that an author can use imagery to communicate his or her feelings about the topic of an essay.

Imagery "The wind could move the branches, but the trunk, thicker than any waist, hugged the ground."

Appeals to Senses and Feelings Explain that the sentence from the story appeals to the senses of touch (wind) and sight (moving branches, trunk hugging the ground). These images help readers understand the importance of the avocado tree to both the grandfather and the narrator. Ask: *How would you describe the narrator's feelings about the tree?*

Plan your own personal essay. Think about what you want to write about, and then plan images that will appeal to different senses. Try to make these communicate your feelings about your topic.

1. Use an image that helps readers picture something.

2. Use an image that helps readers hear something.

3. Use an image that helps readers feel something.

4. Use an image that helps readers taste something.

5. Use an image that helps readers smell something.

Think As A Reader/Writer Have students return to the last few paragraphs of the selection. Ask: *How did Grandfather and the narrator feel about the first avocado that they ate?* Ask students to think about the imagery Soto uses, Grandfather's simple words, and the narrator's actions. Have them rewrite the section, using their own words to communicate the characters' feelings.

VOCABULARY SKILL
Especially for ELL
(15 minutes)
English-language learners will benefit from practice with the additional words below. Go over these words and their meanings with students. Then challenge students to use the words in original oral sentences.

- *bore* (p. 469): past tense of *bear*—produced fruit or offspring
- *abundance* (p. 470) large amount; plenty
- *omen* (p. 470): a sign, suggesting future trouble or danger
- *edible* (p. 470): able to be eaten
- *haggle* (p. 470) to argue, disagree, or bargain over the price of something with the goal of reaching a lower or higher price

READING/WRITING
Especially for WGP
(5 minutes)
Allow writers who are gaining proficiency to write multiple drafts of a personal essay.

"The Grandfather" from A Summer Life by Gary Soto (Dell, 1991) Copyright © 1990 **University Press of New England** and electronic format by permission of **Gary Soto.**

Original content Copyright © by Holt, Rinehart and Winston. Additions and changes to the original content are the responsibility of the instructor.

Differentiating Instruction

Collection 5
Graphic Organizer

from Boy   Roald Dahl

Visualizing Diagram When you see in your mind what you are reading on the page, you are **visualizing**. Visualizing can help make the events, people, and places of a story come alive.

Visualize or reread the description of the scene inside the sweet-shop when the boys discover the Gobstoppers' jar is broken. Use this diagram to fill in the details that help you visualize the scene.

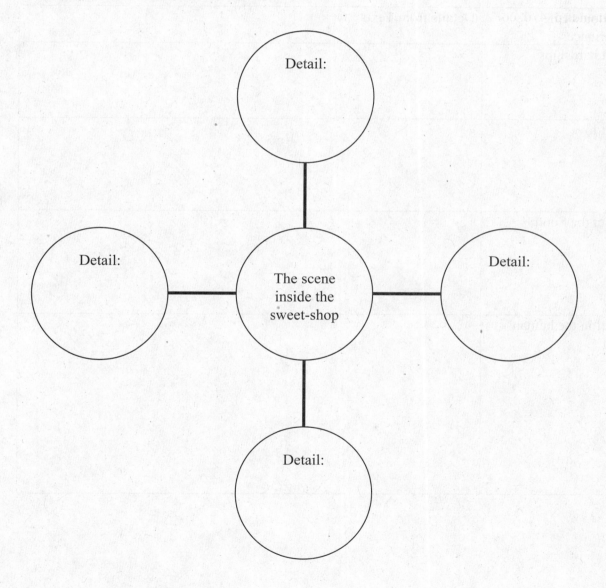

Original content Copyright © by Holt, Rinehart and Winston. Additions and changes to the original content are the responsibility of the instructor.

Collection 5
Graphic Organizer

ANALYZING BIOGRAPHICAL APPROACH

Maya Angelou

Biographical Analysis Chart Writers often use experiences from their personal lives in their works. When you analyze how texts reflect the heritage, attitudes, experiences and beliefs of an author, you are using a **biographical approach.**

Use this chart to analyze the how the life experiences of Maya Angelou are reflected in her writings. Use details from the four selections by Angelou.

Angelou's Life Experiences	Details from Texts
Great hardships	
Great love	
Life in the South	
Belief in the human spirit	

Original content Copyright © by Holt, Rinehart and Winston. Additions and changes to the original content are the responsibility of the instructor.

Differentiating Instruction

Lesson Plan and Teaching Strategies

About Story Corps

Preteach

LISTENING COMPREHENSION SKILLS *(10 minutes)*

Build Background/Set a Purpose Discuss Build Background on p. 504, simplifying words like *intended* (planned) and *destitute* (poor). Explain that at the time the Works Project Administration was created, the U. S. was suffering from the effects of the Great Depression—a time when many people lost their jobs and their savings because businesses and banks failed.

Have students look ahead at the photographs. Together, discuss what the young people in the photographs on pages 504 and 505 are doing. Preview these details from the selection.

- StoryCorps is a program through which all sorts of people record interviews with friends or relatives.

- StoryCorps started in New York City in 2003. (Point out New York City on a map) Now there are also traveling studios in trailers, which go around the country.

- Through StoryCorps, organizers hope to gain a record of many people's lives. Information like this, gained through interviews, is known as "oral history."

Point out that there are many reasons that project organizers would like people to take part in these interviews. Ask: *If you had the chance to ask someone close to you about his or her life, what would you ask?*

VOCABULARY SKILLS *(10 minutes)*

Preteach Vocabulary Words Review the meanings of the vocabulary in the Word Bank. Then give students these sentences to complete.

1. The group's [collective] purpose is to raise money for the poor.

2. You may need a [facilitator] to explain how to use the new technology.

Remind students to watch for these words as they read the story.

LANGUAGE COACH SKILL *(10 minutes)*

Derivations Explain that when we talk about a word's derivation, we mean its history (from where it is derived) and to what words it is related. Point out these examples from the selection.

- The adjective *national* (p. 504) comes from the noun *nation,* which means country,

- The noun *collection* (p. 505) is related to the verb *collect,* which means "to gather."

RESOURCES

In *The Holt Reader:* "About Story Corps" for students who need more scaffolding in a workbook format

In this book: *Vocabulary Skill Builder,* p. 104; "About Story Corps" Selection Test, p. 107.

Consult *Holt Audio Library* for recordings of most selections.

Especially for ELL

(5 minutes or less)
Point out that the word corps in StoryCorps means a group or unit.

WORD BANK

collective
facilitator

ACADEMIC VOCABULARY

Preteaching Academic Vocabulary

(5 minutes)
Write these terms and their meanings on a chalkboard or transparency. Review them with the students before previewing the selection.

Functional Document: A text, such as an article or set of instructions, that explains how to do something
Structure: The way an author organizes and presents his or her ideas
Format: The design of a document, which helps readers to pay attention to important ideas

Original content Copyright © by Holt, Rinehart and Winston. Additions and changes to the original content are the responsibility of the instructor.

Differentiating Instruction

- The noun *humanity* (p. 505).is related to the noun *human*, which means "a person."

Write these sentences on the board. Have students complete each one by adding a word from the box.

national	collection	humanity

1. We can all appreciate acts of [humanity] and kindness.
2. All of her friends enjoy her [collection] of songs.
3. The [national] program helps children all over the country.

LITERARY FOCUS *(20 minutes)*

Structure and Format of Functional Documents Explain: *The structure of a document is the way in which ideas are organized. When we talk about the format of a document, we are talking about its design. The format of a functional document should make it easy to follow and understand. The kind of type that is used is a* formatting element. *The kind of pictures or other visuals used are called* graphic elements. *The way that the graphic elements are placed on the page along with the text is called the* design element. Point out the following examples on page 505 of the selection.

> Teens interview each other in the StoryCorps booth at Grand Central Station in New York City.
>
> **Our Vision**
>
> *How did you and Mom meet?*

Explain that the small text under the photograph is called a caption. It is set in smaller type size to set it apart from the rest of the text. Captions give information about a photograph or illustration.

Note that "Our Vision" is a heading for the second section of the document. It is set in larger, bold type. Headings help readers to find information they need.

The question from the last paragraph of the document is set in italic type. It is an example of the kind of question that someone might want to ask. All of these questions are set in italics, which sets them apart from the rest of the text.

Help students practice using academic vocabulary and concepts. Have small groups work together. Tell students to look at different articles in textbooks or magazines. Encourage them to look at the formatting, graphic, and design elements. Ask: *How do changes in type size make the article easier or harder to follow? Are there any visuals, and if so, what do they add? Are there sections and headings?*

After students have spent time looking at other articles, have them work together to fill out a chart like the one on the right, noting elements in "About StoryCorps." Invite them to share what the different structural elements add to the document.

Original content Copyright © by Holt, Rinehart and Winston. Additions and changes to the original content are the responsibility of the instructor.

Differentiating Instruction

LANGUAGE SKILL
Especially for ELL

(5 minutes or less)

Some English-language learners may have difficulty with the technical term *structure*. Remind students that the *structure* of a piece is the way it is put together. Point out any structural elements that are obvious in the building you are in, such as beams, walls, ceilings, and so on. Explain that the structure of a building is similar to the structure of a document: it holds everything together.

READING FOCUS
Structure and Format

About StoryCorps	
Type Size and Style	
Pictures, Graphs, and Charts	
Placement and Size of Type and Visuals	

Direct Teach

(45 minutes)

Think – Pair - Share Write the following question on the board: *What is the main purpose of the StoryCorps project?* Have students work individually, making notes about their ideas. Then ask students to work in pairs. Encourage them to discuss their notes and ideas.

In order for students to more fully understand what a StoryCorps interview might be like, encourage them to spend some time interviewing each other. Write a few sample questions on the board to get them started, such as "Where were you born?" "What is your middle name?" "What is your happiest memory?" Have the person asking questions take notes during the interview.

Once they are done, encourage students to think about what they learned from doing the interview. Ask: *How was this interview different from one that you would do with StoryCorps?* (In StoryCorps, there would be a facilitator. They would have recording equipment. The interview would be placed on a CD and archived.) Invite students to discuss whether their ideas about StoryCorps' purpose changed after they had taken part in interviews themselves. Then, call on pairs of students to share their answers with the class.

Check for Understanding

WRITING FOCUS *(15 minutes)*

Explain Your Mission Note that in "About StoryCorps," the authors explain the mission of the StoryCorps project.

>   **Example**: "We've tried to make the experience as simple as possible: We help you figure out what questions to ask." (p. 504)

>   **Style** The author keeps the language simple, and addresses the readers as "you."

Read aloud each sentence below. Then have students think about any project on which they are working or would like to work. Ask students to use these sentences as a model for writing their own mission statements for their projects.

1. "StoryCorps is a national project to instruct and inspire people to record one another's stories in sound." (first sentence, p. 504)

2. "To start, we're building soundproof recording studios across the country, called Story Booths." (explains what they are doing) (p. 504)

3. "StoryCorps celebrates our shared humanity and collective identity." (explains why they are doing it) (p. 505)

Think As A Reader/Writer Ask: *If you could interview anyone, who would it be? What questions would you ask?* Have students think about who they would like to question and why. Then ask them to make a list of questions that they would use in such an interview.

Slightly adapted from "About StoryCorps" from *StoryCorps*. Copyright © by Sound Portraits Productions, Inc. Reproduced by permission of the publisher.

READING/WRITING
Especially for WGP
(5 minutes)
For writers gaining proficiency, it is helpful to have very short conferences to check their progress. Make sure students understand the assignment, and remind them that a mission statement tells what the purpose of a project is. If students are having trouble coming up with a project, you might suggest the following ideas: Make a record of your family history (genealogy); set up a recycling center; or put on a play or concert.

Original content Copyright © by Holt, Rinehart and Winston. Additions and changes to the original content are the responsibility of the instructor.

Differentiating Instruction

Graphic Organizer ANALYZING STRUCTURE OF FUNCTIONAL DOCUMENTS

About StoryCorps/Do-It-Yourself Interview

Structural Diagram Functional documents are often divided into sections, which are marked by headings. These headings will help you understand a document's **structure.** Some documents may have one or two sections. Others may have many sections.

Use this diagram to analyze the structure of "About Story Corps" and "Do-It-Yourself Interview." Place the headings of the sections in the boxes.

Do-It-Yourself Interview	About StoryCorps
Section 1:	Section 1:
Section 2:	
Section 3:	
Section 4:	
Section 5:	
Section 6:	
Section 7:	
Section 8:	

Original content Copyright © by Holt, Rinehart and Winston. Additions and changes to the original content are the responsibility of the instructor.

Differentiating Instruction

Targeted Strategies for Learners with Diverse Needs

READING SKILLS

Structure and Format of Functional Documents *(15 minutes)*

Explain that documents are clearer and easier to read if they have a structure and format that suits their function. Publishers carefully consider formatting, graphics, and design elements of books, magazines and newspapers. Posters for movies, concerts, and shows use these elements, too. Even restaurant menus and train schedules use these elements.

Formatting elements	Graphic elements	Design elements
What kind of type best fits the function? (Think of size and style.)	What images would be useful? (Think of photos, illustrations, maps, diagrams, etc.)	What needs to stand out? Which items are related? What overall impression is created?

Have students analyze various documents using the chart above. Challenge them to list examples of each kind of element and how they contribute to the function of the document.

LITERARY SKILLS

Style and Tone *(15 minutes)*
Help students understand style and tone by making a comparison to music. Ask students to give examples of popular songs performed by two different artists or even by the school band. The difference between the two versions often has to do with style and tone. Artists have their own styles and the tone of the song may be slower and sadder or faster and more upbeat. As a group, have students contrast the style and tone of Mark Twain's and Gary Soto's writing.

Then have students vote on which they prefer. Encourage students to give reasons for their preferences.

Style and Imagery *(15 minutes)*
Help students understand style and imagery by making a comparison to the visual arts. Ask students to think of the pictures each writer paints with words. Have partners describe how they might illustrate each story. Have them think about what the images would show and what the style of the art would be.

Invite students to describe the images or even create them, if they so desire. Ask volunteers to share their ideas or work with the class.

- **Readings in Collection 5 Minimum Course of Study**
- "Cub Pilot on the Mississippi", p. 444
- "The Grandfather", p. 466
- "About StoryCorps", p. 502

RESOURCES
In *The Holt Reader,* all three selections help students who need more scaffolding in a workbook format.

Consult *Holt Audio Library* for recordings of most selections.

TEACHING TIP
Illustrating a story is a great way for English-language learners to demonstrate their comprehension. Help them build vocabulary by pointing to details in their drawing and asking them questions about them.

ALTERNATIVE ASSESSMENT *(5 minutes)*
Ask students to answer these questions.

- You could recognize an author's work by its [style].
- [Imagery] is created with details that help readers form a metal picture.
- If you were making a Web page, what elements would you consider? [formatting, graphics, design].

Original content Copyright © by Holt, Rinehart and Winston. Additions and changes to the original content are the responsibility of the instructor.

Differentiating Instruction

Cub Pilot on the Mississippi The Grandfather
About StoryCorps

A. Match words with their opposites. Write the letter of the correct antonym next to each word.

_____ 1. indulgent

_____ 2. judicious

_____ 3. transient

_____ 4. meager

_____ 5. inoffensive

a. foolish

b. generous

c. rude

d. permanent

e. strict

B. Circle the letter of the word that best fits the clue.

1. Clue: Some classmates caught a friend cheating.

   A) hovered   B) confronted

2. Clue: The school team lost the state championship game

   A) sulked   B) scared

3. Clue: The driver's ed class you wanted to take is only offered on Saturday mornings.

   A) constrain   B) gurgle

4. Everyone had to do extra laps at practice because someone arrived late.

   A) facilitate   B) collective

C. Use the academic vocabulary words to complete the following paragraph about "The Grandfather," by Gary Soto.

appeal   attitude   establishes   enhanced

Gary Soto writes about his grandfather with a loving (1) _____. His

grandfather is a hard worker, which Soto (2) _____ with examples from

his grandfather's life. At first, the young Soto doesn't seem to care about his grandfather's fruit

trees. But over time, as the trees grows, Soto's appreciation is (3) _____.

With delicious details that are meant to (4) _____ to the senses, Soto

describes the fruits of his grandfather's labor.

Original content Copyright © by Holt, Rinehart and Winston. Additions and changes to the original content are the responsibility of the instructor.

Selection Test

Cub Pilot on the Mississippi Mark Twain

COMPREHENSION, SKILLS, AND VOCABULARY **Circle the letter of the best answer to each of the following items.**

1. In the selection, what is the narrator's main problem?

   A) He wants to be a pilot but cannot get training.

   B) He has a very mean supervisor.

   C) He is unhappy that his brother is on the boat.

   D) He does not like George Ritchie's teasing.

2. When the captain learns that the narrator has "pounded" Brown, he—

   A) makes the narrator leave the steamboat

   B) punishes the narrator by making him work more with Brown

   C) encourages the narrator secretly to fight Brown off the boat

   D) makes both Brown and the narrator find new jobs

3. When describing Twain's tone in the story, you might say it is—

   A) comical   C) formal

   B) sad   D) bitter

4. Which sentence below is an accurate paraphrase of this quotation from the selection?

   "…but he was not equipped for this species of controversy."

   A) He did not have the correct gear for fishing on the river.

   B) He did not have the strength to move forward.

   C) He did not have weapons for this type of battle.

   D) He did not know how to argue in that way.

5. Which of the following is the best example of someone who is **indulgent**?

   A) She punished the children when they did wrong.

   B) She forgave the children and gave them treats.

   C) She expected children to always do their best.

   D) She disliked children and tried to avoid them.

6. Think about what kind of man Brown is. Use the organizer below to note your ideas. Then write a short character sketch about him.

Introductory statement: Brown has many traits, including ….
Two or three supporting sentences: From the selection, we know that he looks… He acts…. Other characters view Brown as…
Concluding statement: In conclusion, Brown can best be described as….

Original content Copyright © by Holt, Rinehart and Winston. Additions and changes to the original content are the responsibility of the instructor.

Differentiating Instruction

Collection 5
Selection Test

The Grandfather Gary Soto

COMPREHENSION, SKILLS, AND VOCABULARY Circle the letter of the best
answer to each of the following items.

1. About how long does it take for the avocado tree to start bearing fruit?

    A) five years   C) one year

    B) ten years   D) twenty years

2. What is one reason that the grandfather likes to grow fruit trees?

    A) He thinks that meat is bad for you.

    B) He thinks that fruit is good for you.

    C) He thinks that he can save money by growing his own fruit.

    D) He thinks that he can make a lot of money by selling the fruit.

3. The following example of imagery in the story appeals to which sense?

    "A lemon tree hovered over the clothesline."

    A) taste   C) sight

    B) hearing   D) touch

4. Which sentence below is an accurate generalization about the narrator's grandfather?

    A) He is a patient, thrifty man.

    B) He is impatient and unhappy in California.

    C) He cares more about fruit trees than he cares about his family.

    D) He doesn't work hard, but spends time in the backyard instead.

5. Which of the following is the best example of someone who **sulked**?

    A) After she won the game, she did a little dance.

    B) After she lost the game, she pouted in a corner.

    C) After she tied for first place, she shook hands with her teammates.

    D) After she lost the game, she stomped off the field angrily.

6. How did the narrator's feelings about the avocado tree change over time? Use
    the graphic organizer below to gather your ideas. Then write a brief paragraph.

Introductory statement: At first, the narrator….
Two or three supporting sentences: Then, as he got older, he,…By the end of the essay, he …
Concluding statement: Therefore, I think that narrator's feelings changed from….

Original content Copyright © by Holt, Rinehart and Winston. Additions and changes to the original content are the responsibility of the instructor.

Collection 5
Selection Test

About StoryCorps

COMPREHENSION, SKILLS, AND VOCABULARY Circle the letter of the best answer to each of the following items.

1. On what is the StoryCorps project modeled?

    A) the Works Progress Administration of the 1930s

    B) the New Deal of the 1930s

    C) the New Frontier of the 1960s

    D) the Contract with America of the 1990s

2. What do the organizers of StoryCorps hope to accomplish?

    A) They want to record many people's songs.

    B) They want to record many people's short stories.

    C) They want to record many people's life stories.

    D) They want to record many people's likenesses.

3. Which of the following is an example of a graphic element in "About StoryCorps"?

    A) type   C) heading

    B) photograph   D) structure

4. Which sentence below best explains StoryCorps' goal?

    A) "Our first StoryBooth opened in New York City's Grand Central Terminal…"

    B) "We handle all the technical aspects of the recording."

    C) "We've tried to make the experience as simple as possible…"

    D) "StoryCorps celebrates our shared humanity and collective identity."

5. Which of the following is the best example of someone who is a **facilitator**?

    A) As the owner of the company, Gina was in charge of its products.

    B) When the new computers were installed, Carlos helped students use them.

    C) Since he started at a new school, Koji had lots of questions.

    D) As a member of the team, Joanna was a valuable player.

6. Imagine that you took part in a StoryCorps interview. Which one would be more meaningful to you: a CD of the interview or having the interview archived in the Library of Congress? Use the graphic organizer below as you construct your response.

Introductory statement: I believe that getting a CD of the interview is/is not more meaningful because…
Two or three supporting sentences: First of all,…Additionally,….For those reasons,…
Concluding statement: In conclusion, I think…

Original content Copyright © by Holt, Rinehart and Winston. Additions and changes to the original content are the responsibility of the instructor.

Differentiating Instruction

Collection 5
Collection Summative Test

**VOCABULARY SKILLS Complete the sentences below by using the collection
vocabulary words from the list below.**

transient   indulgent   confronted

meager   collective

1. The _____ grandmother gave the children lots of attention.

2. When Juan_____ his sister, she admitted she lost his videogame.

3. The _____ goal of our band is to create great music.

4. The family was _____, having lived in five different cities in five years.

5. The _____ amount of food at lunch left everyone hungry.

LITERARY AND READING SKILLS Circle the letter of the best answer.

6. A writer's **diction** is his or her—
    A) word choice
    B) plot
    C) setting
    D) character

7. **Imagery** is the use of words or phrases that—
    A) rhyme and use alliteration
    B) spring from the imagination
    C) appeal to our senses
    D) describe a document's purpose

8. A set of instructions is an example of which type of writing?
    A) personal essay
    B) functional document
    C) memoir
    D) autobiography

**LANGUAGE AND WRITING SKILLS Correct each run-on sentence by adding
semicolons where they belong.**

9. Jorge, Mia, and Peter played baseball I played tennis.

10. The bicyclist peddled quickly I accidentally walked into her path.

Original content Copyright © by Holt, Rinehart and Winston. Additions and changes to the original content are the responsibility of the instructor.

Collection 6
Graphic Organizer

from An Indian's Views of Indian Affairs Chief Joseph

Emotional Appeals Chart Writers often use **emotional appeals** to persuade readers. Emotional appeals include the use of **loaded words,** or words with strong emotional impact (such as *patriotism*). They also include **anecdotes**, which are brief, true stories that appeal to a reader's emotions.

Use this chart to identify and analyze the emotional appeals that Chief Joseph uses in his speech. Read each passage from the speech. Then write any loaded words in the second column and any anecdotes in the third column.

Passage	Loaded Words	Anecdotes
"I am tired of talk that comes to nothing. It makes my heart sick when I remember all the good words and all the broken promises."		
"When I think of our condition, my heart is heavy. I see men of my race treated as outlaws and driven from country to country or shot down like animals."		
"Let me be a free man – free to travel, free to stop, free to work, free to trade where I choose, free to choose my own teachers, free to follow the religion of my fathers, free to think and talk and act for myself – and I will obey every law and submit to the penalty."		
"Then the Great Spirit Chief who rules above will smile upon this land and send rain to wash out the bloody spots made by brothers' hands from the face of the earth."		

Original content Copyright © by Holt, Rinehart and Winston. Additions and changes to the original content are the responsibility of the instructor.

Differentiating Instruction

Collection 6
Graphic Organizer

Ain't I a Woman? Sojourner Truth

Summarizing Diagram A **summary** is a short restatement of the important ideas in a work. When you summarize, you restate the main idea in a passage.

Use this diagram to summarize some of the passages from "Ain't I a Woman?"
Think about what the passage is saying and then write a one-sentence summary
in the oval.

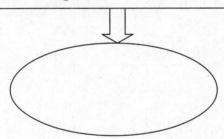

"Then that little man in black there, he says women can't have as much rights as men, 'cause Christ wasn't a woman! Where did your Christ come from? Where did your Christ come from? From God and a woman! Man had nothing to do with Him."

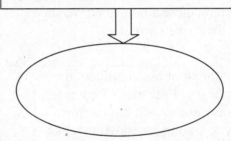

"If the first woman God ever made was strong enough to turn the world upside down all alone, these women together ought to be able to turn it back, and get it right side up again! And now they is asking to it, the men better let them."

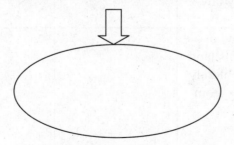

"That man over there says that women need to be helped into carriages, and lifted over ditches, and to have the best place everywhere. Nobody ever helps me into carriages, or over mud-puddles, or gives me any best place! And ain't I a woman?"

Original content Copyright © by Holt, Rinehart and Winston. Additions and changes to the original content are the responsibility of the instructor.

Differentiating Instruction

Lesson Plan and Teaching Strategies

Cinderella's Stepsisters Toni Morrison

Preteach

PREREADING SKILLS *(10 minutes)*

Build Background/Set a Purpose To set a purpose for reading, lead a discussion about role models with students. Ask: *From whom did you learn the most important lessons about how to treat others? What were those lessons? Why were they important?* Explain that in this graduation address Nobel-prize winning author Toni Morrison explores the stepmother as a role-model to her two daughters in the classic tale of "Cinderella." For students unfamiliar with the tale in any of its cultural iterations, an English translation of the original Grimm fairy tale may be found at www.cs.cmu.edu/~spok/grimmtmp. Or you may wish to read a retelling of the story from a picture book for children, e.g. *Cinderella* by Barbara Karlin, illustrated by James Marshall (Little Brown, 1989).

After reading the fairy tale, discuss with students what the stepsisters learned from their mother about the abuse of power. Have students speculate about the relevance of this story to a group of young female graduates about to embark on their own lives and careers. Ask: *In what way might this story be a cautionary tale for women who will potentially wield power?* Have students read to find out what Morrison believes is the answer to this question.

VOCABULARY SKILLS *(10 minutes)*

Preteach Vocabulary Words Review the meanings of the vocabulary in the Word Bank. Then give students these sentences to complete.

1. A bad beginning did not [diminish] our hope for success.

2. Without Tad's [indispensable] help, we might have failed.

3. When there's a big job to be done, no one's help is [expendable].

4. We must stay on task and let nothing [deflect] our attention.

5. We cannot let ambition overcome our kinder, gentler [sensibilities].

Remind students to watch for these words as they read the story.

LANGUAGE COACH SKILL *(10 minutes)*

Synonyms and Antonyms Explain that a *synonym* is a word that has the same or about the same meaning as another word. An *antonym* is a word that has the opposite meaning of another word. Display the Vocabulary Words and read them aloud. Review their meanings, if necessary. Then have students decide which word (or words) on the list:

- is a synonym for *essential* (indispensable)

- is an antonym for *increase* (diminish)

- is an antonym for *necessary* (expendable)

RESOURCES

In *The Holt Reader:* "Cinderella's Sisters" for students who need more scaffolding in a workbook format

In this book: *Vocabulary Skill Builder,* p. 120; "Cinderella's Sisters" Selection Test, p. 121

Consult *Holt Audio Library* for recordings of most selections

WORD BANK

deflect
expendable
indispensable
sensibilities
diminish

ACADEMIC VOCABULARY

Preteaching Academic Vocabulary
(5 minutes)
Write these terms and their meanings on a chalkboard or transparency. Review them with the students before previewing the selection.

Intent: A writer's purpose in writing a work that it meant to persuade the reader.
Tone: The attitude expressed in the work toward the subject or the audience.
Analogy: A comparison used to explain a complicated or unfamiliar concept by relating it to something familiar.
Influence: Persuade or affect someone.

Original content Copyright © by Holt, Rinehart and Winston. Additions and changes to the original content are the responsibility of the instructor.

Differentiating Instruction

- is a synonym for *feelings* (sensibilities)
- is an antonym for *attract* (deflect)
- are antonyms for each other (expendable; indispensable)

As they read "Cinderella's Stepsisters," have students look for examples of Toni Morrison's use of antonyms and synonyms in her writing.

LITERARY FOCUS *(30 minutes)*

Author's Argument and Tone Explain that the selection they are about to read is a speech that is an example of persuasive writing. Point out that persuasive writing tries to get the reader—or in this case the listener—to think or behave in a certain way. Persuasive writing presents an **argument** for a particular idea. Point out that *argument* can mean "quarrel or disagreement," but in this case it means the presentation of facts of ideas with the intention of persuading the reader or listener.

To help students understand the concept of argument in persuasive writing, suggest to your students a topic that is familiar and likely to elicit differing opinions. Select a topic that you think everyone in the group will have an opinion about. A possibility might be global warming. Ask: *Can what we do as individuals make a meaningful difference?* Have students share their opinions and offer reasons to support their positions.

Use the students' statements as a vehicle for talking about **tone**. After each student outlines his or her argument on the chosen topic, comment on the **tone** of the statement, expressing what you perceive to be the student's attitude toward the topic or the audience. For example, you might say that a student's statement shows a sense of urgency, a feeling of hopefulness, or an attitude of disinterest. After you have modeled "reading" the tone of students' statements, involve students in the discussion of the tone of their peers' arguments. Talk together about how tone can impact or influence the effectiveness of a persuasive argument.

READING FOCUS *(30 minutes)*

Questioning Tell students that, in order to get the most out of what they read, they need to be actively engaged in reading. That means thinking about what they are reading and asking questions. Say: *Questioning is a way to get involved with what you are reading and to be sure that what you're reading makes sense.*

Model the strategy of asking questions by reading aloud the first paragraph of "Cinderella's Stepsisters," pausing from time to time to ask questions. For example, you might pause after the sentence ending "a feeling of urgency" to ask: *Why does "Cinderella" cause a feeling of urgency?* You might pause again after "prince with a foot fetish" to ask:

READING SKILL
Especially for LDN
(15 minutes)
This selection was originally delivered as a speech. To help students appreciate the tone of the work, read the work aloud in the way that Morrison might have delivered it. After students have heard the speech "performed," discuss how the tone of the work influenced whether or not the listener was persuaded by the argument.

Especially for ELL
Help students understand the concept of **tone** in writing by relating it to tone of voice. Explain that the tone used in saying something sometimes communicates as much as the words themselves. Use a simple sentence like "I didn't do that" to demonstrate this. Say the sentence in a way that communicates regret, defiance, apology, disgust, scorn. Talk about how the different ways you said the sentence reveal different attitudes toward the listener and toward "that."

READING FOCUS
Question Chart

Questions	Answers

Original content Copyright © by Holt, Rinehart and Winston. Additions and changes to the original content are the responsibility of the instructor.

Differentiating Instruction

Why does she say this about the prince? Pause again after "It is her stepsisters that interest me" to ask: *Why do the stepsisters interest her?* Finally, at the end of the paragraph, ask: *Where is she going with this?*

Point out that as you read on some questions get answered right away—sometimes in the next sentence or two. Some questions require you to make your own judgment. Other questions require you to read further in the text to find the answers. *Where is she going with this?* is that kind of question. Ask students to use a Question Chart to record their questions as they read, especially the ones that remain unanswered when they have finished reading a paragraph. As they find the answers, have them write them in the right column.

Direct Teach
(30 minutes)

Chunk the Text Help students pace their reading by dividing the selection into "chunks" or parts. After the students have read each part, talk about the questions they asked themselves as they read that part and the answers they discovered.

Part 1: ends p. 543, col. 2: "…care of their own mother?"
Part 2: ends p. 544, col 1: "…deflect their anger."
Part 3: ends p. 544, col 2: "…or your stepsister."
Part 4: ends p. 544, col 2: "Just the two of us."

Check for Understanding

WRITING FOCUS *(15 minutes)*

Writing Style Point out that repetition and the contrast of opposites are notable characteristics of Morrison's **writing style** in this speech. To illustrate this, read aloud the paragraph on page 544, column 1, that begins *I am alarmed by* . . . and ends with *is first-order business.* Ask students to listen, as you read, for examples of repetition (three sentences beginning *I am alarmed* . . . the repeated word *violence*) and examples of contrasting opposites (*who shall flourish* . . . *who shall wither; the deserving poor* . . . *the undeserving poor; which life is expendable* . . .*which is indispensable; the power to do it* . . . *the right to do it*).

Have students explore the selection to locate other examples of repetition and contrast. Encourage students to talk about the writing style and tell what, if anything it reminds them of, and why it might be an especially effective style for a speech.

Think As A Reader/Writer Remind students that Morrison's speech gives advice to young women graduating from college. Ask: *What advice would you give students who are just starting at our school?* Have students share their ideas. Explore how the ideas could be expressed using repetition and contrast. Then ask students to write a paragraph that gives advice to new students and uses repetition and contrast to present their argument.

Original content Copyright © by Holt, Rinehart and Winston. Additions and changes to the original content are the responsibility of the instructor.

READING SKILL
Especially for RGP
(10 minutes)
Introduce students to the concept of **analogy**. Explain that an analogy is a comparison that uses something familiar and concrete to introduce or explain a more abstract concept or idea. Talk about how Morrison uses Cinderella's stepsisters as a way of introducing and illustrating abuse of power. Explore what effect this analogy would have had on the audience for this speech.

VOCABULARY SKILL
Especially for ELL
(5 minutes)
Morrison uses some terms in her speech that will be confusing to students learning English. Discuss these with students.
killing floor (p. 544): A reference to the place in a slaughterhouse where animals are killed, this has come to mean any place of difficulty and struggle.
rainbow journey (p. 544): This use of *rainbow* as an adjective may make reference to seeking the pot of gold at the end of the rainbow.

READING/WRITING
Especially for RGP
(5 minutes)
Point out that another feature of Morrison's writing style is the use of incomplete sentences and sentences that begin with conjunctions—*Because, But, Or.* Explain that this is a liberty that experienced writers sometimes take, especially when writing something that is meant to be spoken. Students, however, should make an effort always to write complete sentences and to avoid starting a sentence with a conjunction.

Differentiating Instruction

Graphic Organizer

The Next Green Revolution Alex Nikolai Steffen

Argument Support Chart In persuasive writing, authors make an **argument.** To convince the reader to accept their views, they provide **support**, or evidence. Types of support include facts, statistics, examples, and quotes from experts.

Use this chart to identify the kinds of support that Alex Nikolai Steffen uses in the essay "The Next Green Revolution." In the second column, write what kind of support he uses. He may use more than one kind. In the third column, explain which evidence you found most convincing.

Passage	Type of Support Used	Most Convincing
"For decades, environmentalists have warned of a coming climate crisis. Their alarms went unheeded, and last year we reaped an early harvest: a singularly ferocious hurricane season, record snowfall in New England, the worst-ever wildfires in Alaska, artic glaciers at their lowest ebb in millennia, catastrophic drought in Brazil, devastating floods in India – portents of global warming's destructive potential."		
"Efficiency creates value. The number one U.S. industrial product is waste. Waste is worse than stupid; it's costly; which is why we're seeing businesspeople in every sector getting a jump on the competition by consuming less water, power and materials."		
"Cities beat suburbs. Manhattanites use less energy than most people in North America. Sprawl eats land and snarls traffic. Building homes close together is a more efficient use of space and infrastructure. It also encourages walking, promotes public transit, and fosters community."		

From "The Next Green Revolution" by Alex Nikolai Steffen from *Wired Magazine,* May 2006.
Copyright © 2006 by **Alex Nikolai Steffen.** Reproduced by permission of the author.

Original content Copyright © by Holt, Rinehart and Winston. Additions and changes to the original content are the responsibility of the instructor.

Differentiating Instructions

Collection 6
Graphic Organizer

Why I Wrote Persepolis/Setting the Record Straight/Graphic Novels 101

Persuasive Techniques Chart To persuade readers, authors use different techniques. They use **exposition** to explain or inform, **narration** about a series of events, and **persuasion** to convince readers to believe or act in a certain way.

The three writers in the selections all use the three persuasive techniques. In the chart below, give examples from the texts of each technique. A few examples have been provided.

Persuasive Techniques	Exposition	Narration	Persuasion
Why I Wrote *Persepolis*		"From the time I came to France in 1994, I was always telling stories about life in Iran to my friends. We'd see pieces about Iran on television, but they didn't represent my experience at all. I had to keep saying, 'No, it's not like that there.'	
Setting the Record Straight			"But for comics, this attention has been rare. Let's see if we can help rectify the situation."
Graphic Novels 101	"One of the biggest benefits of graphic novels is that they often attract kids who are considered 'reluctant' readers. This is not just hype – the combination of less text, narrative support from images, and a freeing of reading outside the expected canon often relieves the tension of reader expectations for kids who are not natural readers...."		

Slightly adapted from "On Writing *Persepolis*" (from "Why I Wrote *Persepolis*," "Writing a Graphic Novel is Like Making a Movie," and "What I Wanted to Say") by Marjane Satrapi from *Pantheon Graphic Novels*. Reproduced by permission of **L'Association, Paris, France.**

Original content Copyright © by Holt, Rinehart and Winston. Additions and changes to the original content are the responsibility of the instructor.

Lesson Plan and Teaching Strategies

Kaavya Viswanathan Sandhya Nanknai
Kaavya Syndrome Joshua Foer

Preteach

PREREADING SKILLS *(20 minutes)*

Build Background/Set a Purpose Lead a discussion about **plagiarism** with students. Explain that plagiarism is taking all or part of someone else's work and presenting it as one's own original work. Make it clear that plagiarism is unacceptable and illegal behavior that has different penalties depending upon the situation. Describe some obvious ways that a student might be guilty of plagiarism. (Handing in a paper someone else wrote as their own; picking up material word for word from a reference book without acknowledging the source)

Explore the concept of plagiarism further by having students consider the following situations. In each case, ask the students to decide if they think this is an example of plagiarism, and explain why or why not.

- A student uses information he finds on a history website to write a report on the Whig Party in the United States. He reorganizes the facts and restates them, but he does not identify his source.

- A student completely rewrites a research paper written by an older sibling to make it sound like her own work and hands it in for a class assignment.

- A writer writes a mystery story in which the main character is modeled after Agatha Christie's Miss Marple.

- A writer finds an obscure novel published in the early 20th century. He finds out that the copyright has lapsed, so he inputs the text on his computer, gives it a new title, and submits the manuscript to a publisher as his own work.

VOCABULARY SKILLS *(10 minutes)*

Preteach Vocabulary Words Review the meanings of the vocabulary in the Word Bank. Then give students these sentences to complete.

1. He claimed that copying the idea was [inadvertent], not deliberate.

2. Rhea could write like Dr. Seuss because she had [internalized] the language and rhythm of his books.

3. Will is a diligent researcher who is known for his [perseverance].

Remind students to watch for these words as they read the story.

LANGUAGE COACH SKILL *(20 minutes)*

Word Parts Display the Vocabulary Word *internalized*. Explain that internalize is a verb formed by adding *-ize* to the adjective internal.

RESOURCES

In *The Holt Reader:* "Kaavya Viswanathan" and "Kaavya Syndrome" for students who need more scaffolding in a workbook format

In *Holt Pronunciation Resources* video support of phoneme sounds and spelling

In this book: *Vocabulary Skill Builder,* p.120; "Kaavya Viswanathan/Kaavya Syndrome" Selection Test, p. 122

Consult *Holt Audio Library* for recordings of most selection2

WORD BANK
internalized
perseverance
inadvertent

ACADEMIC VOCABULARY

Preteaching Academic Vocabulary
(5 minutes)
Write these terms and their meanings on a chalkboard or transparency. Review them with the students before previewing the selection.

Pro and con arguments: Opposing views on the same issues.
Counter: Oppose or take issue with
Valid: Supported by facts
Verify: Prove something to be true

Original content Copyright © by Holt, Rinehart and Winston. Additions and changes to the original content are the responsibility of the instructor.

Differentiating Instructions

Name and display some other verbs formed by adding *-ize* to another word: *symbolize, formalize, itemize, idealize, standardize*. Relate the meaning of the word with *-ize* to the meaning of the base word.

Display the word *internal* and compare it with *external*. Point out that *internal* refers to things that are inside and *external* refers to things that are outside. The words are the same except for the prefixes, and they are opposites. Name and display other *in-* and *ex-* opposites, discussing their meaning as you do: *interior/exterior; inhale/exhale; introvert/extrovert; intramural/extramural.*

Point out that *inadvertent* also has the prefix *in-*. In this case, it adds the meaning "not" to the base word. *Inadvertent* means "not intentionally" or "not on purpose." Have students suggest other words they know in which the prefix *in-* adds the meaning "not." Possibilities include: *inadequate, inappropriate, incapable, incomplete, indirect, independent,* and so on.

As students read the two selections about Kaavya Viswanathan, have them look for words with other prefixes that add the meaning "not."

INFORMATIONAL TEXT FOCUS *(30 minutes)*

Evaluating Arguments Pose the following question: *When you think you know how you feel about an issue, and someone comes along and gets you to change your mind, what is it about that person's argument that convinces you?* Invite students to share their ideas.

Model how to evaluate whether an argument is strong or weak by saying: *There's a way to evaluate an argument. Ask yourself these questions:*

1. *What is the claim or position? What support is given?*
2. *Is the argument logical?*
3. *How comprehensive is the support?*

Read this argument aloud.

Students shouldn't be punished for plagiarism. After all, it's not like we are cheating anyone. We don't get paid for the writing we do, so it's not like we're stealing anything if once in a while, when we've got too much homework to do, we take something that someone else has written and put it in our own words. We've got too much to do anyway. People do it all the time. Lots of the stories in Shakespeare's plays are stories that other people wrote. He didn't write them himself, and he's supposed to be this great writer. If he can copy other people, why can't I?

Ask: *What position or claim does this argument make? What support is given?* Help students see that the claim is that students shouldn't be punished for plagiarism. The support offered is (1) they don't get paid for writing so they are not cheating anyone; (2) they have too much to do to be expected to write everything themselves; (3) people do it all the time.

Ask: *Is the argument logical?* Help students recognize how illogical the argument is. The argument is filled with **logical fallacies**. The argument

VOCABULARY SKILL
Especially for ELL
(10 minutes)
Point out that the prefix *in-* is a negative prefix in words like *informal, incomplete,* and *inadequate*. Explain that there are other prefixes that also add a negative meaning to words. Present the negative prefixes *un-* (*unkind, unhappy, uncover*), *non-* (*nonverbal, nonsense, nonfiction*), and *dis-* (*disagree, disadvantage, dishonest*). Explore the meanings of example words with and without the negative prefix.

Original content Copyright © by Holt, Rinehart and Winston. Additions and changes to the original content are the responsibility of the instructor.

Differentiating Instructions

contains lots of examples of **false cause and effect**: student should be immune from punishment because they don't get paid for writing; or they have too much homework; or Shakespeare used stories written by others, so they should be able to do it, too. Note the **hasty generalization** in the paragraph: "People do it all the time." Finally, talk about how mentioning Shakespeare in a completely false and irrelevant way might be seen as a kind of **personal attack**.

Ask: *How comprehensive is the support?* Help students see that the writer makes the point that students shouldn't be punished for plagiarism and then makes a lot of statements that don't offer any valid support.

Have students read the blog about Kaavya Viswanathan. Annotating a chart like the one at the right will help them organize their thinking.

Direct Teach
(30 minutes)

Pin Wheel Discussion Have students work in groups of eight: four students are facing in; four students are facing out. Students in the inside circle remain stationary throughout the discussion, while students in the outside circle move to their right prior to discussing each question.

Read aloud the blog on pages 580 and 581 while students read along. Pause at the letter A, and have a volunteer read the question at the bottom of the page. Allow the student facing each other to discuss the question for about five minutes, then rotate to the next partner. Continue reading the blog as students follow, repeating this procedure for questions: B, C, D, E, and F. Allow students pairs five minutes per question in order to evaluate the argument.

Check for Understanding
WRITING FOCUS *(15 minutes)*

Evaluating Arguments Have students work in groups of three to evaluate the argument in the Web article. Encourage them to use the Evaluation Chart. After they have identified the claim and support presented in the article, they should discuss the logic of the argument and decide if reasons and evidence presented are comprehensive. As the groups discuss the selection, move from group to group to help guide the conversation and assist in evaluating the arguments.

Think As A Reader/Writer Ask: *Which selection to you think presents a more effective argument?* Have student share their opinions and discuss their reasons as a group. Then have each student decide which selection he or she thinks presents the most persuasive argument and write a paragraph explaining why. Students' paragraphs should state their opinion and give at least three reasons why they hold that opinion.

Claim and Support
Logic of Argument
Comprehensiveness

READING SKILL
Especially for RGP
(5 minutes)
Help students distinguish from among the examples cited of photographic memory by helping them create a word web. From a center circle labeled "Photographic Memory," extend five lines to five outer circles. Label them: Elizabeth, Savants; Shass Pollacks; Truman Capote; George Harrison. Work with students to take notes about each example of "photographic memory" before they decide whether or not the writer has supported his claim with sufficient evidence.

READING/WRITING
Especially for WGP
(10 minutes)
When students have completed their work, have them exchange papers with a classmate. Have them use questions similar to those they used to evaluate the selections to evaluate their classmate's paragraphs: (1) What opinion is expressed? What reasons are given? (2) Are the reasons logical? (3) How comprehensive are the reasons?

Original content Copyright © by Holt, Rinehart and Winston. Additions and changes to the original content are the responsibility of the instructor.

Collection 6

Targeted Strategies for Learners with Diverse Needs

READING SKILLS

Evaluating Arguments *(30 minutes)* Explain that arguments are only as strong as the logic or reasoning used to support them. Point out that the term "logical fallacy" means there has been an error in reasoning. Advise students to avoid these common fallacies when making an argument.

Fallacy	The Problem	Example
Bandwagon	Popularity or trends don't prove anything.	Everyone thinks the test was too hard.
Slippery Slope	Argument is based on an incorrect assumption.	If the test is too hard, I won't pass this class, and then I won't graduate.
Circular reasoning	Argument begins and ends with the same point.	If a test is too hard, how can I do well? Since I didn't do well, the test must have been too hard.
Sweeping Generalization	Argument ignores real differences between people or things.	If this test is too hard, all the tests will be too hard.
Ad Hominem	Argues by making a personal attack instead of using logic.	The test was too hard because the teacher is mean.

Have two groups of students hold a brief debate about a topic of interest at your school while another group evaluates the arguments. Ask the student evaluators to document any fallacies listed in the chart above.

LITERARY SKILLS

Author's Argument and Tone *(15 minutes)* Help students understand that an argument is a contest of ideas and not a personal disagreement. Point out that the tone should always be respectful. Discuss the following with the class:

- why a personal attack is a weak form of logic
- the possible consequences of taking a harsh tone
- what kind of language students can use to respectfully disagree with another student about something.

Be sure students understand that saying something negative about a person doesn't disprove his or her argument, and that taking a harsh tone can alienate people, thereby making the "attacker's" point or view far less persuasive.

Have students work with a partner to find quotes from each selection that are examples of each author's tone. Ask: *In which selection is the author's tone most effective? Explain your answer.*

- **Readings in Collection 6 Minimum Course of Study**
- "Cinderella's Stepsisters", p. 540
- "Kaavya Viswanathan; Kaavya Syndrome", p. 578

RESOURCES

In *The Holt Reader,* all three selections help students who need more scaffolding in a workbook format.

Consult *Holt Audio Library* for recordings of most selections.

TEACHING TIP

English-language learners may need to work on phrases that constitute polite criticism. Some graceful ways to point out errors include the following:
-Employs faulty logic
-Makes questionable assumptions
-Makes unproven statements
-Uses outdated facts
-Makes an irrelevant point
-Is confusing the meaning of _____
-Fails to consider _____

ALTERNATIVE ASSESSMENT *(5 minutes)*
Ask students to answer these questions.

- If the logic of an argument is weak the argument probably contains a [logical fallacy].
- [An argument] is not a personal disagreement.
- It's important to keep the [tone/logic] of an argument respectful.

Original content Copyright © by Holt, Rinehart and Winston. Additions and changes to the original content are the responsibility of the instructor.

Differentiating Instructions

Academic and Selection Vocabulary

Cinderella's Stepsisters Kaavya Viswanathan
Kaavya Syndrome

A. Write a "U" for unrelated, an "S" for synonym or an "A" for antonym
next to each pair of words..

_____ 1. expendable, necessary

_____ 2. diminish, reduce

_____ 3. perseverance, determination

_____ 4. internalized, substance

_____ 5. inadvertent, planned

B. Write an "E" for example or an "N" for non-example next to each vocabulary word.

_____ 1. deflect: knocking a ball away just as it is about to go in the basket

_____ 2. indispensable: a bag of used clothes to be donated

_____ 3. internalized: words of wisdom that help you in your life

_____ 4. sensibilities: not noticing a rude attitude

_____ 5. inadvertent: seeing your teaching in line at the supermarket

C. Use the academic vocabulary words to complete the following paragraph about "Cinderella's Sisters," by Toni Morrison.

valid   influence   verifies   counters

Toni Morrison wants to (1) _____ women to treat each other well, unlike

the way Cinderella's stepsisters treated her. Morrison (2) _____ the recent

portrayal of the stepsisters as ugly, clumsy, and stupid. She feels the recent portrayal isn't

(3) _____ because the original story suggests that these women were

powerful and elegant. Morrison (4) _____ this with a quote that states the

stepsisters were "beautiful and fair in appearance." Despite their physical beauty, Morrison

believes they *were* ugly in their abusive treatment of Cinderella!

Original content Copyright © by Holt, Rinehart and Winston. Additions and changes to the original content are the responsibility of the instructor.

Differentiating Instruction

Collection 6
Selection Test

Cinderella's Stepsisters Toni Morrison

COMPREHENSION, SKILLS, AND VOCABULARY Circle the letter of the best
answer to each of the following items.

1. Why do the stepsisters interest Toni Morrison?

    A) They are ugly, clumsy, and stupid.

    B) They are beautiful, elegant, and powerful.

    C) They are not the most memorable characters in "Cinderella" story.

    D) They have watched and joined in the brutal control of another woman.

2. What does Morrison say about the graduates who are hearing her speech?

    A) They share the same background.

    B) They all come from educated families.

    C) They will have the economic and social status of the stepsisters.

    D) They will use their power against other women like the stepsisters.

3. Which sentence best states the author's argument?

    A) Women are responsible for the fate of other women.

    B) Women have always used their power in an abusive way.

    C) Women should make choices based on their personal safety and security.

    D) Women should pursue their goals but also encourage those of other women.

4. Which words best describe the tone of this speech?

    A) humorous and clever

    B) angry and demanding

    C) important and heartfelt

    D) flattering and complimentary

5. Which quality do you think Morrison would find **indispensable** to the success of a women's
rights movement?

    A) the ability of women to nurture other women along the way

    B) the ability of women to fight the status quo and do what's never been done

    C) the ability of women to pursue their highest ambitions, no matter what the cost

    D) the ability of women to focus on a goal that is neither safe not secure

6. What recommendation would you make to students at your school to help them
get along? Use the organizer below to collect your ideas. Then write a short
paragraph.

Introductory statement: Everyone/No one should . . .
Two or three supporting sentences: First….In addition…For that reason…
Concluding statement. Thus I believe that everyone could….

Original content Copyright © by Holt, Rinehart and Winston. Additions and changes to the original content are the responsibility of the instructor.

Differentiating Instruction

Kaavya Viswanathan/Kaavya Syndrome

COMPREHENSION, SKILLS, AND VOCABULARY Circle the letter of the best
answer to each of the following items.

1. Which is the following is an example of plagiarism?

   A) using facts you read in a book in your own writing.

   B) writing something that reminds people of another work.

   C) writing something that is exactly like someone else's work.

   D) writing a story with a plot that is similar to another story's plot.

2. What does Sandhya Nankani say we should learn from Kaavya's experience?

   A) We should write in our own original voices.

   B) We should never try to learn from another writer's style.

   C) We shouldn't allow ourselves to be inspired by other writers.

   D) We should be careful not to memorize the work of other writers.

3. What claim made by Kaavya Viswanathan is challenged in "Kaavya Syndrome"?

   A) She had a photographic memory.

   B) She had internalized another author's work.

   C) She copied another author's style without realizing it.

   D) She had help developing the plot from a book packager.

4. Some examples thought to be photographic memory were actually attributed to—

   A) mental snapshots recalled with perfect accuracy

   B) a strong connection with another writer's style

   C) memorization and mnemonic techniques

   D) an unlimited human memory of people and events

5. Which of the following might happen if you **internalized** something?

   A) You wouldn't be able to repeat it word for word.

   B) You couldn't distinguish it from your own thoughts.

   C) You couldn't remember it unless you were hypnotized.

   D) You wouldn't remember it unless you used mnemonic techniques.

6. What do you think about Kaavya Viswanathan? Was she an unconscious
   copycat or an intentional plagiarist? Use the organizer below to collect your
   ideas. Then write your opinion and support it in a brief paragraph.

Introductory statement: I believe/don't believe that Kaavya was . . .
Two or three supporting sentences: First….In addition…For that reason…
Concluding statement. Thus I believe that Kaavya ….

Original content Copyright © by Holt, Rinehart and Winston. Additions and changes to the original content are the responsibility of the instructor.

Collection 6
Collection Summative Test

VOCABULARY SKILLS Complete the sentences below by using the collection vocabulary words from the list below.

deflect   expendable   indispensable   sensibilities

diminish   internalized   perseverance   inadvertent

1. Completing the job required determination and _____.

2. Every member of the team is important, and no one is _____.

3. The difficulty of the task did not _____ our resolve to succeed.

4. The mistake was _____ and not an attempt to harm the project.

5. Through it all, our teacher's advice and encouragement were _____.

LITERARY AND READING SKILLS Circle the letter of the best answer.

6. Which statement is the best definition of an **argument** in persuasive writing?

   A) disagreement between two characters in a story

   B) opposing views on the same issue expressed in the same work

   C) presentation of facts and ideas for the purpose of persuading

   D) summary of the main points in a speech or article

7. A **tone** of a piece of writing is—

   A) the choice of words used to describe things

   B) the rhythm of the language and length of sentences

   C) the use of figures of speech and imagery

   D) the attitude expressed toward the subject or the audience

LANGUAGE AND WRITING SKILLS Circle the letter of the best answer.

8. *Expendable* is an **antonym** for

   A) costly   B) essential

   C) unnecessary   D) discretionary

9. *Diminish* is a **synonym** for

   A) increase   B) unimportant

   C) disapproval   D) reduce

10. The prefix *in-* means "not" in the word

    A) internal   B) increase

    C) inaccurate   D) integrity

Original content Copyright © by Holt, Rinehart and Winston. Additions and changes to the original content are the responsibility of the instructor.

Lesson Plan and Teaching Strategies

Writing Workshop: Persuasive Essay
PREWRITING
Write an Opinion, or Thesis, Statement *(15 minutes)*

Review the purpose of a persuasive essay: *When you write a persuasive essay, you try to convince your audience to think or act in a certain way about an important issue.* Once students have brainstormed a list of topics, help them form their opinion, or thesis, statement by using thoughtful questions. Model with the examples given below. Advise students to choose an issue that they understand well; otherwise they may need to conduct preliminary research in order to take a position.

Topic/Issue	Question to think about
Rap music	Who do you think is the best rap artist?
Bullies	Do you agree with how bullying is handled in your school?
Pets	Do you think they are worth the trouble?

Collect Evidence *(15 minutes)*

Have students draw a concept web. Ask them to write their opinion statement in the center circle. Around the center circle, have them write their three supporting reasons, each in its own oval. Around each oval, have them add at least two pieces of evidence.

Then have students share their web with a partner and discuss each of these questions.

1. Do my three reasons relate to my opinion? Is each reason clear? Is each one strong?

2. Have I been able to find different kinds of evidence for my reasons? If not, where can I look?

3. Can you think of any arguments against my reasons and evidence? If so, what kind of evidence can make my opinion stronger?

DRAFTING
Organize Details *(10 minutes)*

Make sure students use their webs to draft their essays. Have students number the reasons in the webs to show the order they will discuss them. They can number each piece of evidence, as well. Explain that numbering can help them organize the body of the essay.

Review the framework on page 601 of the Student Edition. Remind students that they will state their opinion in the introduction and conclusion. In the conclusion they will also summarize the reasons that support their opinions. Then have students draft their essays.

TEACHING TIP
Students will find it helpful to work with a partner or group during the prewriting stage. Be sure to articulate what each partner discussion should accomplish during each activity. Scaffold work toward these goals by using the questions in the student book on page 599. Finally, make sure that students take time to adjust or edit their written materials after each discussion. You may need to prompt students to do this.

ESPECIALLY FOR ELL
(10 minutes)
Before English-language learners begin to write, they will need to develop adequate technical vocabulary related to their topic. Partner English-language learners with proficient English speakers. Have proficient speakers help English-language learners list words related to their chosen issue. Give students time to generate and revise their lists and to look up definitions as needed.

ESPECIALLY FOR WGP
Writers gaining proficiency will benefit from more time spent in partner discussions during prewriting. If possible, spend a few minutes alone with students after each partner discussion. Help students summarize what was discussed and plan how to revise their written materials.

Original content Copyright © by Holt, Rinehart and Winston. Additions and changes to the original content are the responsibility of the instructor.

Differentiating Instructions

EVALUATING AND REVISING

Review Content and Organization *(20 minutes)*

Give students time to focus on the following points in Evaluation Questions 1, 2, 3, and 5.

1. Start by identifying the opinion. The opinion should express a strong feeling or idea. It may use words such as *should, ought,* or *must.* Use the student draft on page 603 as an example of a good opening paragraph.

2. Be sure there are three reasons that support the opinion. A reason answers the question "Why?" It often includes the word *because.* Example: *We should have more parks in our city because people who live in places with parks are healthier and happier.*

3. Be sure there are two pieces of evidence to support each reason. Use the chart on page 600 that shows the different types of evidence.

5. Consider a possible counterargument against your point of view. Add a sentence that challenges this counterargument. Example: *Some people think parks are a waste of space, but the top-ranked cities in the nation all have many parks.*

Pair students with a partner to use the guidelines and the points above when they review each other's drafts.

Grammar Link: Parallel Structure *(15 Minutes)*

Parallel structure is a difficult concept for students who are struggling with writing. Work with concrete examples about number and tense. Review how to form number and tense.

Review parallel sentences and phrases. Dictate each set of examples and discuss which is clearer and why.

Confusing	Clear
We will use cell phones responsibly. **We didn't speak** with our friends during class. **I do not cheat** on tests.	**We will use** cell phones responsibly. **We will not speak** with our friends during class. **We will not cheat** on tests.
I promise we **will turn** the phones off before class, **turned** them on only in the halls, and **turning** them off again before the next class starts.	I promise we **will turn** the phones off before class, **will turn** them on only in the halls, and **will turn** them off again before the next class starts.

Then ask students to reread their essays to find and fix sentences or phrases that are not parallel.

TEACHING TIP

Wait until students are at the proofreading stage to introduce the grammar link lessons. Student gaining proficiency with writing will benefit from smaller and fewer steps in the pacing of the writing process and saving considerations of grammar for a later stage.

ESPECIALLY FOR ELL
(10 minutes)

When working with English-language learners on parallel structure, students may need extra practice with the final "s" at the end of third person plural verbs. Depending on level of language proficiency, students may benefit from practice with verb tenses. Ask students to give past and future forms of present tense verbs. Increase complexity according to students' readiness.

ESPECIALLY FOR LDN

Many students will benefit from an oral approach to parallel structure. They'll be able to hear the pattern more easily than recognizing it in their writing. Have students read their essays aloud to a partner or work with students on a one-to-one basis, as necessary.

Original content Copyright © by Holt, Rinehart and Winston. Additions and changes to the original content are the responsibility of the instructor.

Differentiating Instructions

Lesson Plan and Teaching Strategies

Listening and Speaking Workshop: Persuasive Speech

ADAPT THE ESSAY *(30 minutes)*

Explain to students that they will take the persuasive essay they have written and prepare it for an oral presentation. Have them follow these steps to prepare their speeches:

1. Read your persuasive essay aloud to yourself or a partner.

2. As you read, note any sentences or phrases that seem hard to read aloud. Mark those sentences with a colored marker or pen. You may need to revise them so that you can read them more smoothly.

3. Read your persuasive essay again, this time silently. As you read, mark all of the contractions with another color. Practice saying the consonant sounds in each contraction clearly, especially *isn't, don't, and won't,* as well as *shouldn't* and *wouldn't.*

4. Read your persuasive essay aloud a second time to yourself or a partner. This time make notes about gestures you might use to make a point or where you might raise or lower your voice.

5. Prepare your script. Rewrite or retype it in a larger format so that you can refer to it easily when you are speaking. Be sure to number the pages clearly.

6. Rehearse. Practice giving your speech in front of a mirror.

Delivering a Presentation

PRESENTING A GOOD FRONT *(10 minutes)*

Explain that non-verbal techniques can be more effective than words.

1. Eye contact communicates honesty and sincerity. You should make eye contact with as many audience members as possible.

2. Facial expressions are so important that they can take the place of a verbal message. Make sure your expressions are appropriate.

3. Simple gestures, such as nodding for "yes," shaking one's head for "no," and pointing one's finger can be very effective.

4. Posture—standing up straight and looking alert communicates confidence to the audience.

Have students fill out a checklist like the one below as they practice giving their speeches.

Non-verbal Techniques	Regularly	Sometimes	Never
Eye contact			
Facial expressions			
Simple gestures			
Posture			

Teaching Tip

For additional listening and writing practice, have students write down these six steps as you read them aloud.

ESPECIALLY FOR LDN

Have pairs of students read to one another and to rehearse their presentations together.

EVALUATION CRITERIA

Use these criteria to evaluate students' presentations:

- Gave their presentations smoothly with little hesitation or struggling with notes
- Pronounced most words correctly
- Varied phrasing and used good expression
- Focused on three reasons that clearly support the opinion statement
- Offered at least two pieces of evidence that clearly support each reason
- Demonstrated a command of non-verbal techniques

Original content Copyright © by Holt, Rinehart and Winston. Additions and changes to the original content are the responsibility of the instructor.

Differentiating Instructions

Unit 2; Skill Builder 1
Oral Language Skill Builder

Interview

UNDERSTAND THE SKILL A good way to gather information is by conducting an interview. You can learn a lot by asking those who witnessed an event firsthand about their experience.

Work with a partner to complete the chart. Then answer the discussion question below. When you are finished, explain your answers to different partners.

Practicing Interviewing skills	
Who?	Ask questions to learn the key facts about this person.
What?	Ask about interesting things has this person done or experienced.
When?	Ask when these events took place. What is special about that time in history?
Where?	Ask where these events took place. What is special about that place?
Why?	Ask why these events took place and why they were important.
How?	Ask how this person acted at the time. Would they do things differently today, if they were facing the same situation?

Extend Discussion Think about how you might phrase the questions to a friend, a family member, or a famous person. Discuss these situations with a partner.

- Suppose you wanted to make the questions more formal. How would you do that?
- Suppose you knew the person you were interviewing very well. How would you phrase your questions?

Original content Copyright © by Holt, Rinehart and Winston. Additions and changes to the original content are the responsibility of the instructor.

Unit 2; Skill Builder 2
Oral Language Skill Builder

Scoring a Debate

UNDERSTAND THE SKILL Being able to make your point persuasively and back it up can help you participate in class discussions and write better essays. How do you recognize a good argument when you hear one? Look for clear statements, logical thinking, support from facts and examples, and a reason you should care.

Choose an issue to debate about as a small group. Have someone keep score on the chart below. Take turns until everyone has had a chance to keep score. After the debate discuss the score and the questions below with your group.

Topic of Debate:

Pro:	Clear ☐	Unclear ☐
They say…	Logical ☐	Not logical ☐
	Enough support ☐	Not enough support ☐
Because…	Convincing ☐	Not Convincing ☐
Here's why…		

Con:	Clear ☐	Unclear ☐
They disagree…	Logical ☐	Not logical ☐
	Enough support ☐	Not enough support ☐
Because…	Convincing ☐	Not Convincing ☐
Therefore…		

Extend Discussion Discuss your scores with the group. Do you think your scores are fair? Do you think your classmates' scores were fair?

- What makes an argument convincing? Give examples.
- What makes an argument seem weak? Explain.

Original content Copyright © by Holt, Rinehart and Winston. Additions and changes to the original content are the responsibility of the instructor.

Unit 2, Skill Builder 3
English Language Skill Builder

Negative Sentence Patterns

UNDERSTAND THE SKILL In the English language, there are three ways to create a negative phrase or sentence.

- Use the word *not*, for example *I will* <u>not</u> *be attending the meeting.*
- Use a negative word, such as *nothing, never, no one, nowhere,* or *nobody.*
- Put *no* in front of a noun to show zero amount, for example <u>no</u> *cash* or <u>no</u> *time.*

It's important to choose only one type of negative to use within each sentence to avoid double negatives, such as *I* <u>don't</u> *have* <u>no</u> *cash.*

Work with a partner to change each sentence to a negative. Discuss your work with other student pairs. Did you form negatives in the same way?

1. Brown heard Henry deliver the message. (Hint: Use a negative word.)

   _____

2. Brown insisted that someone gave him the message. (Hint: Use a negative word.)

   _____

3. Brown had patience for the young apprentices. (Hint: Add the word <u>no</u>.)

   _____

4. The captain had affection for Brown. (Hint: Add the word <u>no</u>)

   _____

5. The captain was furious with Twain, which is what Twain had expected. (Hint: Add the word <u>not</u>.)

   _____

6. The captain warned Twain to repeat their conversation. (Hint: Add the word <u>not</u>.)

   _____

EXTEND DISCUSSION Answer the questions, using negative sentence patterns.

1. Was Brown ever kind to Twain and the other cub pilots?

   _____

2. What might Gary Soto's grandfather's say to kids jumping over his fruit trees?

   _____

3. Who would be excluded from telling their story through StoryCorps?

   _____

Original content Copyright © by Holt, Rinehart and Winston. Additions and changes to the original content are the responsibility of the instructor.

Differentiating Instruction

Unit 2; Skill Builder 4
English Language Skill Builder

Articles

UNDERSTAND THE SKILL An article is a word that helps identify a noun. An article usually comes before a noun that you can count.

Example: *I found a letter in an envelope in the trunk in the attic.*

• Use *a* and *an* before singular nouns that are not specific. Use *a* before a word that starts with a consonant sound. Use *an* before a word that starts with a vowel sound.

Example: *A girl rode her bike around the block for almost an hour.*

• Use *the* before singular nouns that are specific.

Example: *The newspaper delivery girl rode her bike around the block*

• Use *some*, *few*, *many*, and *a lot of* before plural nouns that are not specific.

Example: *Some children are going on a hayride.*

Write the letter on the line to match each article to its noun.

_____ 1. umbrella   a. some

_____ 2. visitors   b. the

_____ 3. fish   c. a

_____ 4. giant squid   d. an

EXTEND DISCUSSION Fill in the missing articles in these sentences about **Kaavya Viswanathan. Then discuss Kaavya's case with a partner. Do you think she intentionally copied Megan McCafferty's work? Why or why not?**

a	the	some	a lot of
an	few	many	

1. Kaavya read _____ novels while she was growing up.

2. _____ book Kaavya wrote was published.

3. _____ details from Kaavya's book were not original.

4. Kaavya didn't really have _____ explanation for this.

5. _____ people thought Kaavya plagiarized Megan McCafferty's work.

6. Did Kaavya copy McCafferty or does she just have _____ great memory?

Original content Copyright © by Holt, Rinehart and Winston. Additions and changes to the original content are the responsibility of the instructor.

          Differentiating Instructions

Unit 2
Summative Test

LITERARY AND READING SKILLS

A. Circle the letter of the best answer. *(25 points; 5 points each)*

1. An author's **style** is—

   A) the way a writer uses language

   B) the attitude the writer has toward the topic

   C) the point of view a writer uses in his or her writing

   D) the way the characters in a writer's story act and talk

2. Which of these sentences is an example of **imagery**?

   A) She looked him straight in the eye and nodded in agreement.

   B) She was careful about everything and hated any kind of disorder.

   C) She was a large and comfortable woman, with hair the color of Spanish moss.

   D) Before leaving the house, she checked that all the doors and windows were locked.

3. When you **paraphrase** something, you—

   A) read it aloud word for word

   B) put something in your own words

   C) tell what you were thinking about as you read it

   D) read it the way you think the story character would say it

4. In persuasive writing, an **argument** is—

   A) the author's use of logical fallacy

   B) the author's attitude toward the subject matter

   C) the account of a disagreement between two characters

   D) the presentation of facts and ideas to influence the reader's thinking

5. When you make a **generalization**, you—

   A) use specific details to make a larger point

   B) ignore differences between people or things

   C) ask yourself if what you are reading always makes sense

   D) make a statement that is true for everyone in every situation

Original content Copyright © by Holt, Rinehart and Winston. Additions and changes to the original content are the responsibility of the instructor.

Differentiating Instructions

B. Complete each sentence with one of the literary or reading skills shown below. *(25 points; 5 points each)*

questioning   tone   format   style   logical fallacy

6. A functional document should have a. _____ that makes it easy to follow and understand.

7. Short sentences and dialogue flavored with Spanish and Spanglish words are characteristics of Gary Soto's _____.

8. The author's argument was based on _____, and therefore it failed completely to persuade the thoughtful reader.

9. It was clear from the author's _____ that she thought growing up in a big city was an exciting and challenging experience.

10. The strategy of _____ is a way to get involved in what you are reading and to be sure that what you're reading making sense.

Read the question below. Then write a short response on the lines. *(50 points)*

Author's Style

11. How would you describe Toni Morrison's style in "Cinderella's Stepsisters"? What would you say about the way she used language in this work?

_____

_____

_____

_____

_____

Original content Copyright © by Holt, Rinehart and Winston. Additions and changes to the original content are the responsibility of the instructor.

My Father's Song/ First Lesson

Visualizing Diagram When you see in your mind what you are reading on the page, you are **visualizing**. Poetry uses many descriptive words that appeal to the senses of sight, hearing, smell, taste, and touch. Visualizing while you read poetry can help make the poem come alive.

Choose one of the poems and use this diagram to fill in the sensory details that help you visualize the poem's images. Some senses may not be found in the poem.

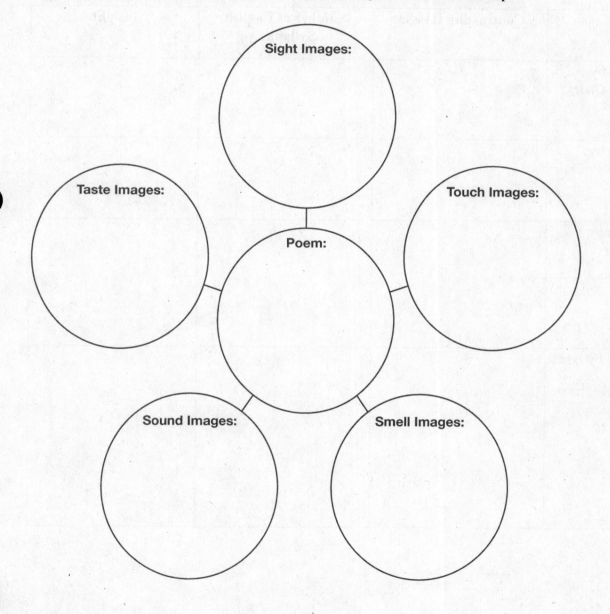

Original content Copyright © by Holt, Rinehart and Winston. Additions and changes to the original content are the responsibility of the instructor.

Differentiating Instruction

Haiku

Elements of Haiku Chart Haiku is a form of Japanese poetry that has three lines. A haiku usually presents two contrasting images—one often from nature. In Japanese, each haiku contains just 17 syllables. It may also contain a seasonal word and end with a moment of insight.

Use this chart to list examples from the four haiku of the form's elements.

	Contrasting Images	Number of English Syllables	Insight
Haiku by Miura Chora			
Haiku by Chiyo			
Haiku by Basho			
Haiku by Issa			

Original content Copyright © by Holt, Rinehart and Winston. Additions and changes to the original content are the responsibility of the instructor.

Differentiating Instruction

Lesson Plan and Teaching Strategies

A Blessing James Wright

Preteach

LISTENING COMPREHENSION SKILLS *(10 minutes)*
Build Background/Set a Purpose Discuss Build Background on p. 653. Explain that James Wright was an important 20th Century American poet who won the Pulitzer Prize for his poetry.

Have students look ahead at the photograph of horses. Explain that the poem tells about the author's experience in the 1950s of seeing two horses in Rochester, Minnesota. Point out Rochester, Minnesota on a classroom map.

Preview these details about the poem:

- "A Blessing" tells about a man going with his friend to look at two horses near a highway.

- Wright uses real details in the poem, such as the location where he sees the two horses (Rochester, Minnesota).

- Wright extends the true-life experience of going to see two horses into something greater.

Point out that animals and natural beauty have inspired poets throughout the ages. In this poem, Wright suggests that the horses have human emotions, such as loneliness. Ask: *Have you ever looked at an animal and thought about what or whether it was thinking and feeling?*

VOCABULARY SKILLS *(10 minutes)*
Preteach Vocabulary Words Review the meanings of the vocabulary in the Word Bank. Then give students these sentences to complete.

1. The deer [bounds] away from the road when it hears a car.
2. The kitten [nuzzled] the girl's arm, purring happily.
3. At [twilight], when it started getting dark, we saw bats flying.
4. The mother began to [caress] her baby's hands to stop his crying.

Remind students to watch for these words as they read the story.

LANGUAGE COACH SKILL *(10 minutes)*
Word Origins Explain that knowing where a word comes from can help you understand its meaning now. Discuss the following—

- The word *highway* comes from the Old English word *heiweg*, which means the main road from one town to another. (p. 654)

- The word *pasture* comes from the Latin word *pastus,* which means "to feed or graze." (p. 654).

- The word *delicate* comes from the Latin word *delicatus,* which means "dainty." (p. 654)

RESOURCES
In *The Holt Reader:* "A Blessing" for students who need more scaffolding in a workbook format

In this book: *Vocabulary Skill Builder,* p. 156; "A Blessing" Selection Test, p. 157.

Consult *Holt Audio Library* for recordings of most selections.

Especially for ELL
(5 minutes or less)
Point out that the word "blessing" can mean a good thing that makes your life better. It can also have a religious meaning similar to a prayer, as in a priest offering his blessing.

WORD BANK
twilight
bounds
nuzzled
caress

ACADEMIC VOCABULARY
Preteaching Academic Vocabulary
(5 minutes)
Write these terms and their meanings on a chalkboard or transparency. Review them with the students before previewing the selection.

Imagery: Words or phrases that appeal to our senses.
Theme: The main message of the piece of writing.

Original content Copyright © by Holt, Rinehart and Winston. Additions and changes to the original content are the responsibility of the instructor.

Differentiating Instruction

Write these sentences on the board. Have students complete each one by adding a word from the box.

| highway | pasture | delicate |

1. The sheep grazed in the [pasture].
2. The [highway] is the fastest route between the two cities.
3. The china doll was [delicate] and dainty.

LITERARY FOCUS (20 minutes)

Imagery and Theme Explain: *Writers, especially poets, use words and phrases that have to do with our five senses. This kind of writing is called imagery. Listen to the following and think about the imagery:*

> "She is black and white,
> Her mane falls wild on her forehead," (page 654)

Explain that these two lines describe one of the horses that the narrator meets. Point out that the colors and the description of the mane help us to see the horse. Discuss with students what other images in the poem appeal to the sense of sight.

Help students use academic vocabulary and concepts. Divide them into groups of three. Tell students to experiment with imagery as they write their own description of one of the horses in the poem. Have students think about which sense or senses they are going to address. Ask volunteers to read their descriptions. Then have them discuss whether the image appeals to sight, smell, touch, hearing, or taste.

READING FOCUS (45 minutes)

Analyze Details Explain that by looking closely at the words and phrases in the poem, students can get a better understanding of the poem's meaning. Read a line from the selection: *They have come gladly out of the willows.* (p. 450). Ask students to think about the language that the poet uses here: *Is it complicated? (no) What kind of mood does it convey? (happy)*

Have students work in pairs to fill out a chart like the one at the right. First, ask students to take turns reading lines from the selection out loud. Then have them work together to make notes about their favorite lines. Encourage them to note the mood that the words convey or what sense the imagery appeals to.

Nuances: Shades of difference in meaning or feeling.
Evoke: Bring a memory or feeling to mind.

LANGUAGE SKILL
Especially for ELL
(10 minutes or less)
Some English-language learners may have difficulty with the technical term *image*. Remind students that images are words and phrases that appeal to one of our senses, and that in this poem, many of the images appeal to our sense of sight. Encourage students to think more about the visual images by having them choose one from the poem and make a drawing of it.

READING FOCUS
Analyze Details

Line	Notes

"A Blessing" from Collected Poems by James Wright. Copyright ©1963, 1971 by James Wright. Reproduced by permission of **Wesleyan University Press, www.wesleyan.edu/wespress.**

Original content Copyright © by Holt, Rinehart and Winston. Additions and changes to the original content are the responsibility of the instructor.

Differentiating Instruction

Direct Teach

(45 minutes)

Think – Pair – Share For students not used to analyzing poetry, the theme in "A Blessing" may be difficult to understand. In order to focus their thinking, read the last three lines of the poem aloud and then pose the following question: *What do the last three lines of the poem mean to you? (*Student answers will vary. One possible response is *The narrator feels a deep connection to nature and feels the connection will last even outside of his own body and life.*) Have students work on the answer to the question individually, making notes. Then have them discuss their responses in pairs. Have partners work toward a shared response. Then, ask students to share their responses with the entire class.

Check for Understanding

WRITING FOCUS *(15 minutes)*

Imagery Explain that when an author uses imagery to appeal to our senses, he or she is also trying to reach our emotions. Use the following example in which Wright uses imagery to help us feel a specific emotion:

> **Image** "They bow shyly as wet swans." (p. 654)
>
> **How It Makes Us Feel** The image appeals to our sense of sight— we can imagine the horses as they behave like the swans. The fact that the imagery is given through the comparison makes us take extra time to envision both the swans and the horses. The image also makes us feel pleasure, as the horses are apparently graceful and lovely.

Read aloud each image below. Have students write what each image makes them feel.

1. "Twilight bounds softly forth on the grass," [anticipation or pleasure.]

2. "At home once more,

    They begin munching the young tufts of spring in the darkness." [contentment]

3. "And the light breeze moves me to caress her long ear" [sweet and serene]

Think As A Reader/Writer Ask: *How can you use imagery to communicate an emotion?* Then ask students to think about an event and to find imagery that appeals to one or more of the senses as they make notes about that event. Encourage them to work on writing an image that communicates their feelings about the event.

READING/WRITING
Especially for WGP
(5 minutes)
Point out that sometimes poets choose words to form phrases that suggest an emotion rather than being a faithful description of what they have seen. For example, in "A Blessing," Wright states that "...the eyes of those two Indian ponies/Darken with kindness." Have students discuss whether eyes really darken with kindness, and why Wright might have chosen this phrase.

Point out to students that they can also write this type of phrase as they work on their images.

"A Blessing" from Collected Poems by James Wright. Copyright ©1963, 1971 by James Wright. Reproduced by permission of **Wesleyan University Press, www.wesleyan.edu/wespress.**

Original content Copyright © by Holt, Rinehart and Winston. Additions and changes to the original content are the responsibility of the instructor.

Differentiating Instruction

Internment/Sanctuary

Figure of Speech Chart Poets often use **figures of speech** to make their language vivid. **Metaphors** compare two unlike things while **similes** make comparisons using words such as *like* or *as*. **Personification** gives human qualities to nonhuman things.

Fill in the chart below as you analyze the use of figures of speech in these poems. The first one is done for you.

Figure of Speech	Type of Figure of Speech	Things Being Compared	What Comparison Suggests
"Corralled, they are herded inland / From Santa Rosa. ("Internment," lines 1 – 2)	Metaphor	Japanese Americans are compared to cattle.	They are being treated like animals, not people.
"which holds them in like stolid cattle" ("Internment," lines 21 – 22)			
"New York came, rampaging." ("Sanctuary," line 1)			
"And my feet, faithful dogs, brought me" ("Sanctuary," line 8)			
"Home to you, my anchor, my light." ("Sanctuary," line 9)			

Original content Copyright © by Holt, Rinehart and Winston. Additions and changes to the original content are the responsibility of the instructor.

Differentiating Instruction

Lesson Plan and Teaching Strategies

Women Alice Walker

Preteach

LISTENING COMPREHENSION SKILLS *(15 minutes)*
Build Background/Set a Purpose Discuss the Meet the Author feature on p. 680. Explain that while growing up in rural Georgia in the 1940s and 1950s, the African-American writer Alice Walker would have faced many hardships, including segregation and poverty. Point out where Georgia is on a classroom map.

Preview this information about the poem:

- The speaker is talking about her mother's generation—that is, the women who were close in age to her mother.

- She explains how the women were like generals, fighting to get their children better opportunities than they themselves had.

Remind students that Walker's own mother was a maid, and that some of the phrases in the poem have to do with that occupation. Point out that Walker's mother did not have a chance to get the kind of education that her daughter did.

LANGUAGE COACH SKILL *(10 minutes)*

Root Words Remind students that words which are related share a common root. Point out that we can better understand these words if we understand their roots. Have students look at the following examples:

- The root for *generation*, *generate*, and *generator* is the Latin *generatio*, which means "to be born."

- *Generation* means "all of the people born and alive at roughly the same time."

- *Generate* means "to bring into being."

- *Generator* means "a machine that brings gas or steam into being."

Write these sentences on the board. Have students complete each one by adding a word from the box.

generation	generate	generator

1. The [generation] of people who were born in the 1920s lived through the Great Depression.

2. The steam engine stopped when the [generator] broke.

3. It is easy to [generate] interest in a product that people want.

RESOURCES
In *The Holt Reader,* "Women" for students who need more scaffolding in a workbook format

In this book: *Vocabulary Skill Builder,* p. 156; "Women Selection Test, p. 158

Consult *Holt Audio Library* for recordings of most selections.

ACADEMIC VOCABULARY
Preteaching Academic Vocabulary
(5 minutes)
Write these terms and their meanings on a chalkboard or transparency. Review them with the students before previewing the selection.

Associate: Connect in thought
Elaborate: Go into greater detail about something
Speaker: The voice in the poem that is speaking to the reader.
Tone: The writer's or speaker's attitude or feeling about what is in the poem or about the readers of the poem.

VOCABULARY SKILL
Especially for ELL
(5 minutes or less)
Explain that the line "battered down / Doors" *(lines 7-8)* probably means that the women had to be insistent and determined to go through doors that were usually closed to them.

Original content Copyright © by Holt, Rinehart and Winston. Additions and changes to the original content are the responsibility of the instructor.

Differentiating Instruction

LITERARY FOCUS *(30 minutes)*

Speaker and Tone To focus students on speaker and tone, write these sentences on the board and read them aloud. Tell students that they describe the same person.

- This woman was determined.
- My mother would risk her life by marching straight across a minefield if she had to.

Ask: *What difference in tone or attitude do these sentences convey?* (The first is strength; the second is dedication and love.) *In each example, what relationship does the speaker have with the woman?* (In the first example, no clear relationship is apparent. In the second example, the speaker is the daughter of the woman she is writing about.) *How does the choice of words help show the speaker's attitude in the second example?* ("Risk her life," "marching…across a minefield" show the depth of dedication and love.)

Help students use academic vocabulary and concepts. Have students work in pairs. Have each pair look at the photograph of the woman on page 681. First, have student pairs experiment with using a different speaker as they work together to write a line or sentence to describe the woman in the photograph. For example, in their first description, they could write as the woman's daughter might. In the second description, they could write as a historian might. Similarly, then, have students experiment with tone. Have each pair write a line or sentence that has a loving tone. Then, have each pair write a line or sentence that has a tone of curiosity (or another tone of their choosing). Encourage students to share their work.

READING FOCUS *(20 minutes)*

Analyzing Details Talk about how readers can look at individual lines and images to better understand a writer's tone. Offer this example:

- The insects were like a disease, destroying plant life all around them.

Ask: *What is the speaker's tone here?* (sorrowful or angry) Explain that by comparing the insects to disease, the speaker shows a negative attitude toward the insects.

Have students work in pairs to fill out a chart like the one at the right. As they read the poem, prompt them to write down examples that best convey the tone of the poem. Have them also describe that tone in the second column of the chart.

VOCABULARY SKILL
Especially for ELL
(5 minutes or less)
ELL students are unlikely to be familiar with the term *booby-trapped.* Explain the term and connect it to the concept of "mined/Fields."

READING FOCUS
Graphic Organizer

Example From Poem	Tone

Original content Copyright © by Holt, Rinehart and Winston. Additions and changes to the original content are the responsibility of the instructor.

Differentiating Instruction

Direct Teach

(60 minutes)

Check Comprehension Read the poem aloud twice. To check comprehension, ask these questions, guiding students to the appropriate lines of the poem.

1. To which women, in particular, is the speaker referring? *(lines 1-2: women of her mother's generation)*
2. How do these women speak and walk? *(lines 3-4: husky voices, strong steps)*
3. What does the speaker mean when she says that the women did not know "a page / Of it"? *(lines 21-26: They were not formally educated.)*

Check for Understanding

WRITING FOCUS *(15 minutes)*

Adjectives Explain that the author uses adjectives to describe the women of her mother's generation. Read the following example:

> *"Husky* of voice—*stout* of / Step." (p. 681)

Then, read the following, and discuss how changing adjectives changes the tone of the lines.

1. *"Smooth* of voice—*silent* of / Step."
2. *"Musical* of voice—*skipping* of /Step."

(In the first example, the tone shifts to calmness. In the second example, the tone shifts to one that is more joyful.)

Think As A Reader/Writer Ask *What words can you use to describe someone important to you?* Have students choose a person to write about. Ask them to brainstorm a list of adjectives that would best describe that person. Then, have students write a short description of that person, using the adjectives that work best.

READING/WRITING
Especially for WGP
(5 minutes)
Writers gaining proficiency are likely to benefit from a word bank of descriptive words. Encourage these students spend a few minutes working in a group. Have them brainstorm adjectives that can be used to describe people's looks, character, and personality. Students can use these lists as a starting point for their own lists of adjectives.

"Women" from *Revolutionary Petunias & Other Poems* by Alice Walker. Copyright © 1970 and renewed © 1998 by Alice Walker. Reproduced by permission of **Harcourt, Inc**. and electronic format by permission of **The Wendy Well Agency, Inc**. This material may not be reproduced in any form or by any means without prior written permission of the publisher.

Lesson Plan and Teaching Strategies

I Wandered Lonely as a Cloud William Wordsworth

Preteach

LISTENING COMPREHENSION SKILLS *(10 minutes)*

Build Background/Set a Purpose Discuss Build Background on p. 686. Point out the pictures of daffodils on page 687, and explain to students that daffodils are one of the first flowers to bloom in spring. Note that William Wordsworth's poetry, though now close to two hundred years old, is still taught and enjoyed through many parts of the world.

Preview these details about the poem:

- "I Wandered Lonely as a Cloud" tells about the speaker's walk by a lake, where he sees thousands of daffodils.

- The speaker begins the poem "lonely as a cloud," but the sight of the beautiful daffodils cheers him during the walk.

- The speaker notes that the memory of the daffodils has cheered him many times since he first saw them.

Point out that the daffodils in this poem show the poet's interest in the beauty of nature, and how it affects us. Ask: *Have you been cheered up when thinking about something beautiful in nature that you have seen?*

VOCABULARY SKILLS *(10 minutes)*

Preteach Vocabulary Words Review the meanings of the vocabulary in the Word Bank. Then give students these sentences to complete.

1. Juan was in a [pensive] mood as he quietly wrote in his journal.

2. The ice skater performed her routine in a [sprightly], playful way.

3. When our team won, I was filled with [glee].

4. After an hour of [solitude], Maria wanted to be around people.

Remind students to watch for these words as they read the story.

LANGUAGE COACH SKILL *(10 minutes)*

Connotation and Denotation Remind students that a word's denotation is its literal meaning, which can be found in a dictionary. Note that a word's connotation is the feelings that we associate with the word. For example, the words *host* and *mob* both describe a crowd. Which word has a positive connotation? *(host)* Which word has a negative connotation? *(mob)*

Write these words from the poem on the board. Have students write two headings at the top of a piece of paper: *Positive* and *Negative*. Ask students to then write each of the words under the heading that describes its connotation.

RESOURCES

In *The Holt Reader:* "I Wandered Lonely as a Cloud" for students who need more scaffolding in a workbook format

In this book: *Vocabulary Skill Builder*, p. 156; "I Wandered Lonely as a Cloud" Selection Test, p. 159.

Consult *Holt Audio Library* for recordings of most selections.

WORD BANK

sprightly
glee
pensive
solitude

ACADEMIC VOCABULARY

Preteaching Academic Vocabulary

(5 minutes)

Write these terms and their meanings on a chalkboard or transparency. Review them with the students before previewing the selection.

Rhythm: A pattern of sound created by repeating certain arrangements of stressed and unstressed syllables.

Meter: A pattern of stressed and unstressed syllables. One example is *iambic*, in which a stressed syllable follows an unstressed syllable, as in the word *beside*.

Original content Copyright © by Holt, Rinehart and Winston. Additions and changes to the original content are the responsibility of the instructor.

Differentiating Instruction

- wandered *(negative)*
- lonely *(negative)*
- golden *(positive)*
- twinkle *(positive)*
- sparkling *(positive)*
- vacant *(negative)*

LITERARY FOCUS *(30 minutes)*

Rhythm and Meter Explain: *The iambic foot (unstressed/stressed) is the most commonly used rhythm in English poetry. Many people feel this rhythm is common in language, music, and dance because it mimics the rhythm of the human heart. This beat is often represented by the sounds "lubb-DUBB."* Ask students to repeat "lubb-DUBB" in rhythm, while tapping their feet on the second syllable, the "DUBB" sound. Guide students to notice that they are tapping on the stressed beat, not the unstressed. Then read the following two lines from the selection, stressing the words and syllables that are capitalized.

> "They FLASH up-ON that IN-ward EYE
> Which IS the BLISS of SO-li-TUDE."

Explain that each of these two lines from the poem has four iambic feet (lubb DUBB). Read the lines again, and have students read along, tapping their feet on the stressed beats.

Help students use academic vocabulary and concepts. Divide them into groups of three. Have them create a list, with the headings Iambic Meter. Tell students to spend a few minutes thinking about lines from other poems they have read that have iambic meter. They can also list lyrics from songs they know that follow this pattern. Alternatively, they can list lines that they write themselves. Encourage students to use academic vocabulary. Ask volunteers for examples from their lists.

READING FOCUS *(45 minutes)*

Summarize Stanzas For students not used to nineteenth century poetry, "I Wandered Lonely as a Cloud" may be difficult to understand. Read the following lines from the poem:

> "For oft, when on my couch I lie
> In vacant or in pensive mood,
> They flash upon that inward eye
> Which is the bliss of solitude."

Discuss with students what these lines mean. Then have a volunteer summarize the lines' meaning. *(Often, when the speaker is lying quietly, he remembers the flowers, which makes him happy.)*

Have students work in small groups. Have volunteers read aloud one stanza at a time. Then have each group write a summary of the stanza, in a chart like the one on the right. Point out that the summaries are in

LANGUAGE SKILL
Especially for ELL
(5 minutes or less)
Remind students that the basic unit of measure for meter is the poetic foot (page 618 in the Student Book).

READING FOCUS
Summarize Stanzas

Stanza	Summary
1.	
2.	
3.	
4.	

Original content Copyright © by Holt, Rinehart and Winston. Additions and changes to the original content are the responsibility of the instructor.

Differentiating Instruction

ordinary, non-rhythmical language and ask: *Which version do you think sounds better? Why?*

Direct Teach
(45 minutes)

Fluency Ask students to work in pairs. Have students take turns reading the poem aloud. Each student should read the poem aloud twice. Allow students to help each other, if necessary. When students have finished their reading, encourage them to discuss the experience. Ask: *Was your reading excellent, good, okay, or does it need work?* Then have them evaluate their own fluency in reading aloud.

Check for Understanding

WRITING FOCUS *(15 minutes)*

Re-Order Difficult Sentences English-language learners will need extra help with unusual word order. Write line 11 on the board. "Ten thousand saw I at a glance." Ask students to rewrite the sentence so that it sounds more like ordinary speech. Tell them to start the sentence with the word I, and ask: *Which word in this line would usually follow the word I? (saw)* They can then rebuild the sentence *(I saw ten thousand at a glance)* to help them understand the meaning more easily.

Have students work in pairs to fill out a chart like the one at the right. Ask students to identify any other sentences that seem to have an odd word order, such as lines 17-18, and change the order. Ask volunteers to read the re-ordered lines aloud. Discuss whether the re-ordered line still has the same rhythm and meter as the original line.

Think As A Reader/Writer Ask: *What do you think of Wordsworth's use of word order in the poem? Do you think it adds to the poem or does the unusual word order make the poem weaker or more difficult to understand?* Then ask students to imagine that William Wordsworth is still alive, and have them write a letter to the poet, explaining their feelings about the word order in his poetry.

WRITING FOCUS
Re-Order Difficult Sentences

Original Line	Re-ordered Line

READING/WRITING
Especially for WGP
(10 minutes)
Review the parts of a letter with students, including the heading, date, greeting, body, closing, and signature. You may show examples of proper format for a friendly letter.

Original content Copyright © by Holt, Rinehart and Winston. Additions and changes to the original content are the responsibility of the instructor.

Differentiating Instruction

from Song of Myself, Number 32 / I Hear America Singing

Rhythm Chart Poets use sounds in a special way to give their works a musical quality, or **rhythm.** One way rhythm is created is by repeating sentence structures, words, and sounds.

Fill in the chart below with examples of Walt Whitman's use of rhythm in his two poems.

Rhythm	Examples from Poems
Repetition of Sentence Structures	
Repetition of Words	
Repetition of Sounds	

Original content Copyright © by Holt, Rinehart and Winston. Additions and changes to the original content are the responsibility of the instructor.

Differentiating Instruction

Lesson Plan and Teaching Strategies

Legal Alien / Extranjera Legal Pat Mora

Preteach
LISTENING COMPREHENSION SKILLS *(15 minutes)*
Build Background/Set a Purpose Discuss Build Background on p. 706. Explain that some people do not like the term "alien" used to describe an individual immigrant, since it sounds too much like a space creature. An even more controversial term is "illegal alien," which implies that the immigrant is here without proper, legal documents.

Preview these details of the poem:

- The speaker of the poem speaks both English and Spanish fluently, and uses both languages in the poems.

- Both versions of the poem include the phrase *"Me'stan volviendo loca"* (page 707). Explain its English translation, *"They're driving me crazy."*

- The speaker feels that Anglos view her as different from them, and that Mexicans also feel she is different from them.

- The speaker is uncomfortable with the fact that she will be judged by both groups of people (Mexicans and Anglos).

Point out that the word "alien" in the title might also refer to the way that the speaker feels as she maneuvers between the Anglo and Mexican communities—she seems to feel *alien*ated. Point out to students that the poem was written in 1984. Ask students if they think that things are easier for Mexican immigrants today.

LANGUAGE COACH SKILL *(10 minutes)*
Prefixes Tell students that a prefix is a word part added to the beginning of a base word, or root, to create a new word with a different meaning. Write the prefix *bi-* on the board. Explain that it means "two." Review with students the meaning of these examples from the poem. Discuss how *bi-* added to each root word creates a word with a new, or more specific, meaning.

- *Bi-lingual*, usually written as *bilingua*l, means knowing two languages

- *Bi-cultural*, usually written as *bicultural*, means knowing two cultures.

- *Bi-lateral*, usually written as *bilateral*, means by two sides or two-sided.

Write these sentences on the board. Have students complete each one by adding a word from the box.

bilingual	bicultural	bilateral

RESOURCES
In *The Holt Reader,* "Legal Alien / Extranjera legal" for students who need more scaffolding in a workbook format

In this book: *Vocabulary Skill Builder,* p. 156; "Legal Alien / Extranjera legal" Selection Test, p. 160

Consult *Holt Audio Library* for recordings of most selection

VOCABULARY SKILL
Especially for ELL
(5 minutes or less)
Introduce these words, which may be new to students:
Paneled: Having wood panels as wall coverings
Drafting: Writing a rough version of
Hyphenated: Divided by a hyphen
Exotic: Strikingly strange
Token: Representative
Fringes: Edges

Original content Copyright © by Holt, Rinehart and Winston. Additions and changes to the original content are the responsibility of the instructor.

Differentiating Instruction

1. Since she was comfortable with the customs of her home country and her father's country, Diane considered herself (bicultural).

2. Marisol was proud that she was [bilingual], speaking English and Spanish.

3. The [bilateral] agreement pleased both sides.

LITERARY FOCUS *(45 minutes)*

Speaker and Persona Ask students to listen as you read aloud the following paragraph:

> I wanted to fly—straight across the sea like no woman had. I became famous for my flying, and no one knew how nervous it made me. A crowd gathered to see me off on my last journey. I waved merrily as I boarded the plane, but I was terrified. Now no one knows where I am—lost at sea. No crowds can see me now—alone and at sea.

Discuss whether students believe that the speaker in the poem is the actual author. *(no.)* Read the text again, and ask students to pay attention to the speaker's voice. Ask: *Does she sound happy? What else can you tell about her?* (She does not sound happy. We can tell that she was ambitious and that her last journey ended badly.) *What does the speaker reveal to the reader that she hid from those around her?* (She was terrified.) Explain to students that the speaker had created a brave persona, or mask, that hid the negative emotions the speaker felt.

Help students use academic vocabulary and concepts. Write the following lines from the poem on the board:

> an American to Mexicans
>
> a Mexican to Americans
>
> a handy token
>
> sliding back and forth
>
> between the fringes of both worlds
>
> by smiling
>
> by masking the discomfort
>
> of being pre-judged
>
> Bi-laterally.

Help students use academic vocabulary and concepts. Ask students to work in pairs. Have each pair take notes about what they learn about the speaker and her persona in this excerpt from the poem. *(Sample response: She feels judged by both Americans and Mexicans as being different. In her public persona, she smiles to hide her negative feelings about being judged)* Bring all student pairs together to share their ideas with the class.

"Legal Alien" and "Extranjera Legal" from *Chants* by Pat Mora.Copyright © 1984 by Pat Mora.Published by **Arte Público Press—University of Houston, Houston, TX , 1985, 2000.**

ACADEMIC VOCABULARY
Preteaching Academic Vocabulary
(5 minutes)
Write these terms and their meanings on a chalkboard or transparency. Review them with the students before previewing the selection.

Speaker: The voice that speaks to readers in a poem. The poet may use his or her own voice as speaker, or may create a new voice.
Persona: The character created by an author when speaking in a voice different from his or her own
Word Play: The use of puns, sound effects, and pairing an unusual set of words
Parallel Structure: When writers express a series of ideas or actions in similar ways. For example, if the first item in a series begins with a noun, the next item in the series will begin with a noun; if the first noun is described by an adjective, the next noun will be described with an adjective.

Original content Copyright © by Holt, Rinehart and Winston. Additions and changes to the original content are the responsibility of the instructor.

Differentiating Instruction

READING FOCUS *(30 minutes)*
Listen to Details in the Poem Use the audio recording to allow students to hear the poem read in both languages. Read aloud—:

> "Bi-lingual, Bi-cultural,
> able to slip from "How's life?"
> to *"Me'stan volviendo loca,"*

Ask: *Do you hear a rhyme?* (No.) *Do you hear a regular rhythm?* (No.) Encourage students to notice that this is a free verse poem, with no rhyme or rhythm. Then have volunteers read several lines aloud in English, emphasizing the tone. Next, have a volunteer read the same lines in Spanish, again emphasizing tone.

As students listen to the CD and the other students' readings, ask them to fill out a chart like the one on the right. Encourage them to take notes each time they listen, about the speaker, the tone of the poem, or new discoveries about its meaning.

Direct Teach

(30 minutes)
Focus on the Speaker After students read the poem once again, discuss the speaker's identity and feelings, prompting students with such questions as *Do you think the speaker is an adult or a child?* (adult) *What details in the poem help you to determine the age of the speaker?* (lines 4-7: The speaker is working and ordering food at a restaurant). *How do you think the speaker feels about being a legal alien? Does the speaker seem to feel accepted by Anglos and Mexicans?* List their answers on the board. Make sure to ask for and include on the list any details in the poem that reveal information about the speaker.

Check for Understanding

WRITING FOCUS *(15 minutes)*
Spanish and English Remind students that Mora uses a Spanish sentence in both versions of the poem, *"Me'stan volviendo loca,"* which means "They're driving me crazy." She also uses an English sentence, *"How's life?"*

Ask students which sentence seems more revealing and what that might say about the speaker's struggle within the two cultures. *(The Spanish sentence seems more revealing. It might show that she is more at home in the Spanish culture.)*

Then have students write original sentences in English or Spanish that sound like something the speaker of the poem might say. Have them keep in mind that the speaker hides her discomfort.
Think As A Reader/Writer Ask: *What advice would you give to the speaker in the poem?* Have students brainstorm ideas, and then choose one idea to write about. Have them write a few sentences explaining their advice to the speaker in the poem.

READING FOCUS
Listening Chart

Reading	Notes
1.	
2.	
3.	

READING/WRITING
Especially for WGP
(5 minutes)
Writers gaining proficiency are likely to benefit from sharing their work with a partner who can suggest improvements before sharing their work with the class.

Original content Copyright © by Holt, Rinehart and Winston. Additions and changes to the original content are the responsibility of the instructor.

Lesson Plan and Teaching Strategies

The History Behind the Ballad Taylor Branch
Ballad of Birmingham Dudley Randall 4 Little Girls Roger Ebert

Preteach

LISTENING COMPREHENSION SKILLS *(10 minutes)*
Build Background/Set a Purpose Discuss Build Background for "The History Behind the Ballad" on p. 713. Explain to students that the Pulitzer Prize is a very prestigious writers' award. Tell students that this account was written in 1989, many years after the event took place.

Next, discuss Build Background for "Ballad of Birmingham" on page 714. Point out Birmingham, Alabama on a classroom map. Finally, discuss Build Background for "4 Little Girls" on page 716. Preview the following details of the story, which all three accounts cover:

- In 1963, African Americans were struggling for their civil rights. Many protests were held in Birmingham, Alabama.

- Four young African American girls went to church early one Sunday in Birmingham. The church was bombed, and all four were killed.

Point out that many works of literature and many movies deal with real historic events. Ask: *Have you seen any movies about real events in history? Were they documentaries, or did they re-imagine the event?*

VOCABULARY SKILLS *(10 minutes)*
Preteach Vocabulary Words Review the meanings of the vocabulary in the Word Bank. Then give students these sentences to complete.

1. The actor had [charisma], which attracted people.
2. The student [literally] danced with joy when she got an A.
3. The small boy gave many [rationalizations] for his bad behavior.
4. The [infamous] criminal was sentenced to life in prison.

Remind students to watch for these words as they read the story.

LANGUAGE COACH SKILL *(10 minutes)*
Word Origins Explain that understanding where a word comes from can help students better understand words' meanings. Discuss these words from the selections.

- In Latin, *evanescere* means "disappear." In English, the word *vanished* means to have disappeared (p. 713).

- In Latin, the word *ferus* means "wild." In English, the word *fierce* refers to something that is violent and brutal (p. 714).

- The Latin word *contextus* means "coming together." The English word *context* means the set of facts surrounding an event (p. 717).

Write these sentences on the board. Have students complete each one by adding a word from the box.

vanished	fierce	context

RESOURCES
In *The Holt Reader:* "The History Behind the Ballad," "Ballad of Birmingham," and "4 Little Girls" for students who need more scaffolding in a workbook format

In this book: *Vocabulary Skill Builder,* p. 156: "The History Behind the Ballad," "Ballad of Birmingham," and "4 Little Girls" Selection Test, p. 161.

Consult *Holt Audio Library* for recordings of most selections.

WORD BANK
literally
Infamous
charisma
rationalizations

ACADEMIC VOCABULARY
Preteaching Academic Vocabulary
(5 minutes)
Write these terms and their meanings on a chalkboard or transparency. Review them with the students before previewing the selections.

Ballad: poems that tell stories, often with rhymes and a strong rhythm.
Historical Accounts: Writing that focuses on real events in history.

Original content Copyright © by Holt, Rinehart and Winston. Additions and changes to the original content are the responsibility of the instructor.

Differentiating Instruction

1. The [fierce] dog attacked strangers.

2. The dinner [vanished] before I had a chance to eat.

3. The book explains the [context] within which the Civil War began.

LITERARY FOCUS *(20 minutes)*

Historical Accounts Across Genres To introduce the poetic form, write *ballad* on the board. Tell students that stories are told in all cultures, and that ballads began as stories in song form. Then write *literary ballad* on the board, and explain that this is a ballad written as a poem, usually with rhyme and meter. Ask: *What do you think the appeal might be of putting a story into poetic form? How might this be different in tone and emotion than the same story told as nonfiction?*

Read the following examples from each of the selections:

> "All four were dressed in white from head to toe, as this was their day to run the main service for the adults at eleven o'clock." (p. 713)
>
> "She has combed and brushed her night-dark hair,
> And bathed rose-petal sweet,
> And drawn white gloves on her small brown hands,
> And white shoes on her feet." (p. 715)
>
> "The little girls had gone to church early for choir practice, and we can imagine them, dressed in their Sunday best, meeting their friends in the room destroyed by the bomb." (p. 716)

Explain that each of these excerpts is describing one or more of the girls on the day that they were killed. Point out that the first example comes from a nonfiction book by Taylor Branch; the second excerpt is from "Ballad of Birmingham," by Dudley Randall; and the third excerpt is from Roger Ebert's review of the movie *4 Little Girls*. Discuss whether students' image of the girls changes when they listen to each of the excerpts. Ask: *How are the descriptions different? (The first covers all four girls, the second focuses on one little girl, the third is more general, without giving specifics about their clothing.)*

Help students use academic vocabulary and concepts. Divide them into groups of three. Tell students to compare and contrast the three excerpts above, discussing the different techniques that the writers use in their

LANGUAGE SKILL
Especially for LDN
(5 minutes or less)
Some learners may have difficulty understanding the term *ballad*. If possible, bring in a recording of the ballad "Barbara Allen" or another folk ballad, to let students hear what a musical ballad is like. Then, explain that a literary ballad is similar, though usually presented without music.

LANGUAGE SKILL
Especially for ELL
(5 minutes or less) Some English-language learners may need to review the difference between the forms of the three selections. Review with students that nonfiction books cover real events in history, and that writers have to do a lot of research to collect the information presented. Ballads, on the other hand, can be based on real events, but can be presented through the author's imagination. A movie review can include the writer's own reflections on the story that the movie covers.

Excerpt [retitled "The History Behind the Ballad"] from *Parting the Waters: America in the King Years, 1956–63*, by Taylor Branch. Copyright © 1988 by Taylor Branch. Reproduced by permission of **Simon & Schuster Adult Publishing Group**.

"Ballad of Birmingham" from *Cities Burning*, by Dudley Randall. Copyright © 1968 by **Broadside Press**. Reproduced by permission of the publisher.

Roger Ebert's review of *4 Little Girls* by Spike Lee from *Chicago Sun Times*, October 24, 1997. Copyright © 1997 by Roger Ebert. Reproduced by permission of **Andrews McMeel Publishing**.

Original content Copyright © by Holt, Rinehart and Winston. Additions and changes to the original content are the responsibility of the instructor.

descriptions. *(The first creates a visual image of the girls dressed in white from head to toe; the second uses imagery that appeals to the senses of touch and sight, as well as strong meter; the third describes how the movie lets us picture the girls who are about to be killed.)* Ask students to jot down their observations; have volunteers share their work.

READING FOCUS *(45 minutes)*

Comparing Messages in Different Forms Explain that when you choose to read a specific genre, such as a ballad or a movie review, you have expectations about what you will find. Explain: *You might read a nonfiction book to learn a lot about a specific event. You might read a ballad to enjoy its rhythm and rhyme, and to feel moved by its story. You might read a movie review to gain quick insights about a movie.* Ask students to work in pairs as they jot down what they expect to learn from each of the selections in this section, using a chart like the one on the right. Have students read each of the selections carefully. As they read, ask them to take time to fill in the second column of the chart on the right. Then have volunteers share their ideas with the class.

Direct Teach

(45 minutes)

Build Fluency To practice fluency, read each stanza of "Ballad of Birmingham" aloud, then give volunteers a chance to take turns reading the same stanza to the class. When you have read through the ballad, read the first sentence of the "History Behind the Ballad" on page 713, and let volunteers read the same sentence after you finish. Then, read the first sentence of "Movie Review: 4 Little Girls." Again have volunteers read the same sentence after you finish. Ask: *What differences do you notice in the rhythm and general feel of the three selections?* (The poem is rhythmical, with a catchy, appealing beat; the first excerpt is prose, and is straight facts. The movie review is also in prose, and covers a movie about the event, rather than the event itself.)

Check for Understanding

WRITING FOCUS *(15 minutes)*

Analyze the Ballad Re-read "Ballad of Birmingham" and analyze the lines together for their rhythm and rhyme. Ask students how many repetitions they see of the word *child.* (3) Divide the class into groups and have each group list as many other examples of repeated words and phrases as they can. Ask each group to share their findings, and make a master list on the board of all the repetitions students found.

Ask students to write 2 to 4 lines of poetry that rhyme, have meter, and include repeated words.

Think As A Reader/Writer Ask students to think about all three of the selections that they read. Ask: *Which of the selections made you feel the tragedy of the event most powerfully?* Have students write a paragraph, explaining their choice.

READING FOCUS
Read Aloud and Paraphrase

What I Expect to Learn and Feel	What I Actually Learned and Felt

VOCABULARY SKILL
Especially for ELL
(5 minutes)
Point out and define hyphenated words in the ballad: "night-dark" (*line 17,* p. 715), as black as night; "rose-petal" (*line 18,* p. 715), like the petals of a rose.

READING/WRITING
Especially for WGP
(5 minutes)
Point out that although using correct grammar is very important in formal writing, such as a nonfiction book, a ballad or poem might include less formal language, including slang.
Explain that any less formal language should accurately reflect the voice of the speaker of the poem, and take into consideration such things as their setting (the time and place in which they live), and their ethnic and/or educational background.

Original content Copyright © by Holt, Rinehart and Winston. Additions and changes to the original content are the responsibility of the instructor.

Differentiating Instruction

Lesson Plan and Teaching Strategies

Generating Research Questions

Preteach

LISTENING COMPREHENSION SKILLS *(10 minutes)*
Build Background/Set a Purpose Explain that the two selections in this section are nonfiction accounts about how the FBI hunts down stolen art. Point out the picture on page 720, and explain that the scientist is collecting evidence to determine if a painting is authentic or not. Discuss the Build Background feature on 724. Explain to students that Rockwell's paintings are known for their American themes, and so the painting described in the article, entitled *Russian Schoolroom*, is unusual. If possible, show more examples of Norman Rockwell's work, collected from library books or the Internet.

Preview these details of the selections:

- The FBI created a special team to deal with the theft of art and cultural property. The team has been successful at recovering many items.

- Director Steven Spielberg learned that he had a stolen painting by Norman Rockwell in his collection. His staff had discovered the painting on an FBI Web site that listed stolen artwork.

Explain that art theft and the theft of cultural artifacts is a continual problem, because many people find these items to be so valuable. Ask: *Beyond their monetary value, why do you think people find artwork and historic cultural items so valuable? Are they important to you?*

VOCABULARY SKILLS *(10 minutes)*
Preteach Vocabulary Words Review the meanings of the vocabulary in the Word Bank. Then give students these sentences to complete.

1. The accountant's [client] needed help with his taxes.

2. Since its [inception], the Neighborhood Watch program has prevented several car thefts.

3. The [ceremonial] robes were used in important religious rituals.

4. Even a [legitimate] salesperson can sometimes sell goods that are stolen.

Remind students to watch for these words as they read the story.

LANGUAGE COACH SKILL *(10 minutes)*
Word Origins Explain that understanding where a word comes from can help us understand its current meaning. Discuss the following examples:

- The Latin word *investigationem* means "looking into." In English, *investigations* are attempts to find out why something happened (p. 722).

RESOURCES

In *The Holt Reader:* "Generating Research Questions" for students who need more scaffolding in a workbook format

In this book: *Vocabulary Skill Builder*, p. 156; "Generating Research Questions" Selection Test, p. 162

Consult *Holt Audio Library* for recordings of most selections

WORD BANK

Inception
ceremonial
legitimate
client

ACADEMIC VOCABULARY
Preteaching Academic Vocabulary
(5 minutes)
Write these terms and their meanings on a chalkboard or transparency. Review them with the students before previewing the selection.

Research Questions: When you need to find out information about a topic, you need to do research. That means you need to look at books, websites, and articles to find out more. Before you start your research, you should think about exactly what you want or need to find out by coming up with questions about the topic. As you find answers to your questions, write them down. Go on to write more specific research questions.

Original content Copyright © by Holt, Rinehart and Winston. Additions and changes to the original content are the responsibility of the instructor.

Differentiating Instruction

- The Greek word *arkhaiologia* means "the study of ancient things." In English, the word *archeological* means something related to archaeology, the study of ancient societies (page 723).

- The Greek word *dekas* means "group of ten." In English, a *decade* is a group of ten years (page 724).

- The Latin word *inspicere* means "to look into." In English, if someone has *inspected* something, it means they have studied it closely (page 724).

Write these sentences on the board. Have students complete each one by adding a word from the box.

investigations	archeological	decades	inspected

1. At the [archaeological] site, they found ancient pottery.
2. Since I am 15 years old now, in two [decades], I will be 35.
3. When she [inspected] the work, she found mistakes.
4. During the [investigations], many people were interviewed.

INFORMATIONAL TEXT FOCUS *(40 minutes)*
Generating Research Questions Explain *In the two selections, you will be reading facts about the FBI's Art Crime Team. Both selections are non-fiction. One focuses on what the Art Crime Team has achieved, and the other focuses on one specific case.*

Remind students that when we do research about a certain topic, it helps to come up with research questions to focus our search. Write the 5W and How questions on the board (Who? What? When? Where? Why? and How?) Explain: *Asking questions such as "Who did something?" "What did they do?" "When did they do it?" "Why did they do it?" and "How did they do it?" helps you to make sure that you are getting a complete look at your subject. Once you have answered these questions about your topic, you can develop new questions for your research.* Read the following example from the selection to students:

> The FBI established a rapid deployment Art Crime Team in 2004. The team is composed of twelve Special Agents, each responsible for addressing art and cultural property crime cases in an assigned geographic region.

Explain: In the first two sentences of their website, the FBI answers a *Who?* question *(the FBI),* a *What* question *(Art Crime Team),* a *When?* question (in 2004), a *Where* question *(in twelve assigned geographic regions)* and a *How?* question *(rapid deployment).*

Have students work in pairs to fill out charts like the one on the right. Before they read the first selection, have them write down what they already know from the excerpt above. Then, have them write a list of

INFORMATIONAL TEXT FOCUS
Generating Research Questions

What We Already Know	
What We'd Like to Find Out	
What We Learned from the Selection	

Original content Copyright © by Holt, Rinehart and Winston. Additions and changes to the original content are the responsibility of the instructor.

Differentiating Instruction

questions about what they would like to find out. As they read the selections, prompt them to write notes about what they learned, especially answers to any of their questions above. Finally, have student share their notes with the class. Discuss with them whether everything that they wanted to learn was covered in the selection.

Direct Teach
(60 minutes)
Chunk the Text Help students pace their reading by dividing the selection into "chunks" or parts. After the students have read each part, have them stop to note what they learned about *Who?, What?, When?, Where?, Why?,* and *How?*
"Art Crime Team"
Part 1: ends p. 722, par. 1: "…for prosecutive support."
Part 2: ends p. 723, bullet 3: "…Chicago, New York, and Tokyo."
Part 3: ends p. 723, bullet 7: "…archaeological sites in Iraq."

"Collection Is Found to Contain Stolen Rockwell Art"
Part 4: ends p. 724, col 1: "….determined," the bureau said."
Part 5: ends p. 725, col 2: "…for *The Saturday Evening Post.*"

Check for Understanding
WRITING FOCUS *(20 minutes)*
Research Questions Review with students that generating questions is an important step in conducting research. Write *Who? What? When? Where? Why?* and *How?* on the chalkboard. Have students look at the following example from "Collection Is Found to Contain Stolen Rockwell Art."

Example "A Norman Rockwell painting stolen from a gallery in Clayton, Mo. more than three decades ago was found in Steven Spielberg's art collection, the F.B.I. said Friday."
Answer *Who?, What?, Where?, When?* Questions Explain that the sentence gives information about *who* was involved (Steven Spielberg), *what* was taken, (a painting) *where* it was found (Spielberg's art collection), and *when* the painting was stolen (three decades ago). Ask students to share any further questions they have after reading this excerpt. For example, "Why was the painting in Spielberg's collection?" Say: *As you re-read, stop after each paragraph to come up with more questions that you would like to research.*

Think As A Reader/Writer Have students re-read the second selection once again. Remind them that this was a true story presented in a newspaper. Have students begin to work on an outline of a short story, based on the same idea. Ask: *How will a short story be different from a newspaper account? What details will you change?*

Slightly adapted from "Spielberg Collection Is Found to Contain Stolen Rockwell Art" as it appears in *The New York Times*, March 4, 2007 by **The Associated Press**. Reproduced by permission of the publisher.

VOCABULARY SKILL
Especially for ELL
(15 minutes)
English-language learners will benefit from practice with the additional words below. Go over these words and their meanings with students.

- *assigned* (p. 722): past tense of *assign*—to give something to someone
- *sting* (p. 722) a trick used for catching someone who is doing something illegal
- *authenticity* (p. 724): proven to be genuine
- *disposition* (p. 724) arrangement or settlement

READING/WRITING
Especially for WGP
(5 minutes)
Students who are developing writing skills may find it easier to make an outline of the short story by drawing pictures for a storyboard instead of writing sentences.

Original content Copyright © by Holt, Rinehart and Winston. Additions and changes to the original content are the responsibility of the instructor.

Differentiating Instruction

Targeted Strategies for Learners with Diverse Needs

READING SKILLS

Generating Research Questions *(15 minutes)* Explain to students that when they generate research questions they should give some thought to the kind of information that they are seeking. A research question can be answered by a single fact. For example, What is the circumference of Earth? Other research questions might lead students to investigate a design or process. For example, *How does a nuclear reactor work?* Finally, research questions could also lead students to explore relationships between things or concepts. For example, *Is the early 21st Century a new Gilded Age?* Review this chart with students:

Facts	Design/process	Relationships
Search for a piece of information; state it.	Investigate how something is made or how it works; explain it.	Explore how one thing affects another, causes, comparisons, context, hypothetical situations; analyze it.

Have partners write three research questions about one or several of the reading selections. Challenge students to brainstorm where they might seek this information.

LITERARY SKILLS

Imagery and Theme *(15 minutes)* Point out that the imagery in a poem supports the theme. The theme is the message about the world or life. Imagery is a big part of that message. For example, a slip on a banana peel could be funny or tragic. The imagery makes the difference. Read these two examples to the class:

- Large shoes flapped in the air, a horn blew, and the audience howled.

- There was blur, then a thud, then a hoarse cry for help.

Then have students take a vote to decide which imagery makes the fall seem humorous and which makes it seem tragic.

Speaker and Persona *(15 minutes)* A persona speaks in a character's voice but has the perspective of a narrator. Help students understand the difference between these literary devices

- A character can be viewed as an object from the outside, like a doll or action figure.

- A narrator can tell a story without being a character, like a person playing with a doll or action figure.

- A persona tells a story like a narrator, but is also a character, like a puppet or ventriloquist's dummy.

Ask students to use the think/pair/share technique to discuss narrators they were most likely to confuse with the authors themselves.

Readings in Collection 7 Minimum Course of Study
"A Blessing", p. 652
"Women", p. 679
"I Wandered Lonely as a Cloud", p. 685
"Legal Alien/ Extranjera Legal", p. 705
"The History Behind the Ballad", "Ballad of Birmingham", and "4 Little Girls", p. 710
Generating Research Questions, p. 720

RESOURCES
In *The Holt Reader,* all three selections help students who need more scaffolding in a workbook format.

Consult *Holt Audio Library* for recordings of most selections.

TEACHING TIP
English-language learners can explore imagery and build their vocabulary by describing visual images.

ALTERNATIVE ASSESSMENT *(5 minutes)*
Have students provide answers for these items.

It's easy to confuse a [persona/theme] with the author.

One way to get to information on a subject is to [generate research questions].

Original content Copyright © by Holt, Rinehart and Winston. Additions and changes to the original content are the responsibility of the instructor.

Poems   History Behind the Ballad/4 Little Girls
FBI Crime

A. Match words and definitions. Write the letter of the correct definition next to each word.

_____ 1. twilight   a. great delight

_____ 2. caress   b. being alone

_____ 3. glee   c. touch gently with affection

_____ 4. pensive   d. thoughtful, serious

_____ 5. solitude   e. just after sunset

B. Circle the letter next to the best answer to each question.

1. Should you take the expression, "I'm on cloud nine" literally?

   A. yes   B. no

2. Which is a better description of an infamous person?

   A. role model   B. negative example

3. If someone told you that you have a lot of charisma, how would you feel?

   A. complimented   B. insulted

4. Which is more likely to end in rationalizations?

   A. studying for an exam   B. cheating on an exam

5. How should you dress for a ceremonial occasion?

   A. formally   B. casually

C. Use the academic vocabulary words to complete the following paragraph about "Ballad of Birmingham," by Dudley Randall.

elaborates   evoke   nuances   associates

In the "Ballad of Birmingham," the mother (1) _____ the church with safety. In

contrast, she (2) _____ on the dangers of the Freedom March, which include

dogs, clubs, hoses, and guns. The girl's rose-petal scent, brushed hair, and white accessories (3)

_____her innocence. The (4) _____ in the poem (the

polite way the child asks to go to the march and the mother's smile when she thinks her child is safe)

add to the tragedy when the church is bombed.

Original content Copyright © by Holt, Rinehart and Winston. Additions and changes to the original content are the responsibility of the instructor.

Differentiating Instruction

Collection 7

Selection Test

A Blessing James Wright

COMPREHENSION, SKILLS, AND VOCABULARY Circle the letter of the best
answer to each of the following items.

1. What does the speaker feel as he sees the horses?

   A) hatred and rage

   B) tenderness and affection

   C) sadness and loss

   D) jealousy and envy

2. How do the horses react to the visitors?

   A) The horses run from them.

   B) .The horses ignore them.

   C) The horses come close to them.

   D) The horses lead them into the fields.

3. "She is black and white" is an example of—

   A) imagery   C) metaphor

   B) simile   D) rhythm

4. Another word for the central idea of a poem is

   A) meter

   B) metaphor

   C) theme

   D) allusion

5. Which is the best example of something that *bounds?*

   A) a dog walking to its owner

   B) a deer running from a hunter

   C) a turtle resting on a bank

   D) a fish swimming in the ocean

6. Write about the emotions that the horses feel in the poem, and whether or not
   horses really feel such emotions. Use this organizer to collection your ideas.

Introductory statement: I think that horses can/cannot feel emotions like . . .
Two or three supporting sentences: At first, the speaker describes them as feeling…Later, he describes them as feeling…In my opinion, horses …
Concluding statement: In conclusion, I believe that horses do/do not feel emotions like those described in the poem

Original content Copyright © by Holt, Rinehart and Winston. Additions and changes to the original content are the responsibility of the instructor.

Differentiating Instruction

Selection Test

Women Alice Walker

COMPREHENSION, SKILLS, AND VOCABULARY Circle the letter of the best answer to each of the following items.

1. How do the women described in the poem help their children?

    A) by encouraging them to do their best

    B) by working hard to provide them with opportunities

    C) by leading armies across fields

    D) by joining the Civil Rights movement

2. What did the speaker have that the women described in the poem did not?

    A) a good education

    B) a job as a maid

    C) a career in the army

    D) concern for other people

3. What is the speaker's tone toward the women she describes?

    A) angry

    B) mocking

    C) proud

    D) cruel

4. To what does the poet compare the women in the poem?

    A) military leaders

    B) political radicals

    C) high school teachers

    D) wild flowers

5. Which words best describes the women in the poem?

    A) weak and defeated

    B) determined and strong

    C) jealous and bitter

    D) rigid and icy

6. Are the women in Walker's poem likable? Use the graphic organizer below to collect your ideas. Then write a paragraph.

| Introductory statement: I think that the women in the poem are/are not likeable because …. |
| Two or three supporting sentences: From the poem, I can tell that… Also, the women… |
| Concluding statement: In conclusion, I do/do not find these women likeable because…. |

Original content Copyright © by Holt, Rinehart and Winston. Additions and changes to the original content are the responsibility of the instructor.

Selection Test

I Wandered Lonely as a Cloud William Wordsworth

COMPREHENSION, SKILLS, AND VOCABULARY Circle the letter of the best
answer to each of the following items.

1. What does the speaker see as he wanders?

    A) a host of angels

    B) thousands of daffodils

    C) fish sparkling in a stream

    D) a beautiful woman

2. How does the speaker feel when he remembers what he saw?

    A) vacant

    B) pensive

    C) happy

    D) sad

3. The poem's repeated pattern of sounds is its—

    A) imagery

    B) simile

    C) metaphor

    D) rhythm

4. An iambic foot, such as "That FLOATS," is one type of—

    A) imagery

    B) metaphor

    C) meter

    D) alliteration

5. Which of the following is the best example of someone who is **pensive**?

    A) Kevin was the life of the party.

    B) Kendra sobbed as she watched the sad movie.

    C) David was determined to get revenge.

    D) Sienna sat quietly, thinking about all she had to do.

6. Do you, like Wordsworth, think that solitude is blissful? That is, does being
   alone make you feel happy? Use the graphic organizer below to collect your
   ideas. Then write a paragraph about your feelings.

| Introductory statement: I think that solitude is/is not blissful. |
| Two or three supporting sentences: The speaker in the poem enjoys solitude because… I feel that… |
| Concluding statement: In conclusion, to me, solitude is … |

Original content Copyright © by Holt, Rinehart and Winston. Additions and changes to the original content are the responsibility of the instructor.

Differentiating Instruction

Collection 7
Selection Test

Legal Alien / Extranjera Legal by Pat Mora

COMPREHENSION, SKILLS, AND VOCABULARY Circle the letter of the best
answer to each of the following items.

1. Between what two cultures does the speaker of the poem move?

   A) French and Mexican

   B) African and Spanish

   C) American and Mexican

   D) Argentinian and Mexican

2. What does the speaker of the poem do?

   A) She works in an office.

   B) She goes to school.

   C) She works at a restaurant.

   D) She works as a judge

3. How does the speaker feel about her situation?

   A) She feels superior to others.

   B) She feels uncomfortable.

   C) She feels happy.

   D) She feels jealous.

4. In poetry, the **speaker** is—

   A) the poet talking to the reader

   B) the voice speaking to the reader

   C) the reader himself or herself

   D) the sound effects

5. The word **alien** can mean all of the following except—

   A) something different or strange

   B) a close relative or friend

   C) someone from another planet

   D) an immigrant or foreigner

6. Write a character sketch of the speaker of the poem. Use the graphic organizer
   below. Then write a paragraph about the speaker.

Introductory statement: The speaker in this poem can best be described as …
Two or three supporting sentences: At the beginning of the poem, she seems … As the poem continues, we realize that…
Concluding statement: In conclusion, I believe that the speaker is….

Original content Copyright © by Holt, Rinehart and Winston. Additions and changes to the original content are the responsibility of the instructor.

Differentiating Instruction

Historical Accounts Across Genres

COMPREHENSION, SKILLS, AND VOCABULARY Circle the letter of the best answer to each of the following items.

1. In "Ballad of Birmingham," what did one girl really want to do that Sunday morning?

   A) go outside to play

   B) study for a school test

   C) join a Freedom March

   D) stay home with her mother

2. Roger Ebert's review of Spike Lee's "4 Little Girls" could be described as being

   A) a mixed review

   B) a negative review

   C) a positive review

   D) a nonsensical review

3. What literary elements are generally included in a **ballad**?

   A) satire and irony

   B) meter and rhyme

   C) imagery and symbolism

   D) singers and an orchestra

4. Which of the following is the best example of someone who is **infamous**?

   A) a popular television star

   B) a best-selling author

   C) a notorious criminal

   D) a ground-breaking inventor

5. Which of the following is the best example of someone who has **charisma**?

   A) a teacher who bores his students

   B) a coach who scares her team

   C) an actor who cannot get a job

   D) a politician who inspires voters

6. Write a paragraph about which genre you would use to describe a historic event. Use the graphic organizer below to collect your ideas.

Introductory statement: If I were to write about a historical event, I would choose to write a ballad/nonfiction account because…
Two or three supporting sentences: I would be comfortable writing a ballad/nonfiction account because … Also, I think that ballads/nonfiction accounts are more…
Concluding statement: For all of these reasons, I would choose to ….

Original content Copyright © by Holt, Rinehart and Winston. Additions and changes to the original content are the responsibility of the instructor.

Generating Research Questions

COMPREHENSION, SKILLS, AND VOCABULARY Circle the letter of the best answer to each of the following items.

1. The information given in the "FBI Art Crime Team" selections is from—
   A) an FBI training manual   C) a newspaper article
   B) an FBI Web site   D) a museum brochure

2. The Norman Rockwell painting discussed in the second selection shows—
   A) a New York City barbershop
   B) a Russian schoolroom
   C) a Midwestern diner
   D) a Greek statue

3. If you did more research on the FBI Art Crime Team, which would be the best question to ask?
   A) How does the FBI locate stolen art work?
   B) What else does the FBI do?
   C) When did the FBI Art Crime Team begin?
   D) Why did the FBI recover a "Trapdoor" rifle?

4. Which of the following is the best example of someone who is a **client**?
   A) a lawyer
   B) an accountant
   C) someone who hires a lawyer
   D) someone who is hired by an accountant

5. Which word means the *opposite* of **legitimate**?
   A) unlawful   C) acceptable
   B) legal   D) authentic

6. Write about whether or not you would make a good investigator for a crime unit. Use the graphic organizer below to collect your ideas.

Introductory statement: I would/would not make a good investigator for a crime unit because . . .
Two or three supporting details: One important quality that an investigator needs is . . . I do/do not possess that quality . . . For that reason, I . . .
Concluding statement: In conclusion, I believe that . . .

Original content Copyright © by Holt, Rinehart and Winston. Additions and changes to the original content are the responsibility of the instructor.

Differentiating Instruction

Collection 7
Collection Summative Test

VOCABULARY SKILLS **Complete the sentences below by using the collection vocabulary words from the list below.**

twilight	nuzzled	glee	solitude
infamous	charisma	inception	ceremonial

1. The politician had such _____ that she attracted many followers.

2. At_____ the light grows dim and we have to stop our ball game.

3. The _____ bandit robbed many stage coaches.

4. Soon after its _____ in 2003, the lucky band had a popular hit.

5. The child laughed with _____ at the clown's juggling act.

LITERARY AND READING SKILLS **Circle the letter of the best answer.**

6. A poem's **theme** is its—

   A) origins

   B) plot

   C) central idea

   D) character

7. The voice that talks to us in a poem is called—

   A) a character

   B) the speaker

   C) an image

   D) the theme

8. The repetition of sound patterns gives a poem its—

   A) rhythm

   B) connotation

   C) theme

   D) image

LANGUAGE AND WRITING SKILLS **Choose the best transition word or words in each answer pair.**

9. First, I headed toward the store. [Then/Now] I bought a toothbrush.

10. On the one hand, Bruno wanted to play with his cousin. [Later/On the other hand], he knew he had to do his homework and he was running out of time.

Original content Copyright © by Holt, Rinehart and Winston. Additions and changes to the original content are the responsibility of the instructor.

Differentiating Instruction

Lesson Plan and Teaching Strategies

Writing Workshop: Response to Literature
PREWRITING
Choose a Poem *(15 minutes)*

Review the definition of a response to literature: *A response to literature is an opinion, feeling, or statement you express and you support with examples from that work.* Help students find a poem that offers the appropriate level of challenge. Advise them to select one of the poems in the collection that they have read with the class (Spanish speakers may prefer to work with "Legal Alien," which appears in English and Spanish. If you wish to help them find a new poem, see the list of recommended poets under the WGP tip on this page.)

Then have students use the recommendations on page 735 in the Student Edition to make their selection.

Write and Support Your Thesis *(15 minutes)*

Before students begin to work on their thesis, be sure they understand the different literary elements. If students need extra help, review with them the language of poetry on pages 616-619 in the Student Edition.

Have students create a full-size chart like the one on page 736 in Student Edition. Before they fill the chart out go over this model with them, based on "First Lesson" on page 624 of the Student Edition.

Literary Element	Detail/Quotation	Elaboration
personification	"lie back, and the sea will hold you."	At first the father holds his daughter and the sea takes over the job. That sounds like what happens when you grow up and enter the world on your own.
Thesis: Philip Booth teaches his daughter about swimming and life.		

Allow them to work with a partner to fill out their charts and discuss what their thesis might be.

DRAFTING
Respond in Style/Grammar Link: Possessives *(10 minutes)*

Have students use their charts when they begin to draft their essays. Review the framework for a Response to Literature on page 737 of the Student Edition. Briefly introduce the Grammar Link so that students can rely on those examples to introduce the poem and author. Be sure students understand how to write in the 3rd person. Have students begin to draft their response.

TEACHING TIP
Before beginning this lesson with the professional model, return to page 654 of the student book and reread "A Blessing" by James Wright with students. Help students with the difficult vocabulary in the poem and in the professional model. Also, explain the concept of "irony" to students (a gap between what might be expected and what really happens).

ESPECIALLY FOR ELL
(10 minutes)
Idiomatic language is a challenge for English-language learners, who cannot simply look up the definitions of individual words to decode meaning. Have them circle phrases that give them trouble and partner with proficient English speakers to get help with these idioms. Invite them to share idioms from their native language with the class.

ESPECIALLY FOR WGP
(10 minutes)
Help students gaining proficiency find poems that they will be able to work with and enjoy. Have them look in the library for books by the following poets:

- Angela Johnson
- Angela Shelf Medearis
- Sandra Cisneros
- Gary Soto
- Walter Dean Myers
- Paul Fleischman

Original content Copyright © by Holt, Rinehart and Winston. Additions and changes to the original content are the responsibility of the instructor.

Differentiating Instruction

EVALUATING AND REVISING
Review Content and Organization *(20 minutes)*

Give students time to focus on the following points in Evaluation Questions 1, 3, 4 and 5. Help them understand how they can use these points to make their literary response better.

1. Have students turn to the corrected first paragraph of the Student Draft at the bottom on page 739. Have students locate the name of the poem and the poet as well as the thesis statement. Ask: *How clear is your thesis statement?*

3. Remind students to refer to their chart of literary elements. If their charts are incomplete, help them to finish individually or have them work with a partner.

4. If students need more help prioritizing the literary elements in their chart, have students work with a partner to number the literary elements on their chart.

5. Have students read the conclusion of the Student Draft on page 740 of the Student Edition. Have them compare the conclusion with the opening paragraph on page 739. Ask: *How did the author expand her thesis in the conclusion*?

Pair students with a partner to evaluate and improve each other's drafts. Have them use this guidance along with the chart on page 738 of the Student Edition.

Grammar Link: Homonyms and Proofread *(15 Minutes)*

Explain to students that these are very common mistakes most writers make if they're not very careful. Demonstrate an easy way that students can check homonyms to see whether they're contractions or possessive case. Have them replace the word in question with the words that make up the contraction. If the sentence makes sense, use the contraction, if not, it's the possessive.

Sentence	Check for contractions
It's/Its raining.	*It is raining.—yes, It's*
It's/Its paws are wet.	*It is paws are wet—no, Its*
Whose/Who's coat is that?	*Who is coat is that—no, Whose*
Whose/Who's at the door?	*Who is at the door—yes, Who's*
Their/They're here.	*They are here—yes, They're*
Their/They're team won.	*They are team won—no, Their*

Then ask students to reread their essays to find and fix sentences in the passive voice.

TEACHING TIP
Motivate students by reminding them that they have already supported a thesis if they have finished the Persuasive Essay in Unit 2. Students will be able to use their sense of accomplishment to tackle this new challenge.

ESPECIALLY FOR ELL
(10 minutes)

Writing in the third person will likely be difficult for English-language learners as they try to distinguish plurals, possessives, and the final "s" on third person present tense verb forms. Most languages do not use "'s" to show possession. Give English language learners extra practice by having them circle plurals, box third person singular "s" endings, and underline possessives. If students' level of language acquisition allows, have them also identify plural possessives.

ESPECIALLY FOR LDN
Even with appropriate text, students may need individual attention to develop elaborations, theses, and conclusions. Help students form elaborations from the examples they find. Help them see what the elaborations have in common to form a thesis. Then help them see how the language of the poem continues to help prove the thesis for the conclusion.

Original content Copyright © by Holt, Rinehart and Winston. Additions and changes to the original content are the responsibility of the instructor.

Differentiating Instruction

Lesson Plan and Teaching Strategies

Listening and Speaking Workshop: Presenting Response to a Poem

ADAPT YOUR RESPONSE TO LITERATURE *(20 minutes)*

Explain that students will now take the response to literature they have written and prepare it for an oral presentation. Have them follow these steps:

1. Read your poem and your response to partner. Have your partner interrupt you with questions if anything is unclear, especially the conclusion. Work together to make corrections.

2. Help listeners know where you on in the poem. Add expressions like, "in the beginning of the poem," or "near the end of the poem" that you might not have needed in your written response.

3. Remember, when you read aloud, your audience can't see the quotes you've put around the words you've taken from the poem. However, it's important to show the difference between your words and the poet's. So even though you don't usually pronounce punctuation marks, you'll want to say the word *quote,* when you get to a quote. Say unquote when you get to the end of it.

4. As always, practice your presentation until your delivery is smooth. Memorize it if you can. Use note cards during the presentation to jog your memory.

Deliver Your Response to Literature

USE VERBAL AND NONVERBAL TECHNIQUES *(20 minutes)*

Explain how to use these techniques.

Emphasis In addition to saying *quote/unquote* to indicate the words taken directly from the poem, tell students that they can alter their diction, using a slightly different volume or tone. Remind students that they don't want to exaggerate this too much or it will sound like they are mocking the poem.

Gestures Another way students call out the language of the poem is to put quotes on the chalkboard before presenting, and point to them as they come up in the presentation.

Have students practice their delivery with a partner. Have the partner fill out a checklist like the one below as feedback.

Non-verbal Techniques	Regularly	Sometimes	Never
Clear Meaning			
Verbal Techniques			
Nonverbal Techniques			
Smooth Use of Note Cards			

Teaching Tip

Students will find it easier to listen to these presentations if you can share the poems with the audience just before the presentation. Provide copies for students to read, or have a volunteer do a dramatic reading.

ESPECIALLY FOR ELL

In some cultures, eye contact is considered impolite. If students are uncomfortable making eye contact during their presentations, you might have them look at the back wall or some point just above the heads of the audience.

EVALUATION CRITERIA

Use these criteria to evaluate students' presentations:

- Gave their presentations smoothly with little hesitation or struggling with notes
- Pronounced most words intelligibly
- Varied tone, volume, and rate of expression
- Focused on a thesis and related literary elements in the poem to that thesis
- Offered evidence from the text
- Demonstrated a command of non-verbal techniques

Original content Copyright © by Holt, Rinehart and Winston. Additions and changes to the original content are the responsibility of the instructor.

Differentiating Instruction

Unit 3; Skill Builder 1
Oral Language Skill Builder

Spoken Word Performance

UNDERSTAND THE SKILL You can bring a poem to life by reading it with feeling. The tone of your voice and the words you chose to emphasize will communicate more than words alone.

Copy the poem "Women" on p.681 into the box below. Work with a group to perform the poem together. Listen to other groups perform. Then discuss the questions below with your group.

How will you stress the words that stand alone and the word in *italics*?	
How will you group the lines into phrases? Which lines go together to complete a thought?	
How loud or soft will your voice be as you read this?	
How can you make your voice show the strength of these older women?	
How can you make your voice convey the pride the poet feels in these older women?	
Additional notes:	

Extend Discussion How did your performance differ from other groups' performances? What worked best about each performance?

Original content Copyright © by Holt, Rinehart and Winston. Additions and changes to the original content are the responsibility of the instructor.

Differentiating Instruction

Unit 3; Skill Builder 2
Oral Language Skill Builder

Cross-Text Discussion

UNDERSTAND THE SKILL Reading about the same subject in different kinds of texts can deepen your understanding. Look for the information the texts have in common. Also look for details that are different.

After reading about the tragedy in Birmingham, work with a partner to discuss the prompts in the chart below. Then answer the discussion question.

How does each text show evidence of sorrow?	The following details show the sorrow of that event…		
	Historical Account	Ballad	Movie Review

How does each test show evidence of anger?	The anger people felt about the injustice is shown by…		
	Historical Account	Ballad	Movie Review

What historical details can you find in each text?	Details that show this event took place in the past include…		
	Historical Account	Ballad	Movie Review

What, if anything, does each text say about the effect on history?	The texts that address the event's effect on history have this to say…		
	Historical Account	Ballad	Movie Review

Extend Discussion Think about how the format of each text affects the message. Think about how you felt as you read each one.

- Which text gives the most information about the subject? Give examples of what you learned. Which text has the greatest emotional impact? Explain.

Original content Copyright © by Holt, Rinehart and Winston. Additions and changes to the original content are the responsibility of the instructor.

Unit 3; Skill Builder 3
English Language Skill Builder

Comparison/Contrast

UNDERSTAND THE SKILL When you compare two things, you tell how they are alike. When you contrast two things, you tell how they are different. When you are comparing and contrasting, choose the conjunctions, or connecting words that show sameness or difference.

Work with a partner to sort the conjunctions into two categories. Write each one beneath the correct heading. Look up any words that are unfamiliar.

> and, but, also, yet, too, still, as well, nevertheless, besides,
> however, in addition, except, furthermore, though,
> moreover, then again

Conjunctions Used to Compare	**Conjunctions Used to Contrast**

EXTEND DISCUSSION Use conjunctions to complete these sentences about the language of poetry. Then discuss the poetry selections you've read in this unit with a partner. Compare and contrast them, using conjunctions.

1. Free verse, catalog poems, _____ haiku do not rhyme. _____, haiku have a rhythm based on the number of syllables per line.

2. A ballad always rhymes. A sonnet does, _____. A lyric may or may not rhyme _____ unlike a ballad, it doesn't tell a story.

3. A simile creates a connection between two things. Metaphors _____ do this. _____ similes have the word "like" to show the comparison is not exact.

4. Alliteration _____assonance repeat sounds; _____ one repeats consonants and the other repeats vowels.

Original content Copyright © by Holt, Rinehart and Winston. Additions and changes to the original content are the responsibility of the instructor.

Unit 3; Skill Builder 4
English Language Skill Builder

Idioms

UNDERSTAND THE SKILL Idioms are expressions that mean something beyond the literal definition of the words. Often the meaning is figurative—or even poetic. The best way to learn these expressions is to memorize them.

Write the letter on the line to match each idiom to its defintion. If you don't know what an idiom means, ask a native speaker. Compose a sentence for each idiom. Compare your work with others in your class.

Idioms

____ 1. in a different light

____ 2. stand up and be counted

____ 3. snap judgments

____ 4. turn your back on

____ 5. on edge

____ 6. cheer someone up

Definitions

a. nervous

b. betray or abandon

c. help improve someone's mood

e. deciding quickly without much thought

f. from another perspective

g. to get what you are entitled to

EXTEND DISCUSSION Use what you know about the selections you have read to answer the question and define the idiom, underlined in each sentence.

1. In the poem "I Wandered Lonely as a Cloud," what <u>cheered up</u> the narrator? _____ How? _____

2. In the poem "A Blessing" did the horses seem <u>on edge</u> when the narrator and his friend enter the pasture? _____ How could you tell? _____

3. How did the women in Alice Walker's poem help their children <u>stand up and be counted</u>? What did they achieve for their children that they didn't have themselves?

   _____

4. In "Legal Alien," who makes <u>snap judgments</u> about the Mexican-American? How does it make the subject of the poem feel? _____

   _____

5. How did the bombing in Birmingham cause people to see racism <u>in a different light</u>? What began to change after that? _____

   _____

Original content Copyright © by Holt, Rinehart and Winston. Additions and changes to the original content are the responsibility of the instructor.

Differentiating Instruction

Unit 3
Summative Test

LITERARY AND READING SKILLS

A. Circle the letter of the best answer. *(25 points; 5 points each)*

1. Which of the following phrases from the poem "A Blessing" is the best example of **personification**?

   A) "bow shyly as wet swans"

   B) "young tufts of spring"

   C) "Twilight bounds softly forth on the grass"

   D) "We step over the barbed wire into the pasture"

2. Which of the following best helps to create an **image** in poetry?

   A) meter

   B) rhyme

   C) repetition

   D) sensory details

3. The **tone** of a poem is—

   A) the writer's attitude toward a subject

   B) its literal dictionary definition

   C) the main message the poem conveys

   D) the emotional quality it evokes

4. In poetry, a musical quality based on repetition is called—

   A) alliteration

   B) assonance

   C) rhythm

   D) symbol

5. Which of the following are all examples of **sound devices** in poetry?

   A) imagery, tone, and rhythm

   B) metaphor, simile, and rhyme

   C) onomatopoeia, assonance, and alliteration

   D) denotation, associations, and personification

Original content Copyright © by Holt, Rinehart and Winston. Additions and changes to the original content are the responsibility of the instructor.

Differentiating Instruction

| Unit 3 Summative Test *continued*

B. Complete each sentence with one of the literary or reading skills shown below. *(25 points; 5 points each)*

ballad   visualizing   speaker   connotation   meter

6. A regular pattern of stressed and unstressed syllables in the lines of a poem is called _____.

7. The _____ of a word are all the meanings, associations, or emotions that have come to be attached to it.

8. The _____ is the voice that talks to us in a poem.

9. When reading poetry, an important skill is _____ because it allows you to use the descriptive words and phrases to see in your mind what you are reading.

10. A type of poem that uses a steady rhythm, strong rhymes, and repetition is a _____.

Read the question below. Then write a short response on the lines. *(50 points)*

Reading Aloud

11. Re-read "Ballad of Birmingham" on page 714 silently and then aloud. How does reading the poem aloud affect your reaction to it? What sound devices does the poet use? What do you notice about the speakers in the poem?

_____

_____

_____

_____

_____

Original content Copyright © by Holt, Rinehart and Winston. Additions and changes to the original content are the responsibility of the instructor.

Differentiating Instruction

Collection 8
Graphic Organizer

from Cyrano de Bergerac   Edmond Rostand

Cause and Effects Chains A **cause** explains why something happens, and an **effect** is the result of something that happens. In plays, you can understand why a character acts in a certain way when you look for the cause of the action. Then you can look to see what effect that action had.

In the scene from "Cyrano de Bergerac," Roxane travels to camp to see Christian. In the cause and effect chain below, analyze the effects of her arrival. Use the 5 events in the box and place them in the right order.

> • Cyrano refuses to tell.
> • Christian worries that she is actually in love with Cyrano, because he wrote the letters.
> • She declares she loves him for his soul, not his looks.
> • Christian goes to tell Roxane the truth.
> • Christian tells Cyrano to tell Roxane that Cyrano wrote the letters.

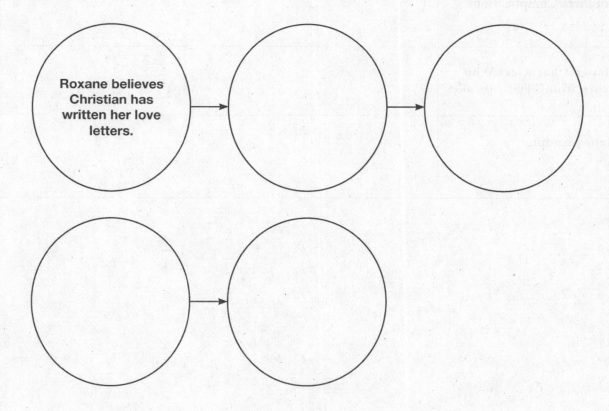

Roxane believes Christian has written her love letters.

Original content Copyright © by Holt, Rinehart and Winston. Additions and changes to the original content are the responsibility of the instructor.

The Frog Prince David Mamet

Elements of Comedy Chart A **comedy** is a play with a happy ending. Along the way to the happy ending, however, characters face **conflicts** and complications and learn from their mistakes.

"The Frog Prince" is a comedy, but it does not possess all the traditional characteristics of a comedy. In the chart below, analyze which elements of comedy the play displays. Fill in the chart with examples from the play. If the play does not contain the element, explain how it is different.

Elements of Comedy	Examples from the Text
Humor	
Conflicts/Complications	
Flawed Characters Who Learn from Their Mistakes	
Happy Ending	

Original content Copyright © by Holt, Rinehart and Winston. Additions and changes to the original content are the responsibility of the instructor.

Differentiating Instruction

Lesson Plan and Teaching Strategies

The Tragedy of Romeo and Juliet, Act I William Shakespeare

Preteach

LISTENING COMPREHENSION SKILLS *(15 minutes)*

Build Background/Set a Purpose Introduce the play by reviewing the list of characters on p. 805 with students. Use a world map to locate Italy and the cities of Verona and Mantua. Explain that the action of the play takes place here. Point out that the play was written in 1596, so the setting of the story is around that time or earlier. Then have students preview Act I by looking at the photographs, beginning with the one on p. 796. Confirm that these images are from stage productions and movies about Romeo and Juliet. Invite students to share anything they know about this play or about movies or plays that are related to it (e.g. *West Side Story* as a modern Romeo and Juliet tale; the 1998 movie *Shakespeare in Love,* which includes a production of Romeo and Juliet as a key part of the plot). Also check for what students know about William Shakespeare. Confirm that he wrote many plays and is considered one of the greatest English writers of all time. He lived and wrote when Queen Elizabeth I ruled England.

To help students set a purpose for reading, preview these details:

- The Montagues and the Capulets are both noble families in Verona.

- The Montagues and the Capulets hate each other and have been feuding for years.

- Romeo Montague and Juliet Capulet meet for the first time in Act I. Juliet is thirteen. Romeo's age is not given but he is also young.

Based on the photo on p. 796, have students explain what they think happens to Romeo and Juliet when they meet, and what problems they may have as a result. Have students read to check their predictions.

VOCABULARY SKILLS *(15 minutes)*

Preteach Vocabulary Words Introduce the vocabulary in the Word Bank. Write each word and its meaning on the board. Discuss each word, and then give students these sentences to complete.

1. Those dark clouds are a [portentous] sign that a storm is coming.

2. In a war, a soldier has to know who the [adversary] is.

3. She has become [rebellious] and will not follow her parents' rules.

4. Spreading a rumor that hurts someone is a [pernicious] thing to do.

5. That player's skills are [augmenting] the strength of our team.

6. Cheating on a test is a serious [transgression].

Remind students to watch for these words as they read Act I.

RESOURCES

In *The Holt Reader:* "The Tragedy of Romeo and Juliet, Act I," for students who need more scaffolding in a workbook format

In this book: *Vocabulary Skill Builder,* p. 187; "The Tragedy of Romeo and Juliet, Act I," Selection Test, p. 188

Consult *Holt Audio Library* for recordings of most selections

WORD BANK

The following words are not identified as vocabulary but will be helpful for students to learn before reading Act I:
rebellious (p. 811): defying authority
pernicious (p. 811): harmful
adversary (p. 812): enemy
augmenting (p. 813): making or becoming greater in size, number, amount, or degree; adding to
portentous (p. 813): threatening; ominous
transgression (p. 815): act of breaking a law or command;

VOCABULARY SKILL
Especially for ELL
(10 minutes)
In addition to the Word Bank terms, English language learners will benefit from previewing these words:
marred (p. 818): spoiled the beauty of; damaged
languish (n. p. 819): lack of energy; weakness
disposition (p. 824): nature; tendency
extremity (p. 825): to an extreme degree
solemnity (p. 834): seriousness

Original content Copyright © by Holt, Rinehart and Winston. Additions and changes to the original content are the responsibility of the instructor.

Differentiating Instruction

LANGUAGE COACH SKILL *(30 minutes)*

Shakespeare's Language Remind students that William Shakespeare wrote his plays more than four hundred years ago. The language he used is different from how we speak today. Some words are not in use anymore. Some have different meanings, such as these examples:

- "*Soft!* I will go along." (line 193, p. 815). Here *soft* means "wait."

- "Tell me in *sadness,* who is it that you love?" (line 196, p. 815) Here *sadness* means "seriousness."

Direct students to the sidenotes on p. 815 that give the meaning of both words. Review strategies students can use to figure out unfamiliar words, such as checking the sidenotes; looking for context clues in dialogue; or using the meaning of lines that come before or after.

Explain that another feature of Shakespeare's language is his use of figures of speech, such as similes and metaphors. Review the dialogue on p. 808, using the sidenotes to explain the servants' joking language. Point out that some of Shakespeare's word play, like this example, is not essential to the plot; students should follow it as well as they can.

Confirm that reading Shakespeare's language is different from everyday speech because he wrote some parts – including many of the most famous lines – in iambic pentameter. Explain that an *iamb* is an unstressed syllable followed by a stressed syllable, and *penta-* comes from the Greek and means "five." In iambic pentameter, there are five stressed syllables, or beats, in each line. Write the opening line of the prologue on the board to emphasize the stressed syllables. Read it aloud and have students listen for the beats:

- "Two HOUSEholds, BOTH aLIKE in DIGniTY, (p. 807)

Have volunteers continue reading lines from the prologue in iambic pentameter, listening for the beats. Then have students pair up with a partner to read aloud the entire prologue together. Circulate to listen to the pairs and help them to get the rhythm of the language as they read.

LITERARY FOCUS *(30 minutes)*

Tragedy Have students give examples of their favorite movies that are comedies. Confirm that a comedy is funny and ends in a good way for the main characters. Point out that a *tragedy* is the opposite of a comedy. Have a volunteer explain what happens to the main characters in a tragedy (e.g. they die or have something very unhappy happen to them). Remind students of lines and phrases they read in the prologue, such as "star-crossed lovers" and "death-marked love." Based on the title of this play and the prologue clues, have student predict what will happen to Romeo and Juliet (e.g. one or both of them will die). Review with students the Literary Focus information on p. 804 to explain the structure of a tragedy. Point out that in Act I, they will be reading the *exposition* and should watch for *rising action* that moves the play along.

READING/WRITING
Especially for RGP
(20 minutes)
Readers gaining proficiency will benefit from more help with the archaic language of the play. Suggest that as students read, they list words they do not understand that are not defined in the sidenotes. After reading, divide the class into small groups. Have the groups work together to define the words using dictionaries and context clues. Have students make a note of which words are no longer in use, which words have changed meanings, and which words are still in common usage.

ACADEMIC VOCABULARY
Preteaching Academic Vocabulary
(5 minutes)
Write the following words and their meanings on the board or on a transparency. Review them with students before introducing the literary focus.
Exposition: The background of a story that explains the setting, main characters, and the main conflict.
Rising Action: Events in a story that cause the conflict to increase.
Complications: Events that make it hard for the main characters to achieve their goals
Production: Presentation of a play; performance.

Original content Copyright © by Holt, Rinehart and Winston. Additions and changes to the original content are the responsibility of the instructor.

Differentiating Instruction

Have students check their understanding of tragedy with this activity. Ask students to work with a partner to think of a story they know – a book or movie – that ends unhappily for a main character. It can be the character's own doing or something that happens to the character. Have each pair explain the "tragedy" for the character.

READING FOCUS *(20 minutes)*

Reading a Play Review the Reading Focus on p. 804. Work with students to check their understanding of each strategy.

- Have pairs of students *read aloud* a few lines from Scene 1, such as p. 810 between Benvolio and Tybalt. Confirm how hearing lines spoken can help students understand the meaning.

- Have volunteers *paraphrase* lines from the prologue on p. 807. Discuss how using their own words can help them clarify meaning.

- Have students use the photo on p. 796 to practice *making inferences*. Discuss how they used clues in the image and how to use word clues.

- Have students use this same photo to explore *cause and effect* – what may *cause* Romeo and Juliet to fall in love and the *effect* it will have.

Then have students work in pairs to create a chart like the one at right.

Direct Teach

(60 minutes or more than one class period)

Chunk the Text Help students pace their reading by dividing Act I into "chunks" or parts. After students read each part, have them work with a partner to record notes in their strategy chart.

Part 1: ends p. 807, "What here shall miss, our toil…strive to mend."
Part 2: ends p. 810, "Have at thee, coward!"
Part 3: ends p. 814, "Come madam, let's away."
Part 4: ends p. 817, "I'll pay that doctrine, or else die in debt."
Part 5: ends p. 821, "But to rejoice in splendor of mine own."
Part 6: ends p. 825, "Go, girl, seek happy nights to happy days."
Part 7: ends p. 831, "Strike, drum."
Part 8: ends p. 837, "Now seeming sweet, convert to bitt'rest gall."
Part 9: ends p. 839, "Come, let's away; the strangers are all gone."

Check for Understanding

WRITING FOCUS *(30 minutes)*

Summarizing Act I Remind students that when they summarize, they identify only the most important events. For example, point out that there are two sword fights in Scene 1. Have students explain which event would belong in a summary. (e.g. Benvolio and Tybalt fighting, because they are more important characters to highlight the feud between the Montagues and Capulets). Have students work with a partner to list the most important events that occur in Act I.

Think as a Reader/Writer Have students use the list of key events they developed with their partners to write a summary of Act I.

Original content Copyright © by Holt, Rinehart and Winston. Additions and changes to the original content are the responsibility of the instructor.

Differentiating Instruction

READING FOCUS
Reading Strategy Chart

Reading Strategy	My Notes
Read aloud/ Paraphrase	
Make Inferences	
Analyze Causes and Effects	

READING/WRITING Especially for ELL
(10 minutes)
English-language learners from non-Western cultures will benefit from a brief review of the Western dramatic form before they read. Tell students that a drama, or play, is written to be performed by actors in front of an audience. The story is told through dialogue — the words characters speak — and the characters' actions. Use examples from Act I to review the following elements of a play:
* Long plays are divided into acts, which in turn are further divided into scenes. These divisions indicate a change of location or the passage of time. Changes in setting are usually noted at the beginning of acts and scenes.
* The written form of the play consists of lines of dialogue. Each character's name appears in dark (bold) type before his or her lines.
* Stage directions tell the actors how to speak and move. In this play, they are set in italics within brackets or parentheses.

Lesson Plan and Teaching Strategies

The Tragedy of Romeo and Juliet, Act II William Shakespeare

Preteach
LISTENING COMPREHENSION SKILLS *(10 minutes)*

Build Background/Set a Purpose Briefly review the setting of the play (e.g. Verona in northern Italy long ago) and ask volunteers to summarize these important events in Act I:

- Have students describe the relationship between the Montague and Capulet families when the play begins. (e.g. They are bitter enemies because of a long-standing feud.)

- Have students explain what happens when Romeo and Juliet meet for the first time. (e.g. They fall in love at first sight.)

- Have students explain what Romeo and Juliet discover about each other at the end of the act. (e.g. Romeo finds out that Juliet is a Capulet and Juliet learns that Romeo is a Montague.)

Check for questions students have about Act I before continuing. As background for Act II, explain that Romeo visits a friar, who is a kind of Catholic priest. Point out that at the time the story takes place, most families in Italy followed the Catholic religion.

Help students set a purpose for reading Act II. Have students preview the photographs of movies and stage productions for clues to events. Share these details with students:

- Romeo and Juliet discover they share the same feelings for each other.

- Romeo and Juliet are determined to be together.

Ask students to predict what actions Romeo and Juliet may take because of how they feel. Have students state their ideas and explain their reasoning. Have students check their ideas as they read.

VOCABULARY SKILLS *(10 minutes)*
Preteach Vocabulary Words Introduce the vocabulary in the Word Bank. Write each word and its meaning on the board. Discuss each word, and then give students these sentences to complete.

1. If we use our thinking skills, we can [devise] a solution that works.

2. We can [incorporate] both of our ideas together for a better plan.

3. A few players got angry and viewed the other team with [enmity].

4. Cleaning up rotten, stinky garbage is a [loathsome] job.

5. It is likely that the cat found in a box was [forsaken] by someone.

6. You can't just [conjure] a friend when you want something to do.

Remind students to watch for these words as they read the story.

RESOURCES
In *The Holt Reader*, "The Tragedy of Romeo and Juliet, Act II," for students who need more scaffolding in a workbook format

In this book: *Vocabulary Skill Builder*, p. 187; "The Tragedy of Romeo and Juliet, Act II," Selection Test, p. 189

Consult *Holt Audio Library* for recordings of most selections

WORD BANK
The following words are not identified as vocabulary but will be helpful for students to learn before reading Act II:
conjure (p. 844): compel to appear by reciting or using magic
enmity (p. 848): feeling enemies have for each other; hatred
forsaken (p. 856): deserted; abandoned
devise (p. 862): think out; plan or contrive
loathsome (p. 869): disgusting
incorporate (p. 869): join or combine

VOCABULARY SKILLS
Especially for ELL
(5 minutes)
In addition to the Word Bank terms, English language learners will benefit from previewing these words:
perverse (p. 849): contrary and willful; stubborn
impute (p. 849): charge with, as a fault
lamentable (p. 858): causing sadness

Original content Copyright © by Holt, Rinehart and Winston. Additions and changes to the original content are the responsibility of the instructor.

Differentiating Instruction

LANGUAGE COACH SKILL *(20 minutes)*

Archaic Language Remind students that Shakespeare wrote his plays more than four hundred years ago. Some of the words he uses are now archaic, or out of use. Write the following examples from *Romeo and Juliet* of archaic terms and their meanings on the board. Review them with students.

Pray: ask

- *Saucy:* rude
- *Ropery:* vulgar ways
- *Secret:* trustworthy
- *Ne'er:* never
- *Had as lieve see:* would as soon see
- *Aweary:* tired
- *Give me leave:* let me rest
- *Jaunce:* tiring journey
- *Hie you hence:* go quickly

Have students work with a partner to use each word or expression in original oral sentences. As students use the words, have them think about which might have been slang terms in Shakespeare's day, such as *saucy.* Refer students to the expression "Marry come up, I trow" (p. 866), which is explained in the sidenote, as another example of slang. Have students watch for more archaic slang as they read Act II.

LITERARY FOCUS *(30 minutes)*

Dramatic Irony Remind students that they read a story with situational irony – which is when we expect one thing to happen but something entirely different occurs instead – in O. Henry's "The Gift of the Magi." Explain that *dramatic irony* is the opposite literary technique. Dramatic irony occurs when the reader or audience knows something important that a character does not. Give students this example to consider.

> Let's say the story "The Gift of the Magi" started in a different way. It begins with Jim, the husband, selling his pocket watch to buy two beautiful combs for Della's long hair. Then the story shifts to Della. She is upset because she does not have money to buy Jim a Christmas gift. So she decides to cut off her long hair and sell it, and then she uses the money to buy a beautiful chain for Jim's watch.

Discuss the dramatic irony in this version of the story. Confirm that the reader knows when Della sells her hair that she will not be able to use Jim's gift. And when Della chooses the watch chain, the reader knows Jim won't be able to use it. The excitement of the story becomes wondering how each character will react when they learn what the reader already knows. Explain that Act II of *Romeo and Juliet* has dramatic irony. A *turning point* in the tragedy occurs in this act that will lead to the *climax* of the play.

READING/WRITING
Especially for LDN
(15 minutes or more)
Learners with diverse needs will benefit from opportunities to read aloud selected scenes before, during, and after reading Act II. Have small groups of students read aloud all or parts of scenes, such as the famous balcony scene. Remind students that characters do not read the setting and stage directions. For each group, assign a narrator to read the stage directions. Discuss with students the experience of reading the lines aloud and ways it aids their understanding of the language, characters, and action of the play.

ACADEMIC VOCABULARY
Preteaching Academic Vocabulary
(5 minutes)
Write these terms and their meanings on a chalkboard or transparency. Review them with the students before introducing the literary focus.
Turning Point: In a tragedy, the moment when the main characters decide on a course of action that determines the outcome of the conflict.
Climax: The moment of greatest emotional intensity in a drama, such as the death of one or more main characters in a tragedy.
Convention: Standard technique.
Interpretation: Portrayal that conveys a particular understanding of a work.

Original content Copyright © by Holt, Rinehart and Winston. Additions and changes to the original content are the responsibility of the instructor.

Differentiating Instruction

Have students check their understanding of dramatic irony with this activity. Have them work with a partner to alter a favorite story or movie to give it dramatic irony. Ask the pairs to explain what they would change so readers or viewers know something important that the characters do not. Bring students together to share their examples.

READING FOCUS *(20 minutes)*

Reading a Play Review with students the different strategies they used in reading Act I. Focus on the process of making inferences. Confirm that students use clues from the text and their own experiences to understand parts of the play that are not stated in the dialogue. Have students return to the image of Romeo and Juliet on p. 796, which shows their first meeting. Ask: *What have you learned about them in Act I? What clues do you get about them from this photo? How do they feel about love? Are they likely to make wise decisions at their age?*

Have students work with a partner to discuss these questions, using clues in the play and what they know about teens their own age. Have students create a chart like the one at right, then pencil in their answers for Romeo and Juliet. Have students check their inferences as they read.

Direct Teach

(60 minutes or more than one class period)

Chunk the Text Help students pace their reading by dividing Act II into "chunks" or parts. After students read each part, have them stop to fill in the chart and make inferences about characters.

Part 1: ends p. 845, "To seek him here that means not to be found."
Part 2: ends p. 850, "Stay but a little, I will come again."
Part 3: ends p. 853, "His help to crave and my dear hap to tell."
Part 4: ends p. 857, "Wisely and slow. They stumble that run fast."
Part 5: ends p. 861, "Here's goodly gear."
Part 6: ends p. 863, "Before, and apace."
Part 7: ends p. 867, "Hie to high fortune! Honest nurse, farewell."
Part 8: ends p. 869, "Till holy church incorporate two in one."

Check for Understanding

WRITING FOCUS *(20 minutes)*

Summarizing Act II Remind students of the summaries they wrote for Act I. Have students work with a partner to list the most important events that occur in Act II.

Think as a Reader/Writer Have students use the list of key events they developed with their partners to write a summary of Act II. Tell students to be sure to explain why Romeo and Juliet's secret marriage is a complication for their families that may be a *turning point* in the play.

READING FOCUS
Inferences Chart

Make Inferences	My Notes
What can I infer about Romeo?	
What can I infer about Juliet?	
What can I infer about the friar?	

READING/WRITING
Especially for WGP
(15 minutes)
To help Writers Gaining Proficiency to summarize the events in Act II, write the following key events out of sequence on the board. Have students work with a partner to place the events in sequence, then copy them in their notebooks. Have students follow the list of events to write a summary of Act II in their own words:
* Romeo enters the Capulets' orchard and overhears Juliet.
* Romeo and Juliet declare their love and make plans to marry in secret.
* Friar Laurence agrees to marry the couple.
* Romeo rejoins his friends, who are pleased by his cheerfulness.
* The nurse carries a message from Romeo to Juliet arranging a time for their meeting.
* Juliet joins Romeo in Friar Laurence's cell, and they exit to perform the marriage ceremony.

Original content Copyright © by Holt, Rinehart and Winston. Additions and changes to the original content are the responsibility of the instructor.

Differentiating Instruction

The Tragedy of Romeo and Juliet, Acts III-V

William Shakespeare

Elements of Drama Chart The characters in drama often speak in **dialogue, monologues, soliloquies,** and **asides.** They use **metaphors** and other figures of speech to communicate their thoughts and feelings.

Fill in the chart by identifying passages from Acts III, IV, or V that contain these elements. Identify who is speaking, describe the passage, and include the line numbers.

Elements of Drama	Examples from Acts III, IV, or V
Dialogue	
Monologue	
Soliloquy	
Metaphor or Other Figure of Speech	
Aside	

Original content Copyright © by Holt, Rinehart and Winston. Additions and changes to the original content are the responsibility of the instructor.

Collection 8
Graphic Organizer

Lost at Sea retold by Mary Pope Osborne
Alcyone and Ceyx Mary Zimmerman

Narratives Across Genres Diagram A myth and a play are both stories, or **narratives**. They share these common elements: plot, setting, theme, and character. A myth, however, uses a **narrator** to tell the story. A play relies on dialogue between characters to tell the story, although many Greek plays also include a narrator.

Compare the differences and similarities between narration and dialogue in the two selections. Fill out the diagram by putting the similarities in the center and the differences in the outer circles of the diagram. Use the elements listed in the box.

- Describes the action of the story.
- Gives information about the characters.
- Reveals the characters' feelings indirectly.
- Reveals the characters' feelings directly.
- Makes the characters seem more personal.
- Doesn't tell the reader what to think about the characters.
- Lets the characters speak for themselves.

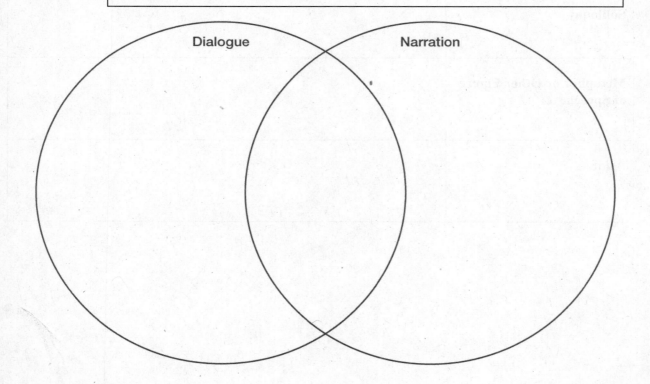

Dialogue   Narration

Original content Copyright © by Holt, Rinehart and Winston. Additions and changes to the original content are the responsibility of the instructor.

Lesson Plan and Teaching Strategies

"Dear Juliet": Seeking Succor from a Veteran of Love
Dinitia Smith *from* The Juliet Club

Preteach

LISTENING COMPREHENSION SKILLS *(10 minutes)*

Build Background/Set a Purpose Discuss the Build Background on p. 974. Review key details of *The Tragedy of Romeo and Juliet* to refresh students' memories. (e.g. The play is set in Verona; Romeo and Juliet are from feuding families; they fall passionately in love and marry secretly; they die tragically as a result of their love.) Be sure students know that a "tomb" is a place where a person is buried. Discuss the photo on p. 972 of the building in Verona that is called Juliet's house. Have student identify a feature of the house they recall from the play (e.g. the balcony where Juliet stood as Romeo declared his love). However, point out that Juliet and Romeo were not actual historical persons. Discuss why the city of Verona would identify places as belonging to Juliet, even though she was not a real person (e.g. to bring tourists to visit; because people are looking for connections to Shakespeare's famous play).

Help students set a purpose for reading by previewing these details:

- The first selection is a newspaper article about the Juliet Club in Verona.

- People from around the world send letters to Juliet in Verona, which are received by the club. As evidence, have students look at the photo on p. 975. (Confirm that Giulietta is Juliet in Italian.)

- The second selection is an example of an actual letter written to Juliet.

Review the title of the newspaper article with students. Refer students to the meaning of *succor* (e.g. comfort; relief). Check understanding of *veteran* (e.g. someone with experience). Ask students to give their ideas of why real people might write to Juliet and how the Juliet Club gets involved. Have students read to check their ideas for accuracy.

VOCABULARY SKILLS *(10 minutes)*

Preteach Vocabulary Words Review the meanings of the vocabulary in the Word Bank. Then give students these sentences to complete.

1. To be a successful student, it is [vital] to have good study skills.

2. When I'm anxious, I feel like a person dangling from a [precipice].

3. If we [collaborate] on a project, we can share ideas and materials.

4. She always includes drawings in the envelope with her [missives].

Remind students to watch for these words as they read.

RESOURCES

In *The Holt Reader*, "'Dear Juliet': Seeking Succor from a Veteran of Love/*from* The Juliet Club," for students who need more scaffolding in a workbook format

In this book: *Vocabulary Skill Builder*, p. 187; "'Dear Juliet': Seeking Succor from a Veteran of Love/*from* The Juliet Club," Selection Test, p. 190

Consult *Holt Audio Library* for recordings of most selections

WORD BANK
precipice
vital
missives
collaborate

VOCABULARY SKILLS
Especially for LDN
(5 minutes)
Learners with diverse needs may benefit from applying the academic vocabulary word *embody* to this discussion of the letters to Juliet. Review that "embody" means to give form to something abstract. Discuss the image of Juliet (and Romeo, too) that students recall from the play. Confirm that each character brings to mind someone deeply in love. Point out that Juliet, especially, has come to embody, or represent, love to many people. So they write to her for guidance about love.

Original content Copyright © by Holt, Rinehart and Winston. Additions and changes to the original content are the responsibility of the instructor.

Differentiating Instruction

LANGUAGE COACH SKILL *(25 minutes)*

Etymology Explain that a word's *etymology* is its history. Knowing where a word comes from can help students understand its meaning and other related words. Discuss these examples from the selections:

- The Latin word *humilis* means "low" or "small." *Humiliation* (p. 974) is a noun that means the act of being humiliated. When you are humiliated, you are made to feel low, small, and insignificant. Explain that another word that comes from *humilis* is *humble*. Have students check its meaning in a dictionary (e.g. low in condition).

- The Old French word *tourner* means "to turn." *Tour*, which means a long trip for sightseeing, comes from it. *Tourists* (p. 976) are people who take a tour. Discuss the connection to *tourner* (e.g. a tour is a turn at doing something different; tourists do not follow their everyday routines).

- *Ineffable* (p. 977) comes from the Latin word *ineffabilis,* which means *in-,* "not," plus *effabilis,* "utterable." *Effabilis* comes from the Latin word *effari,* which means "to speak out." Help students put this word history together to understand the definition on p. 977. Something *ineffable* cannot be spoken of; it's indescribable.

- *Passion* (p. 978) comes from the Latin word *passus,* which means "to endure." Discuss with students why passion – strong feeling – can be something to endure, or get through (e.g. it can be painful to want something or feel something so strongly).

Write these sentences on the board. Have students complete each one by adding a word from the box.

ineffable	humiliation	passion	tourist

1. She will have fun on vacation spending her days as a [tourist].
2. Because of their [passion] for skating, they practice all the time.
3. The view from the mountain was [ineffable] in its beauty.
4. I felt his [humiliation] when he tripped on the way to the stage.

INFORMATIONAL TEXT FOCUS *(20 minutes)*

Primary and Secondary Sources Explain that when students read informational text, they need to pay attention to where the information comes from. *Primary sources* are firsthand accounts. They come directly from a person and express the individual's feelings and thoughts to the reader. *Secondary sources* come through someone else. The writer gathers information and *interprets* it for the reader. Give students these examples to demonstrate the difference between primary and secondary sources:

- You e-mail a friend to describe a basketball game that you attended and your friend did not. You are a *primary source* for your friend, providing your thoughts and feelings about the game directly.

Original content Copyright © by Holt, Rinehart and Winston. Additions and changes to the original content are the responsibility of the instructor.

ACADEMIC VOCABULARY

Preteaching Academic Vocabulary
(5 minutes)
Write these terms and their meanings on a chalkboard or transparency. Review them with students before introducing the informational text focus and reading the selections.
Primary source: A firsthand account that comes directly from a person and reveals the person's thoughts and feelings
Secondary source: A secondhand account that often contains more than one person's views
Embody: Give form to something abstract.
Interpret: To explain or translate ideas or information for others

READING/WRITING
Especially for ELL
(20 minutes)
English-language learners will benefit from concrete experiences with primary and secondary sources. Have ELL students write a letter to a friend or relative about some aspect of life in America. Then compare each student's letter (primary source) to a textbook or encyclopedia entry about the same topic or a general entry on the U.S. (secondary source). Discuss the differences in viewpoint and information provided in the two types of sources.

Differentiating Instruction

the game. So your friend uses your e-mail comments and comments from other students. Your friend also gets information from a sports almanac on basketball and old yearbooks to compare teams. Your friend's Web story is a *secondary source* on the basketball game, with some primary sources – like your quotes – included in it.

Discuss advantages of primary sources (e.g., first-person views) and disadvantages (e.g., the views may be limited or wrong). Discuss advantages of secondary sources (e.g., broader view on a topic) and disadvantages (e.g., the writer interprets information, so you get the information the writer thinks is important to include).

Check students' understanding of different types of sources. Write examples from the lists below randomly on the board. Have students work with a partner to identify each as a primary source or a secondary source. Students' completed lists might look like this:

- Primary: speech, letter, autobiography, quotes from a person
- Secondary: encyclopedia, textbook, biography, newspaper article

Then have students work in pairs to fill out a chart like the one at right. As they read the newspaper article, "Dear Juliet," have them list examples of primary sources (e.g., quotes from people) and secondary sources (e.g., information from books the writer read).

Direct Teach
(40 minutes)

Chunk the Text Help students pace their reading by dividing the selection into "chunks" or parts. After students read each part, have them stop to list primary and secondary sources in the text on the chart.
Part 1: ends p. 974, col. 2: " '…your husband will come back to you.' "
Part 2: ends p. 976, col. 2: "…but is otherwise run by volunteers."
Part 3: ends p. 977, col. 1: " '… one of those ineffable things.' "
Part 4: ends p. 978, col. 2: "…the legend of love. Charlotte"

Check for Understanding
WRITING FOCUS *(30 minutes)*

Comparing Information From Sources Discuss key information students learned from the newspaper article about the Juliet Club (e.g., its members are volunteers who respond to people that write to Juliet; two American sisters wrote a book about the club). Have students describe what they learned from the letter (e.g., the writer's feelings about Juliet and love). Ask students to write a sentence that explains their idea of the biggest difference between the two selections.

Think as a Reader/Writer Check for questions about the writing assignment on p. 979. Encourage students to review the newspaper article, identify the primary sources in it, and think about the purpose they serve. Then have students write their responses on their own.

READING FOCUS
Sources Chart

Primary Sources in the Text	Secondary Sources in the Text

READING/WRITING Especially for WGP
(10 minutes)
Have Writers Gaining Proficiency use a Venn diagram to compare the newspaper article and the letter. On the left, they list information they learned only from the newspaper article. On the right, they list information they learned only from the letter. In the middle, they list similar information they gained from both. Guide students to recognize that the parts of letters to Juliet, which the writer includes in the newspaper article, belong here. Discuss with students why the writer would include quotes from letters (e.g., to hear directly from people who write Juliet and highlight their feelings).

Original content Copyright © by Holt, Rinehart and Winston. Additions and changes to the original content are the responsibility of the instructor.

Differentiating Instruction

Collection 8
Targeted Strategies for Learners with Diverse Needs

READING SKILLS

Primary and Secondary Sources *(15 minutes)* Explain to students that a **primary source** is created by someone who is present at the time and place of an event, while a **secondary source** is created by someone who did not experience that event firsthand. Copy the chart below on the board or on a transparency. Discuss the reasons why a newspaper article might appear in more than one place on the chart.

Primary: from the event itself	Primary: at the time by a witness	Primary: after the event by a witness	Secondary: after the event, from primary sources
-photographs -videos -posters -brochures -maps -records	-interviews -statements -quotes -newspaper article	-diary entries -letters -memoirs -autobiographies -oral histories -newspaper article	-biographies -histories -textbooks -newspaper article

Have partners choose an event and give examples of the kinds of primary and secondary sources they could find. Challenge students to brainstorm where they might seek this information.

LITERARY SKILLS

Tragedy *(15 minutes)* Point out that any story with an unhappy ending can be considered a **tragedy**. Explain that two of the characteristics of a tragedy are a serious problem (often caused by a mistake made by the main character) and the lack of escape or alternative. Guide the class to think about a story that ends unhappily and analyze it together:

- What is the main problem? Why is it so hard to solve?

- Is there another way out of the situation? What is limiting the freedom or choices the main character can make?

Have students work in pairs to discuss another story that ends tragically.

Dramatic Irony *(15 minutes)* Have students think of a time they wished they could warn a character about something they realized but the character didn't know. Explain that when the reader knows something that a character does not know it is called **dramatic irony**. Have students use the think/pair/share technique to discuss this question:

- How does it feel to know more than the characters know?

Ask student to use their answers to brainstorm reasons why an author might use this technique.

Readings in Collection 8
Minimum Course of Study
The Tragedy of Romeo and Juliet, Act I, p. 796
The Tragedy of Romeo and Juliet, Act II, p. 842
"Dear Juliet": Seeking Succor from a Veteran of Love/ from The Juliet Club, p. 972

RESOURCES
In *The Holt Reader*. all three selections help students who need more scaffolding in a workbook format.
Consult *Holt Audio Library* for recordings of most selections.

TEACHING TIP
English-language learners may not be familiar with the range of primary source types. It may help to have them visit the library where they can see examples.

ALTERNATIVE ASSESSMENT *(5 minutes)*
Have students provide answers for these items.

[A tragedy/dramatic irony] is when the reader knows more about the plot than a character does.

A story that ends unhappily is called [a tragedy].

If you wanted to know what it was like to experience an event in the past, you could look for a [primary source].

Original content Copyright © by Holt, Rinehart and Winston. Additions and changes to the original content are the responsibility of the instructor.

Differentiating Instruction

Academic and Selection Vocabulary *Student Edition pages 796–979*

The Tragedy of Romeo and Juliet
Dear Juliet/Letter to Juliet and "Her" Response

A. Circle the word that doesn't belong in each series.

1. precipice, edge, rock, cliff

2. vital, critical, important, fussy

3. missives, numbers, letters, correspondence

4. collaborate, cooperate, score, assist

B. Complete each sentence with one of the vocabulary words below.

conjure   devise   loathsome   incorporate · rebellious

1. The star-crossed lovers tried to _____ a plan to run away and get married.

2. My mom views this as the _____ act of two teens defying their parents.

3. I believe that their actions _____ both rebellion and true love.

4. The idea that both took poison in the end was nothing short of _____!

5. As I watched the play, I longed to _____ a different kind of potion to bring them back to life.

C. Use the academic vocabulary words to complete the following paragraph about "The Tragedy of Romeo and Juliet," by William Shakespeare.

convention   embody   productions   interpretation

Today it is hard to imagine a male actor trying to (1) _____ Juliet's

innocence, youth, and beauty. But in Shakespeare's time it was the (2)

_____ to use all male actors, even in the female roles. Modern (3)

_____ usually cast a talented young actress in the role of Juliet. Audiences

expect a realistic (4) _____ of the tragic young lovers.

Original content Copyright © by Holt, Rinehart and Winston. Additions and changes to the original content are the responsibility of the instructor.

Differentiating Instruction

Selection Test

The Tragedy of Romeo and Juliet, Act I

William Shakespeare

COMPREHENSION, SKILLS, AND VOCABULARY Circle the letter of the best answer to each of the following items.

1. Which explains the situation between the Montagues and the Capulets?

   A) Each family wants to rule Verona.

   B) Both families want to end their fight but don't know how.

   C) The two families have been bitter enemies for years.

   D) The Prince has been stirring up trouble between the two families.

2. Which statement is true of Romeo and Juliet?

   A) They are strangers until they meet at Juliet's home.

   B) They have known each other since they were children.

   C) Romeo pretends to like Juliet to make Rosaline jealous.

   D) Juliet's father thinks Romeo could make a good husband.

3. Which is the most accurate statement about a *tragedy*?

   A) It cannot have any funny lines.

   B) It ends in an unhappy way for the main characters.

   C) It is usually about young people who fall in and out of love.

   D) It has an evil character that fights against the main characters.

4. Which would you learn in the exposition of a play?

   A) how it ends

   B) who the main characters are

   C) what happens to increase the conflict

   D) which decision or event will determine the ending

5. Which statement best describes Shakespeare's language?

   A) He wrote the way people speak today.

   B) He used mainly simple words that rhyme.

   C) He used mainly figures of speech that are not spoken anymore.

   D) He gave some lines a beat with stressed and unstressed syllables.

6. What is your opinion of Romeo in Act I? Do you like him, or not? Why? Use the organizer to collect ideas. Then write a paragraph.

| Introductory statement: I do/do not like Romeo in Act I. |
| Two or three supporting sentences: For one thing, … Also, … But then, … |
| Concluding statement: So, in my opinion, I think Romeo… |

Original content Copyright © by Holt, Rinehart and Winston. Additions and changes to the original content are the responsibility of the instructor.

Collection 8
Selection Test

The Tragedy of Romeo and Juliet, Act II

William Shakespeare

COMPREHENSION, SKILLS, AND VOCABULARY Circle the letter of the best answer to each of the following items.

1. Which is true of Romeo's and Juliet's decision to marry?

   A) Their parents tell them they cannot marry.

   B) Juliet's father says she is too young to marry Romeo.

   C) The Prince encourages them to marry to bring peace to the families.

   D) No one knows about their plans to marry except the friar and the nurse.

2. How long have Romeo and Juliet known each other when they decide to marry?

   A) one night

   B) one week

   C) several years

   D) since they were born

3. Which statement best explains dramatic irony in a play?

   A) the opposite of what you expect takes place

   B) you know something that the characters don't

   C) you can read between the lines to figure out the ending

   D) the main characters speak to the audience and tell what they're thinking

4. When you *make an inference,* you—

   A) restate lines of text in your own words

   B) explain how one event causes another to occur

   C) use clues and your own experiences to guess about a character or event

   D) take a wild guess about why a character acts a certain way or an event happens

5. Which best describes language that is **archaic?**

   A) It comes from Greek or Latin words.

   B) It sounds like everyday speech in English.

   C) It is made up mostly of slang words and phrases.

   D) It is language that is no longer spoken or written.

6. Could marriage between Romeo and Juliet have solved the problem between their families? Use the organizer to help write a paragraph.

Introductory statement: I do/do not think marriage between Rome and Juliet ….
Two or three supporting sentences: For one thing, … Also, … In addition, …
Concluding statement: So, in conclusion, I think …

Original content Copyright © by Holt, Rinehart and Winston. Additions and changes to the original content are the responsibility of the instructor.

Differentiating Instruction

"Dear Juliet": Seeking Succor from a Veteran of Love

Dinitia Smith/ *from* **The Juliet Club**

COMPREHENSION, SKILLS, AND VOCABULARY Circle the letter of the best
answer to each of the following items.

1. What is the Juliet Club?

   A) a club for students who are age thirteen

   B) a club for students who have read *Romeo and Juliet*

   C) a group of people who answer letters written to Juliet

   D) a group of people who like to perform *Romeo and Juliet*

2. Which is a detail from the article about Verona, Italy?

   A) Shakespeare visited Verona before he wrote *Romeo and Juliet*.

   B) There is nothing in Verona that reminds people of Shakespeare's play.

   C) Most people do not know that Shakespeare set *Romeo and Juliet* in Verona.

   D) The place called Juliet's house was first given that name in the 19th century.

3. Which is an example of a *primary source* in the newspaper article?

   A) the quotes from club members

   B) the book title, "Newly Discovered Story of Two Noble Lovers"

   C) the mention of street names in Verona, Italy, such as Via Cappello

   D) the writer's explanation, in parentheses, that no bones are in Juliet's tomb

4. Which statement accurately describes a secondary source?

   A) It usually provides less information than a primary source.

   B) It usually provides information gathered from more than one source.

   C) It is always the next source you find after the first, or primary, source.

   D) It is always the exact words of a person who experienced a specific event.

5. Which phrase describes what you do when you **collaborate**?

   A) team up with others

   B) compete against others

   C) look for ways you are like others

   D) look for ways you are different from others

6. Would you want to be a member of the Juliet Club? Explain your point of view.
   Use the organizer to help you write a paragraph.

Introductory statement: I would/would not want to be a member ….
Two or three supporting sentences: For one thing, … Also, … In addition, …
Concluding statement: So, in conclusion, …

Original content Copyright © by Holt, Rinehart and Winston. Additions and changes to the original content are the responsibility of the instructor.

Collection 8
Collection Summative Test

VOCABULARY SKILLS Complete the sentences below by using the collection vocabulary words from the list below.

vital   collaborate   missives   devise

conjure   rebellious

1. Let's _____ a system for organizing the letters we receive.

2. It is _____ that we get the correct address for each delivery.

3. The children became _____ and refused to wait quietly for the bus.

4. The campers sent many _____ home describing fun activities.

LITERARY AND READING SKILLS Circle the letter of the best answer.

5. In a tragedy, what is the **turning point?**

   A) the halfway point of the play

   B) when the main characters first appear on stage

   C) when the main characters make a choice that decides what happens to them

   D) the most emotional moment of the play, such as when a main character dies

6. Which is an example of **dramatic irony?**

   A) predicting that a character will die

   B) being surprised when a main character dies

   C) having the main character die at the end of the play

   D) knowing a character will die as he or she plans for the future

7. When you look for **primary sources** in a nonfiction article, you

   A) look for information in quotes coming from a person

   B) look for information that comes from an encyclopedia

   C) read between the lines for information not stated by the writer

   D) look for the most important sources the writer used for information

LANGUAGE AND WRITING SKILLS Choose the correct answer in each answer pair.

8. The etymology of a word is its _____ [history/part of speech].

9. One characteristic of William Shakespeare's language in *Romeo and Juliet* is his use of _____ [words in Italian/figures of speech].

10. When you write a summary of a play, you include only the most _____ [enjoyable/important] characters and events.

Original content Copyright © by Holt, Rinehart and Winston. Additions and changes to the original content are the responsibility of the instructor.

Lesson Plan and Teaching Strategies

Writing Workshop: Informative Essay

PREWRITING

Write Your Thesis *(15 minutes)*

Review the purpose of an informative essay: *When you write an informative essay, you give your audience information about a topic that you know well.* Once students have brainstormed a list of topics, and chosen one, help students construct an appropriate thesis. Say, *A thesis can be too broad, if it doesn't focus in on the topic enough. On the other hand, a scope that is too narrow would not give you enough to write about.* Additionally, remind students that the thesis in an informative essay is not an opinion as it is in a persuasive essay. Give students the model below.

Scope	Thesis on the topic of celebrity gossip
Too broad	Where to find news about celebrities
Good	Techniques celebrity magazines use to invent news
Too narrow	The celebrity most searched on the Web this week
Opinionated	America's unhealthy obsession with celebrities

Have students work in small groups to help each other generate their thesis statements.

Gather Information to Support Your Thesis *(15 minutes)*

Help students on an individual basis with potential sources for their topics, so that every student has a plan. Then, once students have decided on a structure for organizing support of their topic, have them generate a flow chart that includes the elements of the structures listed on page 994 of the Student Edition.

Then have students share their flowcharts, showing how each of the three structural parts are represented.

DRAFTING

Organize Details *(10 minutes)*

Make sure students use their flowcharts to draft their essays. Have students code the boxes on the flowchart to related notes they have taken. Explain that doing this will help them put their notes in order.

Review the framework on page 995 of the Student Edition. Remind students that they will begin with a "fun fact" in addition to their thesis in the first paragraph. In the body of the essay, they will use the information they've gathered and organized. The conclusion of the essay should summarize their main points. Once you have reviewed this with students, have them draft their essays.

TEACHING TIP

In this lesson students may need some guidance in where to look for information. The school library, where they can request support, may be the best place. Be sure to have students capture their sources when gathering information. For each note that students take, have them list the author, title of the work, source, and copyright date.

ESPECIALLY FOR ELL

(10 minutes)

Transition words can be challenging for English-language learners since their meaning relies heavily on context. Ask proficient speakers to help you invent or find examples of sentences that include the transition words in the chart on page 995 of the Student Edition. Post these examples so that English-language learners can refer to them and use them as models.

ESPECIALLY FOR WGP

Encourage students to choose a topic that interests them and one they already know something about. Since they have just read about drama, they may want to think about forms of entertainment they enjoy. If they can think of a question that they wish to explore, it will help them remain motivated throughout the assignment.

Original content Copyright © by Holt, Rinehart and Winston. Additions and changes to the original content are the responsibility of the instructor.

Differentiating Instruction

EVALUATING AND REVISING

Review Content and Organization *(20 minutes)*

Give students time to focus on the following points in Evaluation Questions 2, 3, 4, 5 and 6.

2. Start by underlining the thesis. The thesis should clearly state what the essay is going to be about. The thesis often is found in the last sentence of the first paragraph.

3. Use the mini-lesson on adding specific information to give students more guidance. If there is any confusion about the different kinds of evidence students can use to support each reason, have students review the chart on page 600 in the Student Edition on writing a persuasive essay.

4. If students are having trouble with the organization of their essays, have them consult the flowcharts they created during the prewriting activities. Then follow the directions in the chart on page 996 of the Student Edition.

5. For more help with transitions, remind students to use the chart on page 995 of the Student Edition.

6. Point out the conclusion of the Student Draft on page 998 of the Student Edition as a model for students to use as they work on their own conclusions.

Pair students with a partner to use the guidelines and the points above when they review each other's drafts.

Mini-Lesson: How to Make Information Credible *(10 Minutes)*

Give students time to go back into their notes and find the sources of the information they've gathered. If they are lacking in credible sources work with students individually to suggest how they might find some, depending on the topic they've chosen.

Grammar Link: Capitalizing Proper Nouns *(5 Minutes)*

Moving beyond basic capitalization rules can be tricky. Explain to students that the items are capitalized because they are specifically part of a name and that the same words would not otherwise be capitalized.

Review the examples below and discuss which are capitalized and why.

Not Capitalized	Capitalized
We are voting for a new president.	President Johnson is known for his war on poverty.
The local animal shelter needs volunteers.	Town Lake Animal Shelter has strict rules for adoption.
The student applied to college.	Julio attends City College.
I need to see a doctor.	I went to see Dr. Gonzales.

Then ask students to reread their essays to find and fix proper nouns that are not appropriately capitalized.

TEACHING TIP

Wait until students are at the proofreading stage to introduce the grammar link lessons. Student gaining proficiency with writing may be overwhelmed by too many considerations at earlier stages.

ESPECIALLY FOR ELL
(10 minutes)

Since the rules for capitalization vary across languages, the Grammar Link: Capitalizing Proper Nouns provides a great opportunity to practice the basics with English-language learners, for example, names of people and places, days and dates, titles of books and movies, and the names of languages.

ESPECIALLY FOR LDN

Allow students who are familiar with the basic rules of capitalization (names, places, days, and dates) to work with their English-language learning peers. It is often rewarding for these students to be cast in the role of mentor.

Original content Copyright © by Holt, Rinehart and Winston. Additions and changes to the original content are the responsibility of the instructor.

Differentiating Instruction

Lesson Plan and Teaching Strategies

Listening and Speaking Workshop: Analyzing and Evaluating Speeches

ANALYZE THE CONTENT *(20 minutes)*

Help students prepare to analyze a speech by explaining the combination of skills required to do so. They must combine an understanding of the content with sensory observation of the voice and actions of the speaker. Tell students that they will have opportunities while listening to a speech to pause and note examples of both the type of argument the speaker makes and the ways in which he or she uses language to make the message stand out.

- **Type of Argument**: Review the five types of arguments on page 1002 of the Student Edition with the group. Students may be familiar with each argument type from their own experiences: *causation* (if you keep doing that…), *analogy* (it's just like the time…), *appeal to authority* (the teacher said…), *emotional appeal* (I'll be your best friend), and *logical appeal* (it's a fact that…).

- **Rhetorical Devices**: Student who are not yet masters of rhetoric can learn a great deal from the speeches of Martin Luther King, Jr. for example. You may wish to find copies of his speeches in your school or local library or on the Internet. Use them to highlight the rhetorical devices listed on page 1002 of the Student Edition, e.g. *allusion* ("I have been to the mountaintop . . ."); *repetition* ("I have a dream today . . ."); *parallelism* (" . . . when people are not judged by the color of their skin but by the content of their character.")

ANALYZE THE DELIVERY *(10 minutes)*

Instruct students to make charts like those on page 1004 of the Student Edition. Have them replace each description of a verbal and/or nonverbal technique, however, with an example of each technique from the speech they are watching. As students watch the "I Have a Dream" speech, for example, they can readily cite King's delivery of the phrase "I have a dream . . ." as an example of *emphasis*.

EVALUATE A SPEECH *(10 minutes)*

As students prepare to evaluate a speech they have watched, ask them to rate the examples they have gathered for their effectiveness. Have students then use the questions on page 1005 of the Student Edition as a guide for writing a paragraph to evaluate of the quality and impact of a historical speech that they have just viewed.

TEACHING TIP
Students may need help selecting speeches. Help them use library or Internet resources. You may wish to have students listen to speeches in small groups and delegate roles for listening. For additional practice speaking, students may wish to present their evaluations to the class.

ESPECIALLY FOR ELL
Encourage English-language learners to listen to the speech multiple times with a single purpose for listening each time. The first time students listen, they should focus simply on the gist of the speech, who is speaking, the topic, and the effect.

EVALUATION CRITERIA
Use these criteria to evaluate students' work:

- Identifies and evaluates types of arguments
- Identifies and evaluates rhetorical devices
- Analyzes speaker's verbal and nonverbal techniques
- Sums up an evaluation of speech in a single paragraph with some examples of the above

---

Original content Copyright © by Holt, Rinehart and Winston. Additions and changes to the original content are the responsibility of the instructor.

Differentiating Instruction

Unit 4; Skill Builder 1
Oral Language Skill Builder

Paraphrase

UNDERSTAND THE SKILL Paraphrasing a statement, or putting it into your own words, is a great way to check your understanding.

Work with a partner to complete the chart. Paraphrase the quotes from *The Tragedy of Romeo and Juliet* in the third column. Then role-play the conversations between callers and an advice line host. Afterward, discuss the questions below.

Verona Advice Line			
Caller	**Problem**	**Paraphrase**	**Advice**
Prince (calling about Montagues and Capulets)	"Rebellious subjects, enemies to the peace… Will they not hear?"	If I understand your problem correctly, it seems that…	One way that you might handle this situation is…
Romeo (calling about Rosalind)	"I do love a woman…She'll not be hit with Cupid arrow…She hath forsworn to love, and in that vow do I live dead that live to tell it now."	It sounds like you're saying…	Perhaps you might consider…
Juliet (calling about Romeo)	"My only love, sprung from my only hate! Too early seen unknown, and known too late! Prodigious birth of love it is to me that I must love a loathed enemy."	I believe what you're saying is…	In this case, it may be a good idea to…
Friar (calling about Romeo)	"Is Rosalind…so soon forsaken? Young men's love then lies not truly in their hearts, but in their eyes."	So, to put it another way,	As a friend, you might…

Extend Discussion Think of problems that other characters might have in the play. Discuss these situations with a partner.

• Suppose you were Juliet's nurse. How would you advise Juliet?

• Suppose you were Benvolio. How would you advise Romeo?

Original content Copyright © by Holt, Rinehart and Winston. Additions and changes to the original content are the responsibility of the instructor.

Unit 4; Skill Builder 2
Oral Language Skill Builder

Retell

UNDERSTAND THE SKILL Retelling the events in a story is a good way to check your understanding of the plot. When you retell the story, you focus on the action and leave out the details.

Work with a group to complete the chart. When you are finished, have a group retelling of Act Two. Then discuss the questions below.

Scene 1

Benvolio and Mercutio wanted_____. But, Romeo _____
_____. So, _____.

↓

Scene 2

Romeo wanted_____. But, Juliet _____.
So, _____.

↓

Scene 3

Romeo wanted_____. But, the Friar _____.
So, _____.

↓

Scene 4

Nurse wanted_____. But, Romeo's friends _____.
So, _____.

↓

Scene 5

Juliet wanted_____. But, Nurse _____.
So, _____.

↓

Scene 6

Romeo and Juliet wanted_____. But, Friar _____.
So, _____.

Extend Discussion Now that you have retold each scene of Act Two, how would you retell larger chunks of the story? Discuss the following with your group.

- Think about all that has happened in Act Two. How would you retell the events of the entire act?

- Think about all that has happened in both Acts One and Two. How would you retell the events of the play so far?

Original content Copyright © by Holt, Rinehart and Winston. Additions and changes to the original content are the responsibility of the instructor.

Unit 4; Skill Builder 3
English Language Skill Builder

Multiple Meaning Words

UNDERSTAND THE SKILL When a word has more than one meaning, context clues can help you tell which meaning is intended. However, to understand a kind of joke called a *pun*, you need to know both meanings of a word. Shakespeare loved to fill his plays with puns. Today, we need footnotes to understand these jokes, since many of the words or expressions are no longer used.

Work with a partner to complete each pun with a multiple-meaning word. If you don't know both meanings of the word, look it up in a dictionary. Do you think these puns are funny or not? Discuss this with your partner.

Punning with multiple meaning words

    ruins   curb   run

1. The archeologist cried, "My career is in _____!"

    meaning 1: _____ meaning 2: _____

2. A sidewalk café is a great place to _____ your appetite.

    _____ meaning 1: _____ meaning 2: _____

3. My grandfather said large noses _____ in our family.

    _____ meaning 1: _____ meaning 2: _____

EXTEND DISCUSSION Use what you know from reading *The Tragedy of Romeo and Juliet* to give the correct definition of the multiple meaning words.

1. At the beginning of the play, Romeo says that Rosalind is <u>fair</u> but not <u>kind</u>. Choose the

    meanings of "fair" and "kind" in this context: _____.

    What are the other meanings? _____

2. When Romeo first sees Juliet, he compares her to the <u>light</u>. Choose the meaning of "light" in

    this context: _____. What's the other meaning? _____

3. During their first conversation, Romeo and Juliet touch <u>palms</u>. Choose the meaning of "palm"

    in this context: _____. What's the other meaning?_____

4. In the garden, Juliet's balcony is up on the second <u>story</u>. Choose the meaning of "story" in this

    context: _____. What's the other meaning? _____

Original content Copyright © by Holt, Rinehart and Winston. Additions and changes to the original content are the responsibility of the instructor.

Differentiating Instruction

Unit 4; Skill Builder 4
English Language Skill Builder

Stress Patterns

UNDERSTAND THE SKILL Stress is the loudness or emphasis placed on a syllable or a word. Inside words, the stress is placed on the main root. Prefixes and suffixes aren't stressed. In a sentence, the stress is generally placed on the words that carry the most meaning (nouns, verbs, adjectives, and adverbs).

Work in groups to practice this dialogue from *The Tragedy of Romeo and Juliet*, Act 1, Scene 1. Before you speak the line, tap out the stress pattern. Tap loudly for the words that are underlined. Tap softly for all the others. Pause as indicated by punctuation.

Gregory. I will frown as I pass by, and let them take it as they list.

Sampson. Nay, as they dare. I will bite my thumb at them, which is disgrace to them if they bear it.

Abram. Do you bite your thumb at us, sir?

Sampson. I do bite my thumb, sir.

Abram. Do you bite your thumb at us, sir?

Sampson *(aside to Gregory).* Is the law of our side if I say ay?

Gregory *(aside to Sampson).* No.

Sampson. No, sir, I do not bite my thumb at you, sir; but I bite my thumb, sir.

EXTEND DISCUSSION Put the emphasis where you think it belongs on this dialogue by Roxane and Christian in the play *Cyrano de Bergerac*. Compare notes in a small group. Work together to underline the words or syllables where you think the stress should go. Discuss how stress helps communicate meaning.

Roxane: You do not altogether know me…Dear,

There is more of me than there was—with this,

I can love more of you—more of what makes

You your own self—Truly!...If you were less

Lovable—

Christian: No!

Roxane: —Less charming—ugly even—

I should love you still.

Original content Copyright © by Holt, Rinehart and Winston. Additions and changes to the original content are the responsibility of the instructor.

Differentiating Instruction

Unit 4
Summative Test

LITERARY AND READING SKILLS

A. Circle the letter of the best answer. *(25 points; 5 points each)*

1. Which question helps you identify a play as a **tragedy**?

   A) What is the main conflict?

   B) Who is the main character?

   C) How does the main character die?

   D) What does the main character want?

2. Which event marks the **turning point** in *Romeo and Juliet*?

   A) Romeo and Juliet marry in secret.

   B) The Montagues and Capulets begin feuding.

   C) Romeo meets Juliet at the party at her home.

   D) The Prince warns the Montagues and Capulets to stop feuding.

3. Which clue lets you know that a writer is using **dramatic irony**?

   A) There is a surprise ending you didn't expect.

   B) You only get the point of view of one character.

   C) You are getting hints about what is going to happen next.

   D) You want to warn a character about something he or she doesn't know about.

4. Which one explains what you do when you **paraphrase**?

   A) repeat a character's exact words

   B) put what a character says in your own words

   C) make a prediction about what a character may do

   D) use your own experiences to understand a character's actions

5. The **climax** of a drama is the—

   A) ending

   B) beginning

   C) most exciting emotional moment

   D) moment when the main character first appears

B. Complete each sentence with one of the literary or reading skills shown below. *(25 points; 5 points each)*

primary source   secondary   resolution   exposition   rising action
                  source

6. The setting, main characters, and main conflict of a drama are introduced in the
    _____ .

7. Loose ends, such as what happens to minor characters, are tied up in the
    _____ of a drama.

8. During the _____ of a drama, the conflict escalates.

9. A biography of William Shakespeare is a(n) _____ on the playwright.

10. A magazine interview with the actors who are starring as Romeo and Juliet is a(n)
    _____ because you get their views directly.

Read the question below. Then write a short response on the lines. *(50 points)*

Making Inferences

11. What would you infer about the people who write to Juliet and whose letters are answered by
    the Juliet Club? Identify details from *Romeo and Juliet*, the articles, and what you know from
    everyday life, to explain your answer.

    _____

    _____

    _____

    _____

    _____

    _____

    _____

    _____

Original content Copyright © by Holt, Rinehart and Winston. Additions and changes to the original content are the responsibility of the instructor.

Differentiating Instruction

Collection 9
Graphic Organizer

Paris and Queen Helen retold by Robert Graves

Elements of Myth Chart Myths are stories with specific elements. They often explain acts of nature, teach moral lessons, explain history, and express the hopes and fears of a culture. They also tell about gods and goddesses and often contain a heroic character.

Fill in the chart by identifying examples from "Paris and Queen Helen" that demonstrate these elements.

Elements of Myth	Examples from Text
Explains History	
Heroic Character	
Rivalry among Gods	
Moral Lesson	

Original content Copyright © by Holt, Rinehart and Winston. Additions and changes to the original content are the responsibility of the instructor.

Lesson Plan and Teaching Strategies

Odyssey, Part One Homer

Preteach
PREREADING SKILLS *(15 minutes)*
Build Background/Set a Purpose Ask: *Have you ever heard the word* odyssey*?* Explore with students uses of the word *Odyssey* that may be familiar to them, e.g. the movie *2001: A Space Odyssey*; the science magazine *Odyssey*; NASA's Mars Odyssey mission; a minivan called Odyssey, and so on. Point out that *odyssey* has come to mean a long journey filled with adventure or a spiritual or intellectual quest, and it all began with the work that they are about to read. Explain that this work is very important because of the influence it has had on Western culture.

Prepare students to read by sharing this synopsis of the events that led up to the *Odyssey:*

> The story told in the *Odyssey* is the last part of a very long story that begins with, of all things, a beauty contest. Paris, the son of the king of Troy, must decide which goddess is the most beautiful: Athena, the goddess of wisdom; Hera, the goddess of honor and marriage; or Aphrodite, the goddess of love. Paris chooses Aphrodite, and she rewards him by promising him the most beautiful woman in the world. Unfortunately, the most beautiful woman in the world is Helen of Sparta, who is already married to Menelaus, but that doesn't stop Paris. He goes to Sparta, which is in Greece, steals Helen away from Menelaus, and takes her back with him to Troy. Menelaus, with all his men, goes to Troy to retrieve Helen, and all the kings of Greece, including Odysseus, the king of Ithaca, are duty-bound to go with him. This is the beginning of the Trojan War, which lasts for ten years. Eventually, the Greeks win, Menelaus gets Helen back, and the Greeks head back home. But for Odysseus, the trip back to Ithaca takes another ten years, and the misfortunes and adventures that he has along the way are the subject of the epic poem the *Odyssey*.

VOCABULARY SKILLS *(10 minutes)*
Preteach Vocabulary Words Review the meanings of the vocabulary in the Word Bank. Then give students these sentences to complete.

1. The snow and driving wind created a wintry [tumult] outside.
2. The blowing snow created a [profusion] of snow drifts.
3. It's hard to accept that nature can be your [adversary].
4. Dealing with the cold and snow can be a [formidable] challenge.
5. People must learn to deal with the [adversity] of extreme weather.

Remind students to watch for these words as they read the story.

RESOURCES
In *The Holt Reader:* "Odyssey, Part One" for students who need more scaffolding in a workbook format

In this book: *Vocabulary Skill Builder,* p. 212; "Odyssey, Part One" Selection Test, p. 213

Consult *Holt Audio Library* for recordings of most selections

TEACHER TIP
Reading the *Odyssey* may present a challenge for students, yet, the stories are engaging. You may want to prepare students to read Fitzgerald's translation of the original epic poem by having students first read simpler retellings of the stories. Mary Pope Osborne's six-volume *Tales from the Odyssey* provides faithful retellings written for students at the intermediate level, grades 4 through 6.

WORD BANK
adversity
formidable
profusion
adversary
tumult

ACADEMIC VOCABULARY
Preteaching Academic Vocabulary
(5 minutes)
Write these terms and their meanings on a chalkboard or transparency. Review them with the students before previewing the selection.

Original content Copyright © by Holt, Rinehart and Winston. Additions and changes to the original content are the responsibility of the instructor.

Differentiating Instruction

LANGUAGE COACH SKILL *(10 minutes)*

Related Words Display the two Vocabulary Words *adversity* and *adversary*. Explain that both words are related to the word *adverse* which means "harmful" or "unfavorable." Discuss with students how the meaning of *adverse* relates to the meaning of *adversity* (a situation that is harmful or unfavorable) and *adversary* (someone who is harmful or unfavorable to another).

Display the first word in each set and define it. Then display the other words and explore with students how their meanings are related to the meaning of the base word.

- *passion* "powerful emotion" *passionate, impassioned*
- *courage* "bravery" *encourage, courageous*
- *mortal* "subject to death" *mortality, immortal*
- *person* "a human being" *personal, personify*
- *extra* "more than usual or necessary" *extraordinary, extraneous*

As they read, encourage students to think about how words they are reading might be related to other words they know.

LITERARY FOCUS *(20 minutes)*

Epic Heroes and Conflict The counterpart of the epic hero in modern culture is the superhero. Discuss familiar superheroes with students, encouraging students to tell what a superhero is and what happens in a superhero movie or in an episode of a superhero TV show. Relate the relevant traits of the superhero—the extraordinary powers and abilities—to the larger than life qualities of the epic hero—uncommon strength and exceptional knowledge, cunning, courage, and daring. Relate the superhero's repeated fights against evil with the epic hero's battles against the forces of nature, gods, and other beings who try to hinder his progress on his quest. Make the point that Odysseus is like the superhero of Greek culture, and students may find his adventures as exciting and engaging as the adventures of Superman or Batman.

READING FOCUS *(20 minutes)*

Reading an Epic Explain that *The Odyssey* is a long poem that was originally written in Greek. It has been translated into English, but it still looks like a poem and reads like a poem, and the language provides a number of challenges for the reader. Discuss two strategies that will help students read with understanding.

- **Paraphrasing** Explain that *paraphrasing* is restating something in your own words. Demonstrate how you would paraphrase the line *When the young Dawn with fingertips of rose / lit up the world.* Tell students that if you can say it in your own words, you are probably making sense of what you're reading.
- **Summarizing** Explain that *summarizing* is another way to check if you are making sense of what you are reading. Point out that students will be reading the *Odyssey* in chunks. Each chunk tells a part of the

---

Epic: A long narrative poem that tells of the adventures of a hero who in some way embodies the values of his civilization
Conflict: An obstacle—either external or internal—that a hero experiences in his quest
Express: To put into words
Portrayed: Showed
Destiny: A person's fate or unavoidable future

READING SKILL
Especially for LDN
The placement of the type of the page may be puzzling for students who think that new lines should always begin at the left. Read aloud the first 15 lines of the selection and help students see that *The Odyssey* is a poem and is written in lines, each of which has a regular meter. When a new sentence begins in the middle of a line, as in line 5, the beginning of the next line is actually the continuation of the sentence.

READING FOCUS
5W-How Chart

Questions	Answers
Who are the main characters?	
What happened in this part of the story?	
Where and **when** did the events take place?	
Why did this happen?	
How does the hero deal with the conflict?	

Original content Copyright © by Holt, Rinehart and Winston. Additions and changes to the original content are the responsibility of the instructor.

Differentiating Instruction

story. After they have read each chunk, they should try to tell in their own words what just happened. This is called *summarizing*. Tell students that thinking about these questions can help them to consider the most important details: **Who** are the main characters? **What** happened in this part of the story? **Where** and **when** did the events take place? **Why** did this happen? **How** does the hero deal with the conflict?

Encourage students to use the 5W-How Chart shown in the margin to help them summarize each chunk as they read.

Direct Teach
(120 minutes)
Chunk the Text Help students pace their reading by dividing the selection into "chunks" or parts. After the students have read each part, have students summarize what happened in that part of the story.
Part 1: ends p. 1043, l. 118: "...for the sight of home. . . ."
Part 2: ends p. 1047, l. 218: "...moved out again on our seafaring. . . ."
Part 3: ends p. 1051, l. 329: "...and I made five as captain."
Part 4: ends p. 1055, l. 432: ". . . we waited until morning."
Part 5: ends p, 1058, l. 538: ". . . to bitter days at home. . . ."
Part 6: ends p. 1061, end of note: ". . . *the blind prophet Teiresias.*
Part 7: ends p. 1064, l. 658: ". . . shall be just as I foretell'. . . ."
Part 8: ends p. 1071, l. 843: ". . . the world's delight, the Sun. . . ."
Part 9: ends p. 1074, end of final note: "*. . . until the next night."*

Check for Understanding
WRITING FOCUS *(15 minutes)*
Characterization Remind students of the ways readers get information about characters. They learn about characters *directly* from things the author says about a character, what other characters say about the character, and what the character tells the reader about him/herself. Readers also learn about characters *indirectly* from what the character says, does, thinks, and how the character interacts with other people.

Invite students to describe Odysseus and the kind of person he is. As students mention particular character traits, ask: *How to we know this?* Have students indicate whether their knowledge comes from something that is stated directly by the author, Odysseus, or another character; or if it is indirectly demonstrated through Odysseus's words and actions.

Think As A Reader/Writer Ask: *What do you think are Odysseus's most notable character traits? What trait gets him into trouble? What trait helps him get out of trouble?* Discuss with students how two mental qualities—curiosity and cleverness—both exist in Odysseus. Then ask students to write a brief character sketch of Odysseus. For each character trait they mention, encourage them to give examples from the text that show how this trait is demonstrated in Odysseus's speech or actions.

Especially for LDN
Use the map of Odysseus's journey on page 1034 of the Student Edition to help students recall story events and keep them in the right order. Encourage students to use the visual images as prompts for recall and a way to envision the story's many settings. Work with students to identify each stopping place on a modern day map. As a bonus, help students replace each of the 16 key names with those of their contemporary counterparts.

READING SKILL
Especially for RGP
(10 minutes each)
Have students read and discuss the Links found with this selection. Encourage them to talk about why this material was chosen to accompany the *Odyssey* and how it enhances the reader's appreciation of the work.

READING SKILL
Especially for ELL
(5 minutes or less)
Remind students that much of the story is told by Odysseus himself. Review with students the point at which the narrator's voice stops being the poet Homer and starts being Odysseus himself. Point out the use of single and double quotes to remind the reader that it is Odysseus who is speaking.

READING/WRITING
Especially for WGP
(10 minutes)
Tell students that in art a sketch is a preliminary drawing. It doesn't have all the details, but it shows the most important features. The same is true for a character sketch. It doesn't have to tell everything; instead it should concentrate on what is most important.

Original content Copyright © by Holt, Rinehart and Winston. Additions and changes to the original content are the responsibility of the instructor.

Differentiating Instruction

Collection 9
Graphic Organizer

from the Odyssey, Part Two Homer

"Somebody Wanted But So" Chart To help you keep track of all the events and characters in an epic, you can **summarize** the plot by writing a statement about the section's most important events.

Complete this chart to summarize two of the books in Part Two: Coming Home. Under "Somebody" write the character's name. Under "Wanted," describe the character's main goal. Under "But" describe what is keeping the character from achieving the goal. Write the outcome of the struggle under "So." You may have more than one character from each section.

Book # ___			
Somebody	**Wanted**	**But**	**So**

Book # ___			
Somebody	**Wanted**	**But**	**So**

Original content Copyright © by Holt, Rinehart and Winston. Additions and changes to the original content are the responsibility of the instructor.

Collection 9
Graphic Organizer

The Fenris Wolf retold by Olivia Coolidge

Archetypes Chart Archetypes are patterns that recur in stories. They often
include a familiar character, such as a brave hero or evil character. Archetypes are
also found in familiar plots, and settings. You will recognize them in fairy tales,
epics, and other timeless stories.

**Fill in the chart by identifying examples from "The Fenris Wolf" that
demonstrate archetypal elements.**

Archetypal Elements	Examples from Text
Trickster Character	
Heroic Character	
Gods or Humans against a Beast	
Battle between Good and Evil	
Prophecy	

Original content Copyright © by Holt, Rinehart and Winston. Additions and changes to the original content are the responsibility of the instructor.

Differentiating Instruction

Collection 9
Graphic Organizer

Mexico Next Right Sandra Cisneros
The Boy Left Behind Sonia Nazario

Themes Across Genres Chart Themes, or insights about life, are important to all **genres,** or forms of literature. **Themes** are conveyed through the characters, plots or problems, and topics in the works. Another clue to discovering themes in different genres is to look at the tone the writer displays. **Tone** is revealed through the words, images, and details that the writer uses. The tone may suggest a theme that is formal or casual, serious or playful, inspiring or depressing.

Use this chart to understand how the genre affects the theme of a work. First, fill in the top three rows. Then read the passages and identify the tone of each work. Finally, develop a theme or insight that each work reveals.

Mexico Next Right		The Boy Left Behind	
Genre		Genre	
Main Character		Main Character	
Problem		Problem	
Passage: "No more billboards announcing the next Stuckey's candy store, no more truck-stop donuts or roadside picnics with bologna-and-cheese sandwiches and cold bottles of 7-Up. Now we'll drink fruit-flavored sodas, tamarind, apple, pineapple; Pato Pascual with Donald Duck on the bottle, or Lulú, Betty Boop soda, or the one we hear on the radio, the happy song for Jarritos soda."		Passage: "His mother never returns, and that decides Enrique's fate. As a teenager – indeed, still a child – he will set out for the United States on his own to search for her. Virtually unnoticed, he will become one of an estimated 48,000 children who enter the United States from Central America and Mexico each year, illegally and without either of their parents."	
Tone		Tone	
Theme		Insight	

From "Mexico Next Right" from *Caramelo* by Sandra Cisneros. Copyright © 2002 by Sandra Cisneros. Published by Vintage Books in paperback in 2003 and originally in hardcover by Alfred A. Knopf, a division of Random House, Inc., 2002. Reproduced by permission of **Susan Bergholz Literary Services, New York, NY and Lamy, NM.**

Original content Copyright © by Holt, Rinehart and Winston. Additions and changes to the original content are the responsibility of the instructor.

Lesson Plan and Teaching Strategies

Shipwreck at the Bottom of the World Jennifer Armstrong
Tending Sir Ernest's Legacy

Preteach
PREREADING SKILLS *(15 minutes)*

Build Background/Set a Purpose Explain that the two selections students will read are about the same historic event: Sir Ernest Shackleton's expedition to cross Antarctica. Point out Antarctic on a classroom map. Have students preview the photographs that accompany the selections. Explain these photos were taken by a photographer who accompanied Shackleton on his expedition. Then share this background with students:

Sir Ernest Shackleton was an Antarctic explorer who lived a hundred years ago. In 1914, he set out in a ship called *Endurance* with a crew of 27 men on an expedition to cross the Antarctic by way of the South Pole. You have to remember that back then ships had sails and were made of wood, and there were no communications systems and no GPS. A ship sailing through this part of the world was pretty much on its own.

Early in 1915, the *Endurance* got trapped in the ice. When spring came, moving ice masses crushed the ship and it sank. In April 1916, Shackleton and his crew, sailing in three lifeboats, made it to Elephant Island. Shackleton knew that they couldn't survive for very long on the island, so with five crew members, he sailed off again, in one of the lifeboats, to get help from a whaling station on South Georgia Island, 800 hundred miles away.

Explain that the first selection is an excerpt from a biography, which is based on records and diaries kept by Sir Ernest Shackleton and other men on the expedition. The second selection is an interview with Sir Ernest Shackleton's granddaughter. Both selections deal with the same events.

VOCABULARY SKILLS *(10 minutes)*
Preteach Vocabulary Words Review the meanings of the vocabulary in the Word Bank. Then give students these sentences to complete.

1. When ice started to crush the ship, the crew had to [abandon] it.

2. The survival of his crew was Shackleton's first [priority].

3. When their [provisions] ran out, the men would be hungry.

4. When the storm hit, the temperature [plummeted].

Remind students to watch for these words as they read the story.

RESOURCES
In *The Holt Reader:* "Shipwreck at the Bottom of the World" and "Tending Sir Ernest's Legacy" for students who need more scaffolding in a workbook format

In this book: *Vocabulary Skill Builder,* p. 212; "Shipwreck at the Bottom of the World/Tending Sir Ernest's Legacy" Selection Test, p. 214

Consult *Holt Audio Library* for recordings of most selections

WORD BANK
provisions
plummeted
abandon
priority

ACADEMIC VOCABULARY
Preteaching Academic Vocabulary
(5 minutes or less)
Write these terms and their meanings on a chalkboard or transparency. Review them with the students before previewing the selection.

Synthesize: To put together information and ideas from different sources in order to get a richer and better understanding of a topic or an event.
Primary sources: Actual records that provide firsthand evidence or accounts of an event. Diaries, letters, and

Original content Copyright © by Holt, Rinehart and Winston. Additions and changes to the original content are the responsibility of the instructor.

Differentiating Instruction

LANGUAGE COACH SKILL *(10 minutes)*

Word Derivations Point out that the Vocabulary Word *priority* has the base word *prior* which means "coming first." Explain that *priority* is formed by adding the suffix *-ity* to *prior*. Explore with students how the meaning of *prior* relates to the meaning of *priority*.

Work with students to analyze these words from the selections. Help students identify the base word from which each word is derived and how the meaning of the base word relates to the meaning of the new word:

- *preparation* (*prepare* "get ready"; "the process of getting something ready")
- *provisions* (*provide* "supply"; "things that are provided or supplied")
- *arrangements* (*arrange* "plan or prepare"; "things that are planned or prepared')
- *exposure* (*expose* "lay open"; "condition of being exposed and without shelter")
- *prismatic* (*prism* "glass that separates beams of light into the colors of the spectrum"; "containing all the colors of the spectrum")

As they read the selections, have students look for more examples of words that are derived from other words.

INFORMATIONAL TEXT FOCUS *(30 minutes)*

Primary and Secondary Sources Explain that when we want to learn about an event that happened in the past, there are two kinds of sources we can turn to: **primary sources** and **secondary sources**. *Primary sources* are documents created by the people who took part in the events or witnessed them. These can be letters, journals, diaries, newspaper articles, reports, and photographs. *Secondary sources* are written some time after the event has taken place, by people who know a lot about the topic but did not take part in the events nor did they witness them.

Explain that "Shipwreck at the Bottom of the World" and "Tending Sir Ernest's Legacy" are both secondary sources, but they include primary sources and rely on primary sources for their information. Explain that the photographs that accompany both selections are primary sources. With the exception of the photograph of Alexandra Shackleton, they were all taken by a photographer who participated in the Antarctic expedition. Both selections also quote primary sources. The biography quotes Shackleton himself, who kept a diary of the expedition, and Captain Wosley, who wrote about the adventure. Similarly, in the interview, Alexandra Shackleton quotes things her grandfather wrote in his diary and in his letters. Have students be on the lookout for quotes from primary sources as they read the selections.

Synthesizing Sources Engage students in an exercise to demonstrate what happens when you synthesize sources. Name a historic event of which students have some knowledge. Then ask each of them to tell something they know about the event. What each student says does not have to be unique, but everyone should contribute something. Record what each student says. Then work together to *synthesize* the information into one defining statement about the event.

photographs are examples of primary sources.

Secondary sources: Accounts of the past written after the events happened by people who did not directly experience the events.
Expedition: A journey undertaken for a specific purpose, often for the purpose of scientific exploration.
Mutual: Done, said, or felt by each toward the other

VOCABULARY SKILL
Especially for ELL

(15 minutes)
Some of the difficult words in this story are designated vocabulary words or defined in footnotes. Other words students might not know are listed below. Pronounce each word and explain its meaning. Help students locate each word in the story and explore the context for clues to its meaning.
stores (p. 1137, col. 1): supplies
sorcery (p. 1140, col. 1): magic
albatross (p. 1040, col. 2): a large web-footed sea bird not unlike a gull. It is a common nautical superstition that to kill an albatross will bring back luck to a ship and everyone on it.

Especially for LDN
Sir Ernest Shackleton published his diary of the *Endurance* expedition as a book entitled *South: The Story of Shackleton's 1914-1917 Expedition.* The text the book and all of the photographs are available online at www.Gutenberg.org/etext/15 19

Original content Copyright © by Holt, Rinehart and Winston. Additions and changes to the original content are the responsibility of the instructor.

Differentiating Instruction

Explain: *What we just did is called* synthesizing. *We took information from different sources—you were the different sources—and we put it all together to create one inclusive statement about the topic.*

Point out that we synthesize all the time when we read, putting together the things we already know about a topic and things we know that are related to a topic. We also synthesize when we read different texts on the same topic. Explain that synthesizing when you read involves **making connections** and **comparing**. When you make connections, you let the things you are reading remind you of things you've read in other texts and things you already know. You compare when you think about how the information in one text is like the information or different from the information in another text or what you already know.

Tell students that there will many opportunities to make connections and compare as they read the two selections about Shackleton's Antarctic expedition. Encourage them to create a Question Chart like the one at the right and use it to record their responses as they read "Shipwreck at the Bottom of the World" and "Tending Sir Ernest's Legacy."

Direct Teach
(30 minutes)

Chunk the Text Help students pace their reading by dividing the selection into "chunks" or parts. After the students have read each part, talk about primary sources and secondary sources and have students identify which passages, if any, come from primary sources.

"Shipwreck at the Bottom of the World"
Part 1: ends p. 1139, col.12: "…fueling themselves constantly."
Part 2: ends p. 1141, col 2: "…ever been forced to do."
Part 3: ends p. 1142, col 2: "…half the distance left to go."
"Tending Sir Ernest's Legacy"
Part 4: ends p. 1145: "…a complete waste of valuable time."
Part 5: ends p. 1148: "…where no man has trod before."

Check for Understanding

WRITING FOCUS *(15 minutes)*

Comparing Texts Remind students that "Shipwreck at the Bottom of the World" is an excerpt from a biography and "Tending Sir Ernest's Legacy" is the text of an interview. Discuss how the texts are alike and how they are different. Ask: *How did reading about the first half of the journey to South Georgia help you understand the interview? How did getting a family member's perspective in the interview contribute to your appreciation of Sir Ernest?* Encourage students to tell the connections they made as they read the interview.

Think As A Reader/Writer In the interview, Alexandra Shackleton tells the qualities that her grandfather believed were most important for a polar explorer: optimism, patience, imagination, and courage. Discuss those qualities. Then ask students to write a paragraph telling how, in the excerpt from the biography, Sir Ernest demonstrates each one of them.

INFORMATIONAL TEXT FOCUS
Question Chart

Questions	Responses
How are these sources similar? How are they different?	
What other works on this topic do these pieces remind me of?	
How have these sources added to my under-standing of life?	

READING/WRITING
Especially for ELL
The photographs that accompany the selections will help students visualize the things being described, particularly in the excerpt from the biography. Help English language learners refer to the photographs as they read.

READING/WRITING
Especially for RGP
(5 minutes)
Discuss with students how, in both selections, quotations from primary sources have been used to illustrate and give credibility to the work. Encourage students to use quotes from the selections in a similar way in their writing to illustrate how Sir Ernest displayed the qualities he valued.

Original content Copyright © by Holt, Rinehart and Winston. Additions and changes to the original content are the responsibility of the instructor.

Differentiating Instruction

Targeted Strategies for Learners with Diverse Needs

READING SKILLS

Primary and Secondary Sources/Synthesizing Sources *(15 minutes)* Explain to students that when they read from *Shipwreck at the Bottom of the World* and part of the interview "Tending Sir Ernest's Legacy," they will encounter information from both primary and secondary sources. The selections are secondary sources because they are written by people who did not go on the expedition. However, the selections include photos taken during the expedition, quotes from expedition members, and Shackleton's diary excerpts, which are primary sources. Remind students that primary sources are artifacts of an event or an account from a witness or participant. Share the chart with students and discuss what they can learn from each type of source:

Primary: Photos	Primary: Quotes/Excerpts	Secondary: Commentary
What details can you see in the images that are not mentioned in the text?	What can the participants tell you about events that no one else can?	What advantages does someone looking back on events have over the participants?

Have partners find examples of unique information from each type of source. Challenge students to discuss how the combination of sources creates a fuller picture of events.

LITERARY SKILLS

Epic Heroes and Conflict *(15 minutes)* Point out that "heroes" across cultures face conflict in very similar ways. Share these typical features of a hero's journey:

- **Birth**: There is usually something special about a hero's creation.
- **Call**: The hero may willingly or reluctantly answer the call to adventure.
- **Helpers**: People or supernatural beings appear and give the hero aid.
- **Tests**: The hero must complete some task that no one else can accomplish.
- **Victory**: The hero must defeat the person or object that stands in the way of success.
- **Return**: The hero's return from adventure makes life better for all.

Then have a class discussion about examples of heroes in popular culture. Superheroes are an obvious example. Ask: *What about fairy tales? Do the main female characters qualify as heroes?* What other stories can students think of that follow this pattern?

Readings in Collection 9 Minimum Course of Study

- from *The Odyssey*, Part One, p. 1035
- "Shipwreck at the Bottom of the World"/ "Tending Sir Ernest's Legacy", p. 1134

RESOURCES

In *The Holt Reader,* all three selections help students who need more scaffolding in a workbook format.

Consult *Holt Audio Library* for recordings of most selections.

Especially for ELL

Discussing heroes from different cultures is a great way to engage English-language learners in storytelling. Give them an opportunity to share stories from their culture. If they are more comfortable using imagery, have them tell the story as an original comic strip. Or have them direct their classmates in a play to act out the story.

ALTERNATIVE ASSESSMENT *(5 minutes)*
Have students provide answers for these items.

You can learn more by synthesizing information from [primary and secondary sources] than from either type alone.

A special person who does something that no one else can is a [hero/narrator].

Original content Copyright © by Holt, Rinehart and Winston. Additions and changes to the original content are the responsibility of the instructor.

Differentiating Instruction

Collection 9

Academic and Selection Vocabulary

The Odyssey
Shipwreck at the Bottom of the World
Interview with Alexandra Shackleton

A. Choose the word that best fits into each category.

priority	adversity	profusion	formidable	plummeted

1. Not a good time: difficulty, hardship, struggle, _____

2. On the decline: fell, dropped, tumbled, _____

3. As soon as possible: main concern, right away, urgent, _____

4. More than enough: lots, plenty, abundance, _____

5. Frightening: fearsome, dreadful, tough, _____

B. Write a "T" for true or "F" for false next to each sentence.

_____ 1. An adversary is someone who is willing to help.

_____ 2. If you abandon something, you no longer have it.

_____ 3. Most people would find tumult stressful.

_____ 4. Picnic provisions include ants and bees.

_____ 5. A priority can wait till later.

C. Use the academic vocabulary words to complete the following paragraph about "The Odyssey" by Homer.

destiny   mutual   express   portrays

Homer (1) _____ Odysseus as a clever mortal. But even Odysseus cannot

escape his (2) _____. Every time the gods get angry at him they

(3) _____ their displeasure by making his journey longer and more

dangerous. Still he and his men bravely face every challenge. They are motivated by their

(4) _____ desire to return home to Ithaca.

Original content Copyright © by Holt, Rinehart and Winston. Additions and changes to the original content are the responsibility of the instructor.

Differentiating Instruction

Collection 9
Selection Test

The Odyssey, Part One

COMPREHENSION, SKILLS, AND VOCABULARY Circle the letter of the best
answer to each of the following items.

1. What is the goal of Odysseus's quest?

    A) He is trying to get back home to Ithaca.

    B) He is trying to get to Troy to fight in the war.

    C) He is trying to prove he is worthy of Athena's favor.

    D) He is trying to make sure he will be happy in the afterlife.

2. What is the long-term effect for Odysseus of blinding the Cyclops?

    A) Odysseus and his men are trapped in the Cyclops's cave.

    B) All the other Cyclopes vow to take revenge on Odysseus.

    C) Poseidon, god of the sea, is angry with Odysseus for blinding his son.

    D) The Cyclops throws boulders at Odysseus's ships and nearly sinks them.

3. Which of the following is Odysseus's most significant character trait?

    A) his love of boasting

    B) his foolhardy behavior

    C) his compassion for his men

    D) his desire to know and experience everything

4. When you **paraphrase** something, you—

    A) restate it in your own words

    B) read it line by line just as it was written

    C) read it aloud while other people can listen

    D) summarize it and tell only the most important parts

5. Each one is an **adversary** for Odysseus except—

    A) Circe, the sorceress

    B) Polyphemus, the Cyclops

    C) Poseidon, the god of the sea

    D) Athena, the goddess of wisdom

6. *The Odyssey* is required reading for most students in high school. Do you
   think reading it is worthwhile? Use the organizer below to collect your ideas.
   Then write a short paragraph stating your opinion.

Introductory statement: I think/don't think it's important to read *The Odyssey*.
Two or three supporting sentences: First….In addition…For that reason…
Concluding statement. Thus I believe that ….

Original content Copyright © by Holt, Rinehart and Winston. Additions and changes to the original content are the responsibility of the instructor.

Differentiating Instruction

Shipwreck at the Bottom of the World Jennifer Armstrong
Tending Sir Ernest's Legacy

COMPREHENSION, SKILLS, AND VOCABULARY Circle the letter of the best
answer to each of the following items.

1. Which of these details about Shackleton is mentioned in both selections?

   A) His men called him "the Boss."

   B) He was not much good at anything except being an explorer.

   C) He threw two of the slimy and revolting sleeping bags overboard.

   D) He ordered hot milk for everyone whenever one crew member looked tired.

2. For Shackleton, the most important qualities for an explorer were optimism, patience,
   imagination, and—

   A) courage   C) love of adventure

   B) self-sacrifice   D) desire to face the unknown

3. When you *synthesize*, you—

   A) put the text in your own words

   B) summarize the main ideas of a text

   C) read about the same topic in different sources

   D) put together information from different sources

4. Which of the following is a secondary source of information about a historic event?

   A) photos taken at the time the event occurred

   B) a diary of someone who took part in the event

   C) a letter written by someone who witnessed the event

   D) a book written by someone who had discovered some old records

5. What was Shackleton's **priority** at all times?

   A) his men

   B) becoming famous

   C) reaching the South Pole

   D) getting back home

6. Alexandra Shackleton compares her grandfather's Antarctic expedition to being
   in space. Is this a good comparison? Use the organizer below to collect your
   ideas. Then write a short paragraph.

Introductory statement: Shackleton's expedition was/was not like exploring space . . .
Two or three supporting sentences: First….In addition…For that reason…
Concluding statement. Thus I believe that Shackleton's expedition was….

Original content Copyright © by Holt, Rinehart and Winston. Additions and changes to the original content are the responsibility of the instructor.

Collection 9
Collection Summative Test

VOCABULARY SKILLS Complete the sentences below by using the collection vocabulary words from the list below.

abandon   adversity   formidable   profusion
plummeted   provisions   priority   tumult

1. The early explorers of the Antarctic had to endure a lot of _____.

2. Surviving in the cold and ice required _____ endurance.

3. When the temperature _____, it was hard to stay warm.

4. Protecting oneself from frostbite became everyone's _____.

5. In a world of ice, there was little to eat if one's _____ ran out.

LITERARY AND READING SKILLS Circle the letter of the best answer.

6. **Paraphrasing** is a way to—

    A) become a better public speaker

    B) improve your ability to read aloud

    C) get the gist of a text without reading the whole thing

    D) prove to yourself that you understand what you're reading

7. Which is the best definition of **conflict** in a work of literature?

    A) a competition between two characters

    B) the author's attitude toward the characters

    C) a conversation that involves two or more characters

    D) an external or internal problem that a hero encounters

8. Which of these would be a **primary source** of information about a famous author?

    A) a biography written after she died

    B) a copy of the first book she published

    C) an article written about her by her editor

    D) the letters she and her editor wrote to each other

LANGUAGE AND WRITING SKILLS Of the two related words, write the one that fits the sentence.

9. You pull all the information together when you _____ synthesis/synthesize.

10. Patience is an important quality of a leader's _____ temporary/temperament.

Original content Copyright © by Holt, Rinehart and Winston. Additions and changes to the original content are the responsibility of the instructor.

Differentiating Instruction

Lesson Plan and Teaching Strategies

Writing Workshop: Research Paper

PREWRITING

Form a Research Question *(15 minutes)*

Before they select a topic, remind students that their research paper should be something that interests them and will interest others. To generate ideas they might consider pooling from current events, their own interests, history, or something as specific as a place they'd like to visit. Once students have brainstormed topics, help them pose question stems to apply to their topics, for example—

Question	Sample Application to a Topic
What is?	What is global warming?
Which one?	Which U.S. city is the most livable?
How?	How can scientists predict a volcano eruption?
What if?	What if the Allies had lost World War II?
Should?	Should the U.S. send more aid to Africa?
Why?	Why is steroid use considered cheating?

Once students have a question to investigate, they will need to think of related questions to explore. These questions can be used as organizing principles later in the process.

Find Sources *(15 minutes)*

For preliminary research, help point students to library or Internet resources. Explain that a good research report will make use of primary, as well as secondary, sources. While some primary sources may be too archaic or technical, remind students that photos, postcards, posters, maps, and works of art are also primary sources. Encourage students to search the websites of different libraries and organizations that include primary sources in multimedia presentations.

Evaluate Sources *(15 minutes)*

Once students find sources, remind them that they do not need to read every word. Using skimming (for overall gist) and scanning (for key words and phrases), students can sort through a source to find the exact page or paragraph that offers the information they need.

Only after students have determined that a source is relevant to their topic should they apply the criteria on page 1163 of the Student Edition. Also, when students are evaluating online sources, have them notice the number of ads. Lots of ads on a site is a warning sign: the site's purpose might be to sell something rather than provide unbiased information.

TEACHING TIP

Before beginning this lesson be sure students have access to the complete writer's model online. Visit **go.hrw.com L9-1161** You may also wish to consider having students work on this project in groups, since students gaining proficiency and English-language learners may need more time than their peers to complete this assignment.

ESPECIALLY FOR ELL

After students have chosen a topic, encourage them to do some preliminary research in their first language. Academic language skills can take time to develop, and if students can get background on a subject before they tackle difficult academic texts in English, their comprehension will improve.

ESPECIALLY FOR WGP

Remind students how to focus on a topic as you showed them in the Teacher's Guide lesson on writing an Informative Essay, (see pages 198 and 199 of this guide).

Original content Copyright © by Holt, Rinehart and Winston. Additions and changes to the original content are the responsibility of the instructor.

Differentiating Instruction

PREWRITING (CONTINUED)
Take Notes *(30 minutes)*

Point out to students that taking notes does not mean copying down every word on the subject. Explain that the purpose of note taking is to find quotes, facts, and ideas that they want to include in their research papers. In addition to quoting, summarizing, and paraphrasing others, encourage students to add their own original insights about the subject. For example,

Kennedy Speech 4	Original Idea:
"Our goal is not the victory of might, but the vindication of right, not peace at the expense of freedom, but both peace and freedom, here in this hemisphere, and, we hope, around the world. God willing, that goal will be achieved." Page 8	The U.S. is a much bigger, stronger, and richer country than Cuba. I think that Kennedy was trying to show the world that the U.S. wasn't trying to bully Cuba.

Organize Information *(15 minutes)*

Review the organizational structures offered on page 1165 in the Student Edition. If students don't have a clear chronology or order of importance to guide their organization, suggest that students organize their notes around a series of questions they ask about their topic.

Have students create a content web that shows the central question that will become their thesis statement and the related questions they are investigating. Have them treat this as an ongoing document, deleting dead-end questions and adding new questions as they arise. This visual aid will likely help students in the drafting stage.

Encourage students to share their graphic organizers with a partner, if they are not already part of group. Have students use this opportunity to explain their thinking and find out if someone unfamiliar with the topic might have other questions.

DRAFTING
Document Sources *(10 minutes)*

When reviewing the guidelines for documenting sources, explain to students that, in addition to exact quotes, ideas that are paraphrased from someone also need to be credited. A summary or an original idea, however, does not need to be credited since each one emanates from the student's own thinking.

Have students use their content webs when they begin to draft their essays. Review the framework for a Research Paper on page 1167 of the Student Edition. Remind students that they will also be expected to create a list of works cited or a bibliography. To avoid overload, you may wish to introduce the Grammar Link, Punctuating Titles, when students are ready to begin this task.

TEACHING TIP

If students are conducting any of the research online, you may wish to help them construct effective search terms. Give them practice choosing key words that relate to their subject. Show them how to put quotes around any exact phrase they are looking for. Tell them to avoid prepositions, conjunctions, articles in the search terms. Explain that they want to be as specific as possible. For example, use "Bay of Pigs" rather than "Invasion."

ESPECIALLY FOR ELL

You can help Spanish and French-speaking students expand their academic vocabularies in English by having them look for Latin cognates, words with similar spelling and meaning.

ESPECIALLY FOR LDN

Be sure to break this assignment into a number of small assignments that are carefully explained to students. Deadlines and check-ins with students should be frequent so that students don't waste effort or become frustrated.

Original content Copyright © by Holt, Rinehart and Winston. Additions and changes to the original content are the responsibility of the instructor.

Differentiating Instruction

EVALUATING AND REVISING

Review Content and Organization *(20 minutes)*

Give students time to focus on the following points in Evaluation Questions 1, 2, 4 and 6. Help them understand how they can use these points to make their research paper better.

1. Have them read the first paragraph of the Student Draft on page 1169 of the Student Edition. Explain that the last sentence of the first paragraph is often where the thesis statement is placed in research papers. Above it is some engaging fact, quote, or relevant piece of background. Ask: *Does your thesis statement tell the reader what your research paper is about?*

3. If students are unsure of how to integrate quotations into their research paper, go over the Grammar Link: Integrating Quotations on page 1171 in the Student Edition. Remind students that all quotations need to be credited on their list of works cited.

4. Citing the sources properly is complex and may be difficult for students. Review the Guidelines for Recording Source Information on a chart that spans pages 1163-4 in the Student Edition. Review the Guidelines for Giving Credit Within a Paper as well as Grammar Link: Punctuating Titles on page 1167 of the Student Edition.

5. Print out the complete model of a research paper (Visit **go.hrw.com L9-1161**). Point out where the author returns to the thesis in the conclusion. Ask: *How did the author expand her thesis in the conclusion?*

Pair students with a partner to evaluate and improve each other's drafts. Have them use this guidance along with the chart on page 1168 of the Student Edition.

Mini-lesson: How to Revise for a Formal Tone *(15 Minutes)*

Explain to students that an easy way to make the tone of their writing sound more formal is to look for contractions and spell out the complete words instead.

Words that usually are contracted include pronouns (he, she, they, it,), question words (who, what, where, when, why, how), helping verbs (would, could, should, can, might, must), and some common verbs (to be, to have, to do)

Contractions	Words
's, 're, 'll, 'd	Is/Are/Will/Would
've, 's, 'd	Have/Has/Had
n't	Not

Then ask students to reread their essays to find and fix sentences that contain contractions.

TEACHING TIP
You may wish to post the complete model of the research paper (Visit **go.hrw.com L9-1161**) as well as examples of correct citation forms in the classroom for students' easy reference while they work.

ESPECIALLY FOR ELL
English-language learners may be confused by contractions that use the same ending but mean something different. For example, the *'s* ending on a contraction can stand for "is" or "has." The *'d* ending can stand for "had" or "would." If students are working in heterogeneous groups on their research paper, have more proficient speakers assist students with contractions as well as help them recognize slang words.

ESPECIALLY FOR LDN
Some students with learning differences may overestimate what the reader knows and fail to provide sufficient background or explanation for their information. Help them gauge what they can safely assume and what information needs to be revised for accuracy.

Original content Copyright © by Holt, Rinehart and Winston. Additions and changes to the original content are the responsibility of the instructor.

Differentiating Instruction

Lesson Plan and Teaching Strategies

Listening and Speaking Workshop: Presenting Research

ADAPT YOUR RESEARCH PAPER *(30 minutes)*

Explain to students that they will take the research paper they have written and prepare it for an oral presentation. Have them follow these steps to prepare their speeches:

1. Review the content webs you made during the prewriting phase to create subheads for each section of the paper. You can turn the questions into statements or leave them as questions.

2. If you have written your research paper as part of a group, decide who will read each section. Make sure you have a smooth transition between sections, so that it is easy for your classmates to follow the presentation.

3. Create visual aids and props for your presentation. If your research is about a place, you might have maps and photographs. If your research is about a kind of technology, you might have a diagram. If your research is about a famous figure in recent history, you might have a recording of that person. Be sure your props are large enough for the rest of the class to see and make sure they are clearly labeled.

4. Read your research aloud a second time to yourself or a partner. This time make notes about gestures you might use to make a point or where you might raise or lower your voice.

5. Prepare your script. Rewrite or retype on cards so that you can refer to it easily when you are speaking. Be sure to number the pages clearly.

Delivering Your Research Presentation

USE VERBAL/NONVERBAL TECHNIQUES *(10 minutes)*

Explain that non-verbal techniques can help students make their presentation more effective.

Verbal Technique In addition to saying *quote/unquote* to indicate the words taken directly from a source, tell students that they can alter their diction, using a slightly different volume or tone. Remind students that they don't want to exaggerate this too much or will it sound like they are making fun of the source being quoted.

Nonverbal Technique If students are using visual aids and props with their presentation, tell them to remember to incorporate them by cuing them at the proper time.

Have students practice their delivery with a partner or in front of mirror until the delivery is smooth.

Teaching Tip
For additional listening and writing practice, have students write down the five steps for preparing their papers, as you read them aloud.

ESPECIALLY FOR LDN
You may also wish to give students some alternative forms for presenting their material, such as Microsoft Powerpoint™ or as a photo essay.

EVALUATION CRITERIA
Use these criteria to evaluate students' presentations:

- Engages the attention of the audience
- Supports the thesis with relevant evidence
- Uses a clear pattern of organization with helpful transitions
- Varied phrasing and used good expression
- Demonstrated a command of non-verbal techniques

Original content Copyright © by Holt, Rinehart and Winston. Additions and changes to the original content are the responsibility of the instructor.

Differentiating Instruction

Unit 5; Skill Builder 1
Oral Language Skill Builder

Aspects of Epic Stories

UNDERSTAND THE SKILL Epic stories, such as myths and legends, are an important part of a culture. The heroes help us understand the qualities that are admired by that culture. The challenges the hero faces suggest that culture's fears.

Complete the Venn diagram on your own. Then work with a partner to take turns explaining how the *Odyssey* compares to a myth or legend from your own culture. Finally, discuss the question below with your partner.

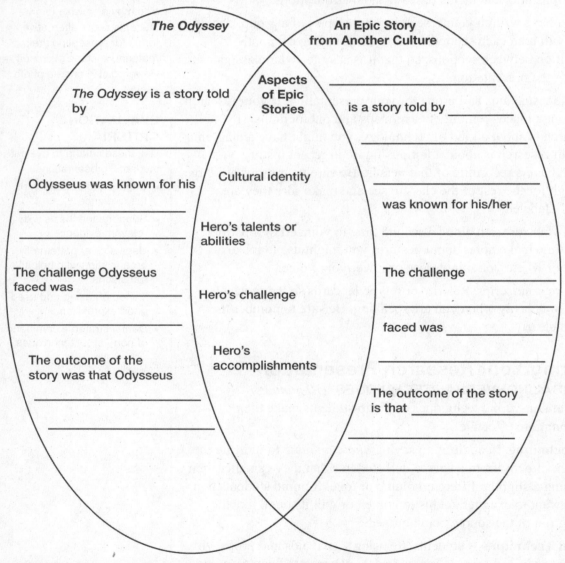

The Odyssey

An Epic Story from Another Culture

The Odyssey is a story told by _____ _____

Odysseus was known for his _____ _____

The challenge Odysseus faced was _____ _____

The outcome of the story was that Odysseus _____ _____

Aspects of Epic Stories

Cultural identity

Hero's talents or abilities

Hero's challenge

Hero's accomplishments

_____ is a story told by _____ _____

was known for his/her _____

The challenge _____ _____ faced was _____ _____

The outcome of the story is that _____ _____ _____

Extend Discussion What do these myths tell us about the cultures that created them?

- What can we tell about the culture that created the *Odyssey*?

- What are we able to learn about other cultures from aspects of their epic stories?

Original content Copyright © by Holt, Rinehart and Winston. Additions and changes to the original content are the responsibility of the instructor.

Unit 5; Skill Builder 2
Oral Language Skill Builder

Vocabulary Discussion

UNDERSTAND THE SKILL Using new vocabulary words helps you learn them faster and more easily than memorizing definitions. Consider the vocabulary words you learned before you started reading about epics. Now practice using them.

Finish each sentence. First, fill in the boxes marked "Think" on your own. Next, fill in the boxes marked "Pair" with a partner. Then share your sentences in a group. Write down another way to finish the sentence in the boxes marked "Share." Finally, discuss the questions below with the group.

An epic is exciting when…		
Think	**Pair**	**Share**

An internal/external conflict is challenging because…		
Think	**Pair**	**Share**

If a hero is portrayed as strong, courageous, and clever, the foil would be portrayed as…		
Think	**Pair**	**Share**

Extend Discussion How did your ideas change as you discussed them with a partner and then with a group?

- How similar or different were the ideas that you and your classmates came up with? Give examples.

- What was the best idea you offered the group? What was the best one you heard?

Original content Copyright © by Holt, Rinehart and Winston. Additions and changes to the original content are the responsibility of the instructor.

Differentiating Instruction

Unit 5; Skill Builder 3
English Language Skill Builder

Spelling

UNDERSTAND THE SKILL In English, spelling can be a challenge even to native speakers. Common sounds are often spelled in more than one way. Some examples appear below.
Look in the reading selections to find words that have the same the sounds and spellings as the sample words below. How many different words can you find? If necessary, use an extra sheet of paper to list them.

Sounds and Common Spellings

/k/	/f/	/ō/	/ē/	/ī/	/ū/
Examples:	**Examples:**	**Examples:**	**Examples:**	**Examples:**	**Examples:**
<u>c</u>an, <u>k</u>i<u>ck</u>	<u>f</u>ake, <u>ph</u>ony	t<u>o</u>ld, b<u>oa</u>st, n<u>ose</u>, gr<u>ow</u>	r<u>e</u>lax, sl<u>ee</u>p, dr<u>ea</u>m, laz<u>y</u>	b<u>i</u>cycle, b<u>i</u>ke	<u>u</u>nite, f<u>use</u>

1. Words with /k/ and words with /f/:

   _____

2. Words with /ō/ and words with /ē/:

   _____

3. Words with /ī/ and words with /ū/:

   _____

EXTEND DISCUSSION Use the spelling clues below and what you know from the story to guess the names of these characters from the *Odyssey*. Check your answers with a partner.

1. Who said a sad goodbye to Odysseus? Clue: /k/ and /ō/_____

2. Who ate the sweet plant and forgot everything? Clue: /ō/ _____

3. Who does the poet ask for inspiration? Clue: /ū/ _____

4. Who is the queen of the underworld? Clue: /f/ and /ē/ _____

5. Who sings a dangerous song? Clue: /ī/ _____

Original content Copyright © by Holt, Rinehart and Winston. Additions and changes to the original content are the responsibility of the instructor.

Unit 5; Skill Builder 4
English Language Skill Builder

Prepositions

UNDERSTAND THE SKILL Prepositions show relationships between two things.
Many show relationships between time or place.

Work with a partner to draw a picture of the prepositions of place in relation to the "X" in the middle of the box. Put the prepositions of time on the timeline. Be creative to show the meanings of the words. Then share your work with other classmates.

Prepositions of place

on	in	above	near	across	through
off	out	below	far	around	past

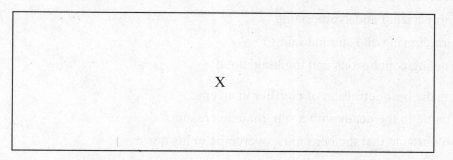

X

Prepositions of time

before	at	by	since
after	during	until	about

earlier ←——————————————————|——————————————————→ later

EXTEND DISCUSSION Work with a partner to fill in the missing prepositions, using what you know from reading about Shackleton. HINT: There may be more than one correct answer.

1. Shackleton and his men were exposed to temperatures _____ freezing.

2. Ice cold seawater splashed _____ the boat's deck.

3. _____ the ordeal, Shackleton gave his men hot milk to help keep them warm.

4. _____the gale ended, the men began to realize that the ship was trapped _____ the ice.

Original content Copyright © by Holt, Rinehart and Winston. Additions and changes to the original content are the responsibility of the instructor.

Differentiating Instruction

Unit 5
Summative Test

LITERARY AND READING SKILLS

A. Circle the letter of the best answer. *(25 points; 5 points each)*

1. Which statement is the best definition of an **epic**?

   A) a dramatic series on TV

   B) a long historic account of a city or a nation

   C) a drama set to music that tells of war or conflict

   D) a long narrative poem that tells the adventures of a hero

2. Which two strategies are most helpful when reading a challenging work like *The Odyssey*?

   A) predicting and visualizing

   B) summarizing and synthesizing

   C) paraphrasing and summarizing

   D) drawing conclusions and thinking aloud

3. Which is the best definition of **conflict** in an epic?

   A) a battle to the death with a superhuman creature

   B) an obstacle that the hero must overcome in his quest

   C) a challenge the hero must undertake to prove himself

   D) a struggle between what the hero wants to do and what he must do

4. Newspapers, letters, diaries, and photographs are all examples of

   A) primary sources

   B) secondary sources

   C) functional documents

   D) first-person accounts functional documents

5. What is involved in **synthesizing** when you read?

   A) comparing and making connections

   B) distinguishing between fact and opinion

   C) contrasting primary sources and secondary sources

   D) asking questions and consulting different sources to find the answers

Original content Copyright © by Holt, Rinehart and Winston. Additions and changes to the original content are the responsibility of the instructor.

Differentiating Instruction

| Unit 5 Summative Test *continued*

B. Complete each sentence with one of the literary or reading skills shown below. *(25 points; 5 points each)*

primary sources   epic hero   paraphrase   synthesize   conflicts

6. Odysseus is the classic example of the _____.

7. Odysseus must struggle with both internal and external _____ as he tries to make his way home to Ithaca.

8. When you read a difficult text, it's a good idea to _____ what you read to be certain that you understand it.

9. The biographer of Sir Ernest Shackleton used such _____ as Sir Ernest's own journal and the journals of some of his crew members.

10. When writing a research paper, you need to _____ information from many different sources.

Read the question below. Then write a short response on the lines. *(50 points)*

Conflict

11. What conflicts did Sir Ernest Shackleton have to overcome on his expedition? How was his expedition like the quest in an epic poem?

_____

_____

_____

_____

_____

_____

_____

_____

_____

_____

Consumer Documents

Elements of Consumer Documents Chart Consumer documents give you important information about an item you have bought. They give specific details through the **production information, instruction manuals, warranties, and contracts.**

Use this chart to give an example of the information you found in each element for the WYSIWY Game Arts Computer Game. In the third column, explain how or when you might use this information.

Consumer Document Element	Example	How/When I Would Use This Information
Product Information		
Instruction Manual		
Warranty		

Original content Copyright © by Holt, Rinehart and Winston. Additions and changes to the original content are the responsibility of the instructor.

Differentiating Instruction

Lesson Plan and Teaching Strategies

Following Technical Directions

Preteach

LISTENING COMPREHENSION SKILLS *(15 minutes)*
Build Background/Set a Purpose Ask students to preview the selection by looking at the illustrations on pages 1194-1196. Discuss with students what they think the selection is about.

Preview this information about the selection:

- This nonfiction article is about how to add graphics to a web site by using a scanner.

- The article takes readers through the steps of scanning a photograph, editing the photograph, and saving it.

Remind students that when they are following technical directions like these, they need to do the steps in the order indicated by numbers. Ask: *Have you ever become frustrated trying to follow written directions? What happened?*

VOCABULARY SKILLS *(10 minutes)*
Preteach Vocabulary Words Review the meanings of the vocabulary in the Word Bank. Then give students these sentences to complete.

1. When you [scan] a paper document, you can edit it and save it on your computer.

2. Dina had a hard time choosing what to eat for lunch because there were so many [options].

3. The company used an [image] of a tiger in its ads.

Remind students to watch for these words as they read the story.

LANGUAGE COACH SKILL *(10 minutes)*
Multiple Meaning Words Remind students that some words have more than one meaning, including some words from this selection. Review these other meanings with students:

- *Scan* means "a medical test in which a picture of the inside of part of your body is taken."

- *Image* means "a picture that you have in your mind."

- *Resolution* means "a promise to try hard to do something."

Write these sentences on the board. Have students complete each one by adding a word from the box.

scan	image	resolution

1. Mom's New Year's [resolution] was to work fewer hours and spend more time with the family.

RESOURCES

In *The Holt Reader:* "Following Technical Directions" for students who need more scaffolding in a workbook format

In this book: *Vocabulary Skill Builder*, p. 236; "Following Technical Directions" Selection Test, p. 237

Consult *Holt Audio Library* for recordings of most selections.

WORD BANK
scan
image
options

ACADEMIC VOCABULARY
Preteaching Academic Vocabulary
(5 minutes)
Write these terms and their meanings on a chalkboard or transparency. Review them with the students before previewing the selection.

Technical directions: These tell how to use or fix machines, tools, or equipment.
Skimming: Getting the main idea of a document by glancing at the title, heads and subheads. To get a better idea of the document, read the first sentence or two in each paragraph.
Scanning: Focusing on specific information in a document, such as boldfaced words or graphics.
Coherent: Clear; connected logically; understandable.
Function: Typical action of something.

Original content Copyright © by Holt, Rinehart and Winston. Additions and changes to the original content are the responsibility of the instructor.

Differentiating Instruction

2. The poem's words created a clear [image] in my mind.

3. Carlos had a [scan] of his abdomen, but the doctors found nothing wrong.

LITERARY FOCUS *(30 minutes)*
Following Technical Directions Explain: *Reading technical directions is different from reading other nonfiction articles in that when you read technical directions, your purpose is to learn how to do something.*

Read the following lines to students:

1. Make sure the scanner is turned on.

2. Place your image in the scanner. The image should lie face down on the glass, aligned according to the page-size indicators on the scanner.

Ask: *Would you know what to do after reading or hearing this information once?* (Student answers may vary.) *Are there any words that you are unfamiliar with in these directions?* (Answers may vary. Students may be unfamiliar with *scanner, aligned,* and *indicators.)* Review the meaning of any unfamiliar words with students, and discuss how they can find the meaning of any words they do not know by using the dictionary or asking others for help.

Help students use academic vocabulary and concepts. Have students work in pairs. Have each pair look at the labeled illustration on pages 1194–1196. First, have each pair make a list of any words with which they are unfamiliar Then, have each pair find out what the words mean, and have them to jot down the definitions. Encourage students to share their work.

READING FOCUS *(20 minutes)*
Skimming and Scanning Explain: *Skimming documents helps you get a broad idea of what they are about. When you skim, you look at the title, the heads, the illustrations, and you may read one or two lines under each head.* Write the following heads on the chalkboard:

Setting Up
Making Calls
Making a Contact List
Using Voice Mail

Ask: *In what kind of document would you find these heads?* (technical directions for a phone) Explain that simply by skimming heads, you can get a good idea of what a document is all about.

VOCABULARY SKILL
Especially for ELL
(5 minutes or less)
Review the meaning of the word t*echnical (specialized, especially relating to practical or mechanical arts).* Break it into syllables *(tech ni cal),* and note that the *ch* is pronounced like a *k.* You may also consider having Spanish-speaking students read or listen to the summary in Spanish.

READING FOCUS
Graphic Organizer

Skimming	Scanning

Original content Copyright © by Holt, Rinehart and Winston. Additions and changes to the original content are the responsibility of the instructor.

Differentiating Instruction

Then, explain: *Scanning helps you to find specific information in a document. Suppose that you were trying to find out how to add phone numbers to your telephone. Under which of the heads above would you expect to find that information?* (Making a Contact List). *You can also scan to find specific terms or graphics in the text.*

Have students work in pairs to fill out a chart like the one on the preceding page. Before they read the directions carefully, have them jot down the heads under "skimming." Then, as they read, have them note information about particular terms or other details under "Scanning."

Direct Teach
(60 minutes)

Three-Minute Review Start to read the document out loud. Pause at any time during the reading, and ask students to work independently. Set a timer for three minutes. Have students spend three minutes rereading material, reviewing their notes from the Reading Focus activity and writing any questions they have. Then, ask: *What did you notice in your review?* Discuss students' responses.

Check for Understanding

WRITING FOCUS *(15 minutes)*

Adjectives Explain that the author uses heads and numbers to make it clear what should be done first, second, third, and so on. Read aloud the following example to students: :

> *1. Make sure the scanner is turned on.*

Explain that this step is supposed to be done first, and that nothing else can be done until this step is followed. Now ask students to choose something that they know how to use, and to write directions that someone else could follow. Encourage them to use numbered steps, and to think carefully about what needs to be done first, second, and so on.

Think As A Reader/Writer Ask *Do you have any difficulty in understanding technical directions? How do you think writers could make them easier to follow?* Students might suggest that writers could make sure steps are clear and that they should use clear illustrations. Ask students to review the instructions that they have already worked on, to make sure that they are simple and clear. They may wish to trade papers with a partner to gather feedback on their work. Then, have students rewrite the instructions with their partner's comments in mind.

READING/WRITING
Especially for WGP
(5 minutes)
Writers who are gaining proficiency will benefit from short conferences in which they receive explicit instruction on how to correct errors.

Original content Copyright © by Holt, Rinehart and Winston. Additions and changes to the original content are the responsibility of the instructor.

Differentiating Instruction

Citing Internet Sources

Notecards When you do research on the Internet, you should keep track of the sources through **notecards.** Notecards will help you keep track of certain basic information on your sources.

In the notecards below, record information from the sources listed on page 1201 of the text. First locate the source with the information already provided on the card. Then fill in the rest of the information from the source onto the notecard.

Source Type: Product Information from a Commercial Site
Author:
Title:
URL:
Source Type:
Author: Loyd Case
Title:
URL:
Source Type:
Author:
Title:
URL: www.loc.gov/copyright/forms/formva.pdf

Original content Copyright © by Holt, Rinehart and Winston. Additions and changes to the original content are the responsibility of the instructor.

Analyzing Functional Workplace Documents

Preteach
LISTENING COMPREHENSION SKILLS *(10 minutes)*
Build Background/Set a Purpose

Introduce the lesson by explaining: *All of the selections you will be reading are workplace documents. You will be reading a business letter, an e-mail, a Web site, and a contract. Though the documents are different in their format and their purpose, they all relate to a game that one young person has designed.*

Preview the following details of the documents:

- In the business letter, the young game designer asks for help and advice from an editor of a gaming magazine.

- In the e-mail, the editor replies to the game designer and offers her opinions on ways to improve the Web site. She also offers to meet with the game designer.

- On the Web site, the game designer gives information about the game, along with a description of the game, and offers a way for users to download the game.

- On the Shareware Agreement, the game designer presents the legal agreement between the user and the software maker.

Point out that you might read a Web site differently than a business letter. Have students look ahead at the pages to get an idea of what each document looks like. Ask: *Which do you think you could read more quickly—the business letter or the web site? Why?*

VOCABULARY SKILLS *(10 minutes)*
Preteach Vocabulary Words Review the meanings of the vocabulary in the Word Bank. Then give students these sentences to complete.

1. To [differentiate] between the candidates for class president, look at their positions.

2. The most [diligent] students tend to get good grades.

3. As Rita was [en route] to her soccer game, she saw her friend Sara.

Remind students to watch for these words as they read the story.

LANGUAGE COACH SKILL *(10 minutes)*
Oral Fluency Point out to students that some words that begin with *di-* have the long *i* sound, like *diaphragm*, while others have the short *i* sound, like *dismiss*.

Write these words from the selections on the board. Have students write two headings at the top of a piece of paper: *Long i Sound* and *Short i*

RESOURCES
In *The Holt Reader:* "Analyzing Functional Workplace Documents" for students who need more scaffolding in a workbook format

In this book: *Vocabulary Skill Builder,* p. 236; "Analyzing Functional Workplace Documents" Selection Test, p. 238.

Consult Holt Audio Library for recordings of most selections.

WORD BANK
diligent
differentiate
en route

ACADEMIC VOCABULARY
Preteaching Academic Vocabulary
(5 minutes)
Write these terms and their meanings on a chalkboard or transparency. Review them with the students before previewing the selection.
Structure: the overall arrangement of a document on a page or screen. This includes the order, or sequence, of elements; graphics; and some formatting choices.
Format: the design of a document, especially choices related to emphasizing key elements
Graphics: drawings, photos, and other artwork

Original content Copyright © by Holt, Rinehart and Winston. Additions and changes to the original content are the responsibility of the instructor.

Differentiating Instruction

Sound. Ask students to then write each of the words under the heading that describes the sound of the letter *i* in each word.

- diaper *(long i)*
- dialogue *(long i)*
- difference *(short i)*
- diminish *(short i)*
- dispute *(short i)*
- diagram *(long i)*
- diner *(long i)*
- disagree *(short i)*

INFORMATIONAL TEXT FOCUS *(30 minutes)*
Analyzing Functional Workplace Documents Explain: *Some documents have a certain "look" that makes them easier to use and read. A document's look is often achieved through the use of a certain structure. Optional elements such as graphics and formatting choices help give the document its structure and look.*

Read the following excerpt from the Shareware Agreement aloud to students and write it on the chalkboard.

Shareware Agreement

This is a legal agreement between you, the end user, and WYSIWYGame Arts, the proprietor. By using WYSIWYGame Arts software [hereafter called the SOFTWARE], you indicate your acceptance of these terms.

Ask students whether any graphics or formatting choices are obvious in this excerpt. (no, except that the title is set apart) Then ask students to discuss what the terms *end user* and *proprietor* mean here. Discuss with students whether, if they wanted a thorough understanding, they would expect to read the full document quickly or slowly. *(slowly)* Point out that the paragraph above serves as an introduction to the document, and explains why the document is important.

Then ask students to look at the Shareware Agreement in their student book, and discuss the format and design of the Shareware Agreement. Ask: *How are the elements on the page arranged?* (by number). *How does the format help the reader to understand the document?* (each legal issue has its own heading) *Are there any graphic elements on the page?* (yes, there is the game company logo)

Help students use academic vocabulary and concepts. Have students work in pairs. Guide students to preview the web site document in the lesson as they did the Shareware Agreement. Ask them to create a three-column chart with the headings: *Structure, Format, Graphics*. Tell students to spend five minutes discussing the structure, format, and the graphics used on the document. Then have them note their

Vocabulary *(cont.)*
Consequences: Results; outcomes.
Specify: State in detail.

LANGUAGE SKILL
Especially for ELL
(5 minutes or less)
Encourage students to use the academic vocabulary words *consequences* and *specify* in original sentences that relate to contractual agreements, such as the Shareware Agreement.

LANGUAGE SKILL
Especially for ELL
(5 minutes or less)
Draw a web on the board with the term *legal issues* in the center. Cluster the following terms, and explain how and why they are legal issues: *copyright* (and the copyright symbol), *contract, license,* and *shareware agreement.*

Original content Copyright © by Holt, Rinehart and Winston. Additions and changes to the original content are the responsibility of the instructor.

Differentiating Instruction

observations on the chart. Ask volunteers for examples from their charts.

READING FOCUS *(45 minutes)*
Model Reading Strategies As You Read Aloud Explain to students that they are about to read for the purpose of analyzing. Model how to skim the material to get an overview. Then model varying your reading rate and going back to reread the text. For example, quickly read the introductory text on page 1204 of the Student Edition (for an overview), but slowly study the information about structure on page 1205 (so that you can apply it to the readings). Invite volunteers to read different sections of the documents aloud in the same way.

After the class has finished its reading, have students fill out a chart like the one on the right. Ask students to write down which documents they read quickly, which took them a little longer, and which they read the slowest.

Direct Teach

(45 minutes)
Chunk the Text Help students pace their reading by dividing the selection into "chunks" or parts. After students read each part, stop to help them identify reasons why their reading rates might change.
Part 1: ends p. 1206, Business letter
Part 2: ends p. 1207, E-mail
Part 3: ends p. 1209, Web site
Part 4: ends p. 1210 Contract

Check for Understanding

WRITING FOCUS *(15 minutes)*
Compare and Contrast the Documents Provide practice with the terms structure and format, as well as with other important terms, and review key content. Write the Web site title "The Show Must Go On" on the chalkboard, and draw the logo (WYSI WYGAME ARTS) to the left. Ask students to state what academic vocabulary word they would use to describe the logo (graphic). Ask students to discuss the format and structure of the Web page, and what they find most effective. Then, guide students to create a chart or Venn diagram, comparing and contrasting the structure and format of the sample Web page with the structure and format of the sample Shareware Agreement. Encourage students to look back at their notes from the Informational Text Focus activity on the Shareware Agreement.

Think As A Reader/Writer Ask: *Of all the workplace documents in this lesson, which did you find easiest to follow? What made that document easiest to follow?* Ask students to write a paragraph explaining their reasons.

READING FOCUS
Reading Rate Chart

Reading Rate	Document
Quick	
Slower	
Slowest	

READING/WRITING
Especially for WGP
(10 minutes)
Point out to students that in a Venn diagram or chart, they will probably not have room to write full sentences. They will need to make sure to include enough information, however, so that their chart is understandable to an outside reader. Draw a model of a Venn diagram on the chalkboard. Ask student volunteers for comparisons between two of the other documents in this section. Write down these comparisons where appropriate, modeling how much information to include.

Original content Copyright © by Holt, Rinehart and Winston. Additions and changes to the original content are the responsibility of the instructor.

Differentiating Instruction

What Is Wrong with This Document/ WYSIWYGame Arts

Evaluating Logic Chart When you evaluate functional documents, you pay attention to the **logical sequencing** of the document. You want to analyze whether the document is logical and thorough.

In the chart below, read the evaluation questions you might ask when reading a functional document. If the question will help you evaluate the logic of a functional document, check the *Yes* column.

Evaluation Questions	Yes	No
Is enough information given for the article to make sense?		
Is the article funny and/or entertaining?		
Are all the steps given?		
Is the author famous?		
Are the steps given in the right order?		
Is there any missing information?		

Original content Copyright © by Holt, Rinehart and Winston. Additions and changes to the original content are the responsibility of the instructor.

Differentiating Instruction

Targeted Strategies for Learners with Diverse Needs

READING SKILLS

Analyzing Functional Workplace Documents *(15 minutes)* Explain to students that the goal of functional workplace documents is to present information clearly. The tone should be professional. When students read workplace documents, they should pay close attention to how information is arranged. Emphasis is placed on the most important information, which should be reflected by type size and placement. Important items are likely to appear before unimportant items. The way information is grouped or organized may have some relationship to how the information is meant to be used, such as steps in a process. The document should be as brief as possible. Short sentences and bulleted lists are more common than thick blocks of text. The structure is more like an outline than an essay. Clear headings should make items easy to find. Share this chart with students, which they can use to help analyze workplace documents:

Purpose	Audience	Visual Cues
Why has this document been written? Does it explain something or is it requesting that someone take action?	Who is supposed to be using this document? How much knowledge is that person expected to have?	How can you use the visual cues, such as: -headings -boldfaced text -white space -graphics?

Have partners find examples of elements in each document that help to answers these questions. Challenge students to debate whether or not each kind of document would be as successful in a different format.

LITERARY SKILLS

Following Technical Directions *(15 minutes)* Point out that technical directions explain how to make or do something. Ask students if they have ever used a recipe to cook something new. If so, then they have used technical directions. Explain that there is more than one way to approach technical directions. The idea is to find a way that gets the job done. Let students know that they should expect to read the directions more than once. Here are some techniques to try:

- Scan the directions. Be sure you have everything you need to begin.

- Read one step at a time, performing the action before going on to read the next step.

- Have someone read the steps aloud to you while you follow them.

Then have a class discussion about these techniques. Invite students to share any other techniques they have used.

Readings in Collection 10 Minimum Course of Study
Following Technical Directions, p. 1192
Analyzing Functional Workplace Documents, p. 1204

RESOURCES
In *The Holt Reader,* all three selections help students who need more scaffolding in a workbook format.

Consult *Holt Audio Library* for recordings of most selections.

TEACHING TIP
Reading directions is challenging for native speakers and is especially so for English-language learners who may lack some of the technical vocabulary. Advise English-language learners to look for and rely on diagrams, when possible. Diagrams often will include labels that can help students build vocabulary.

ALTERNATIVE ASSESSMENT *(5 minutes)*
Have students provide answers for these items.

[Functional workplace documents] are written for a specific purpose and a specific audience, and are formatted to achieve that purpose as clearly and briefly as possible.

If you carefully follow the steps in [technical directions] you should be able to make or do something new.

Original content Copyright © by Holt, Rinehart and Winston. Additions and changes to the original content are the responsibility of the instructor.

Differentiating Instruction

Collection 10
Academic and Selection Vocabulary

Reading Workplace Documents
Following Technical Directions   Analyzing Function

A. **Write the letter of the correct synonym next to each word.**

_____ 1. diligent   a. choices

_____ 2. chart   b. distinguish

_____ 3. options   c. hard-working

_____ 4. differentiate   d. table

B. **Circle the letter next to vocabulary word that best matches the clue.**

1. Clue: You need to copy this page onto your computer.

   A. scan   B. differentiate

2. Clue: Fix a presentation that looks boring.

   A. agreement   B. image

3. Clue: A new computer isn't working right.

   A. warranty   B. scanner

4. Clue: A check is in the mail.

   A. en route   B. options

5. Clue: The employee of the month has perfect attendance.

   A. differentiate   B. diligent

C. **Use the academic vocabulary words to complete the following paragraph about workplace documents.**

coherent   specify   function   consequences

All workplace documents have a purpose, or (1) _____. They must be

(2) _____ and communicate their purpose clearly. Workplace documents

should (3) _____ any issue or problem and, if possible, offer a solution.

Responsibilities and the (4) _____ of avoiding them should be clearly

stated as well, so that all parties know what is expected of them.

Original content Copyright © by Holt, Rinehart and Winston. Additions and changes to the original content are the responsibility of the instructor.

Differentiating Instruction

Selection Test

Following Technical Directions

COMPREHENSION, SKILLS, AND VOCABULARY Circle the letter of the best answer to each of the following items.

1. Which step should come first?

   A) saving your image

   B) editing your image

   C) scanning the image

   D) checking to make sure the scanner is on

2. When you save your photo, make sure that you use which format?

   A) JPEG   C) DOC

   B) PICT   D) TXT

3. When you get an overview of a document by reading heads, you are—

   A) perusing   C) skimming

   B) scanning   D) studying

4. When you are looking for a particular piece of information, you are—

   A) perusing   C) skimming

   B) scanning   D) studying

5. Which of the following is the best example of **options**?

   A) a menu with many choices

   B) a menu with one excellent choice

   C) a restaurant with many customers

   D) a restaurant with one loyal customer

6. Write a paragraph about a product for which it would be helpful to have clear technical directions. What would you like included in these directions? Use the graphic organizer below to collect your ideas.

Introductory statement: To me, it would be very helpful to have technical directions for…
Two or three supporting sentences: In the technical directions, I would hope that there would be…Also, it would be helpful to have…
Concluding statement: In conclusion, I think that technical directions for …. would be good to have.

Original content Copyright © by Holt, Rinehart and Winston. Additions and changes to the original content are the responsibility of the instructor.

Differentiating Instruction

Functional Workplace Documents

COMPREHENSION, SKILLS, AND VOCABULARY Circle the letter of the best
answer to each of the following items.

1. In which workplace document did the game designer ask for advice?

    A) business letter

    B) e-mail message

    C) Web site

    D) contract

2. The game described on the WYSISYGame Arts Web site is about—

    A) learning to write workplace documents

    .B) learning to read workplace documents

    C) trying to get to a stadium where your character can sing

    D) trying to get to a railroad where your character can travel

3. **Charts**, **diagrams**, and **illustrations** are all types of—

    A) structures   C) graphics

    B) formats   D) letters

4. Which of the following should you take care to read slowly?

    A) the address on a business letter

    B) the closing on a business letter

    C) the title of an e-mail message

    D) the entire text of a contract

5. Which of the following is the best example of someone who is **diligent**?

    A) a student who does not work hard

    B) a waiter who frequently makes mistakes

    C) a police officer who tracks down every lead

    D) a speaker who speaks enthusiastically

6. Write a note to the game designer about the Web site document in this lesson.
   What do you like the best about the Web site? What could be improved? Use the
   graphic organizer below to collect your ideas.

Introductory statement: Dear G. Designer: The best part of the Web site for WYSIWIGame Arts is…because…
Two or three supporting sentences: In my opinion, one part of the Web site that could be stronger is…. A specific suggestion I can offer is …
Concluding statement: In conclusion, I hope that you will consider my opinions about…as you continue to work on your Web site.

Original content Copyright © by Holt, Rinehart and Winston. Additions and changes to the original content are the responsibility of the instructor.

Collection 10
Collection Summative Test

VOCABULARY SKILLS Complete the sentences below by using the collection vocabulary words from the list below.

scan	image	options	diligent
differentiate	en route		

1. As I was _____ to my appointment, I got stuck in traffic.

2. If you _____ the paper document, you can edit it on the computer.

3. The _____ on the Web site was blurry.

4. On Saturday, we have three _____; we can clean, hike, or go biking.

5. To _____ between a business letter and a friendly letter, check the greeting.

LITERARY AND READING SKILLS Circle the letter of the best answer.

6. When you need to get an overview of a technical document, try—
   A) skimming
   B) scanning
   C) imaging
   D) optioning

7. The overall arrangement of a document on a page or screen is its—
   A) graphics
   B) text
   C) structure
   D) feel

8. Which type of document is most likely to include graphics?
   A) business letter
   B) e-mail message
   C) Web site
   D) contract

LANGUAGE AND WRITING SKILLS Choose from the multiple-meaning words below to complete each sentence.

scan	image	options

9. When Peter read the poem about a tiger, he had a clear _____ of the wild cat in his mind.

10. After the brain _____, the doctors were convinced that there was no disease.

Original content Copyright © by Holt, Rinehart and Winston. Additions and changes to the original content are the responsibility of the instructor.

Differentiating Instruction

Lesson Plan and Teaching Strategies

Writing Workshop: Business Communications

PREWRITING

Gather Ideas for a Business Communication *(15 minutes)*

Review the purpose of a business communication: *When you write a business communication, you are passing along accurate information for a specific purpose, using a formal tone.* Once students are ready to select their form of business communication, e.g. business letter or meeting notes, offer the following guidance.

Business Letter Help students recognize that the purpose of a business may to be to inform or to persuade. Depending on which kind of letter is being written, have students review the criteria for including evidence as studied in prior Writing Workshops (e.g. informative and persuasive essay writing) in the Student Edition. You also may wish to review the types of arguments that were presented in Listening/Speaking Activity on Evaluating Speeches.

Meeting Notes When taking notes, students will need to pay careful attention not just to what is said but who is saying it. Students may need to get a list of attendees prior to the meeting. They will also need someone to help them match all the speakers to the list of names, if they do not know everyone present. If the meeting structure is a roundtable discussion, it may help to make a small map on a sticky note of the speakers and their names. Tell students that can use initials to keep track of speakers in their notes.

Have students work with partner who has chosen a similar assignment to help share in the preparation.

Follow the Proper Format/Taking Meeting Notes *(15 minutes)*

Remind students that they can use the professional samples and Student Draft examples of a business letter on pages 1224 and 1229 or of the meeting notes on pages 1224 and 1230 of the Student Edition.

DRAFTING

Organize Details *(10 minutes)*

Encourage students to use the charts on page 1225 of the Student Edition as they draft their essays. Have students review the formatting instructions, as well as the professional samples and Student Draft examples on page 1226 of the Students Edition.

Review with students the "Your Turn" section on page 1227 of the Student Edition. Remind students who are working on a business letter to focus on the purpose they are trying to accomplish. Remind students who are working on meeting notes that they need to focus on an accurate summary of what was discussed in chronological order.

TEACHING TIP

Taking meeting notes will offer special challenges to English-language learners and learners with diverse needs. If students wish to select this form of business communication, be sure they have a supportive setting that will allow students to record the proceedings as well as seek clarification, if needed. You may wish to have students work on either assignment with a partner or in a small group.

ESPECIALLY FOR ELL

(10 minutes)

Aside from the obvious challenges, taking meeting notes is also a wonderful opportunity for English-language learners to work on their listening skills in a real-world setting. As students listen to a recording of the meeting, they may wish to partner with a native speaker who can clarify any words or phrases that they cannot comprehend.

ESPECIALLY FOR WGP

If students are choosing to work on a business letter be sure that they are very clear on the scenario—real or invented—before they begin. You may wish to have students work in pairs to role-play or interview each other in order to draw out the details.

Original content Copyright © by Holt, Rinehart and Winston. Additions and changes to the original content are the responsibility of the instructor.

Differentiating Instruction

EVALUATING AND REVISING

Review Content and Organization *(20 minutes)*

If students have chosen to write a business letter, give them time to focus on points 1, 3, and 4 in the Evaluation Questions. If students have chosen to take meeting notes, give them time to focus on points 3 and 5.

1. If students can't find a sentence to underline that expresses the purpose their business letter, ask them to describe the purpose of the letter. Have students begin their letter with this statement, as in the professional writing model on page 1224 in the Student Edition, or at the end of the first paragraph, as in the Student Draft on page 1229.

3. Use the mini-lesson on How to Use Precise Language on page 1229 of the Student Edition to give students an example of the type of changes they are looking to make. As a general rule, formal language is the way in which they would be expected to speak if they were invited to dinner at the White House. Informal language is the way in which they speak to their friends.

4. You may wish to enlarge and post the formatting instructions on page 1226 of the Students Edition, as well as the professional samples and Student Draft examples. In that way, students will have them as a handy reference as they revise their work.

5. Ask students to listen to the recording of the meeting as they revise their notes to be sure they have accurately conveyed the meeting's content. Students can try to improve their summaries, too, by making them more concise and to the point.

Pair students with a partner to use the guidelines and the points above when they review each other's drafts.

Grammar Link: Correcting Sentence Fragments *(15 Minutes)*

Be sure when giving this grammar link lesson to help students understand why the fragments are not sentences. This will help them recognize fragments when they check their own work.

Review the examples below and discuss which are sentences and why.

Fragment	Why?	Fragment Fixed
Suggested that I contact you for a job.	The subject is missing. Who did the suggesting?	Mr. Jones suggested that I contact you for a job.
I have experience with filing. And typing, too.	"And typing, too" has no subject or verb.	I have experience with filing <u>and typing, too</u>.
Jackson has a problem with.	The thought is unfinished.	Jackson has a problem with <u>the agenda.</u>

Then ask students to reread their essays to find fragments and turn them into sentences.

TEACHING TIP

Wait until students are at the proofreading stage to introduce the grammar link lessons. Student gaining proficiency with writing may be overwhelmed by too many considerations to juggle while drafting.

ESPECIALLY FOR ELL
(5 minutes)

Recognizing the difference between formal and informal tone is sometimes difficult for language learners because it requires experience in a variety of social situations. One subtlety that English-language learners may not realize is that English speakers tend to use the conditional tense (could, would) rather than the imperative form (can, will) as a way to make the tone more polite and less challenging or confrontational.

ESPECIALLY FOR LDN

Learners with diverse needs may have trouble summarizing on the spot as they would need to do while taking meeting notes. You may wish to work with students individually on how to use key words so they don't attempt to transcribe every word that is uttered during a meeting.

Original content Copyright © by Holt, Rinehart and Winston. Additions and changes to the original content are the responsibility of the instructor.

Differentiating Instruction

Lesson Plan and Teaching Strategies

Listening and Speaking Workshop: Debating an Issue

PREPARE TO DEBATE *(20 minutes)*

Explain to students that they are going to form teams to debate an issue. Review the section called Take Sides on p. 1234 of the Student Edition. Clarify the preparation goals of each team in the following way:

- **Affirmative Team**: Explain to this team that they are going to argue for something to change. Their task will be to show why the existing way doesn't work and to prove why their way is better. The Affirmative Team will have to find evidence that supports this position. In addition to finding examples, quotes, and facts, they will have to be sure that the information is true and related to the issue. The Affirmative team will have to look at the negative evidence for this idea to anticipate attacks and prepare counterarguments.

- **Negative Team**: These students will argue against this change or new idea. They may argue that things are fine the way they are. Or they may admit that things are not ideal, but they must show why the Affirmative Team's suggestion is a bad one. They will have to find examples, quotes, and facts that point to problems with this idea. They will also have to look at the evidence in favor of the idea, so they can prepare their attacks and counterarguments.

CONDUCT THE DEBATE *(10 minutes)*

You may wish to further structure the debate so that teams can use their members to specialize. This will ensure that everyone participates while no one is put on the spot. See below chart for an example and adapt to suit any proposition or number of students.

Proposition: Turning a Classroom into a Computer Lab		
Issue 1: Space	2 students from Affirmative Team	2 students from Negative Team
Issue 2: Money	2 students from Affirmative Team	2 students from Negative Team
Issue 3: Grades	2 students from Affirmative Team	2 students from Negative Team

JUDGE THE DEBATE *(10 minutes)*

You may wish to make your scoring explicit during the debate. When a student makes a good point, you might say, "Good delivery!" and post a point in that team's favor. Immediate feedback such as this will help model what good debating skills are all about.

TEACHING TIP

You may wish to take the role of the Chairperson unless there is a student is suited to that role. Keep in mind that the Chairperson is responsible for keeping an orderly tone to the debate. Although teams are allowed to refute or attack the other team's evidence or logic, it must be made clear that no personal attacks will be tolerated. Model an acceptable refutation: *The Affirmative Team is using outdated facts.* Or: *The Negative Team has made a mistake in logic.*

ESPECIALLY FOR ELL

Support English-language learners by allowing them to suggest some subjects for debate. Having subject matter that is familiar will make it easier for English-language learners to participate.

EVALUATION CRITERIA

Use these criteria to evaluate students' debate:

- Offers sound reasons for a particular position
- Gives credible, valid, and relevant evidence for reasons
- Can refute and rebut the other position
- Delivery shows preparedness and confidence
- Tone and manner is respectful

Original content Copyright © by Holt, Rinehart and Winston. Additions and changes to the original content are the responsibility of the instructor.

Differentiating Instruction

Unit 6; Skill Builder 1
Oral Language Skill Builder

Asking and Answering Questions

UNDERSTAND THE SKILL When you ask a question, it's best to be specific about the type of information or action you are requesting. When you ask the right questions, you get closer to solving the problem.

Work with a partner to complete the chart. Then role-play the conversations between customers and each company's or organization's customer service representative. Afterward, discuss the questions below.

Customer Service Department			
Company or Organization	**Problem or Issue**	**Question**	**Answer**
Department of Sanitation	Customer is sprayed with sewage and clothes are ruined.	What kind of compensation…	Please accept our apologies and…
Museum of Modern Art	Art student would like to know the name of the artist who created the "Indian Art" poster.	I was wondering if you could tell me….	Our records show…
WYSIWYGame Arts	WYSIWYGame breaks down 91 days after customer purchase. Within 90 days, game is repaired free of charge. After 90 days, customer must pay labor and shipping costs.	Would it be possible….	Our company's policy…
PhotoEdit	Preview image of item to be scanned doesn't appear on customer's computer screen.	Is there anyone there who can help me with…	According to the directions…

Extend Discussion Have you ever had a real-world experience like the ones you just role-played? What was that like?

• How would you deal with a customer representative who is being rude?

• If you were working as a customer representative, how would you deal with a difficult customer?

Original content Copyright © by Holt, Rinehart and Winston. Additions and changes to the original content are the responsibility of the instructor.

Differentiating Instruction

Oral Language Skill Builder

Taking Notes

UNDERSTAND THE SKILL Taking notes requires more that just good listening skills. You also need to know what the most important information is because it would be too hard to write down everything word for word.

Meet with a small group to discuss forming a summer book club. Take turns taking notes. After the meeting compare your notes and discuss the questions below with your group.

Meeting Attendees:

_____

_____

Purpose for meeting:

The reason for this meeting is

_____

Issues discussed:

_____

_____

Decisions made:

The group has decided_____

_____

_____

Items for further discussion:

Next time we meet, _____

_____should be at the top of the agenda.

Extend Discussion Discuss your notes with the group. Create a complete record of your meeting, using all the notes.

- How difficult was it to listen and take notes during the meeting?

- Do you have any tips to share with your classmates?

Original content Copyright © by Holt, Rinehart and Winston. Additions and changes to the original content are the responsibility of the instructor.

Differentiating Instruction

Unit 6; Skill Builder 3
English Language Skill Builder

Words Often Confused

UNDERSTAND THE SKILL Many words in English have a similar sound and spelling, but they have different meanings.

Write the word that goes with the definition below. If you don't know a word, look it up in a dictionary. Compare your answers with a classmate's.

1. Giving credit to a source _____ (cite/site)

2. To balance or go with something else _____ (compliment/complement)

3. Willing to receive or tolerate _____ (accept/except)

4. A result _____ (affect/effect)

5. A distance beyond _____ (farther/further)

6. An opinion about what others should do _____ (advise/advice)

7. Tolerating delays or difficulties without complaint _____ (patience/patients)

EXTEND DISCUSSION Read each sentence below. If the boldfaced word is used correctly, write "No change." If the boldfaced word is incorrect, write the correct word on the line.

1. What kind of **affect** might a letter of complaint have? _____

2. If you need **further** assistance after reading the manual, you can call the company's help desk.

   _____

3. The phone lines are often busy, so **patients** will be required. _____

4. You can buy insurance in the store to **compliment** the coverage from your warranty.

   _____

5. Reread the technical directions for trouble-shooting **advice**. _____

6. All the replacement costs are covered under the warranty **accept** shipping.

   _____

7. The product must be shipped to the factory, since repairs are done on **cite**.

   _____

Original content Copyright © by Holt, Rinehart and Winston. Additions and changes to the original content are the responsibility of the instructor.

Differentiating Instruction

Unit 6; Skill Builder 4
English Language Skill Builder

Fixed Expressions
UNDERSTAND THE SKILL Fixed expressions are words that go together to mean something specific. Many fixed expressions are used in the business world.

Discuss each expression with a partner. Then read each sentence below. Rewrite each one with the correct expression to replace the underlined words.

Fixed Expressions Used in Business

company policy	human resources	quality control
instruction manual	job satisfaction	follow instructions

1. If you have trouble with the scanner, check your <u>directions booklet</u>.

   _____

2. Please give your application to the <u>person value</u> department.

   _____

3. "Service with a smile" is the <u>business custom</u> around here.

   _____

4. A good assistant knows how to <u>pursue directions</u>.

   _____

5. Some think that <u>work contentment</u> is as important as salary.

   _____

6. Many complaints show that <u>excellence management</u> needs work.

   _____

EXTEND DISCUSSION Use your understanding of these expressions and the reading selections to discuss these real-world situations.

1. Why do you think company policy would put a time limit on warranties?

   _____

2. What kind of changes could a company make to increase job satisfaction?

   _____

3. Why is quality control important?

   _____

Original content Copyright © by Holt, Rinehart and Winston. Additions and changes to the original content are the responsibility of the instructor.

Unit 6
Summative Test

INFORMATIONAL TEXT AND READING SKILLS

A. Circle the letter of the best answer. *(25 points; 5 points each)*

1. Which of the following are the best examples of **workplace documents**?

   A) newspapers and government records

   B) warranties and instruction manuals

   C) business letters and e-mails

   D) friendly letters and greeting cards

2. If you use **skimming** when looking over a document, you

   A) read the title, heads, and subheads

   B) look for key words and phrases

   C) read carefully and slowly

   D) only look at graphics

3. If you are shopping for a product and want to find out if an item has the features you need, you should look at the

   A) contract

   B) warranties

   C) instruction manuals

   D) product information

4. **Numbered steps** and **clear diagrams** are commonly found in

   A) business letters

   B) technical directions

   C) contracts

   D) e-mails

5. If a document is **coherent**, then it

   A) states information in detail

   B) is difficult to follow

   C) is clear and understandable

   D) includes unlabeled graphics

Original content Copyright © by Holt, Rinehart and Winston. Additions and changes to the original content are the responsibility of the instructor.

Differentiating Instruction

| Unit 6 Summative Test *continued*

B. Complete each sentence with one of the informational text or reading skills shown below.
(25 points; 5 points each)

taking notes   scanning   adjust your   warranties   instruction manuals
                                      reading rate

6. By _____ you can find particular information in a document by looking for key words or other important details.

7. You might _____ to better understand technical directions if you have started by reading them quickly.

8. If you want to remember important information in a functional document, try _____ in a notebook, in the margins, or on a computer.

9. In _____ you can find how to set up and use a product.

10. If you need to get products repaired or replaced, check their _____.

Read the question below. Then write a short response on the lines. *(50 points)*

Reading Workplace Documents

11. Review the e-mail from Donna Pulsipher to G. Designer regarding the WYSIWIGame Arts Website. Then, look at the Website itself. What advice from Donna Pulsipher did G. Designer follow? How can you tell?

_____

_____

_____

_____

_____

_____

Original content Copyright © by Holt, Rinehart and Winston. Additions and changes to the original content are the responsibility of the instructor.

Differentiating Instruction

Fluency Passage 1

Read aloud the passage from "The Treasure of Lemon Brown" by Walter Dean Myers, following the instructions from your teacher. After you read, complete the fluency checklist that your teacher provides.

> Greg went to the window and saw three men, neighborhood thugs, on [12] the stoop. One was carrying a length of pipe. Greg looked back toward [13] Lemon Brown, who moved quietly across the room to the window. The [12] old man looked out, then beckoned frantically for Greg to follow him. For [13] a moment Greg couldn't move. Then he found himself following Lemon [11] Brown into the hallway and up darkened stairs. Greg followed as closely [12] as he could. They reached the top of the stairs, and Greg felt Lemon [14] Brown's hand first lying on his shoulder, then probing down his arm until [13] he finally took Greg's hand into his own as they crouched in the darkness. [14]
>
> "They's bad men," Lemon Brown whispered. His breath was [09] warm against Greg's skin. [04]
>
> "Hey! Ragman!" a voice called. "We know you in here. What you got [13] up under them rags? You got any money?" [08]
>
> Silence. [01]
>
> "We don't want to have to come in and hurt you, old man, but we don't [16] mind if we have to." [05]
>
> Lemon Brown squeezed Greg's hand in his own hard, gnarled fist. [11]
>
> [Total 181]

The Treasure of Lemon Brown" by Walter Dean Myers from Boys' Life Magazine, March 1983. CopyrCopyright © 1983 by Walter Dean Myers. Reproduced by permission of **Miriam Altshuler Literary Agency on behalf of Walter Dean Myers.**

Original content Copyright © by Holt, Rinehart and Winston. Additions and changes to the original content are the responsibility of the instructor.

Fluency Passage 2

Read aloud the passage from "The Inn of Lost Time" by Lensey Namioka,
following the instructions from your teacher. After you read, complete the
fluency checklist that your teacher provides.

> The sun was just beginning to set. We passed a bamboo grove, and in [14]
> the low evening light the thin leaves turned into little golden knives. I saw [14]
> a gilded clump of bamboo shoots. The sight made me think of the [13]
> delicious dish they would make when boiled in soy sauce. [10]
> We hurried forward. To our delight we soon came to a clearing with a [14]
> thatched house standing in the middle. The fragrant smell of rice was now [13]
> so strong that we were certain a meal was being prepared inside. [12]
> Standing in front of the house was a pretty girl beaming at us with a [15]
> welcoming smile. "Please honor us with your presence," she said, [10]
> beckoning. [01]
> There was something a little unusual about one of her hands, but, being [13]
> hungry and eager to enter the house, I did not stop to observe closely. [14]
> You will say, of course, that it was my duty as a bodyguard to be [15]
> suspicious and to look out for danger. Youth and inexperience should not [12]
> have prevented me from wondering why an inn should be found hidden [12]
> away from the highway. As it was, my stomach growled, and I didn't even [14]
> hesitate but followed Tokubei to the house. [07]
>
> [Total 203]

"The Inn of Lost Time" by Lensey Namioka from *Short Stories by Outstanding Writers for Young Adults*,
edited by Donald R. Gallo. Copyright © 1989 by Lensey Namioka. All rights reserved. Reproduced by
permission of **Ruth Cohen, for Lensey Namioka.**

Original content Copyright © by Holt, Rinehart and Winston. Additions and changes to the original content are the responsibility of the instructor.

Fluency Passage 3

Read aloud the passage from the textbook *Physical Science,* following the instructions from your teacher. After you read, complete the fluency checklist that your teacher provides.

Forming a Hypothesis [03]

Once you've asked your questions and made observations, you are ready [11] to form a **hypothesis** (hie PAHTH uh sis). A hypothesis is a possible [13] explanation or answer to a question. You can use what you already know [13] and what you have observed to form a hypothesis. [09]

     A good hypothesis is testable. In other words, information can be [11] gathered or an experiment can be designed to test the hypothesis. A [12] hypothesis that is not testable isn't necessarily wrong. But there is no way [13] to show whether the hypothesis is right or wrong. [09]

Making Predictions [02]

Before scientists test a hypothesis, they often predict what they think will [12] happen when they test the hypothesis. Scientists usually state predictions [10] in an if-then statement. The engineers at MIT [Massachusetts Institute of [11] Technology] might have made the following prediction: *If* two flippers are [11] attached to a boat, *then* the boat will be more efficient than a boat [14] powered by propellers. [03]

[Total 157]

Original content Copyright © by Holt, Rinehart and Winston. Additions and changes to the original content are the responsibility of the instructor.

Differentiating Instruction

Fluency Passage 4

Read aloud the passage from "A Retrieved Reformation" by O. Henry, following the instructions from your teacher. After you read, complete the fluency checklist that your teacher provides.

> One afternoon Jimmy Valentine and his suitcase climbed out of the [11] mail hack in Elmore, a little town five miles off the railroad down in the [15] blackjack country of Arkansas. Jimmy, looking like an athletic young [11] senior just home from college, went down the board sidewalk toward the [12] hotel. [01]
>
> A young lady crossed the street, passed him at the corner, and entered [13] a door over which was the sign "The Elmore Bank." Jimmy Valentine [12] looked into her eyes, forgot what he was, and became another man. She [13] lowered her eyes and colored slightly. Young men of Jimmy's style and [12] looks were scarce in Elmore. [05]
>
> Jimmy collared a boy that was loafing on the steps of the bank as if [15] he were one of the stockholders, and began to ask him questions about the [14] town, feeding him dimes at intervals. By and by the young lady came out, [14] looking royally unconscious of the young man with the suitcase, and went [12] her way. [02]
>
> "Isn't that young lady Polly Simpson?" asked Jimmy, with specious [10] guile. [01]
>
> "Naw," said the boy. "She's Annabel Adams. Her pa owns this bank. [12] What'd you come to Elmore for? Is that a gold watch chain? I'm going to [15] get a bulldog. Got any more dimes?" [07]
>
> [Total 206]

Original content Copyright © by Holt, Rinehart and Winston. Additions and changes to the original content are the responsibility of the instructor.

Fluency Passage 5

Read aloud the passage from "The Wise Old Woman" as retold by Yoshiko Uchida, following the instructions from your teacher. After you read, complete the fluency checklist that your teacher provides.

> Many long years ago, there lived an arrogant and cruel young lord [12] who ruled over a small village in the western hills of Japan. [12]
>
> "I have no use for old people in my village," he said haughtily. [13] "They are neither useful nor able to work for a living. I therefore decree [14] that anyone over seventy-one must be banished from the village and left in [14] the mountains to die." [4]
>
> "What a dreadful decree! What a cruel and unreasonable lord we [11] have," the people of the village murmured. But the lord fearfully punished [12] anyone who disobeyed him, and so villagers who turned seventy-one were [11] tearfully carried into the mountains, never to return. [8]
>
> Gradually there were fewer and fewer old people in the village and [12] soon they disappeared altogether. Then the young lord was pleased. [10]
>
> "What a fine village of young, healthy, and hard-working people I have," [12] he bragged. "Soon it will be the finest village in all of Japan." [13]
>
> [Total 158]

"The Wise Old Woman" from *The Sea of Gold and Other Tales from Japan,* adapted by Yoshiko Uchida. Copyright © 1965 byYoshiko Uchida. Reproduced by permission of **Bancroft Library, University of California, Berkeley.**

Original content Copyright © by Holt, Rinehart and Winston. Additions and changes to the original content are the responsibility of the instructor.

Differentiating Instruction

Fluency Passage 6

Read aloud the passage from "Mrs. Flowers" by Maya Angelou, following the instructions from your teacher. After you read, complete the fluency checklist that your teacher provides.

> There was a little path beside the rocky road, and Mrs. Flowers [12]
> walked in front swinging her arms and picking her way over the stones. [13]
> She said, without turning her head, to me, "I hear you're doing very good [14]
> schoolwork, Marguerite, but that it's all written. The teachers report that [11]
> they have trouble getting you to talk in class." We passed the triangular [13]
> farm on our left and the path widened to allow us to walk together. I hung [16]
> back in the separate unasked and unanswerable questions. [08]
> "Come and walk along with me, Marguerite." I couldn't have refused [11]
> even if I wanted to. She pronounced my name so nicely. Or more [13]
> correctly, she spoke each word with such clarity that I was certain a [13]
> foreigner who didn't understand English could have understood her. [09]
> "Now no one is going to make you talk—possibly no one can. But bear in [15]
> mind, language is man's way of communicating with his fellow man and [12]
> it is language alone which separates him from the lower animals." That [12]
> was a totally new idea to me, and I would need time to think about it. [16]
>
> [Total 188]

Excerpts (retitled "Mrs. Flowers") from *I Know Why the Caged Bird Sings* by Maya Angelou. Copyright © 1969 and renewed © 1997 by Maya Angelou. Reproduced by permission of **Random House, Inc.,** **www.randomhouse.com.**

Original content Copyright © by Holt, Rinehart and Winston. Additions and changes to the original content are the responsibility of the instructor.

Fluency Passage 7

Read aloud the passage from "Don't Know Much About Liberty," following the
instructions from your teacher. After you read, complete the fluency checklist
that your teacher provides.

> Although Americans failed the First Amendment pop quiz, they [09]
> passed the Bart Simpson section of the survey with flying colors. More [12]
> than half of the respondents could name at least two of the main [13]
> characters of *The Simpsons*. Twenty-two percent could name all five. [11]
> Those findings made Gene Policinski, executive director of the First [10]
> Amendment Center, want to eat his shorts (as Bart Simpson would say). [12]
> "These are such basic freedoms, and they're in our lives every day," he [13]
> told Senior Edition. "All we have to do is look around." [11]
> No matter how old you are or what state you live in, you exercise First [15]
> Amendment freedoms every day, Policinski says. When you turn on the [11]
> television, you can choose the show you want to watch. If you disagree [13]
> with a law, you can write a letter to your state representative. If you don't [15]
> like something the government is doing, you can say so without getting in [13]
> trouble. [01]
>
> [Total 158]

From "Don't Know Much About Liberty" from *Weekly Reader Senior Edition,* April 21, 2006. Copyright
© 2006 by **Weekly Reader Corporation;** illustrations copyright © 2006 by **Chris Murphy.** All rights
reserved. Reproduced by permission of the publisher and the illustrator.

Original content Copyright © by Holt, Rinehart and Winston. Additions and changes to the original content are the responsibility of the instructor.

Fluency Passage 8

Read aloud the passage from "The Medicine Bag" by Virginia Driving Hawk
Sneve, following the instructions from your teacher. After you read, complete the
fluency checklist that your teacher provides.

> I knew everybody felt as bad as I did. Yet I was proud of this eighty- [16]
> six-year-old man, who had never been away from the reservation, having [11]
> the courage to travel so far alone. [07]
>
> "You found the money in my boots?" he asked Mom. [10]
>
> "Martin did," she answered, and roused herself to scold. "Grandpa, [10]
> you shouldn't have carried so much money. What if someone had stolen it [13]
> from you?" [01]
>
> Grandpa laughed. "I would've known if anyone tried to take the boots [12]
> off my feet. The money is what I've saved for a long time—a hundred [14]
> dollars—for my funeral. But you take it now to buy groceries so that I [14]
> won't be a burden to you while I am here." [10]
>
> "That won't be necessary, Grandpa," Dad said. "We are honored to [11]
> have you with us and you will never be a burden. I am only sorry that we [17]
> never thought to bring you home with us this summer and spare you the [15]
> discomfort of a long trip." [05]
>
> [Total 165]

"The Medicine Bag" by Virginia Driving Hawk Sneve. Copyright © by **Virginia Driving Hawk Sneve.**
Reproduced by permission of the author.

Name _____ Class _____ Date_____

Fluency Passage 9

Read aloud the passage from "A Shot at It" by Esmeralda Santiago, following the instructions from your teacher. After you read, complete the fluency checklist that your teacher provides.

> The auditions are in less than a month. You have to learn a [13] monologue, which you will perform in front of a panel. If you do well, [14] and your grades here are good, you might get into the school." [12]
> Mr. Barone took charge of preparing me for my audition to Performing [12] Arts. He selected a speech from *The Silver Cord,* a play by Sidney [13] Howard, first performed in 1926, but whose action took place in a New [13] York drawing room circa 1905. [05]
> "Mr. Gatti, the English teacher," he said, "will coach you. . . . And Mrs. [15] Johnson will talk to you about what to wear and things like that." [13]
> I was to play Christina, a young married woman confronting her mother- [12] in-law. I learned the monologue phonetically from Mr. Gatti. It opened [11] with "You belong to a type that's very common in this country, Mrs. [13] Phelps—a type of self-centered, self-pitying, son-devouring tigress, with [09] unmentionable proclivities suppressed on the side." [06]
> "We don't have time to study the meaning of every word," Mr. Gatti said. [14] "Just make sure you pronounce every word correctly." [08]
>
> [Total 183]

Original content Copyright © by Holt, Rinehart and Winston. Additions and changes to the original content are the responsibility of the instructor.

Differentiating Instruction

Fluency Passage 10

Read aloud the first four stanzas from "How I Learned English," by Gregory Djanikian, following the instructions from your teacher. After you read, complete the fluency checklist that your teacher provides.

It was in an empty lot [6]
Ringed by elms and fir and honeysuckle. [7]
Bill Corson was pitching in his buckskin jacket, [8]
Chuck Keller, fat even as a boy, was on first, [10]
5 His t-shirt riding up over his gut, [8]
Ron O'Neill, Jim, Dennis, were talking it up [8]
In the field, a blue sky above them [8]
Tipped with cirrus.[1] [3]

And there I was, [4]
10 Just off the plane and plopped in the middle [9]
Of Williamsport, Pa., and a neighborhood game, [7]
Unnatural and without any moves, [5]
My notions of baseball and America [6]
Growing fuzzier each time I wiffed. **[ARD]** [7]

15 So it was not impossible that I, [7]
Banished to the outfield and daydreaming [6]
Of water, or a hotel in the mountains, [8]
Would suddenly find myself in the path [7]
Of a ball stung by Joe Barone. [7]
20 I watched it closing in [5]
Clean and untouched, transfixed[2] [4]
By its easy arc before it hit [7]
My forehead with a thud. [5]

I fell back. [3]
25 Dazed, clutching my brow. [4]
Groaning, "Oh my shin, oh my shin," [7]
And everybody peeled away from me [6]
And dropped from laughter, and there we were, [8]
All of us writhing on the ground for one reason [10]
30 Or another. **[ARD]** [3]

[Total 192]

"How I Learned English" from *Falling Deeply into America* by Gregory Djanikian. Copyright © 1989 by **Gregory Djanikian**. First published in *Poetry*, 1986. Reproduced by permission of the author.

Original content Copyright © by Holt, Rinehart and Winston. Additions and changes to the original content are the responsibility of the instructor.

Differentiating Instruction

Fluency Passage 11

Read aloud the passage from "Lewis and Clark: Into the Unknown" following the instructions from your teacher. After you read, complete the fluency checklist that your teacher provides.

Welcome Additions [02]

In late October, the explorers began building a winter fort near a large [13] community of Mandan and Hidatsa Indians in what is now North Dakota. [12] During their stay at "Fort Mandan," Lewis and Clark learned that horses [12] were needed to cross the mountains. The tribes told them the Shoshone [12] might provide the animals, if they could strike a bargain. [10]

Lewis and Clark found a Shoshone woman to help with these [11] negotiations: Sacagawea, who had been captured by the Hidatsa years [10] earlier. Lewis and Clark hired her and her husband, the French Canadian [12] fur trapper Touissant Charbonneau, as translators. When the corps set out [11] in spring, Charbonneau, Sacagawea, and their new baby son, Jean [10] Baptiste, went along. [03]

Sacagawea's ability to speak Shoshone was, indeed, of great benefit. She [11] helped the corps procure horses and provided aid in many ways. The [12] tribes the explorers encountered were sometimes fearful and suspicious. [09] But when they saw Sacagawea and her baby son, they felt more at ease. [14] Surely a woman and infant wouldn't be included with a war party. [12]

[Total 176]

Original content Copyright © by Holt, Rinehart and Winston. Additions and changes to the original content are the responsibility of the instructor.

Fluency Passage 12

**Read aloud the passage from "The Tell-Tale Heart," by Edgar Allen Poe,
following the instructions from your teacher. After you read, complete the
fluency checklist that your teacher provides.**

> True!—nervous—very, very dreadfully nervous I had been and am; [10]
> but why *will* you say that I am mad? The disease had sharpened my [14]
> senses—not destroyed—not dulled them. Above all was the sense of [11]
> hearing acute. I heard all things in the heaven and in the earth. I heard [15]
> many things in hell. How, then, am I mad? Hearken! and observe how [13]
> healthily—how calmly I can tell you the whole story. [09]
>
> It is impossible to say how first the idea entered my brain; but once [14]
> conceived, it haunted me day and night. Object there was none. Passion [12]
> there was none. I loved the old man. He had never wronged me. He had [15]
> never given me insult. For his gold I had no desire. I think it was his eye! [17]
> Yes, it was this! One of his eyes resembled that of a vulture—a pale blue [15]
> eye, with a film over it. Whenever it fell upon me, my blood ran cold; and [16]
> so by degrees—very gradually—I made up my mind to take the life of the [15]
> old man and thus rid myself of the eye forever. [10]
>
> [Total 187]

Original content Copyright © by Holt, Rinehart and Winston. Additions and changes to the original content are the responsibility of the instructor.

Fluency Passage 13

Read aloud the passage from "Raymond's Run" by Toni Cade Bambara, following the instructions from your teacher. After you read, complete the fluency checklist that your teacher provides.

There is no track meet that I don't win the first-place medal. I used to [15] win the twenty-yard dash when I was a little kid in kindergarten. [12] Nowadays, it's the fifty-yard dash. And tomorrow I'm subject to run the [13] quarter-meter relay all by myself and come in first, second, and third. The [13] big kids call me Mercury cause I'm the swiftest thing in the [12] neighborhood. Everybody knows that—except two people who know [08] better, my father and me. He can beat me to Amsterdam Avenue with me [14] having a two-fire-hydrant head start and him running with his hands in his [14] pockets and whistling. But that's private information. Cause can you [10] imagine some thirty-five-year-old man stuffing himself into PAL shorts to [10] race little kids? So as far as everyone's concerned, I'm the fastest and that [14] goes for Gretchen, too, who has put out the tale that she is going to win [16] the first-place medal this year. Ridiculous. In the second place, she's got [13] short legs. In the third place, she's got freckles. In the first place, no one [15] can beat me and that's all there is to it. [10]

[Total 186]

"Raymond's Run" from *Gorilla, My Love* by Toni Cade Bambara. Copyright © 1960, 1963, 1964, 1965, 1968, 1970, 1971, 1972 by Toni Cade Bambara. Reproduced by permission of **Random House, Inc.,** www.randomhouse.com.

Fluency Passage 14

Read aloud the passage from "Ray Bradbury's On Fire!" by James Hibberd,
following the instructions from your teacher. After you read, complete the
fluency checklist that your teacher provides.

> By mocking the electronic shortcuts and distracting entertainment that [9]
> replace human contact and active thinking, Bradbury shows his science-[10]
> fiction label is misplaced. He cares little for science or its fictions. The [12]
> author of more than thirty books, six hundred short stories, and numerous [12]
> poems, essays, and plays, Bradbury is a consistent champion of things [11]
> human and real. There is simply no ready label for a writer who mixes [14]
> poetry and mythology with fantasy and technology to create literate tales [11]
> of suspense and social criticism; no ideal bookstore section for the author [12]
> whose stories of rockets and carnivals and Halloween capture the [10]
> fascination of twelve-year-olds, while also stunning adult readers with his [10]
> powerful prose and knowing grasp of the human condition. [9]
>
> One secret to Bradbury's lifelong productivity is that his play and his [12]
> work are the same. When asked, "How often do you write?" Bradbury [12]
> replies, "Every day of my life—you got to be in love or you shouldn't do [16]
> it." [1]
>
> . . . When I phoned his Los Angeles home for a 9:00 a.m. interview, [12]
> Bradbury was thoughtful and cranky, and told me he'd already written a [12]
> short story. [2]
>
> [Total 189]

From "Ray Bradbury is on fire!" by James Hibberd from *Salon.com* Web site, accessed December 23,
2002 athttp://dir.salon.com/people/feature/2001/08/29/bradbury/index.html?pn=2.Copyright © 2002
Salon Media Group, Inc. Reproduced by permission of **Salon.com.**

Original content Copyright © by Holt, Rinehart and Winston. Additions and changes to the original content are the responsibility of the instructor.

Fluency Passage 15

Read aloud the passage from "The Flying Machine" by Ray Bradbury, following the instructions from your teacher. After you read, complete the fluency checklist that your teacher provides.

"Sit down with me here," said the Emperor. "Drink some tea. It must [13] be a strange thing, if it is true, to see a man fly. You must have time to [18] think of it, even as I must have time to prepare myself for the sight." [15]

They drank tea. [03]

"Please," said the servant at last, "or he will be gone." [11]

The Emperor rose thoughtfully. "Now you may show me what you have [12] seen." [01]

They walked into a garden, across a meadow of grass, over a small bridge, [14] through a grove of trees, and up a tiny hill. [10]

"There!" said the servant. [04]

The Emperor looked into the sky. [06]

And in the sky, laughing so high that you could hardly hear him laugh, [14] was a man; and the man was clothed in bright papers and reeds to make [15] wings and a beautiful yellow tail, and he was soaring all about like the [14] largest bird in a universe of birds, like a new dragon in a land of ancient [16] dragons. [01]

[Total 168]

"The Flying Machine" from *Golden Apples of the Sun* by Ray Bradbury. Copyright © 1953 and renewed © 1986 by Ray Bradbury. Reproduced by permission of **Don Congdon Associates, Inc.** [NO WEB]

Original content Copyright © by Holt, Rinehart and Winston. Additions and changes to the original content are the responsibility of the instructor.

Differentiating Instruction

Fluency Passage 16

Read aloud the passage from Ray Bradbury's comments about his story "The Dragon," following the instructions from your teacher. After you read, complete the fluency checklist that your teacher provides.

"It is hard to talk about 'The Dragon' without giving away its secret, [13] telling you the surprise. So all I can talk about is the boy I was that [16] became the young man who thought about, and the older man who wrote, [13] this story. I loved dinosaurs from the age of five, when I saw the film *The* [16] *Lost World,* filled with prehistoric monsters. I became even more [10] enamored with these beasts when at age thirteen, *King Kong* fell off the [13] Empire State and landed on me in the front row of the Elite Theater. I [15] never recovered. Later, I met and became friends with Ray Harryhausen, [11] who built and film-animated dinosaurs in his garage when we were both [12] eighteen. We dedicated our lives to these monsters, to dragons in all their [13] shapes and forms. Simultaneously, we loved airplanes, rocket ships, [09] trolley cars, and trains. From this amalgam of loves came our lives and [13] careers. We wound up doing *The Beast from 20,000 Fathoms* as our first [13] film. Not very good, but a beginning. He went on to *Mighty Joe Young* [14] and I to *Moby Dick* and its great sea-beast. When I was in my thirties I [16] wrote 'The Dragon' and combined two of these loves." [09]

[Total 206]

Introduction to *The Dragon* (Graphic Version) by Ray Bradbury with art by Vicente Segrelles. Copyright © 1955 and renewed © 1983 by Ray Bradbury. Reproduced by permission of **Don Congdon Associates, Inc.** [NO WEB]

Original content Copyright © by Holt, Rinehart and Winston. Additions and changes to the original content are the responsibility of the instructor.

Differentiating Instruction

Fluency Passage 17

Read aloud the passage from "Steam Rising: The Revolutionary Power of Paddleboats" by Jessica Cohn, following the instructions from your teacher. After you read, complete the fluency checklist that your teacher provides.

River Commerce [02]

Early steamboats were inefficient and sometimes dangerous. But [08] engineers learned from mistakes and improved their design. In addition, [10] Congress authorized major improvements along the Mississippi and Ohio [09] rivers, which encouraged development of the science of waterway [09] engineering. These factors, along with industrial growth, contributed to [09] the steamboat's rapid rise. In 1814, records show, 21 steamboats visited [11] New Orleans. By 1833, that number had grown to more than 1,200. [12]

By the 1850s, when Twain was on the river, paddleboats had become [12] fancy affairs. "And the boat IS a rather handsome sight, too," he wrote in [14] *Life on the Mississippi,* going on to describe gingerbread trim atop the [12] pilothouse, shiny white railings, and the flapping flag. These vessels had [11] come to define the Mississippi, the principal U.S. waterway. Until [10] railroads crisscrossed the country in the 1870s, nothing replaced the great [11] U.S. steamboat, and in many ways, nothing ever has. [09]

[Total 149]

Original content Copyright © by Holt, Rinehart and Winston. Additions and changes to the original content are the responsibility of the instructor.

Fluency Passage 18

Read aloud the passage from *Harriet Tubman: Conductor on the Underground Railroad* by Ann Petry, following the instructions from your teacher. After you read, complete the fluency checklist that your teacher provides.

Along the Eastern Shore of Maryland, in Dorchester County, in [10] Caroline County, the masters kept hearing whispers about the man named [11] Moses, who was running off slaves. At first they did not believe in his [14] existence. The stories about him were fantastic, unbelievable. Yet they [10] watched for him. They offered rewards for his capture. [09]

They never saw him. Now and then they heard whispered rumors to the [13] effect that he was in the neighborhood. The woods were searched. The [12] roads were watched. There was never anything to indicate his [10] whereabouts. But a few days afterward, a goodly number of slaves would [12] be gone from the plantation. Neither the master nor the overseer had heard [13] or seen anything unusual in the quarter. Sometimes one or the other would [13] vaguely remember having heard a whippoorwill call somewhere in the [10] woods, close by, late at night. Though it was the wrong season for [13] whippoorwills. [01]

[Total 151]

"Go On or Die" and "The Railroad Runs to Canada" from *Harriet Tubman: Conductor on the Underground Railroad* by Ann Petry. Copyright © 1955 and renewed © 1983 by Ann Petry. Reproduced by permission of **Russell & Volkening as agents for Ann Petry.**

Original content Copyright © by Holt, Rinehart and Winston. Additions and changes to the original content are the responsibility of the instructor.

Differentiating Instruction

Fluency Passage 19

Read aloud the passage from "Fragment on Slavery, 1854" by Abraham Lincoln, following the instructions from your teacher. After you read, complete the fluency checklist that your teacher provides.

> If A can prove, however conclusively, that he may of right enslave [12] B—why may not B snatch the same argument, and prove equally that he [13] may enslave A? [03]
>
> You say A is white, and B is black. It is color, then, the lighter having the [17] right to enslave the darker? Take care. By this rule you are to be slave to [16] the first man you meet with a fairer skin than your own. [12]
>
> You do not mean color exactly? You mean the whites are intellectually [12] the superior of the blacks and, therefore, have the right to enslave them? [13] Take care again. By this rule, you are to be slave to the first man you meet [17] with an intellect superior to your own. [07]
>
> But, say you, it is a question of interest; and, if you can make it your [16] interest, you have the right to enslave another. Very well. And if he can [14] make it his interest, he has the right to enslave you. [11]
>
> [Total 164]

Original content Copyright © by Holt, Rinehart and Winston. Additions and changes to the original content are the responsibility of the instructor.

Differentiating Instruction

Fluency Passage 20

Read aloud the passage from "What to the Slave Is the Fourth of July?" by Frederick Douglass, following the instructions from your teacher. After you read, complete the fluency checklist that your teacher provides.

Fellow citizens, pardon me, and allow me to ask, why am I called [13] upon to speak here today? What have I or those I represent to do with [15] your national independence? Are the great principles of political freedom [10] and of natural justice, embodied in that Declaration of Independence, [10] extended to us? And am I, therefore, called upon to bring our humble [13] offering to the national altar, and to confess the benefits, and express [12] devout gratitude for the blessings resulting from your independence to [10] us? . . . [01]

Fellow citizens, above your national, tumultuous joy, I hear the [10] mournful wail of millions, whose chains, heavy and grievous yesterday, [10] are today rendered more intolerable by the jubilant shouts that reach [11] them. . . . My subject, then, fellow citizens, is "American Slavery." I shall [14] see this day and its popular characteristics from the slave's point of view. [13] Standing here, identified with the American bondman, making his wrongs [10] mine, I do not hesitate to declare, with all my soul, that the character and [15] conduct of this nation never looked blacker to me than on this Fourth of [14] July. [01]

[Total 185]

Original content Copyright © by Holt, Rinehart and Winston. Additions and changes to the original content are the responsibility of the instructor.

Fluency Passage 21

Read aloud the directions for downloading music from "SweetPlayer Documents." Follow the instructions from your teacher. After you read, complete the fluency checklist that your teacher provides.

---

1. You may rip tracks from a CD you own to a computer or to the [15] Internet as long as they are for your own use and not for the use of other [17] people. [01]

2. You may download free promotional tracks. This is an increasingly [10] popular way for artists to introduce their work to you. All music is legal [14] on sites where the works are posted by the artists and record companies [13] that created them. Free and promotional tracks are clearly marked, usually [11] under the heading "Free Music." There are often CDs for sale by the artist [14] too. Watch out, though. If a friend wants the same track, he or she will [15] have to download it. It is not legal for you to copy a CD you downloaded [16] from the Net. [03]

3. You may buy the track for your own use. Many sites, including those of [14] more and more record companies, are now offering tracks for sale in this [13] manner. [01]

[Total 160]

Original content Copyright © by Holt, Rinehart and Winston. Additions and changes to the original content are the responsibility of the instructor.

Differentiating Instruction

Fluency Passage 22

Read aloud the directions for downloading music from "Guide to Computers."
Follow the instructions from your teacher. After you read, complete the fluency
checklist that your teacher provides.

Computer Hardware [02]

Input Devices [02]

An input device is a piece of hardware that feeds information to the [13]
computer. You can enter information into a computer by using a [11]
keyboard, mouse, scanner, digitizing pad and pen, or digitizing camera— [10]
or even your own voice. [05]

Central Processing Unit [03]

A computer performs tasks within an area called the central processing [11]
unit, or CPU. In a personal computer, the CPU is a microprocessor. Input [13]
goes through the CPU for immediate processing or for storage in memory. [12]
The CPU is where the computer does calculations, solves problems, and [11]
executes the instructions given to it. Some computers now come with [11]
two—or more—CPUs to process information more effectively. [07]

[Total 111]

Original content Copyright © by Holt, Rinehart and Winston. Additions and changes to the original content are the responsibility of the instructor.

Differentiating Instruction

Fluency Passage 23

Read aloud the passage from "The City Beat" by N. Parker, following the
instructions from your teacher. After you read, complete the fluency checklist
that your teacher provides.

> A lively debate occurred at last Tuesday's packed city council [10]
> Meeting on the subject of whether to establish a skateboard park. Mayor [12]
> Gridlock made a few opening remarks and then turned the microphone [11]
> over to J. Cool, Director of Parks and Recreation. Mr. Cool read front [13]
> portions of a report prepared by his staff, who had investigated the need [13]
> for and the liability, risks, cost, and possible location of a park. Several [13]
> members of the community spoke. [05]
>
> K. Skater said, "Skateboarding is a challenging sport: It's good for us. [12]
> But right now we have no place to skate, and so kids are getting tickets [15]
> for illegal skating. Lots of people say it's too dangerous; but that's not [13]
> true. Kids get hurt in every sport, but you can make it a lot less dangerous [16]
> for us if you give us a smooth place to practice. Still, we skaters have to [16]
> be responsible and only take risks we can handle. That teaches us a lot." [14]
>
> [Total 163]

Original content Copyright © by Holt, Rinehart and Winston. Additions and changes to the original content are the responsibility of the instructor.

Differentiating Instruction

Fluency Passage 24

Read aloud the passage from "Valentine for Ernest Mann" by Naomi Shihab Nye, following the instructions from your teacher. After you read, complete the fluency checklist that your teacher provides.

Once I knew a man who gave his wife [09]

two skunks for a valentine. [05]

He couldn't understand why she was crying. [07]

"I thought they had such beautiful eyes." [07]

And he was serious. He was a serious man [09]

who lived in a serious way. Nothing was ugly [09]

just because the world said so. He really [08]

liked those skunks. So, he re-invented them [08]

as valentines and they became beautiful. [06]

At least, to him. And the poems that had been hiding [11]

in the eyes of skunks for centuries [07]

crawled out and curled up at his feet. [08]

Maybe if we reinvent whatever our lives give us [09]

we find poems. Check your garage, the odd sock [09]

in your drawer, the person you almost like, but not quite. [11]

And let me know. [04]

[Total 95]

"Valentine for Ernest Mann" from *Red Suitcase: Poems* by Naomi Shihab Nye. Copyright © 1994 by Naomi Shihab Nye. Reproduced by permission of **BOA Editions, Ltd.**

Original content Copyright © by Holt, Rinehart and Winston. Additions and changes to the original content are the responsibility of the instructor.

Fluency Passage 25

Read aloud the passage from "Paul Revere's Ride" by Henry Wadsworth Longfellow, following the instructions from your teacher. After you read, complete the fluency checklist that your teacher provides.

> Beneath, in the churchyard, lay the dead, [07]
>
> In their night encampment on the hill, [07]
>
> Wrapped in silence so deep and still [07]
>
> That he could hear, like a sentinel's tread, [08]
>
> The watchful night wind, as it went [07]
>
> Creeping along from tent to tent, [06]
>
> And seeming to whisper, "All is well!" [07]
>
> A moment only he feels the spell [07]
>
> Of the place and the hour, and the secret dread [10]
>
> Of the lonely belfry and the dead; [07]
>
> For suddenly all his thoughts are bent [07]
>
> On a shadowy something far away; [06]
>
> Where the river widens to meet the bay– [08]
>
> A line of black that bends and floats [08]
>
> On the rising tide, like a bridge of boats. [09]
>
>
> Meanwhile, impatient to mount and ride, [06]
>
> Booted and spurred, with a heavy stride [07]
>
> On the opposite shore walked Paul Revere. [07]
>
> [Total 132]

Original content Copyright © by Holt, Rinehart and Winston. Additions and changes to the original content are the responsibility of the instructor.

Differentiating Instruction

Fluency Passage 26

Read aloud the passage from "On the Grasshopper and the Cricket" by John Keats, following the instructions from your teacher. After you read, complete the fluency checklist that your teacher provides.

The poetry of earth is never dead: [07]

When all the birds are faint with the hot sun, [10]

And hide in cooling trees, a voice will run [09]

From hedge to hedge about the new-mown mead; [08]

That is the Grasshopper's—he takes the lead [08]

In summer luxury—he has never done [06]

With his delights; for when tired out with fun [09]

He rests at ease beneath some pleasant weed. [08]

Of the place and the hour, and the secret dread [10]

The poetry of earth is ceasing never: [07]

On a lone winter evening, when the frost [08]

Has wrought a silence, from the stove there shrills [09]

The Cricket's song, in warmth increasing ever, [07]

Where the river widens to meet the bay– [08]

And seems to one in drowsiness half lost, [08]

The Grasshopper's among some grassy hills. [06]

[Total 130]

Original content Copyright © by Holt, Rinehart and Winston. Additions and changes to the original content are the responsibility of the instructor.

Fluency Passage 27

Read aloud the passage from *The Diary of Anne Frank* by Frances Goodrich and Albert Hackett, following the instructions from your teacher. After you read, complete the fluency checklist that your teacher provides.

> **Mr. Frank:** No, you must never go beyond that door. [10]
>
> *[For the first time ANNE realizes what "going into hiding" means.]* [11]
>
> **Anne:** I see. [03]
>
> **Mr. Frank:** It'll be hard, I know. But always remember this, Anneke. [12] There are no walls, there are no bolts, no locks that anyone can put on [15] your mind. Miep will bring us books. We will read history, poetry, [12] mythology. *(He gives her the glass of milk.)* Here's your milk. *(With his* [13] *arm about her, they go over to the couch, sitting down side by side.)* As a [16] matter of fact, between us, Anne, being here has certain advantages for [12] you. For instance, you remember the battle you had with your mother the [13] other day on the subject of overshoes? You said you'd rather die than [13] wear overshoes? But in the end you had to wear them? Well now, you see, [15] for as long as we are here, you will never have to wear overshoes! Isn't [15] that good? [02]
>
> [Total 162]

From *The Diary of a Young Girl: The Definitive Edition* by Anne Frank, edited by Otto H. Frank and Mirjam Pressler, translated by Susan Massoty. Copyright © 1995 by Doubleday, a division of Random House, Inc. Reproduced by permission of **Doubleday, a division of Random House, Inc.,**

Original content Copyright © by Holt, Rinehart and Winston. Additions and changes to the original content are the responsibility of the instructor.

Fluency Passage 28

Read aloud the passage from "A Tragedy Revealed: A Heroine's Last Days" by Ernst Schnabel, following the instructions from your teacher. After you read, complete the fluency checklist that your teacher provides.

> Last year in Amsterdam I found an old reel of movie film on which [14] Anne Frank appears. She is seen for only ten seconds and it is an accident [15] that she is there at all. [06]
>
> The film was taken for a wedding in 1941, the year before Anne [13] Frank and seven others went into hiding in their "Secret Annex." It has a [14] flickering, Chaplinesque quality, with people popping suddenly in and out [10] of doorways, the nervous smiles and hurried waves of the departing bride [12] and groom. [02]
>
> Then, for just a moment, the camera seems uncertain where to look. It [13] darts to the right, then to the left, then whisks up a wall, and into view [16] comes a window crowded with people waving after the departing [10] automobiles. The camera swings farther to the left, to another window. [11] There a girl stands alone, looking out into space. It is Anne Frank. [13]
>
> [Total 149]

A Tragedy Revealed: A Heroine's Last Days" by Ernst Schnabel translated by Richard and Clara Winston from *Life,* vol. 45, no. 7, August 18, 1958. Copyright © 1958 by Time, Inc.; copyright renewed © 1986 by Justina Winston Gregory and Krishna Winston. Reproduced by permission of **Krishna**

Original content Copyright © by Holt, Rinehart and Winston. Additions and changes to the original content are the responsibility of the instructor.

Name _____ Class _____ Date _____

Collection 1
Fluency Passage

Read aloud the passage from "The Most Dangerous Game" by Richard Connell, following the instructions from your teacher. After you read, complete the fluency checklist that your teacher provides.

An abrupt sound startled him. Off to the right he heard it, and his [14] ears, expert in such matters, could not be mistaken. Again he heard the [13] sound, and again. Somewhere, off in the blackness, someone had fired a [12] gun three times. [3]

Rainsford sprang up and moved quickly to the rail, mystified. He [11] strained his eyes in the direction from which the reports had come, but it [14] was like trying to see through a blanket. He leapt upon the rail and [14] balanced himself there, to get greater elevation; his pipe, striking a rope, [12] was knocked from his mouth. He lunged for it; a short, hoarse cry came [14] from his lips as he realized he had reached too far and had lost his [15] balance. The cry was pinched off short as the blood-warm waters of the [14] Caribbean Sea closed over his head. [6]

He struggled up to the surface and tried to cry out, but the wash from [15] the speeding yacht slapped him in the face and the salt water in his open [15] mouth made him gag and strangle. [6]

[Total 178]

"The Most Dangerous Game" by Richard Connell. Copyright © 1924 by Richard Connell; copyright renewed © 1952 by Louise Fox Connell. Reproduced by permission of **Brandt & Hochman Literary Agents, Inc**. Any electronic copying or distribution of this text is strictly forbidden.

Original content Copyright © by Holt, Rinehart and Winston. Additions and changes to the original content are the responsibility of the instructor.

Differentiating Instruction

Collection 1
Fluency Passage

Read aloud the passage from "Liberty" by Julia Alvarez, following the instructions from your teacher. After you read, complete the fluency checklist that your teacher provides.

The little black-and-white puppy yanked at Papi's trouser cuff with his [13] mouth. "What shall we call you?" Papi asked him. [9]

"Trouble," Mami suggested, kicking the puppy away. He had left [10] Papi's trousers to come slobber on her leg. [8]

"We will call him Liberty. Life, liberty, and the pursuit of happiness." [12] Papi quoted the U.S.A. Constitution. "Eh, Liberty, you are a lucky sign!" [12] Liberty barked his little toy barks and all us kids laughed. "Trouble." [12] Mami kept shaking her head as she walked away. Liberty trotted behind [12] her as if he agreed that that was the better name for him. [13]

Mami was right, too—Liberty turned out to be trouble. He ate all of [14] Mami's orchids, and that little hyperactive baton of a tail knocked things [12] off the low coffee table whenever Liberty climbed on the couch to leave [13] his footprints in among the flower prints. He tore up Mami's garden [12] looking for buried treasure. Mami screamed at Liberty and stamped her [11] foot. "Perro sin vergüenza!" But Liberty just barked back at her. [11]

"He doesn't understand Spanish," Papi said lamely. "Maybe if you [10] correct him in English, he'll behave better!" [7]

[Total 191]

"Liberty" by Julia Alvarez. Copyright © 1996 by Julia Alvarez. First published in *Writer's Harvest 2*, edited by Ethan Canin, published by Harcourt Brace and Company, 1996. All rights reserved. Reproduced by permission of **Susan Bergholz Literary Services, New York**.

Original content Copyright © by Holt, Rinehart and Winston. Additions and changes to the original content are the responsibility of the instructor.

Collection 1
Fluency Passage

Read aloud the passage from "The Great Escape" by Thomas Fleming from
Boys' Life, **following the instructions from your teacher. After you read, complete
the fluency checklist that your teacher provides.**

The seven hundred fliers in the prisoner of war camp called Stalag [12]
Luft III came from many countries—the United States, England, Canada, [11]
Poland, Czechoslovakia, Australia, South Africa. They had two things in [10]
common. All had been shot down fighting Germany during World War II [12]
in the early 1940s. [4]

And all were determined to escape. [6]

They had tried to escape from many other camps and had been caught. [13]
That was why these prisoners had ended up in Stalag Luft III, deep in [14]
eastern Germany. It was supposed to be escape-proof. [9]

Two nine-foot high barbed wire fences surrounded the camp. Between [11]
the fences were big towers equipped with searchlights and machine guns. [11]
The prisoners called the towers "goon boxes." Day and night specially [11]
trained groups of Germans, whom the fliers called "ferrets," prowled [10]
inside the camp, looking for escape activity. [7]

Anyone the ferrets caught planning an escape was sent to "the [11]
cooler"—a block of solitary confinement cells where the prisoners would [12]
live on nothing but bread and water. [7]

[Total 184]

From "The Great Escape" by Thomas Fleming from Boys' Life, March 1997. Copyright © 1997.
Copyright © 1997 by **Thomas Fleming**. Reproduced by permission of the author.

Original content Copyright © by Holt, Rinehart and Winston. Additions and changes to the original content are the responsibility of the instructor.

Collection 2
Fluency Passage

Read aloud the passage from "Thank You, M'am" by Langston Hughes, following the instructions from your teacher. After you read, complete the fluency checklist that your teacher provides.

"Lady, I'm sorry," whispered the boy. [5]

"Um-hum! Your face is dirty. I got a great mind to wash your face for [16] you. Ain't you got nobody home to tell you to wash your face?" [13]

"No'm," said the boy. [4]

"Then it will get washed this evening," said the large woman starting [12] up the street, dragging the frightened boy behind her. [9]

He looked as if he were fourteen or fifteen, frail and willow-wild, in [14] tennis shoes and blue jeans. [5]

The woman said, "You ought to be my son. I would teach you right [14] from wrong. Least I can do right now is to wash your face. Are you [15] hungry?" [1]

"No'm," said the being-dragged boy. "I just want you to turn me [13] loose." [1]

"Was I bothering *you* when I turned that corner?" asked the woman. [12]

"No'm." [1]

"But you put yourself in contact with *me,*" said the woman. "If you [13] think that that contact is not going to last awhile, you got another thought [14] coming. When I get through with you, sir, you are going to remember [13] Mrs. Luella Bates Washington Jones." [5]

[Total 180]

"Thank You, Ma'm" from *Short Stories* by Langston Hughes. Copyright © 1996 by Ramona Bass and Arnold Rampersad. All rights reserved. Reproduced by permission of **Hill and Wang, a division of Farrar, Straus, and Giroux, LLC.**

Collection 2
Fluency Passage

Read aloud the passage from "American History" by Judith Ortiz Cofer, following the instructions from your teacher. After you read, complete the fluency checklist that your teacher provides.

Once school started, I looked for him in all my classes, but PS 13 was [15] a huge, overpopulated place and it took me days and many discreet [12] questions to discover that Eugene was in honors classes for all his [12] subjects, classes that were not open to me because English was not my [13] first language, though I was a straight-A student. After much maneuvering [12] I managed to "run into him" in the hallway where his locker was—on the [15] other side of the building from mine—and in study hall at the library, [14] where he first seemed to notice me but did not speak, and finally, on the [15] way home after school one day when I decided to approach him directly, [13] though my stomach was doing somersaults. [6]

I was ready for rejection, snobbery, the worst. But when I came up to [14] him, practically panting in my nervousness, and blurted out: "You're [10] Eugene. Right?" he smiled, pushed his glasses up on his nose, and [12] nodded. I saw then that he was blushing deeply. Eugene liked me, but he [14] was shy. [2]

[Total 179]

Slight adaptation of "American History" from *The Latin Deli: Prose and Poetry* by Judith Ortiz Cofer. Copyright © 1993 by Judith Ortiz Cofer. Reproduced by permission of **The University of Georgia Press**.

Original content Copyright © by Holt, Rinehart and Winston. Additions and changes to the original content are the responsibility of the instructor.

Collection 2
Fluency Passage

Read aloud the passage from "An Interview with Dave Eggers" from *Writing*,
following the instructions from your teacher. After you read, complete the
fluency checklist that your teacher provides.

Writing: A lot of people complain that kids today don't read. Some blame [13]
TV, computers, fast food. (Just kidding, but who knows?) What are your [12]
thoughts about it? [3]

Eggers: I watched a whole lot of TV when I was growing up. I lived in a [17]
house where the TV was on most of the day and night, but I still found a [17]
lot of time to read, and I spent most of my time outside, running around in [16]
the woods. I think there's a balance—you have to get out there and see the [16]
world, learn from books, and also know what's happening via the TV, the [13]
Web, and other media. Any young person who's interested in writing [11]
should be reading (outside of school) about 10 books a year. That's only [13]
one a month—you could definitely read more—but 10 a year is a [14]
guideline. I still keep track of my reading, making sure I'm reading a book [14]
every week or two. Again, it's part of the balance, because I still love TV. [15]

[Total 174]

From "A Staggering Genius Talks About Writing, Fame, and . . . Trout An Interview with Dave Eggers"
from *Writing Magazine*, vol. 27, no 4, January 2005. Copyright © 2005 by Weekly Reader Corporation.
All rights reserved. Reproduced by permission of **Weekly Reader Corporation**.

Original content Copyright © by Holt, Rinehart and Winston. Additions and changes to the original content are the responsibility of the instructor.

Collection 3
Fluency Passage

Read aloud the passage from "The Interlopers" by Saki, following the instructions from your teacher. After you read, complete the fluency checklist that your teacher provides.

> If only on this wild night, in this dark, lone spot, he might come across [15] Georg Znaeym, man to man, with none to witness—that was the wish that [14] was uppermost in his thoughts. And as he stepped round the trunk of a huge [15] beech he came face to face with the man he sought. [11]
>
> The two enemies stood glaring at one another for a long silent moment. [13] Each had a rifle in his hand, each had hate in his heart and murder uppermost [16] in his mind. The chance had come to give full play to the passions of a [15] lifetime. But a man who has been brought up under the code of a restraining [15] civilization cannot easily nerve himself to shoot down his neighbor in cold [12] blood and without a word spoken, except for an offense against his hearth [13] and honor. And before the moment of hesitation had given way to action, a [14] deed of Nature's own violence overwhelmed them both. A fierce shriek of [12] the storm had been answered by a splitting crash over their heads, and ere [14] they could leap aside, a mass of falling beech tree had thundered down on [14] them. [1]
>
> [Total 194]

Original content Copyright © by Holt, Rinehart and Winston. Additions and changes to the original content are the responsibility of the instructor.

Differentiating Instruction

Collection 3
Fluency Passage

Read aloud the passage from "The Cask of Amontillado" by Edgar Allan Poe, following the instructions from your teacher. After you read, complete the fluency checklist that your teacher provides.

> We passed through a range of low arches, descended, passed on, and, [12] descending again, arrived at a deep crypt in which the foulness of the air [14] caused our flambeaux rather to glow than flame. [8]
>
> At the most remote end of the crypt there appeared another less [11] spacious. Its walls had been lined with human remains, piled to the vault [13] overhead, in the fashion of the great catacombs of Paris. Three sides of [13] this interior crypt were still ornamented in this manner. From the fourth [12] the bones had been thrown down and lay promiscuously upon the earth, [12] forming at one point a mound of some size. Within the wall thus exposed [14] by the displacing of the bones, we perceived a still interior recess, in depth [14] about four feet, in width three, in height six or seven. It seemed to have [15] been constructed for no especial use within itself, but formed merely the [12] interval between two of the colossal supports of the roof of the catacombs [13] and was backed by one of their circumscribing walls of solid granite. [12
>
> [Total 175]

Name _____ Class _____ Date_____

Fluency Passage

Read aloud the passage from "Poe's Final Days" by Kenneth Silverman, following the instructions from your teacher. After you read, complete the fluency checklist that your teacher provides.

> Through the chilly wet streets Poe was driven to the hospital of [12] Washington Medical College, set on the highest ground of Baltimore. An [11] imposing five-story building with vaulted gothic windows, it afforded [10] both public wards and private rooms, advertised as being spacious, well [11] ventilated, and directed by an experienced medical staff. Admitted at five [11] in the afternoon, Poe was given a private room, reportedly in a section [13] reserved for cases involving drunkenness. He was attended by the resident [11] physician, Dr. John J. Moran, who apparently had living quarters in the [12] hospital together with his wife. Moran had received his medical degree [11] from the University of Maryland four years earlier and was now only [12] about twenty-six years old. But he knew the identity of his patient—a [14] *"great* man," he wrote of Poe, to whose "rarely gifted mind are we [13] indebted for many of the brightest thoughts that adorn our literature." He [12] as well as the medical students, nurses, and other physicians—all [11] considered Poe, he said, "an object of unusual regard." [9]
>
> [Total 173]

From excerpt retitled "Poe's Final Days" from *Edgar A. Poe: Mournful and Never-ending Remembrance* by Kenneth Silverman. Copyright © 1991 by Kenneth Silverman. Reproduced by permission of **Harper Collins Publishers, Inc.**

Original content Copyright © by Holt, Rinehart and Winston. Additions and changes to the original content are the responsibility of the instructor.

Differentiating Instruction

Collection 3
Fluency Passage

Read aloud the passage from "Poe's Death Is Rewritten as a Case of Rabies, Not Telltale Alcohol" from *The New York Times*, following the instructions from your teacher. After you read, complete the fluency checklist that your teacher provides.

Although it has been well established that Poe died in the hospital, [12] legend has it that he succumbed in the gutter, a victim of his debauched [14] ways. [1]

The legend may have been fostered by his doctor, who in later years [13] became a temperance advocate and changed the details to make an object [12] lesson of Poe's death. [4]

The curator of the Edgar Allan Poe House and Museum in Baltimore, [12] Jeff Jerome, said that he had heard dozens of tales but that "almost [13] everyone who has come forth with a theory has offered no proof."[12]

Some versions have Poe unconscious under the steps of the Baltimore [11] Museum before being taken to the hospital. Other accounts place him on [12] planks between two barrels outside a tavern on Lombard Street. In most [12] versions, Poe is wearing someone else's clothes, having been robbed of [11] his suit. [2]

Poe almost surely did not die of alcohol poisoning or withdrawal, Mr. [12] Jerome said. The writer was so sensitive to alcohol that a glass of wine [14] would make him violently ill for days. Poe may have had problems with [13] alcohol as a younger man, Mr. Jerome said, but by the time he died at [15] forty he almost always avoided it. [6]

[Total 201]

"Poe's Death is Rewritten as a Case of Rabies, Not Telltale Alcohol" from *The New York Times*, September 15, 1996. Copyright © 1996 by **The Associated Press**. All rights reserved. Reproduced by permission of the copyright holder.

Original content Copyright © by Holt, Rinehart and Winston. Additions and changes to the original content are the responsibility of the instructor.

Differentiating Instruction

Collection 4
Fluency Passage

Read aloud the passage from "The Gift of the Magi" by O. Henry, following the instructions from your teacher. After you read, complete the fluency checklist that your teacher provides.

> Now, there were two possessions of the James Dillingham Youngs in [11] which they both took a mighty pride. One was Jim's gold watch that had [14] been his father's and his grandfather's. The other was Della's hair. Had [12] the Queen of Sheba lived in the flat across the air shaft, Della would have [15] let her hair hang out the window some day to dry just to depreciate Her [15] Majesty's jewels and gifts. Had King Solomon been the janitor, with all [12] his treasures piled up in the basement, Jim would have pulled out his [13] watch every time he passed, just to see him pluck at his beard from envy.[15]
>
> So now Della's beautiful hair fell about her rippling and shining like a [13] cascade of brown waters. It reached below her knee and made itself [12] almost a garment for her. And then she did it up again nervously and [14] quickly. Once she faltered for a minute and stood still while a tear or two [15] splashed on the worn red carpet. [6]
>
> [Total 167]

Original content Copyright © by Holt, Rinehart and Winston. Additions and changes to the original content are the responsibility of the instructor.

Collection 4
Fluency Passage

Read aloud the passage from "The Scarlet Ibis" by James Hurst, following the instructions from your teacher. After you read, complete the fluency checklist that your teacher provides.

As long as he lay all the time in bed, we called him William [14] Armstrong, even though it was formal and sounded as if we were referring [13] to one of our ancestors, but with his creeping around on the deerskin rug [14] and beginning to talk, something had to be done about his name. It was I [15] who renamed him. When he crawled, he crawled backward, as if he were [13] in reverse and couldn't change gears. If you called him, he'd turn around [13] as if he were going in the other direction, then he'd back right up to you to [16] be picked up. Crawling backward made him look like a doodlebug so I [13] began to call him Doodle, and in time even Mama and Daddy thought it [14] was a better name than William Armstrong. Only Aunt Nicey disagreed. [11] She said caul babies should be treated with special respect since they [12] might turn out to be saints. Renaming my brother was perhaps the kindest [13] thing I ever did for him, because nobody expects much from someone [12] called Doodle. [2]

[Total 175]

"The Scarlet Ibis" by James R. Hurst from *The Atlantic Monthly*, July 1960. Copyright © 1960 by **James R. Hurst**. Reproduced by permission of the author.

Original content Copyright © by Holt, Rinehart and Winston. Additions and changes to the original content are the responsibility of the instructor.

Differentiating Instruction

Collection 4
Fluency Passage

Read aloud the passage from *Einstein on Peace* from an interview with George Sylvester Viereck, following the instructions from your teacher. After you read, complete the fluency checklist that your teacher provides.

It may not be possible in one generation to eradicate the combative [12] instinct. It is not even desirable to eradicate it entirely. Men should [13] continue to fight, but they should fight for things worthwhile, not for [12] imaginary geographical lines, racial prejudices, and private greed draped [9] in the colors of patriotism. Their arms should be weapons of the spirit, not [14] shrapnel and tanks. [3]

Think of what a world we could build if the power unleashed in war were [14] applied to constructive tasks! One tenth of the energy that the various [11] belligerents spent in the World War, a fraction of the money they exploded in [13] hand grenades and poison gas, would suffice to raise the standard of living in [14] every country and avert the economic catastrophe of worldwide [9] unemployment. [1]

We must be prepared to make the same heroic sacrifices for the cause of [14] peace that we make ungrudgingly for the cause of war. There is no task that is [16] more important or closer to my heart. [7]

[Total 162]

From "Einstein's interview with George Sylvester Viereck" from *Einstein on Peace*, edited by Otto Nathan and Heinz Norden. Copyright © 1960 by Otto Nathan. Reproduced by permission of **The Albert Einstein Archives, The Hebrew University of Jerusalem, Israel.**

Original content Copyright © by Holt, Rinehart and Winston. Additions and changes to the original content are the responsibility of the instructor.

Name _____   Class _____   Date_____

Collection 4
Fluency Passage

Read aloud the passage from "Letter to President Roosevelt" by Albert Einstein, following the instructions from your teacher. After you read, complete the fluency checklist that your teacher provides.

> I believe therefore that it is my duty to bring to your attention the [14] following facts and recommendations: [5]
>
> In the course of the last four months it has been made probable— [13] through the work of Joliot in France as well as Fermi and Szilard in [14] America—that it may become possible to set up a nuclear chain reaction [13] in a large mass of uranium, by which vast amounts of power and large [14] quantities of new radium-like elements would be generated. Now it [11] appears almost certain that this could be achieved in the immediate future. [12]
>
> This new phenomenon would also lead to the construction of bombs, [11] and it is conceivable—though much less certain—that extremely powerful [11] bombs of a new type may thus be constructed. A single bomb of this type, [15] carried by boat and exploded in a port, might very well destroy the whole [14] port together with some of the surrounding territory. However, such [10] bombs might very well prove to be too heavy for transportation by air. [13]
>
> [Total 170]

"Letter to President Roosevelt" from Dr. Einstein's Warning to President Roosevelt, by Albert Einstein. Copyright © 1939 by Albert Einstein. Reproduced by permission of **The Albert Einstein Archives, The Hebrew University of Jerusalem, Israel.**

Original content Copyright © by Holt, Rinehart and Winston. Additions and changes to the original content are the responsibility of the instructor.

⬤

Collection 4
Fluency Passage

Read aloud the passage from "On the Abolition of the Threat of War" from *Ideas and Opinions* by Albert Einstein, following the instructions from your teacher. After you read, complete the fluency checklist that your teacher provides.

> My part in producing the atomic bomb consisted in a single act: I [12] signed a letter to President Roosevelt, pressing the need for experiments [11] on a large scale in order to explore the possibilities for the production of [13] an atomic bomb. [3]
>
> I was fully aware of the terrible danger to mankind in case this attempt [14] succeeded. But the likelihood that the Germans were working on the same [12] problem with a chance of succeeding forced me to this step. I could do [14] nothing else although I have always been a convinced pacifist. To my [12] mind, to kill in war is not a whit better than to commit ordinary murder. [15]
>
> As long, however, as the nations are not resolved to abolish war [12] through common actions and to solve their conflicts and protect their [11] interests by peaceful decisions on a legal basis, they feel compelled to [12] prepare for war. They feel obliged to prepare all possible means, even the [13] most detestable ones, so as not to be left behind in the general armament [14] race. This road necessarily leads to war, a war which under the present [13] conditions means universal destruction. [4]
>
> [Total 185]

"On the Abolition of the Threat of War" from Ideas and Opinions by Albert Einstein. Copyright © 1954 and renewed © 1982 by **Crown Publishers, Inc. a division of Random House, Inc.,** **www.randomhouse.com.** Reproduced by permission of the publisher.

Original content Copyright © by Holt, Rinehart and Winston. Additions and changes to the original content are the responsibility of the instructor.

Collection 5
Fluency Passage

Read aloud the passage from "Cub Pilot on the Mississippi" by Mark Twain, following the instructions from your teacher. After you read, complete the fluency checklist that your teacher provides.

> "So you have been fighting, Mr. Brown? [7]
>
> I answered meekly— [3]
>
> "Yes, sir." [2]
>
> "Do you know that that is a very serious matter?" [10]
>
> "Yes, sir." [2]
>
> "Are you aware that this boat was plowing down the river fully five [13]
> minutes with no one at the wheel?" [7]
>
> "Yes, sir." [2]
>
> "Did you strike him first?" [5]
>
> "Yes, sir." [2]
>
> "What with?" [2]
>
> "A stool, sir." [3]
>
> "Hard?" [1]
>
> "Middling, sir." [2]
>
> "Did it knock him down?" [5]
>
> "He—he fell, sir." [4]
>
> "Did you follow it up? Did you do anything further?" [10]
>
> "Yes, sir." [2]
>
> "What did you do?" [4]
>
> "Pounded him, sir." [3]
>
> "Pounded him?" [2]
>
> "Yes, sir." [2]
>
> "Did you pound him much?—that is, severely?" [8]
>
> "One might call it that, sir, maybe." [7]
>
> "I'm deuced glad of it! Hark ye, never mention that I said that. You [14]
> have been guilty of a great crime; and don't you ever be guilty of it again, [16]
> on this boat. BUT—lay for him ashore! Give him a good sound thrashing, [14]
> do you hear? I'll pay the expenses. Now go—and mind you, not a word of [16]
> this to anybody. [3]
>
> [Total 171]

Original content Copyright © by Holt, Rinehart and Winston. Additions and changes to the original content are the responsibility of the instructor.

Differentiating Instruction

Collection 5
Fluency Passage

Read aloud the passage from "The Grandfather" by Gary Soto, following the instructions from your teacher. After you read, complete the fluency checklist that your teacher provides.

> Birds nested in the tree, quarreling jays with liquid eyes and cool, [12] pulsating throats. Wasps wove a horn-shaped hive one year, but we [12] smoked them away with swords of rolled up newspapers lit with matches. [12] By then, the tree was tall enough for me to climb to look into the [15] neighbor's yard. But by then I was too old for that kind of thing and went [16] about with my brother, hair slicked back and our shades dark as oil. [13]
>
> After twenty years, the tree began to bear. Although Grandfather [10] complained about how much he lost because pollen never reached the [11] poor part of town, because at the market he had to haggle over the price of [15] avocados, he loved that tree. It grew, as did his family, and when he died, [15] all his sons standing on each other's shoulders, oldest to youngest, could [12] not reach the highest branches. The wind could move the branches, but the [13] trunk, thicker than any waist, hugged the ground. [8]
>
> [Total 164]

"The Grandfather" from A Summer Life by Gary Soto (Dell, 1991) Copyright © 1990 **University Press of New England** and electronic format by permission of **Gary Soto.**

Original content Copyright © by Holt, Rinehart and Winston. Additions and changes to the original content are the responsibility of the instructor.

Differentiating Instruction

Collection 5
Fluency Passage

Read aloud the passage from "About StoryCorps," following the instructions from your teacher. After you read, complete the fluency checklist that your teacher provides.

We've modeled StoryCorps—in spirit and in scope—after the Works [11] Progress Administration (WPA) of the 1930s, through which oral-history [10] interviews with everyday Americans across the country were recorded. [10] These recordings remain the single most important collection of American [10] voices gathered to date. We hope that StoryCorps will build and expand [12] on that work, becoming a WPA for the 21st Century. [10]

To us, StoryCorps celebrates our shared humanity and collective [9] identity. It captures and defines the stories that bond us. We've found that [13] the process of interviewing a friend, neighbor, or family member can have [12] a profound impact on both the interviewer and interviewee. We've seen [11] people change, friendships grow, families walk away feeling closer, [9] understanding each other better. Listening, after all, is an act of love. [12]

A StoryCorps interview is an opportunity to ask the questions that [11] never get asked because the occasion never arises. *How did you come to* [13] *this country? How did you and mom meet? How did Uncle Harry get the* [14] *nickname "Twinkles?"* [2]

[Total 169]

Slightly adapted from "About StoryCorps" from *StoryCorps*. Copyright © by Sound Portraits Productions, Inc. Reproduced by permission of the publisher.

Original content Copyright © by Holt, Rinehart and Winston. Additions and changes to the original content are the responsibility of the instructor.

Differentiating Instruction

Collection 6
Fluency Passage

Read aloud the passage from "Cinderella's Stepsisters" by Toni Morrison, following the instructions from your teacher. After you read, complete the fluency checklist that your teacher provides.

I am alarmed by a growing absence of decency on the killing floor of [14] professional women's worlds. You are the women who will take your [10] place in the world where *you* can decide who shall flourish and who shall [14] wither; you will make distinctions between the deserving poor and the [11] undeserving poor; where you can yourself determine which life is [10] expendable and which is indispensable. Since you will have the power to [12] do it, you may also be persuaded that you have the right to do it. As [16] educated women the distinction between the two is first-order business. [11]

I am suggesting that we pay as much attention to our nurturing [11] sensibilities as to our ambition. You are moving in the direction of [12] freedom and the function of freedom is to free somebody else. You are [13] moving toward self-fulfillment, and the consequences of that fulfillment [10] should be to discover that there is something just as important as you are [14] and that just-as-important thing may be Cinderella—or your stepsister. [12]

[Total 170]

"Cinderella's Stepsister's" by Toni Morrison from *Ms. Magazine*, September, 1979. Copyright C 1979 by **Toni Morrison**. Reproduced by permission of the author.

Original content Copyright © by Holt, Rinehart and Winston. Additions and changes to the original content are the responsibility of the instructor.

Collection 6
Fluency Passage

Read aloud the passage from "Kaavya Viswanathan: Unconscious Copycat or Plagiarist?" by Sandhya Nankani, following the instructions from your teacher. After you read, complete the fluency checklist that your teacher provides.

> Plagiarism is copying someone else's writing without noting the [9] source. That's very different from being inspired by another writer and [11] learning from his or her style. [6]
>
> You see why this is so complicated? I'm still trying to wrap my brain [14] around it. What I think we should take away from this is not a sense of [16] glee ("Aha! Kaavya got caught. Serves her right!" I've been hearing a lot [13] of that out there.) Rather, we should step away from this situation and use [14] Kaavya's experience to remind us of the importance of consciously [10] choosing our words. We should use it to remind ourselves that when it [13] comes to writing, there's nothing better than writing in our own voices. [12]
>
> At the end of the day, when Kaavya's book has disappeared from [12] bookshelves and her life has returned to a sense of normalcy, I hope that [14] she will pick up a pen again and ask herself: What is my original writing [15] voice? I wish her good luck in finding it. From what I've seen so far, it is [17] a voice that glimmers with wit. [6]
>
> [Total 182]

Slightly adapted from "Kaavya Viswanathan" Unconscious Copycat or Plagiarist?" by Sandhya Nankani from *WORD: Official Blog of Read and Writing* magazines, Friday, April 28, 2006. Reproduced by permission of **Weekly Reader Corporation**.

Original content Copyright © by Holt, Rinehart and Winston. Additions and changes to the original content are the responsibility of the instructor.

Collection 7
Fluency Passage

**Read aloud the poem "A Blessing" by James Wright, following the instructions
from your teacher. After you read, complete the fluency checklist that your
teacher provides.**

Just off the highway to Rochester, Minnesota, [7]

Twilight bounds softly forth on the grass, [7]

And the eyes of those two Indian ponies [8]

Darken with kindness. [3]

They have come gladly out of the willows [8]

To welcome my friend and me. [6]

We step over the barbed wire into the pasture [9]

Where they have been grazing all day, alone. [8]

They ripple tensely, they can hardly contain their happiness [9]

That we have come. [4]

They bow shyly as wet swans. They love each other. [10]

There is no loneliness like theirs. [6]

At home once more, [4]

They begin munching the young tufts of spring in the darkness. [11]

I would like to hold the slenderer one in my arms, [11]

For she has walked over to me [7]

And nuzzled my left hand. [5]

She is black and white, [5]

Her mane falls wild on her forehead, [7]

And the light breeze moves me to caress her long ear [11]

That is delicate as the skin over a girl's wrist. [10]

Suddenly I realize [3]

That if I stepped out of my body I would break [11]

Into blossom. [2]

[Total 172]

"A Blessing" from Collected Poems by James Wright. Copyright ©1963, 1971 by James Wright.
Reproduced by permission of **Wesleyan University Press, www.wesleyan.edu/wespress.**

Original content Copyright © by Holt, Rinehart and Winston. Additions and changes to the original content are the responsibility of the instructor.

Collection 7
Fluency Passage

Read aloud the passage from a review of Spike Lee's film "4 Little Girls" by Roger Ebert, following the instructions from your teacher. After you read, complete the fluency checklist that your teacher provides.

The little girls had gone to church early for choir practice, and we can [14] imagine them, dressed in their Sunday best, meeting their friends in the [12] room destroyed by the bomb. We can fashion the picture in our minds [13] because Lee has, in a way, brought them back to life, through [12] photographs, through old home movies and especially through the [9] memories of their families and friends.[6]

By coincidence, I was listening to the radio not long after seeing "4 [13] Little Girls," and I heard a report from Charlayne Hunter-Gault. In 1961, [13] when she was 19, she was the first black woman to desegregate the [13] University of Georgia. Today she is an NPR correspondent. That is what [12] happened to her. In 1963, Carole Robertson was 14, and her Girl Scout [13] sash was covered with merit badges. Because she was killed that day, we [13] will never know what would have happened in her life. [10]

[Total 153]

Roger Ebert's review of *4 Little Girls* by Spike Lee from *Chicago Sun Times*, October 24, 1997. Copyright © 1997 by Roger Ebert. Reproduced by permission of **Andrews McMeel Publishing**

Original content Copyright © by Holt, Rinehart and Winston. Additions and changes to the original content are the responsibility of the instructor.

Differentiating Instruction

Collection 7
Fluency Passage

Read aloud the passage from the Federal Bureau of Investigation's Web page about the FBI's Art Crime Team, following the instructions from your teacher. After you read, complete the fluency checklist that your teacher provides.

The FBI established a rapid deployment Art Crime Team in 2004. The [12] team is composed of twelve Special Agents, each responsible for [10] addressing art and cultural property crime cases in an assigned geographic [11] region. The Art Crime Team is coordinated through the FBI's Art Theft [12] Program, located at FBI Headquarters in Washington, D.C. Art Crime [10] Team agents receive specialized training in art and cultural property [10] investigations and assist in art-related investigations worldwide in [9] cooperation with foreign law enforcement officials and FBI Legal Attaché [10] offices. The U.S. Department of Justice has assigned three Special Trial [11] Attorneys to the Art Crime Team for prosecutive support. [9]

Since its inception, the Art Crime Team has recovered over 850 items [12] of cultural property with a value exceeding $65 million. These include: [11]

- Approximately 700 pre-Columbian artifacts. The objects recovered in [9] Miami were the result of a sting operation in coordination with the [12] Ecuadorian authorities. [2]

- Three paintings by the German painter Heinrich Buerkel (1802–1869), [10] stolen at the conclusion of World War II and consigned for sale at an [14] auction house near Philadelphia in 2005. [6]

[Total 180]

Slightly adapted from "Spielberg Collection Is Found to Contain Stolen Rockwell Art" as it appears in *The New York Times*, March 4, 2007 by **The Associated Press**. Reproduced by permission of the publisher.

Original content Copyright © by Holt, Rinehart and Winston. Additions and changes to the original content are the responsibility of the instructor.

Collection 8
Fluency Passage

Read aloud the passage from Act I of *The Tragedy of Romeo and Juliet* by William Shakespeare, following the instructions from your teacher. After you read, complete the fluency checklist that your teacher provides.

Rebellious subjects, enemies to peace, [5]

Profaners of this neighbor-stainèd steel— [6]

Will they not hear? What, ho! You men, you beasts, [10]

That quench the fire of your pernicious rage [8]

With purple fountains issuing from your veins! [7]

On pain of torture, from those bloody hands [8]

Throw your mistempered weapons to the ground [7]

And hear the sentence of your movèd prince. [8]

Three civil brawls, bred of an airy word [8]

By thee, old Capulet, and Montague, [6]

Have thrice disturbed the quiet of our streets [8]

And made Verona's ancient citizens [5]

Cast by their grave beseeming ornaments [6]

To wield old partisans, in hands as old, [8]

Cankered with peace, to part your cankered hate. [8]

If ever you disturb our streets again, [7]

Your lives shall pay the forfeit of the peace. [9]

For this time all the rest depart away. [8]

You, Capulet, shall go along with me; [7]

And, Montague, come you this afternoon, [6]

To know our farther pleasure in this case, [8]

To old Freetown, our common judgment place. [7]

Once more, on pain of death, all men depart. [9]

[Total 169]

Original content Copyright © by Holt, Rinehart and Winston. Additions and changes to the original content are the responsibility of the instructor.

Differentiating Instruction

Collection 8
Fluency Passage

Read aloud the passage from Act II of *The Tragedy of Romeo and Juliet* by William Shakespeare, following the instructions from your teacher. After you read, complete the fluency checklist that your teacher provides.

The clock struck nine when I did send the nurse; [10]

In half an hour she promised to return. [8]

Perchance she cannot meet him. That's not so. [8]

O, she is lame! Love's heralds should be thoughts, [9]

Which ten times faster glide than the sun's beams [9]

Driving back shadows over low'ring hills. [6]

Therefore do nimble-pinioned doves draw Love, [7]

And therefore hath the wind-swift Cupid wings. [8]

Now is the sun upon the highmost hill [8]

Of this day's journey, and from nine till twelve [9]

Is three long hours; yet she is not come. [9]

Had she affections and warm youthful blood, [7]

She would be as swift in motion as a ball; [10]

My words would bandy her to my sweet love, [9]

And his to me. [4]

But old folks, many feign as they were dead— [9]

Unwieldy, slow, heavy, and pale as lead. [7]

O God, she comes! O honey nurse, what news? [9]

Hast thou met with him? Send thy man away. [9]

[Total 164]

Original content Copyright © by Holt, Rinehart and Winston. Additions and changes to the original content are the responsibility of the instructor.

Name _____ Class _____ Date _____

Collection 8
Fluency Passage

Read aloud the passage from "'Dear Juliet': Seeking Succor From a Veteran of Love" by Dinitia Smith, following the instructions from your teacher. After you read, complete the fluency checklist that your teacher provides.

Every week, hundreds of letters pour into the office of the Club di [13] Giulietta, in Verona, Italy, the city that is the setting for Shakespeare's [12] "Romeo and Juliet." Some are addressed simply "To Juliet, Verona," but [11] the postman always knows to deliver them to the club's Via Galilei [12] headquarters. Every letter is answered by the club's group of volunteers, [11] no matter what the language, sometimes with the assistance of outside [11] translators. (In the past, the owner of a local Chinese restaurant helped.) [12]

"Help me! Save me!" wrote an Italian woman whose husband had left [12] her. "I feel suspended on a precipice. I am afraid of going mad."[13]

Her answer came from Ettore Solimani—who was the custodian of [11] Juliet's tomb for nearly 20 years, beginning in the 1930's. [10]

"Have faith...," Mr. Solimani added later in the letter. "The day of [12] humiliation will come for the intruder, and your husband will come back [12] to you." [2]

Now two American sisters, Lise and Ceil Friedman, have put some of [12] the letters and a few of the responses into a book, "Letters to Juliet," along [15] with the story of the club and the play's historical background. [11]

[Total 180]

From "Juliet of Verona Gets a Lot of Love Letters from the Lovelorn" by Lisa Bannon from *The Wall Street Journal*, November 10, 1992. Copyright © 1992 by Dow Jones & Company, Inc. All rights reserved worldwide. Reproduced by permission of **The Wall Street Journal**.

Original content Copyright © by Holt, Rinehart and Winston. Additions and changes to the original content are the responsibility of the instructor.

Differentiating Instruction

Collection 9
Fluency Passage

Read aloud the passage from *The Odyssey* by Homer, following the instructions from your teacher. After you read, complete the fluency checklist that your teacher provides.

"Upon the tenth [3]
we came to the coastline of the Lotus Eaters, [9]
who live upon that flower. We landed there [8]
to take on water. All ships' companies [7]
mustered alongside for the midday meal. [6]
Then I sent out two picked men and a runner [10]
to learn what race of men that land sustained. [9]
They fell in, soon enough, with Lotus Eaters, [8]
who showed no will to do us harm, only [9]
offering the sweet Lotus to our friends— [7]
but those who ate this honeyed plant, the Lotus, [9]
never cared to report, nor to return: [7]
they longed to stay forever, browsing on [7]
that native bloom, forgetful of their homeland. [7]
I drove them, all three wailing, to the ships, [9]
tied them down under their rowing benches, [7]
and called the rest: 'All hands aboard; [7]
come, clear the beach and no one taste [8]
the Lotus, or you lose your hope of home.' [9]
Filing in to their places by the rowlocks [8]
my oarsmen dipped their long oars in the surf, [9]
and we moved out again on our seafaring. . . ." [2]

[Total 165]

From "Book 9: New Coasts and Poseidon's Son" from *The Odyssey* by Homer, translated by Robert Fitzgerald. Copyright © 1961, 1963 by Robert Fitzgerald; copyright renewed © 1989 by Benedict R.C. Fitzgerald, on behalf of the Fitzgerald children. Reproduced by permission of **Benedict R.C. Fitzgerald.**

Original content Copyright © by Holt, Rinehart and Winston. Additions and changes to the original content are the responsibility of the instructor.

Name _____ Class _____ Date_____

Collection 9
Fluency Passage

Read aloud the passage from *Shipwreck at the Bottom of the World* by Jennifer Armstrong, following the instructions from your teacher. After you read, complete the fluency checklist that your teacher provides.

As the storm continued, a large buildup of ice on the sea anchor's rope [14] had kept the line swinging and sawing against the stern. Before noon on [13] the ninth day, the sea anchor broke away, and the boat lurched heavily as [14] seas hit her broadside. Before the gale ended that afternoon, the men had [13] had to crawl onto the deck three times to get rid of the boat's shell of ice. [17] The men all agreed that it was the worst job any of them had ever been [16] forced to do. [3]

By the time the gale ended, everything below was thoroughly soaked. [11] The sleeping bags were so slimy and revolting that Shackleton had the [12] two worst of them thrown overboard. Even before the storm, however, the [12] men had been suffering from the constant wet. "After the third day our [14] feet and legs had swelled," Worsley wrote later, "and began to be [12] superficially frostbitten from the constant soaking in seawater, with the [10] temperature at times nearly down to zero; and the lack of exercise. During [13] the last gale they assumed a dead-white color and lost surface feeling." [13]

[Total 187]

"The Open Boat Journey: The First Ten Days" from *Shipwreck at the Bottom of the World: The Extraordinary True Story of Shackleton and the* Endurance by Jennifer Armstrong. Copyright © 1998 by Jennifer M. Armstrong. Reproduced by permission of Crown Publishers, a division of Random House, Inc., www.randomhouse.com

Original content Copyright © by Holt, Rinehart and Winston. Additions and changes to the original content are the responsibility of the instructor.

Differentiating Instruction

Collection 9
Fluency Passage

Read aloud the passage from "Tending Sir Ernest's Legacy: An Interview with Alexandra Shackleton" from NOVA Online, following the instructions from your teacher. After you read, complete the fluency checklist that your teacher provides.

NOVA: Even today that journey is seen as nothing short of miraculous. [12]

Shackleton: Yes. They had accomplished what many regard as the [11] greatest small boat journey in the world, 800 miles across the stormiest [12] seas in the world in a little boat not even 23 feet long—all the while [16] encountering extremely harsh weather and suffering gales, privations of [9] thirst, hunger, and everything. It was a colossal achievement, and when [11] they saw the black peaks of South Georgia, they felt huge relief and [13] happiness. [1]

NOVA: Was the *Endurance* expedition the greatest achievement of his [10] life? [1]

Shackleton: I think so, because against almost impossible odds he [11] brought his 27 men home safely. The boat journey to South Georgia was [13] an epic in itself, and climbing across the uncharted, unmapped island of [12] South Georgia with no equipment was remarkable. To this day, no one has [13] ever beaten his record of 30 miles in 36 hours. [10]

[Total 155]

From "Tending Sir Ernest's Legacy: An Interview with Alexandra Shackleton" by Kelly Tyler from NOVA Online Web site, 2002, accessed May 27, 2007 at http://pbs.org/wgbh/nova/shackleton/1914/alexandra.html Copyright © 2002 by WGBH Educational Foundation. Reproduced by permission of the publisher http://pbs.org/wgbh/nova/shackleton/1914/alexandra.html

Original content Copyright © by Holt, Rinehart and Winston. Additions and changes to the original content are the responsibility of the instructor.

Collection 10
Fluency Passage

Read aloud the passage from "Documents for Life" by Carol Jago, following the instructions from your teacher. After you read, complete the fluency checklist that your teacher provides.

Consumer Documents [2]

A consumer is someone who buys or uses something. That includes you, [12] your parents, and even your pets. Most of the things you buy come with [14] consumer documents—even a backpack. An advertisement may have [9] convinced you to try it, for example, or you may have read the features on [15] a tag attached to it. The more complicated the product, the more [12] complicated the documents. Here are some consumer documents you may [10] find with a video computer game. [6]

- Product information is often found on the box or label. It tells you if a [15] tee-shirt is your size or a computer game has the features you are looking [15] for. [1]

- Instruction manuals usually include more detailed product information. [8] They also tell you how to set up and use the product. [12]

- Warranties explain what happens if the product does not work as [11] guaranteed and what you have to do to get it repaired. [11]

- Contracts give information on the legal use of the product. [10]

[Total 153]

Original content Copyright © by Holt, Rinehart and Winston. Additions and changes to the original content are the responsibility of the instructor.

Differentiating Instruction

Lesson 1: Introductions

WORD DRILL *3 MINUTES*

(Teach/Guided Practice) Greet the class, and wave while saying, *Hello!* Gesture to the class to repeat: *Hello*. After class has repeated, say *Hello* again and elicit a second repetition. This establishes a rhythm that can be used to introduce new or difficult words: teacher first and then the class.

(Guided Practice) After students have echoed as a class, point to random individual students, say hello, and invite the student to repeat the word. This routine should always be used when introducing new words in order to keep the students involved. It ensures that the words are being pronounced correctly by everybody.

BUILD BACKGROUND *10 MINUTES*

(Teach/Guided Practice/Practice) This is a continuation activity and can be used as a way of introducing yourself. Write the short dialogue below on the board, read the first two lines aloud, and elicit repetition from the students after each line.

Let each student practice introducing him or herself, starting the dialogue from the beginning each time. After each student has had a turn, continue with the remaining four lines of the dialogue. Repeat until students are comfortable pronouncing the words. Then say the first line (A), and elicit the class to respond (B). Reverse roles. When results are satisfactory, allow students to practice the new routine in pairs while you circulate and monitor progress.

A: Hello! I am _____. What is your name?

B: Hello! I am _____.

A: How are you?

B: I'm fine, thanks. How are you?

A: I'm fine, thanks. It is nice to meet you.

B: It is nice to meet you too.

INDEPENDENT RECITATION *4 MINUTES*

(Apply) Give students two minutes to memorize the dialogue on the board. When the time is up, erase the dialogue and chose a few pairs to recite it from memory.

LESSON OBJECTIVES
Students will:

- respond to basic questions used in a greeting
- learn plural and describe themselves and their peers
- speak in complete, coherent sentences to make introductions
- use declarative sentences to identify peers and describe themselves
- listen to instructions and to their peers' dialogue

LESSON VOCABULARY
student, teacher, friend, class, teammate, coach, artist, musician, athlete, cook, girl, boy

Teaching Tip This is an opportunity to explain how English speakers sometimes use a contraction in informal English. Explain the difference between "I am" and "I'm" and the way that the speaking occasion affects the use of this contraction.

Original content Copyright © by Holt, Rinehart and Winston. Additions and changes to the original content are the responsibility of the instructor.

Differentiating Instruction

Lesson 2: Personal Information

WORD DRILL *2 MINUTES*

(Teach/Guided Practice) Greet the class, and wave while saying: *Hello!* Gesture to the class to repeat: *Hello.* This establishes a rhythm that will be used to introduce new or difficult words: teacher first and then the class. After the class has repeated, *Hello!* say: *My name is ____.* Point to a student and ask: *What is your name?* Cue the student to answer by saying: *My name is _____.*

(Guided Practice) Continue to establish the pattern by repeating *My name is ____.* and pointing to a student and asking: *What is your name?* Cue the student to answer: *My name is _____.* Once the pattern is familiar, continue by having the student point to a classmate and ask: *What is your name?* Cue the next student answer: *My name is _____.* and point to another student, asking: *What is your name?* End the exercise after each student has had a turn to ask and answer. Help students make sure that they pronounce the words correctly.

BUILD BACKGROUND *8 MINUTES*

(Teach/Guided Practice/Practice) This is a continuation of the word drill. Preteach the necessary vocabulary for the dialogue by using pictures, acting out words, or drawing items on the board. Write the short dialogue below on the board, read the first pair of lines aloud, and then point to random individual students, asking the question in line A and eliciting the correct response for line B. Repeat the dialogue until students are comfortable pronouncing the words.

Choose several students to ask you the questions in line A. Respond to their questions using text in line B. Next, divide students into pairs. Have each pair practice asking and answering the dialogue questions. Then have students switch roles. Allow students to practice the new routine while you circulate and monitor progress.

A: What is your name?

B: My name is _____.

A: Where do you live?

B: I live in the city of _____. I live in the state of _____.

A: What is your favorite food?

B: My favorite food is _____.

INDEPENDENT RECITATION *3 MINUTES*

(Apply) Give the students two minutes to memorize the dialogue on the board. When their time is up, erase the dialogue and ask them to recite it from memory in front of the class.

LESSON OBJECTIVES
Students will:

- respond with appropriate short phrases or sentences when asked personal information questions
- ask and answer personal information questions by using simple sentences and phrases
- use interrogative sentences correctly to obtain information from peers
- listen to instructions and to their peers' dialogue

LESSON VOCABULARY
name, city, state, birth date, street, address, phone number, favorite food, favorite book, favorite movie

Teaching Tip Using realia or pictures is a good way for students to quickly grasp the concepts of certain vocabulary items.

Original content Copyright © by Holt, Rinehart and Winston. Additions and changes to the original content are the responsibility of the instructor.

Lesson 3: In Case of Emergency

WORD DRILL *2 MINUTES*
(Teach/Guided Practice) Greet the class and say that you are going to play a game called "Emergency." Say: *I'll tell you the emergency and you say, 'Call for help!'* Model saying: *Call for help!* enthusiastically and have students echo. Now establish a rhythm in which you say: *Emergency!* and students reply: *Call for help!*

(Guided Practice) After students have established this pattern, replace *Emergency* with the following: *Earthquake!*, *Fire!*, *Flood!*, while students reply to each with: *Call for help!* Draw pictures of each emergency situation as you call out the word. Help students as needed to ensure that they are pronouncing words correctly.

BUILD BACKGROUND *8 MINUTES*
(Teach/Guided Practice/Practice) Write the three short dialogues below on the board. Preteach or review the vocabulary necessary for the dialogues. Read the first pair of lines aloud and then point to random students, asking them to say these lines out loud. Repeat this exercise for all three pairs of lines. Help students with proper pronunciation. Point to the words on the board as you read.

Now, erase the word, *firefighters*, from the first dialogue. Choose several students to read aloud the first dialogue, filling in the blank with the proper word. Repeat with the second dialogue, erasing the word, *police*, and then the third dialogue, erasing the word *paramedics*. Allow each student to try this exercise, offering help as needed.

A: Help! Fire! Call the firefighters!

B: I will call 911!

A: Help! Robbers! Get the police!

B: I'll call 911!

A: Help! I hurt myself! Call the paramedics!

B: I'll call 911!

INDEPENDENT RECITATION *3 MINUTES*
(Apply) If students grasp the dialogue practice quickly, give them two minutes to memorize each of the three pairs of lines on the board. When the time is up, erase that pair of lines and chose a few students to recite them from memory in front of the class.

LESSON OBJECTIVES
Students will:

- recognize and correctly pronounce words when reading aloud
- produce vocabulary to communicate emergency needs
- demonstrate comprehension of vocabulary by using 1-2 words or a simple sentence response
- learn how to construct simple imperative sentences
- use imperative sentences correctly in speaking
- listen to instructions and to their peers' dialogue

LESSON VOCABULARY
Go to the doctor, call the police, call for help, police officer, paramedic, firefighter, nurse, hospital, police station, bandage, earthquake, fire, flood

Original content Copyright © by Holt, Rinehart and Winston. Additions and changes to the original content are the responsibility of the instructor.

Differentiating Instruction

Lesson 4: Time

WORD DRILL *2 MINUTE*
(TEACH/GUIDED PRACTICE) Look at the clock on the wall. Ask
students: *What time is it?* Then say, *It is (time) o'clock.* Ask students to
repeat this phrase with you.
(PRACTICE)
After students have echoed as a class, write the following words on the
board: *lunch, gym, home.* Explain to students that they usually go to
these places or classes at a certain time. Ask the class: *When do you go
to lunch?* Ask students if they know when their class goes to lunch.
Have the class repeat the correct time: *We go to lunch at (time) o'clock.*
Repeat this exercise by asking students to explain when they go to gym
class and when they go home for the day.

UNDERSTANDING TIME, *8 MINUTES*

(TEACH/GUIDED PRACTICE) This is a continuation of the word
activity and can be used to show students how to explain when (the
time) they do specific activities during the day. This can also help them
explain events that have already taken place. Write these sentences on
the board and read them aloud to the class:

I go to sleep at nine o'clock.

I get to school at eight o'clock.

I eat lunch at twelve o'clock.
Circle the word *at* in each of these sentences. Explain that *at* helps us
understand when the events take place. Ask students to repeat the
sentences on the board with you. Have a volunteer point out the times
on the clock as you say them. This will help students connect the
sentences on the board with the numbers on the clock.

Explain that the word *at* identifies a specific time that an activity takes
place. The word *at* is usually used to explain things that we do on a
regular basis.

INDEPENDENT RECITATION, *3 MINUTES*
(APPLY)
Have students work in pairs to practice the following dialogue.

A: When do you wake up in the morning?

B: I wake up at (time) o'clock.

Students should take turns asking and answering the question. When
they have finished, ask volunteers to tell their partners' answers.

(Student's name) wakes up at (time) o'clock.

LESSON OBJECTIVES
Students will:

• learn and understand
  important words
  associated with time
  (morning, afternoon,
  evening, a.m., p.m.)

• understand how to use *at*
  when describing a specific
  time

• work with partners to
  create dialogues that
  describe specific events

• listen to instructions and to
  peers' dialogue

LESSON VOCABULARY
Time, o'clock, wake, when,
one, two, three, four, five,
six, seven, eight, nine, ten,
eleven, twelve, at

Teaching Tip When
teaching time, review the
spellings of numbers one
through twelve. Write each
number and have students
write the correct spelling next
to each number.

Original content Copyright © by Holt, Rinehart and Winston. Additions and changes to the original content are the responsibility of the instructor.

Differentiating Instruction

Lesson 5: Types of Classes

WORD DRILL *2 MINUTES*
(Teach/Guided Practice) Say to students: *Our class is Language Arts.* Gesture to the class to repeat: *Our class is Language Arts.* After class has repeated, say the sentence again and gesture for the class to repeat.

(Guided Practice) After students have echoed as a class, point to random individual students. Say: *Our class is Language Arts*, and invite the student to repeat the sentence. Use this routine when introducing new words to ensure that the words are being pronounced correctly by everybody, not only by the more outgoing students.

BUILD BACKGROUND *8 MINUTES*
(Teach/Guided Practice/Practice) Write the short dialogue below on the board. Preteach the necessary vocabulary for the dialogue by using pictures, acting out words, or drawing items on the board. Read the first two lines aloud, and elicit repetition from the students after each line.

Go around the room and let each student have a chance to speak alone. Then continue with the rest of the dialogue. Repeat until students are comfortable pronouncing the words. Say the first line (A), and have the class respond (B). Reverse roles. When results are satisfactory, divide the class into pairs and assign each partner a role. Allow students to practice the dialogue while you circulate and monitor progress. Students may vary the dialogue by adding the names of other subjects.

A: Which class do you have before lunch?

B: I have Math class before lunch.

A: I have Science class before lunch. Which class does Amy have?

B: She has Chemistry class before lunch.

A: I think Amy has Math class before lunch.

B. No, she has Chemistry class before lunch.

INDEPENDENT RECITATION *3 MINUTES*
(Apply) Give students two minutes to memorize the dialogue on the board. When the time is up, erase the dialogue and chose a few pairs of students to recite it from memory for the class.

ADDITIONAL LANGUAGE ACTIVITY *15 MINUTES*
(Teach/Guided Practice/Practice) Ask students how high they can count in English. Start with one and count until the students have stopped. Work on pronunciation and drill difficult numbers. After students can count to fifty as a class, go around the room, pointing to individual students until each student has said a number.

LESSON OBJECTIVES
Students will:
- respond to basic questions regarding different types of classes at school
- speak in simple sentences to communicate different types of classes at school
- use interrogative sentences to ask peers about different types of classes at school
- listen to instructions and to their peers' dialogue
- use words for numbers

LESSON VOCABULARY
Language Arts, Math, Physical Education (Phys Ed), Social Studies, Homeroom, Chemistry, Art, Music, Science, Biology, History

Teaching Tip Substitution drills can be a good way to reinforce structures while practicing target vocabulary. Prompt students by cuing them with words or images

Original content Copyright © by Holt, Rinehart and Winston. Additions and changes to the original content are the responsibility of the instructor.

Differentiating Instruction

Lesson 6: Classroom Objects and Supplies

WORD DRILL *2 MINUTES*
(Teach/Guided Practice) Point to the board and say *board*. Gesture to the class to repeat: *board*. After class has repeated, say: *board* again and gesture for the class to repeat. This establishes a rhythm that is used to introduce new or difficult words: instructor first and then the class.

(Guided Practice) After students have echoed as a class, point to random individual students. Say: *board*, and invite the student to repeat alone. Use this routine to introduce the other new words to ensure that everybody is pronouncing the words correctly, not only by the more outgoing students. Point to or hold up the other classroom objects to teach the vocabulary.

BUILD BACKGROUND *8 MINUTES*
(Teach/Guided Practice/Practice) Write the short dialogue below on the board. Preteach the necessary vocabulary for the dialogue by using pictures, acting out words, or drawing items on the board. Read the first two lines aloud, and elicit repetition from the students after each line.

Go around the room and let each student have a chance to speak alone. Then continue with the rest of the dialogue. Repeat until students are comfortable pronouncing the words. Say the first line (A), and have the class respond (B). Reverse roles. Divide the class into pairs and assign each partner a role. Allow students to practice the dialogue while you circulate and monitor progress. Students may vary the dialogue by adding other school and classroom activities.

A: Excuse me, can you tell me what the homework is?

B: We need to read a chapter in the textbook.

A: Thank you.

B: You are welcome. Do you have a pencil I can use?

A: Yes, I have a pencil you can use.

B: Thank you.

INDEPENDENT RECITATION *3 MINUTES*
(Apply) If students grasp the partner activity quickly, give them two minutes to memorize the dialogue on the board. When the time is up, erase the dialogue and chose a few pairs of students to recite it from memory in front of the class.

LESSON OBJECTIVES
Students will:

- respond to basic questions regarding classroom objects and activities
- learn nouns used after present tense verbs to describe classroom objects and activities
- speak in complete, coherent sentences to describe classroom objects and activities
- use interrogative sentences to ask peers about classroom objects and activities
- listen to instructions and to their peers' dialogue

LESSON VOCABULARY
desk, board, clock, computer, map, chair, ruler, eraser, pencil, paper, textbook, notebook (and pass tests, ask questions, finish homework, solve problems, take notes, teach lessons, help classmates)

Original content Copyright © by Holt, Rinehart and Winston. Additions and changes to the original content are the responsibility of the instructor.

Differentiating Instruction

Lesson 7: Comparing Places Inside a School

WORD DRILL 2 MINUTES

(Teach/Guided Practice) Say to students: *This is our classroom.*
Gesture to students to repeat: *This is our classroom.* After class has
repeated, say the sentence again and gesture for the class to repeat.
(Guided Practice) After class has echoed, point to individual students,
say: *This is our classroom.* and invite the student to repeat after you.
Use this routine when introducing new words so that the words are
being pronounced correctly by everybody.

BUILD BACKGROUND 8 MINUTES

(Teach/Guided Practice/Practice) Write the short dialogue below on
the board. Read the first two lines aloud, and elicit repetition from the
students after each line. Go around the room and let each student have a
chance to speak. Continue with the rest of the dialogue, having students
repeat after you until they are comfortable pronouncing the words. Say
the first line (A), and have the class respond (B). Reverse roles. When
results are satisfactory, divide the class into pairs and allow them to
practice the routine for a few minutes while you circulate and monitor
progress. Have students name different places in the school as part of
the dialogue.

A: We need to talk. Let's talk in the gym.

B: The gym is too noisy. Where else can we talk?

A: Let's talk in the auditorium.

B: The auditorium is too noisy. Why don't we talk in the library?

A: No. We are not allowed to talk in the library.

B: Let's talk in the hall. I need to stop at my locker anyway.

INDEPENDENT RECITATION 3 MINUTES

(Apply) Give students two minutes to memorize the dialogue on the
board. When the time is up, erase the dialogue and chose a pair of
students to recite from memory in front of the class.

ADDITIONAL LANGUAGE ACTIVITY 10 MINUTES

(Teach/Guided Practice/Practice) Draw an arrow on the board
pointing to students' left. Say: *left,* and gesture for students to repeat
left. Draw an arrow pointing right, say: *right,* and have students point
and repeat the word. Then go around the room and call on individual
students. Ask: *Who is sitting to your left?* and *Who is sitting to your
right?* until each student has answered at least one question.

LESSON OBJECTIVES
Students will:

- respond to simple
  questions about different
  places at school
- speak in simple sentences
  to communicate directions
- use *left* and *right* to give
  simple directions
- use interrogative
  sentences to obtain
  information about the
  school
- listen to instructions and to
  their peers' dialogue

LESSON VOCABULARY
auditorium, gym, library,
cafeteria, hallway,
classroom, locker, office, big,
clean, dirty, small, long,
short, tall, fat, thin, ugly,
pretty, left, right

Teaching Tip Take students
on a school tour to introduce
them to school vocabulary
words, such as library,
auditorium, office, gym, and
so on.

Original content Copyright © by Holt, Rinehart and Winston. Additions and changes to the original content are the responsibility of the instructor.

Differentiating Instruction

Lesson 8: What Are You Doing?

WORD DRILL *2 MINUTES*
(Teach/Guided Practice) Pantomime holding a phone in your hand and dialing a number. Hold the phone close to your ear. Say: *Hello, Jane. What are you doing?* Gesture to the class to repeat. After repetition, say the question again and cue the class to repeat. This establishes a rhythm that will be used to introduce new or difficult words: teacher first and then the class.

(Guided Practice) After class has echoed, point to individuals and say: *Hello, Jane. What are you doing?* Cue the student to repeat the dialogue. Use this routine when introducing new words so that the words are being pronounced correctly by everybody, not only by the more outgoing students.

BUILD BACKGROUND *8 MINUTES*
(Teach/Guided Practice/Practice) Write the short dialogue below on the board. Preteach the necessary vocabulary by using pictures, acting out words, or drawing items on the board. Read the first two lines aloud, and elicit repetition from the students after each line.

Let each student have a chance to speak alone. Then continue with the dialogue. Repeat until students are comfortable pronouncing the words. Divide the class into pairs and assign each partner a role. Allow students to practice the dialogue for one minute while you circulate and monitor progress. Students may vary the dialogue with other activities.

A: Hello, _____. How are you?

B: I'm fine, thank you.

A: What are you doing?

B: I am reading a book. What are you doing?

A: I am going to the park.

B. I will see you there when I finish reading.

INDEPENDENT RECITATION *3 MINUTES*
(Apply) Give students two minutes to memorize the dialogue on the board. When the time is up, erase the dialogue and chose a few pairs of students to recite it from memory to the class.

ADDITIONAL LANGUAGE ACTIVITY *10 MINUTES*
(Teach/Guided Practice/Practice) Ask students to name the current month. Write it on the board. Ask students to name the other months of the year. Write them on the board. Point to each month, say it aloud, and have students repeat until they are comfortable pronouncing all the names of the months.

LESSON OBJECTIVES
Students will:

- respond to basic questions regarding daily activities in the context of a telephone conversation
- speak in complete, coherent sentences to communicate daily activities in social situations
- use interrogative sentences in social situations, such as a telephone conversation
- listen to instructions and to their peers' dialogue
- learn the names of the months of the year

LESSON VOCABULARY
playing a game, reading a book, listening to music, singing a song, eating a meal, walking to school, going out, watching a movie, talking on the phone, Who? What? When? Where? Why? How?

Teaching Tip Randomly calling on students can be a good way to keep the class alert and active in an activity.

Original content Copyright © by Holt, Rinehart and Winston. Additions and changes to the original content are the responsibility of the instructor.

Differentiating Instruction

Vocabulary for Newcomers

DIRECTIONS: The following lists of words are grouped by topic or function. Write a list on the chalk board or a transparency and have students practice and memorize. Practice activities may include peer conversations, whole class discussion, sentences with missing words, matching, echo reading, etc.

Numerals and Words

1 – one	11 – eleven	21 – twenty-one	40 – forty	500 – five hundred
2 – two	12 – twelve	22 – twenty-two	50 – fifty	600 – six hundred
3 – three	13 – thirteen	23 – twenty-three	60 – sixty	700 – seven hundred
4 – four	14 – fourteen	24 – twenty-four	70 – seventy	800 – eight hundred
5 – five	15 – fifteen	25 – twenty-five	80 – eighty	900 – nine hundred
6 – six	16 – sixteen	26 – twenty-six	90 – ninety	1000 – one thousand
7 – seven	17 – seventeen	27 – twenty-seven	100 – one hundred	
8 – eight	18 – eighteen	28 – twenty-eight	200 – two hundred	
9 – nine	19 – nineteen	29 – twenty-nine	300 – three hundred	
10 – ten	20 – twenty	30 – thirty	400 – four hundred	

Ordinal Numbers

1st First	6th Sixth	11th Eleventh	16th Sixteenth	21st Twenty-first	26 Twenty-sixth
2nd Second	7th Seventh	12th Twelfth	17th Seventeenth	22nd Twenty-second	27 Twenty-seventh
3rd Third	8th Eighth	13th Thirteenth	18th Eighteenth	23rd Twenty-third	28 Twenty-eighth
4th Fourth	9th Ninth	14th Fourteenth	19th Nineteenth	24th Twenty-forth	29 Twenty-ninth
5th Fifth	10th Tenth	15th Fifteenth	20th Twentieth	25 Twenty-fifth	30 Thirtieth

Days of the Week

Sunday (Weekend!)	Monday (School)	Tuesday (School)	Wednesday (School)	Thursday (School)	Friday (School)	Saturday (Weekend!)

Original content Copyright © by Holt, Rinehart and Winston. Additions and changes to the original content are the responsibility of the instructor.

Prepositions of Place

at	above	before	beside	below	behind	down	in	over	under	within

Comparatives and Superlatives

good, better, best	helpful, less helpful, least helpful
bad, worse, worst	helpful, more helpful, most helpful
little, less, least	fast, faster, fastest

Pronouns and Verbs

To Be		
Pronoun	Present Tense Verb	Past Tense Verb
I	am	was
you	are	were
he/she/it	is	was
we	are	were
you	are	were
they	are	were

To Have		
Pronoun	Present Tense Verb	Past Tense Verb
I	have	had
you	have	had
he/she/it	has	had
we	have	had
you	have	had
they	have	had

Nouns of Place

bank	restaurant	library	school	church	shopping center
pharmacy	bus stop	supermarket	park	movie theater	post office

Question Words

Who...?	What...?	When...?	How...?	Where...?	Why...?	Do/Does...?

Original content Copyright © by Holt, Rinehart and Winston. Additions and changes to the original content are the responsibility of the instructor.

Differentiating Instruction

Answer Key

UNIT 1, COLLECTION 1

Academic and Selection Vocabulary

Section A
1. careful
2. attentive
3. delighted
4. commendations
5. advancing
6. annoying

Section B
1. F
2. T
3. T
4. F
5. F
6. T

Section C
1. convey
2. excerpt
3. support
4. effect
5. outcome

THE MOST DANGEROUS GAME
RICHARD CONNELL

Selection Test
Comprehension, Skills, and Vocabulary
1. C
2. D
3. A
4. B
5. C

6. Students' responses will vary. A sample response follows:

I think that Rainsford became kinder from the experience of being hunted. First, he felt the terror of being hunted, which he had not thought about before. He also was disgusted by the general's ideas about killing people for fun. For those reasons, I think he would be changed by the experience in positive ways. As a result, Rainsford would be kinder to animals and people, too.

LIBERTY JULIA ALVAREZ

Selection Test
Comprehension, Skills, and Vocabulary
1. B
2. A
3. D
4. C
5. D

6. Students' responses will vary. A sample response follows:

I think the father means that you have to give up some things to be free. For example, the girl gave up the dog, Liberty, which she loves very much. She also forces herself to be mean to the dog, which must have hurt very much, to be sure it's safe from the thugs and keeps its freedom. For those reasons, I agree with the father's statement.

THE GREAT ESCAPE
THOMAS FLEMING

Selection Test
Comprehension, Skills, and Vocabulary
1. B
2. D
3. C
4. C
5. D

6. Students' responses will vary. A sample response follows:

I do think that Roger Bushell was an escape genius. To start with, he was clearly an amazing leader who got all of the prisoners organized around one main escape plan. Also, he planned the escape to have the best chance of succeeding, such as going deep enough that the Germans couldn't hear the digging and having a disguise and forged papers for each prisonerwho was escaping. In addition, when one tunnel was discovered, he was wise enough to stop work completely for a while to fool the Germans into thinking the men stopped trying to escape. In conclusion, I believe Roger Bushell deserves the title of "escape genius," even though he was killed as a result of the Great Escape.

COLLECTION 1 SUMMATIVE TEST

Vocabulary Skills
1. impression
2. distracted
3. prowled
4. resort
5. imprudent

Literary and Reading Skills
6. C
7. D
8. B

Language and Writing Skills
9. definition
10. unusual

UNIT 1, COLLECTION 2

Academic and Selection Vocabulary

Section A
1. E
2. D
3. C
4. A
5. B

Section B
1. elation
2. solace
3. discreet
4. infatuated
5. vigilant

Section C
1. complex
2. observation
3. incident
4. significant

Original content Copyright © by Holt, Rinehart and Winston. Additions and changes to the original content are the responsibility of the instructor.

THANK YOU, M'AM
LANGSTON HUGHES

Selection Test
Comprehension, Skills, and Vocabulary

1. C   3. A   5. B
2. B   4. B

6. Students' responses will vary. A sample response follows:

Based on his actions, Roger seems to be a complicated character. From what he tells Mrs. Jones, his home life seems troubled. He does not seem to have parents at home to care for him. From the way he speaks to Mrs. Jones, we can tell that he is honest and polite. All in all, Roger seems to be a decent boy who is driven to do bad things because of unfortunate circumstances.

AMERICAN HISTORY
JUDITH ORTIZ COFER

Selection Test
Comprehension, Skills, and Vocabulary

1. A   3. C   5. B
2. A   4. D

6. Students' responses will vary. A sample response follows:

Today it might still be a problem for a girl from one ethnic group to fall in love with a boy from another group. First, many people still feel prejudice toward ethnic groups different from their own. In addition, adults often try to encourage their children to choose friends who they themselves feel comfortable with. For that reason, many adults today would still discourage a relationship between teenagers of two different ethnic groups. Thus I believe that a girl from one ethnic group might still experience pain if she fell in love with a boy from a different ethnic group.

AN INTERVIEW WITH DAVE EGGERS

Selection Test
Comprehension, Skills, and Vocabulary

1. B   3. A   5. B
2. C   4. D

6. Students' responses will vary. A sample response follows:

I think that the best piece of advice that Dave Eggers shares is to read ten books a year. From my own experience, I know that I get lots of ideas from other books. Also, it makes sense that we can learn from other writers. All in all, Eggers' advice seems important because writers should also be readers.

COLLECTION 2 SUMMATIVE TEST

Vocabulary Skills

1. barren   3. permit   5. vigilant
2. frail   4. discreet

Literary and Reading Skills

6. C   7. C   8. B

Language and Writing Skills

9. but   10. so

UNIT 1, COLLECTION 3

Academic and Selection Vocabulary
Section A

1. conspicuous
2. reconciliation
3. exasperation
4. retribution
5. obstinate

Section B

1. E   3. N   5. E
2. N   4. E

Section C

1. distinct   3. impression
2. portrays   4. insight

THE INTERLOPERS SAKI

Selection Test
Comprehension, Skills, and Vocabulary

1. C   3. C   5. A
2. A   4. B

6. Students' responses will vary. A sample response follows:

Today, weather and natural disaster bring people together. For example, the Tsunami that hit the coast of Thailand during Christmas of 2004 was an event that brought the global community together. People from all over the world tried to contribute to the relief effort with food and clothing. Also, countries donated people resources to help find victims of the disaster and aid in reuniting families. In addition, the world community provided money and supplies to help rebuild homes. As I have shown, people—even people who are complete strangers and live halfway around

Original content Copyright © by Holt, Rinehart and Winston. Additions and changes to the original content are the responsibility of the instructor.

    Differentiating Instruction

the world from one another—come together in times of natural disasters and emergencies.

THE CASK OF AMONTILLADO
EDGAR ALLAN POE

Selection Test
Comprehension, Skills, and Vocabulary
1. A 　　3. C 　　5. C
2. B 　　4. D

6. Students' responses will vary. A sample response follows:

What you did to Fortunato was cruel and more than a little nuts. First you claim that Fortunato did you a thousand injuries, but you never say what those injuries were except that he insulted you. In addition, you plot your revenge without ever letting on that you are angry with Fortunato. You might have worked things out if you had talked to him. Besides, nothing justifies killing another human being in the cruel and heartless way that you killed him. For these reasons, I believe that you should not have been able to punish with impunity as you did and you should be punished for your crime.

FOUR READINGS ABOUT POE'S DEATH

Selection Test
Comprehension, Skills, and Vocabulary
1. B 　　3. D 　　5. B
2. B 　　4. D

6. Students' responses will vary. A sample response follows:

We will never know for sure how Poe died because of the time in which he lived. At that time doctors had limited means of diagnosing the causes of death,. while doctors today have many modern ways in which to determine the exact cause of death. Also, the evidence available to us is reports from people who may not be absolutely reliable. Even the doctor, who should be trustworthy, became a temperance advocate and changed the details of his account to make a lesson of Poe's death about the evils of drink. For these reasons I believe that we will never know for certain how Poe died.

COLLECTION 3 SUMMATIVE TEST

Vocabulary Skills
1. disputed

2. obstinate
3. exasperation
4. chronic/conspicuous
5. imposing

Literary and Reading Skills
6. C 　　7. C 　　8. A

Language and Writing Skills
9. impressive 10. striking

UNIT 1, COLLECTION 4

Academic and Selection Vocabulary
Section A
1. S 　　4. S 　　7. S
2. A 　　5. S 　　8. S
3. S 　　6. A
Section B
1. A 　　3. A
2. B 　　4. A

Section C
1. associated 　3. ambiguous
2. imply 　　　4. literal

THE SCARLET IBIS JAMES HURST

Selection Test
Comprehension, Skills, and Vocabulary
1. A 　　3. A 　　5. B
2. C 　　4. D

6. Students' responses will vary. A sample response follows:

I agree that James Hurst wrote "The Scarlet Ibis" to comment on the bloodshed between nations in World War I. For one thing, he has one brother trying to change another, which is what war is usually about—countries trying to change the behavior of other countries. Also, he mentions battles in the war and a soldier who has died that the family knows. In addition, he includes the color red in the story, such as the red bird, a bleeding tree, and a red bush. So, in conclusion, I think the author wrote the story to make people think about the war and the sadness and death it caused.

THE GIFT OF THE MAGI O. HENRY

Selection Test
Comprehension, Skills, and Vocabulary
1. B 　　3. C 　　5. A
2. D 　　4. D

6. Students' responses will vary. A sample response follows:

I think that the greatest gift in the story is the love that Della and Jim have for each other. For example, Della cuts and sells her hair, so she can buy Jim a wonderful gift. Jim also sells something precious, his watch, which belonged to his father and grandfather in order to buy Della the combs she wants. They both sacrifice something important for the happiness of the other. So, in conclusion, I think the story shows that their love for each other is ar and away more valuable than their finest possessions and the greatest gift they could ever give.

SYNTHESIZING WORKS BY ONE AUTHOR ALBERT EINSTEIN

Selection Test
Comprehension, Skills, and Vocabulary
1. A   3. C   5. C
2. D   4. B
6. Students' responses will vary. A sample response follows:

I think Albert Einstein was a very smart person who cared about people and the world he lived in. I feel this way because he realized that war was a terrible waste and spoke out against it. But he also realized that a dangerous country like Nazi Germany was such a threat to people everywhere that he had to sacrifice his own views on war to argue for nuclear weapons. I agree with his views to abolish war, even though I don't think it will ever happen. In conclusion, my respect for Einstein has increased because he always took stands based on what he thought was right.

COLLECTION 4 SUMMATIVE TEST

Vocabulary Skills
1. reiterated   4. prudence
2. scrutiny   5. conceivable
3. ardent

Literary and Reading Skills
6. D   7. A   8. C

Language and Writing Skills
9. origin   10. quotations

UNIT 1, ORAL LANGUAGE SKILL BUILDER

Summarize
Students' responses will vary. A sample response follows:

What is the first problem? The action begins when Rainsford falls off the boat and is left behind.

How does Rainsford solve this problem? He decides to swim for the island. So he thinks he is safe.

What is the next problem? Even though he didn't drown, his problems aren't over yet because his host wants to hunt him like a big game animal.

How does he try to solve it? Rainsford decides to run. But that doesn't work so he tries to hide and set a trap.

What is the climax? The situation is at its most exciting when Rainsford realizes his host is just playing with him because he know the General is crazy and that his own life is in danger.

What is the turning point? Things begin to change when Rainsford comes up with a new plan because he is desperate to save his own life.

What is the conclusion? Finally, the problem is solved when Rainsford swims around the island. He knows he has to kill or be killed. So he sneaks up on his host and kills him.

Extend Discussion
Students' responses will vary. A sample response follows:

If the General had been the better hunter or the more clever man, Rainsford would have died on this island.

If both men had enjoyed the game, perhaps Rainsford would have participated in this "sport" engaging other victims.

UNIT 1, ORAL LANGUAGE SKILL BUILDER

Comparisons
Students' responses will vary. Sample responses follow:

Original content Copyright © by Holt, Rinehart and Winston. Additions and changes to the original content are the responsibility of the instructor.

Who is stronger? In comparison to Roger, Mrs. Jones is stronger. We think this because she can keep him from running away.

Who needs more help? Compared to Mrs. Jones, Roger needs more help. We think this because he is young and has no one at home.

Who gives more help? Even though Roger tried to steal from her, Mrs. Jones wanted to help him.

Who is more trusting? Mrs. Jones is more trusting. The part of the story that shows us this is when she is cooking and turns her back to him.

Who needs to be trusted? Roger needs to be trusted. The part of the story that shows us this is when Roger moves away from the purse.

Who learns more? In our opinion, Roger learns more. One reason we think this is because he expected to be arrested. Another reason is he was surprised by kindness.

Extend Discussion
Students' responses will vary. A sample response follows:

Mrs. Jones would want Roger to do well in school. Accept all reasonable responses that demonstrate this.

Mrs. Jones would be disappointed if Roger tried to steal again. Accept all reasonable responses that demonstrate this.

UNIT 1, ENGLISH LANGUAGE SKILL BUILDER

Shades of Meaning
1. tenement; destitute
2. apartment; house
3. middle class (low); middle class (well off)
4. house; prosperous

UNIT 1, ENGLISH LANGUAGE SKILL BUILDER

Phonemic Awareness
Understand the Skill
1. taught/thought; sigh/shy; seem/theme
2. breathe/breeze; search/surge; price/prize; harsh/hearth; face/faith

Extend Discussion
1. thought   4. searches   7. faith
2. price   5. breathe   8. seem
3. harsh   6. sigh

UNIT 1 SUMMATIVE TEST
Literary and Reading Skills
A.
1. C   3. A   5. D
2. D   4. D

B.
6. antagonist   8. flashback   10. mood
7. inference   9. visualizing

Making Predictions
11. Students' responses will vary. A sample response follows:

I predict that Jim and Della will overcome the disappointment of their Christmas gifts and will continue to be very much in love, perhaps even more so. The details in the story that support this prediction are primarily Jim's responses to Della when he learns she has cut her hair and bought him a beautiful chain for the watch he no longer owns. Since most of the story is about Della's sacrifice for Jim, we already have evidence of how much she loves him. But in Jim's actions and reactions, there is evidence of how much he loves her. First, he sold his watch to buy her the combs that he knew she wanted very much. Then he tells Della that he loves her no matter whether her hair is long or short. That confirms his feelings for her are not just based on her physical beauty created by her lovely hair. He also reacts calmly to the sight of the watch chain and simply tells Della they should put their gifts away for a while. Della's hair, after all, will grow back and, in time, she can use the combs. But his response to the loss of the watch shows that his love for her is greater than his attachment to any material object. Based on their mutual love for each other, I predict they remain happy together for years to come.

UNIT 2, COLLECTION 5
Academic and Selection Vocabulary
Section A
1. E   3. D   5. C
2. A   4. B

Section B
1. B   3. A
2. A   4. B

Section C
1. attitude   3. enhanced
2. establishes   4. appeal

Original content Copyright © by Holt, Rinehart and Winston. Additions and changes to the original content are the responsibility of the instructor.

CUB PILOT ON THE MISSISSIPPI
MARK TWAIN

Selection Test
Comprehension, Skills, and Vocabulary

1. B   3. A   5. B
2. C   4. D

6. Students' responses will vary. A sample response follows:

Brown has many traits, including a fine memory and a sharp tongue. From the selection, we know that he looks middle aged and is thin, with a long face. He acts impatient and yells constantly. Other characters view Brown as being a pest and as being unfair. In conclusion, Brown can best be described as "an unkind man."

THE GRANDFATHER GARY SOTO

Selection Test
Comprehension, Skills, and Vocabulary

1. D   3. C   5. B
2. C   4. A

6. Students' responses will vary. A sample response follows:

At first, the narrator did not care about the tree. When he was small he jumped over it, and nearly knocked it over. Then, as he got older, he shared fruit from the tree with his grandfather. By the end of the essay, he loves the tree since it reminds him of his grandfather. Therefore, I think that the narrator's feelings changed from not caring about the tree to caring very deeply.

ABOUT STORYCORPS

Selection Test
Comprehension, Skills, and Vocabulary

1. A   3. B   5. B
2. C   4. D

6. Students' responses will vary. A sample response follows:

I believe that getting a CD is more meaningful because it would be a record for me of what I learned about a loved one and/or what I shared with them. First of all, we would be more interested in our stories than anyone at the Library of Congress. Additionally, the stories would be available to others in our families for years to come. For those reasons, the CD would be more important to me. In conclusion, although I think that the archive is important, the CD would be more meaningful.

COLLECTION 5 TEST

Vocabulary Skills

1. indulgent   3. collective   5. meager
2. confronted   4. transient

Literary and Reading Skills

6. A   7. C   8. B

Language and Writing Skills

9. Jorge, Mia, and Peter played baseball; I played tennis.
10. The bicyclist peddled quickly; I accidentally walked into her path.

UNIT 2, COLLECTION 6

Academic and Selection Vocabulary
Section A

1. A   3. S   5. A
2. S   4. U

Section B

1. E   3. E   5. E
2. N   4. N

Section C

1. influence   3. valid
2. counters   4. verifies

CINDERELLA'S STEPSISTERS

Selection Test
Comprehension, Skills, and Vocabulary

1. D   3. D   5. A
2. C   4. C

6. Students' responses will vary. A sample response follows:

No one should be unkind to other students. First, being mean serves no useful purpose. Some people think it makes them feel powerful and important. It doesn't. It just makes them someone no one likes. In addition, if you're mean to other people, they will probably be mean to you. For that reason, meanness just leads to more meanness. Thus I believe that we could all get along better if everyone stopped being thoughtless and unkind.

Original content Copyright © by Holt, Rinehart and Winston. Additions and changes to the original content are the responsibility of the instructor.

KAAVYA VISWANATHAN/KAAVYA SYNDROME

Selection Test
Comprehension, Skills, and Vocabulary
1. C   3. A   5. B
2. A   4. C
6. Students' responses will vary. A sample response follows:

I don't believe that Kaavya was an intentional plagiarist. First, she couldn't have been foolish enough to copy from another person's work without realizing she'd get caught. In addition, it seems like it would be more work to find parts of someone else's story that fit into yours than just writing it yourself. For that reason I think that she just accidentally repeated things she read. Thus I believe that Kaavya was an unconscious copycat.

COLLECTION 6 TEST

Vocabulary Skills
1. perseverance
2. expendable
3. diminish
4. inadvertent
5. indispensable

Literary and Reading Skills
6. C   7. D
Language and Writing Skills
8. B   9. D   10. C

UNIT 2, ORAL LANGUAGE SKILL BUILDER

Interview: Ask and answer questions
Students' responses will vary. Sample responses follow:

Who: What's your name? What are you known for?

What: What experiences most changed you? What experience was most meaningful?

When: When did these important events happen?

Where: Where did these important events happen?

Why: Why were these events important to you? Why were they important to your family; your community; the world?

How: How do you feel about what happened; your actions? Would you do anything differently?

Extend Discussion
Students' responses will vary. Sample responses follow:

An interview can be made more formal by avoiding contractions and slang, and by addressing the interviewee as Mr. Miss, or Ms.

Questions can be more specific and less formal if you are interviewing someone you know.

UNIT 2, ORAL LANGUAGE SKILL BUILDER

Scoring a Debate: Listening/Notetaking
Students should score one point for each check mark that the "pro" or "con" respondents earn. The side of the argument that earns the greatest number of check marks or points wins the debate.

Extend Discussion (possible answers)
Students' responses will vary. Sample responses follow:

A convincing argument is clear, logical, and has enough support.

A weak argument is not clear, not logical, and lacks support.

Students should cite specific examples from the debate they just heard to support their evaluations of weak and strong arguments.

UNIT 2, ENGLISH LANGUAGE SKILL BUILDER

Negative Sentences
1. Brown *never* heard Henry deliver the message.
2. Brown insisted that *no one* gave him the message.
3. Brown had *no* patience for the young apprentices....
4. The captain had *no* affection for Brown.
5. The captain was *not* furious with Twain, which is *not* what Twain expected.
6. The captain warned Twain *not* to repeat the conversation.

Extend Discussion
1. Brown was never kind to Twain and the other cub pilots.

Original content Copyright © by Holt, Rinehart and Winston. Additions and changes to the original content are the responsibility of the instructor.

2. Soto's grandfather might have said, "Please do not jump over my fruit trees."
3. No one would be excluded from telling their story to StoryCorp.

UNIT 2, ENGLISH LANGUAGE SKILL BUILDER

Articles
1. an   3. a
2. some   4. the

Extend Discussion (possible answers)
1. a lot of/many
2. The
3. Some/Many/A lot of
4. an
5. Some/Many
6. a

UNIT 2 SUMMATIVE TEST

Literary and Reading Skills
A.
1. A   3. B   5. A
2. C   4. D

B.
6. format
7. style
8. logical fallacy
9. tone
10. questioning

Author's Style
11. Students' responses will vary. A sample response follows:

Toni Morrison's style in "Cinderella's Stepsisters" is quite challenging and not easy to read. She uses big words and difficult words. Some of the sentences are very long, and some of the sentences, although they are quite long, are actually not sentences at all but sentence fragments. But although her style may be a little hard to read, once you get into it, you realize that it has a nice kind of pattern and rhythm. She uses parallel sentences and repetition to achieve that. She also uses colorful words—for example, when she talks about the "nick-of-time prince" and the "rainbow journey toward realization of personal goals."

UNIT 3, COLLECTION 7

Academic and Selection Vocabulary
Section A
1. E   3. B   5. B
2. C   4. D

Section B
1. B   3. A   5. A
2. B   4. B

Section C
1. associates   3. evoke
2. elaborates   4. nuances

A BLESSING JAMES WRIGHT

Selection Test
Comprehension, Skills, and Vocabulary
1. B   3. A   5. B
2. C   4. C
6. Students' responses will vary. A sample response follows:

I think that horses cannot feel emotions like those described in the poem. At first, the speaker describes them as feeling kindness. Later, he describes them as feeling lonely. In my opinion, horses cannot really experience these feelings because they cannot think. as we do. In conclusion, I believe that horses do not feel emotions like those described in the poem.

WOMEN ALICE WALKER

Selection Test
Comprehension, Skills, and Vocabulary
1. B   3. C   5. B
2. A   4. A
6. Students' responses will vary. A sample response follows:

I think that the women in the poem are likeable because they are so giving. From the poem, I can tell that they sacrifice a lot to help their children. Also, they don't just try, they succeed! In conclusion, I find these women likable because they are so admirable.

I WANDERED LONELY AS A CLOUD WILLIAM WORDWORTH

Selection Test
Comprehension, Skills, and Vocabulary
1. B   3. D   5. D
2. C   4. C

Original content Copyright © by Holt, Rinehart and Winston. Additions and changes to the original content are the responsibility of the instructor.

6. Students' responses will vary. A sample response follows:

I think that solitude is not blissful. The speaker in the poem enjoys solitude because he enjoys the "inward eye" of images from the past. I feel that both happy and unhappy memories may return. Also, I get bored when I am alone. In conclusion, to me, solitude is not blissful.

LEGAL ALIEN / EXTRANJERA LEGAL PAT MORA

Selection Test
Comprehension, Skills, and Vocabulary
1. C   3. B   5. B
2. A   4. B
6. Students' responses will vary. A sample response follows:

The speaker in "Legal Alien / Extranjera legal" can best be described as feeling distanced. At the beginning of the poem, she seems proud that she can "slip back and forth" between two languages and cultures. As the poem continues, we realize that she feels very alone. In conclusion, I believe that the speaker, while very capable, feels that she is at a distance from both of her home cultures.

HISTORICAL ACCOUNTS ACROSS GENRES

Selection Test
Comprehension, Skills, and Vocabulary
1. C   3. B   5. D
2. C   4. C
6. Students' responses will vary. A sample response follows:

If I were to write about a historical event, I would choose to write a nonfiction account, because I could include lots of facts. I would be comfortable writing a nonfiction account because it is a straightforward form. Also, I think nonfiction accounts are more educational than ballads or other genres. For all of these reasons, I would write a nonfiction account of a historical event.

GENERATING RESEARCH QUESTIONS

Selection Test
Comprehension, Skills, and Vocabulary
1. B   3. A   5. A

2. B   4. C
6. Students' responses will vary. A sample response follows:

I would make a good investigator for a crime unit because I'm very observant. One important quality that an investigator needs is curiosity. I possess that quality. For that reason, I think I would be successful. In conclusion, I believe that investigation is a good field for me because I am curious and observant.

COLLECTION 7 SUMMATIVE TEST

Vocabulary Skills
1. charisma   3. infamous   5. glee
2. twilight   4. inception

Literary and Reading Skills
6. C   7. B   8. A

Language and Writing Skills
9. Then   10. On the other hand,

UNIT 3, ORAL LANGUAGE SKILL BUILDER

Spoken Word Performance
Note students' use of expression in their reading of the poem:

Extend Discussion
Students' responses will vary. Encourage a lively discussion of the different ways in which different groups of students interpreted and performed the poem.

UNIT 3, ORAL LANGUAGE SKILL BUILDER

Cross Text Discussion
Students' responses will vary. A sample response follows:
Evidence of sorrow:
Historical Account describes a typical Sunday until the unthinkable happens and a bomb kills four little girls. This describes one mother's desperate search for her child and the helplessness of the child's grandfather when he finds her shoe.
Ballad describes the same mother's fear of what her child might find at a freedom march and her certainty that their church will be a safe haven Again, she paws through the rubble to find nothing but her child's shoe.

Original content Copyright © by Holt, Rinehart and Winston. Additions and changes to the original content are the responsibility of the instructor.

Movie Review talks about what the girls' lives might have been and describes the recollections of Denise McNair's father of the sadness of having to expose his child to racism in all its forms.

Evidence of anger:
Historical Account ends with a quote from Denise McNair's grandfather saying that he wanted to blow up the whole town of Birmingham.
Ballad has none.
Movie Review describes movie images that are "in the face" of the audience to force them to view the fallout from racism, e.g. the girls' bodies in a morgue; the patronizing treatment of his black male personal assistant by George Wallace

Historical Details
Historical Account mentions the date, the time, who was in the church, what happened leading up to the moment of the bomb blast and what happened afterward.
Ballad fictionalizes the account but has some accurate allusions to the Freedom Marches as a place where violence against protestors was quite common
Movie Review explains that Spike Lee recreated the entire day through newsreel footage, photos, and eyewitness reports.

Effect on History
Historical Account doesn't say. It is "in the moment."
Ballad doesn't say; it is also "in the moment."
Movie Review explains that because Lee made the film many years after the event he had an ending to the story in the conviction of the bomber, Robert Chambliss. He was also able to present this as a "turning point" in the Civil Rights Movement and the event that forced everyone to take a good, hard look at racism in America.

Extend Discussion
Students' responses will vary. A sample response follows:

The historical account gives the most information. However, the ballad has the greatest emotional impact because it gives you a sense of what the mother of one of the little girls must have thought and felt before and after the bombing of the church. That personal perspective is so heartbreaking.

UNIT 3, ENGLISH LANGUAGE SKILL BUILDER

Comparison/Contrast
Conjunctions Used to Compare
and, also, too, as well, besides, in addition, furthermore, moreover

Conjunctions Used to Contrast
but, yet, still, nevertheless, however, except, though, then again

Extend Discussion
Students' responses will vary. Sample responses follow:
1. Free verse, catalog poems, <u>and</u> haiku do not rhyme. <u>Nevertheless</u>, haiku have a rhythm based on the number of syllables per line.
2. A ballad always rhymes. A sonnet does, <u>too</u>. A lyric may or may not rhyme <u>but</u> unlike a ballad, it doesn't tell a story.
3. A simile creates a connection between two things. Metaphors <u>also</u> do this. <u>In addition</u>, similes have the word "like" to show the comparison is not exact.
4. Alliteration <u>and</u> assonance repeat sounds, <u>however</u> one repeats consonants and the other repeats vowels.

UNIT 3, ENGLISH LANGUAGE SKILL BUILDER

Idioms/Definitions

1. F	3. E	5. A
2. G	4. B	6. C

Extend Discussion
Students' responses will vary. Sample responses follow:
1. Daffodils; they danced and shone in the sunlight; the memory of them continues to fill him with joy.
2. No; the poet says that they come gladly out of the willows and one horse nuzzles the speaker's hand.
3. By working at the most menial of jobs, they enabled their daughters to have the education that they never received.
4. Both the Mexicans and the Anglos seem to make snap judgments about the speaker. This makes her feel distanced from both worlds and both cultures.
5. After the bombing of the church, people did see racism in a different light—one of senseless brutality.

Original content Copyright © by Holt, Rinehart and Winston. Additions and changes to the original content are the responsibility of the instructor.

Differentiating Instruction

UNIT 3 SUMMATIVE TEST

Literary and Reading Skills

A.

1. C   3. A   5. C
2. D   4. C

B.

6. meter   8. speaker   10. ballad
7. connotation 9. visualizing

Reading Aloud

11.. Students' responses will vary. A sample response follows:

I appreciated the poem more after reading it aloud. I was especially able to notice how effectively the poet used the sound devices of rhythm, rhyme, and alliteration Reading the poem aloud also made me more aware of the different speakers in the poem. First there is a conversation between the daughter and the mother. Then the speaker who tells us the story continues. Finally, the last two lines of the poem are in the mother's sad voice.

UNIT 4, COLLECTION 8

Academic and Selection Vocabulary

Section A

1. rock   3. numbers
2. fussy   4. score

Section B

1. devise   3. incorporate   5. conjure
2. rebellious   4. loathsome

Section C

1. embody   3. productions
2. convention   4. interpretation

THE TRAGEDY OF ROMEO AND JULIET, ACT I
WILLIAM SHAKESPEARE

Selection Test
Comprehension, Skills, and Vocabulary

1. C   3. B   5. D
2. A   4. B

6. Students' responses will vary. A sample response follows:

I do not like Romeo in Act I. For one thing, when we first meet him, he is feeling sad and moping because he is in love with Rosaline but she does not love him back. Also, even though his friend and cousin Benvolio tries to talk to him and cheer him up, Romeo continues to feel sorry for himself. But then when he goes to the party at the Capulets, he meets Juliet and immediately forgets all about Rosaline. So, in my opinion, I think Romeo is an immature young man whose attitude and behavior I do not like.

THE TRAGEDY OF ROMEO AND JULIET, ACT II
WILLIAM SHAKESPEARE

Selection Test
Comprehension, Skills, and Vocabulary

1. D   3. B   5. D
2. A   4. C

6. Students' responses will vary. A sample response follows:

I do not think marriage between Romeo and Juliet would have solved the problem between their families. For one thing, Romeo and Juliet were very young to get married. Also, they hardly knew each other, which means they would probably learn things about each other they would not like. In addition, their parents didn't know about the marriage and would most likely be very angry when they found out. So, in conclusion, I think the marriage would create more problems between the families, especially if Romeo and Juliet found that they were not happy together.

"DEAR JULIET": SEEKING SUCCOR FROM A VETERAN OF LOVE DINITIA SMITH/ FROM THE JULIET CLUB

Selection Test
Comprehension, Skills, and Vocabulary

1. C   3. A   5. A
2. D   4. B

6. Students' responses will vary. A sample response follows:

I would not want to be a member of the Juliet Club. For one thing, I think it would be sad to read so many letters from people who are unhappy because of love. Also, I would not want to give people advice on what to do, in case I tell them the wrong thing and make matters worse for them. In addition, I think it would make me fearful that I will have the same problems in the future with love as the people who write. So, in conclusion, I'm sure it's a good thing that some people want to be members of the Juliet Club, but I am not one of them.

Original content Copyright © by Holt, Rinehart and Winston. Additions and changes to the original content are the responsibility of the instructor.

COLLECTION 8 SUMMATIVE TEST

Vocabulary Skills
1. devise
2. vital
3. rebellious
4. missives

Literary and Reading Skills
5. C   6. D   7. A

Language and Writing Skills
8. history
9. figures of speech
10. important

UNIT 4, ORAL LANGUAGE SKILL BUILDER

Paraphrasing
Students' responses will vary. A sample response follows:

Prince: The town's trouble-makers won't listen to my warnings.

Romeo: I love a woman who has decided she doesn't want to be in a relationship.

Juliet: My first love is from a family that my family hates.

Friar: Romeo is so shallow.

Extend Discussion
Accept any reasonable advice.

UNIT 4, ORAL LANGUAGE SKILL BUILDER

Retelling
Students' responses will vary. A sample response follows:

Benvolio and Mercutio wanted to find Romeo. But Romeo was not to be found. So they looked and called for him.

Romeo wanted to climb up on Juliet's balcony. But Juliet was afraid someone would catch them. So they agreed to meet the next day.

Romeo wanted to get married. But the Friar thought he was still in love with Rosaline. So Romeo explained he met someone new.

Nurse wanted to give Romeo a message. But Romeo's friends were rude. So Romeo had to make her feel better.

Juliet wanted to hear what Romeo said. But Nurse was tired. So Juliet had to beg her.

Romeo and Juliet wanted to be together. But Juliet had to sneak out to meet Romeo. So they met secretly so the Friar could marry them.

Extend Discussion
Accept all reasonable retellings.

UNIT 4, ENGLISH LANGUAGE SKILL BUILDER

Multiple-Meaning Words
1. ruins; ancient crumbling structures; broken, shattered
2. curb; the edge of a street; to limit
3. run; are genetically inherited; drip

Extend Discussion
1. pretty, nice; just, type
2. bright; not heavy
3. hand part; tree
4. level of a building; tale

UNIT 4, ENGLISH LANGUAGE SKILL BUILDER

Stress Patterns
(First activity to be done orally; no written responses)

Extend Discussion
Place stress on the words that convey meaning, for example: not, know, Dear, is, more, me, was, this, love, more, you, more makes, self, Truly, If, less, Lovable, No, less, charming, ugly, love, still.

UNIT 4 SUMMATIVE TEST

Literary and Reading Skills
A.
1. C   3. D   5. C
2. A   4. B

B.
6. exposition
7. resolution
8. rising action
9. secondary source
10. primary source

Making Inferences
11. Students' responses will vary. A sample response follows:

Original content Copyright © by Holt, Rinehart and Winston. Additions and changes to the original content are the responsibility of the instructor.

    Differentiating Instruction

One inference I would make about people who write letters to Juliet is that they want to keep their feelings a secret from people they know. I would infer this because from my own experience, you keep feelings to yourself that you are embarrassed about revealing. Otherwise, you would talk to someone you know about a problem, rather than writing a character in a play. Juliet keeps her feelings for Romeo a secret from everyone except Romeo and her nurse, so people who write her would identify with her actions. In the article, the woman whose husband left her is an example of someone who is hurt and probably embarrassed, too. Another inference I would make is that people who write Juliet think of love in a very romantic way. Juliet and Romeo fall deeply in love immediately. So people who are swept off their feet, like the boy who writes about the girl he fell in love with, or the woman who writes the letter longing for a great love like Juliet's, connect Juliet with a passionate love they have felt or want to experience.

UNIT 5, COLLECTION 9

Academic and Selection Vocabulary
Section A
1. adversity	3. priority	5. formidable
2. plummeted	4. profusion	

Section B
1. F	3. T	5. F
2. T	4. F	

Section C
1. portrays	3. express
2. destiny	4. mutual

THE ODYSSEY, PART ONE

Selection Test
Comprehension, Skills, and Vocabulary
1. A	3. D	5. D
2. C	4. A	

6. Students' responses will vary. A sample response follows:

I think it's important to read *The Odyssey*. First, it's a good story, once you get used to reading the complicated language. In addition, there are lots of characters and things that you realize you've heard about in other places. For that reason, the source of all those references is important. Thus I believe that reading *The Odyssey* is worthwhile for everyone who wants to be educated and knowledgeable.

SHIPWRECK AT THE BOTTOM OF THE WORLD/TENDING SIR ERNEST'S LEGACY

Selection Test
Comprehension, Skills, and Vocabulary
1. D	3. D	5. A
2. A	4. D	

6. Students' responses will vary. A sample response follows:

Shackleton's expedition was not like exploring space. First, astronauts who explore space are in constant communication with ground control. People on Earth know at all times what's going on. In addition, if anything goes wrong, astronauts don't have to figure out what to do on their own. For that reason they do not have to fend for themselves as Shackleton and the crew of the *Endurance* did. Thus I believe that Shackleton's expedition took more courage and resourcefulness than today's space missions do.

COLLECTION 9 TEST

Vocabulary Skills
1. adversity	3. plummeted	5. provisions
2. formidable	4. priority	

Literary and Reading Skills
6. D	7. D	8. D

Language and Writing Skills
9. synthesize 10. temperament

UNIT 5, ORAL LANGUAGE SKILL BUILDER

Aspects of Epic Stories

The Odyssey is a story told by the ancient Greeks.

Odysseus was known for his cleverness.

The challenge Odysseus faced was getting back home.

The outcome of the story was that Odysseus finally made it home.

Extend Discussion (possible answer)
You could tell the Greeks respected the qualities of cleverness and persistence because that is what their hero displays.

Original content Copyright © by Holt, Rinehart and Winston. Additions and changes to the original content are the responsibility of the instructor.

Differentiating Instruction

UNIT 5, ORAL LANGUAGE SKILL BUILDER

Vocabulary Discussion
Students' responses will vary. A sample response follows:

An epic is exciting when...the hero is in danger.

An internal conflict is challenging because...the hero must struggle with himself.

An external conflict is challenging because...the hero must struggle with outside forces, such as an enemy or the natural environment.

If a hero is portrayed as strong, courageous, and clever, his or her enemy would be portrayed as...weak, cowardly, and dull.

Extend Discussion
Accept all reasonable answers.

UNIT 5, ENGLISH LANGUAGE SKILL BUILDER

Common Spellings
Accept all reasonable answers

Extend Discussion
1. Calypso   3. Muse   5. Sirens
2. Lotus Eaters 4. Persephone

UNIT 5, ENGLISH LANGUAGE SKILL BUILDER

Prepositions of Place/Time
Accept all reasonable answers.

Extend Discussion (possible answers)
1. below or under
2. over, across or onto
3. During
4. After or once; in, inside, within or by

UNIT 5 SUMMATIVE TEST

Literary and Reading Skills
A.
1. D   3. B   5. A
2. B   4. A

B.
6. epic hero
7. conflicts

8. paraphrase
9. primary sources
10. synthesize

Conflict
11. Students' responses will vary. A sample response follows:

Sir Ernest Shackleton was in conflict with nature. Even if nothing had gone wrong, the cold and inhospitable climate presented enough of an obstacle to succeeding in this quest: to travel across Antarctica. When the ship got crushed by the ice and sank, Shackleton had to give up his original quest. It was replaced by a new quest—one similar to Odysseus's: to get all of his men home safely. Again nature—the cold and the fierce storm-- was the obstacle he had to overcome to achieve his goal.

UNIT 6, COLLECTION 10

Academic and Selection Vocabulary
Section A
1. C   3. A
2. D   4. B

Section B
1. A   3. A   5. B
2. B   4. A

Section C
1. function   3. specify
2. coherent   4. consequences

FOLLOWING TECHNICAL DIRECTIONS

Selection Test
Comprehension, Skills, and Vocabulary
1. D   3. C   5. A
2. A   4. B
6. Students' responses will vary. A sample response follows:

To me, it would be very helpful to have technical directions for my alarm clock. In the technical directions, I would hope that there would be illustrations, diagrams, and clear heads. Also, it would be helpful to have numbered steps. In conclusion, I think that technical directions for my alarm clock would be good to have because right now I'm not sure how to use it!

Original content Copyright © by Holt, Rinehart and Winston. Additions and changes to the original content are the responsibility of the instructor.

FUNCTIONAL WORKPLACE DOCUMENTS

Selection Test
Comprehension, Skills, and Vocabulary

1. A   3. C   5. C
2. C   4. D

6. Students' responses will vary. A sample response follows:

Dear G. Designer: The best part of the Web site for the WYSIWYGame Arts is the choice of icons on the buttons because they are so cute! In my opinion, one part of the Web site that could be stronger is the logo for your company. A specific suggestion I can offer is to add a picture to the words in the logo. In conclusion, I hope that you will consider my opinions about the strengths and weaknesses of your design as you continue to work on your Web site.

COLLECTION 10 SUMMATIVE TEST

Vocabulary Skills

1. en route   4. options
2. scan   5. differentiate
3. image

Literary and Reading Skills

6. A   7. C   8. C

Language and Writing Skills

9. image   10. scan

UNIT 6, ORAL LANGUAGE SKILL BUILDER

Asking and Answering Questions
Students' responses will vary. Sample responses follow

Row 1:
What kind of compensation can I expect for my ruined clothes?
Please accept our apologies and we'll get a check to you in the mail.

Row 2:
I was wondering if you could tell me who created the "Indian Art" poster?
Our records show that it's Pistchal.

Row 3:
Would it be possible to have my WYSIWYGame replaced under the 90-day warranty, even though it expired yesterday?
Our company's policy is to honor the warranty for 90 days, but I'll check with my supervisor.

Row 4:
Is there anyone here who can help me with a problem I'm having with previewing? According to the directions, you should make sure the scanner is on, put your image face down on the glass aligned to page indicators, open the PhotoEdit program, and choose import from the File menu.

Extend Discussion (possible answers)
Students' responses will vary. Sample responses follow:

I would deal with a rude representative by asking to speak to a supervisor.

I would deal with a difficult customer by offering reassurance and focusing on a solution to the problem.

UNIT 6, ORAL LANGUAGE SKILL BUILDER

Take Notes
Students' responses will vary. Sample responses follow

Purpose for meeting:
The reason for this meeting is to establish a summer reading book club.

Issues discussed:
Where to meet, when to meet, how often to meet; who selects the books; what kind of books will we read

Decisions made:
We will meet at the public library on Tuesday and Friday mornings.

Items for further discussion:
Where to obtain enough copies of the book for everyone; whether or not to have a group leader each week; what will be on the reading list

Extend Discussion
Students' responses will vary. Sample responses follow:

It was hard to follow the discussion because I was taking notes about the last thing we discussed.

Just note down key words to help you remember the important things that were said, but continue to follow the conversation. Ask people to pause to allow everyone time to record things after important decisions are made.

Original content Copyright © by Holt, Rinehart and Winston. Additions and changes to the original content are the responsibility of the instructor.

UNIT 6, ENGLISH LANGUAGE SKILL BUILDER

Frequently Confused Words

1. cite
2. complement
3. accept
4. effect
5. farther
6. advice
7. patience

Extend Discussion

1. effect
2. No change
3. patience
4. complement
5. No change
6. except
7. site

UNIT 6, ENGLISH LANGUAGE SKILL BUILDER

Fixed expressions

1. If you have trouble with the scanner, check your instruction manual.
2. Please give your application to the human resources department.
3. "Service with a smile" is the company policy around here.
4. A good assistant knows how to follow instructions.
5. Some people think that job satisfaction is as important as salary.
6. Many complaints show that quality control needs work.

Extend Discussion

Students' responses will vary. Sample responses follow

1. Eventually, all products will wear out. So warranties on old products would cost a company a lot of money. Also, they want you to buy new products eventually to replace the old ones.

2. Companies could give more rewards for a job well done, like the opportunity to get promoted, earn more money, or get more time off.
3. It is important to maintain high standards in the goods or services you produce. If not, in this competitive society, you will lose customers to the competition.

UNIT 6 SUMMATIVE TEST

Literary and Reading Skills

A.

1. C	3. D	5. C
2. A	4. B	

B.

6. scanning
7. adjust your reading rate
8. taking notes
9. instruction manuals
10. warranties

Reading and Workplace Documents

11.. Students' responses will vary. A sample response follows:

In Donna Pulsipher's e-mail, she advises G. Designer to add a page where users can make suggestions or comments. On the WYSIWIGame Arts Web Site, there is an area where users can "Post Your Opinion." This indicates that G. Designer took Ms. Pulsipher's advice. Also, as Ms. Pulsipher advised, there is now a Shareware Agreement.

Donna Pulsipher's other advice to G. Designer was to improve graphics. Since the graphics on the web site look fine to me, I assume that G. Designer also followed that advice. However, I cannot be sure that the graphics were updated without seeing an earlier version.

Original content Copyright © by Holt, Rinehart and Winston. Additions and changes to the original content are the responsibility of the instructor.

Differentiating Instruction